INDUSTRIAL REFORM
IN SOCIALIST COUNTRIES

Industrial Reform in Socialist Countries

From Restructuring to Revolution

Edited by
Ian Jeffries

Department of Economics
University of Swansea

Edward Elgar

Published by
Edward Elgar Publishing Limited
Gower House
Croft Road
Aldershot
Hants GU11 3HR
England

Edward Elgar Publishing Limited
Distributed in the United States by
Ashgate Publishing Company
Old Post Road
Brookfield
Vermont 05036
USA

A CIP catalogue record for this book is available from the British Library

Library of Congress Cataloguing in Publication Data
Industrial reform in socialist countries: from restructuring to
    revolution/edited by Ian Jeffries.
         p.   cm.
      1. Europe, Eastern–Economic conditions–1989–   2. Communist
    countries–Economic conditions.   3. Industrial management–Europe,
    Eastern.   4. Industrial management–Communist countries.   5. Mixed
    economy–Europe, Eastern.   6. Mixed economy–Communist countries.
    I. Jeffries, Ian.
    HC244.I49   1992
    338.947–dc20   91–34962
                                                                        CIP

ISBN 1 85278 380 X

Printed and bound in Great Britain by
Billing and Sons Ltd, Worcester

Contents

vi   *Industrial reform in socialist countries*

Tables

Preface

1989 was the year of 'revolution' in Eastern Europe. I have been fortunate to gather together leading world authorities to analyse industrial reform in 14 remaining or former socialist countries. New and formidable challenges face the Eastern European countries and Mongolia as they make the transition from predominantly state-owned, planned economies to market economies based on private property. North Korea and Cuba cling to their more traditional socialist regimes, while China and Vietnam grapple with market-orientated economic reforms in the firm grip of the Communist Party.

I am very grateful for the comments of the other contributors on my chapters. I am particularly indebted to Aidan Foster-Carter and Robert Bideleux for vetting the chapter on North Korea at short notice; I did not intend to write this, but the scheduled author failed to meet the deadline.

Siân Davies and Carolyn Phillips deserve medals for typing my three chapters and other things like the index; they cheerfully coped with the irritation of constantly amending material in the light of fast moving events.

The library staff at the University College of Swansea has, as always, treated me royally in ensuring rapid and reliable access to the many sources. The following deserve particular praise: Gwen Bailey, Merlyn Brown, Leslie Holland, David Painting, Hazel Pember, Ann Preece, Jane Richards, Clive Towse and Carole Williams.

The porters in the Abbey and in Fulton House again went out of their way to ensure early morning availability of the quality newspapers and the porters in the library were their usual obliging selves.

Ian Jeffries
Swansea

Contributors

Melanie Beresford Department of History and Politics, University of Wollongong, PO Box 1144, Northfields Avenue, Wollongong, NSW 2500, Australia.

George Blazyca School of Social Studies, Thames Polytechnic, Wellington Street, Woolwich, London SE18 6PF, UK.

Saul Estrin Department of Economics, London School of Economics, Houghton Street, London WC2A 2AE, UK.

Paul Hare Department of Economics, Heriot-Watt University, PO Box 807, Riccarton, Edinburgh EH14 4AT, UK.

Robert C. Hsu Office of Economics, Clarke University, 950 Main Street, Worcester, Massachusetts, 01610, USA.

Ian Jeffries Department of Economics and Centre of Russian and East European Studies, University College of Swansea, Singleton Park, Swansea SA2 8PP, UK.

Michael Kaser Institute of Russian, Soviet and East European Studies, 3 Church Walk, Oxford OX2 6LY, UK.

Robert J. McIntyre Department of Economics, Smith College, Northampton, Massachusetts, 01063, USA.

Ludek Rychetnik Department of Sociology, University of Reading, Whiteknights, Reading RG6 2AA, UK.

Adi Schnytzer Department of Economics and Business Administration, Bar-Ilan University, Ramat-Gan, 52900, Israel.

Gertrude E. Schroeder Department of Economics, University of Virginia, Charlottesville, Virginia, 22901, USA.

Alan H. Smith School of Slavonic and East European Studies, University of London, Senate House, Malet Street, London WC1E 7HY, UK.

Lina Takla Centre for Economic Performance, London School of Economics, Houghton Street, London WC2A 2AE, UK.

Andrew Zimbalist Department of Economics, Smith College, Northampton, Massachusetts, 01063, USA.

1   Industrial reform in historical perspective

Ian Jeffries

1.   THE INDUSTRIAL ENTERPRISE IN THE TRADITIONAL SOVIET ECONOMIC SYSTEM

Under command planning central state agencies take the basic allocative decisions about what to produce and in what quantities, but in reality the whole economic hierarchy has to be involved in decision making, e.g. the enterprise director has some marginal decision-making authority with regard to input substitution and output choice within the aggregate plan target. In highly simplified form the hierarchy has the State Planning Commission at its apex, branch ministries at its intermediate level and enterprises at its base. As in other walks of life the Communist Party plays a crucial role in formulating and implementing policies.

The State Planning Commission receives instructions about basic economic magnitudes from the Party (especially the Politburo). These instructions are relayed via the state apparatus (especially the Council of Ministers) and the Commission combines these with the data/requests/proposals flowing upwards from the hierarchy to draw up plans of varying duration by means of 'material balances'. In this planning technique major sources of supply and demand for particular commodities are drawn up, with the aim of attaining a rough balance. The crudity of such planning typically results in excess demand, one reason for the endemic supply problems afflicting command economies (the allocation of non-labour inputs is handled by the materials allocation system). The annual, quarterly and monthly plans are operational. The five-year and longer-term plans are much more highly aggregated and are only operational in relation to the investment plan; many projects are spread over a number of years and thus longer-term plans are needed for guidance. Since it is impossible for central planners to produce detailed, concrete plans in the abstract, the whole economic hierarchy has to be involved; the emphasis in the traditional economic system is on vertical linkages. Specifically, tentative, crudely balanced output targets ('control figures') are passed down the planning pyramid to be increasingly disaggregated by ministries and enterprises. Eventually the enterprise receives its technical–industrial–financial plan, but only after a haggling and bargaining process up and down the hierarchy.

The command planning solution of labour direction has been ruled out in more normal circumstances. Market forces are needed when the planners determine basic wage differentials. Pay differentials help induce workers to move into desired sectors and regions and to acquire desired skills. The non-market elements in manpower allocation include forced labour camps, while moral pressure is used, for example, to persuade students and workers to help out at harvest time. Trade unions are an arm of the state and help carry out state plans.

The typical industrial enterprise was a state-owned plant, operating on the principle of 'one-man responsibility and control' by a director appointed by the state or more strictly the party: positions of any importance were to be found on its *nomenklatura* or list of key posts. Lower levels of management included the deputy director and chief engineer, complemented by the party cell and the trade union branch.

The basic function of the industrial enterprise was to fulfil its 'technical, industrial and financial plan'. The operational plans (annual, quarterly and monthly) were expressed in terms of plan targets (success indicators), varying over time in terms of number and priority as particular problems arose. Output targets, however, were paramount. Gross output measures the value of finished output plus net change in the value of goods in the process of production; output in physical terms involves units of measurement such as weight, numbers and length; and targets for more heterogeneous output were broken down into main assortment (product-mix) indicators. On the input side there was a plan for material-technical supply and for labour utilization indicators, namely the wage fund (the total amount to be paid out in the plan period), productivity, average wage and number of workers by skill brackets. There were usually many other indicators, such as cost reduction, profit (as a percentage of cost rather than capital), investment, innovation, delivery schedules and equipment utilization.

The industrial enterprise was a financially separate and accountable unit operating on a *khozraschyot* (economic accounting) basis, for the purpose of efficiently implementing the plan. Prices, based on branch average cost, were fixed by the state and did not reflect the interaction of supply with demand. The enterprise account had to be kept in the local branch of the State Bank. The purpose of this was to help ensure plan compliance, the idea being that only payments in conformity with the plan should be permitted. Budgetary grants covered fixed capital needs and the State Bank had a monopoly over the granting of short-term credit, available at a nominal rate of interest which was fixed only to cover administrative costs. Management motivation involved negative consequences for non-fulfilment of plan, such as loss of bonuses, expulsion from the party and its associated privileges, and possible imprisonment or even capital punishment for 'economic sabotage' during the darkest periods. Positive incentives were associated with fulfilment and overfulfilment. Bonus, socio-cultural and investment funds were linked to success indicators, especially output.

Enterprises producing goods for export or using imported commodities were shielded from the world market by the state monopoly of foreign trade and payments. The industrial enterprise was assigned to a foreign trade corporation (FTC). The FTC, in turn, was subject to the authority of the Ministry of Foreign Trade and the ministry to the State Planning Commission. The price paid to the enterprise producing the goods for export was the domestic and not the world price; imports were paid for at the prices of comparable domestic commodities. This divorce of domestic and world market prices, coupled with arbitrarily determined exchange rates (the rouble is an inconvertible currency), led to accounting 'profits' and 'losses' being made by the FTCs. Due to a penchant for overvaluation of the rouble there were typically losses on exports and profits on imports. This is the mechanism by means of which exports and imports are involved in a sort of price equalization with world and domestic price, respectively. This separation of Soviet and foreign industrial firms greatly aggravated the problems already experienced with product quality. Although the traditional system played a crucial role in carrying out Stalin's basic goal of catching up with and surpassing the leading capitalist countries in terms of heavy industrial capacity and military power, microeconomic problems of a severe kind arose. These were:

Neglect of user need   Output only had to be produced and not sold in the traditional Soviet economic system, while emphasis on one indicator led to neglect of others. The result was that quantity was stressed at the expense of quality. For example, physical indicators such as weight, number, or length resulted in too large, small, or narrow objects respectively being produced, relative to user need. Gross output provides an incentive to use expensive inputs if these are reflected in product price and to orientate product assortment towards those goods incorporating large amounts of these inputs. This neglect of the qualitative aspects of production was especially acute in low-priority sectors involved in heterogeneous output, such as textiles, and helps explain the seemingly paradoxical phenomenon of stockpiles of unsaleable products in a situation of general consumer goods scarcity.

A tendency to understate productive capacity   The director has an incentive to provide such false information in the hope of achieving a 'slack' plan, one that calls for less than feasible output, since no bonuses were paid for anything less than 100 per cent fulfilment ('taut' planning generally prevails, with pressure to maximize output from given resources). Although extra bonuses were available for overfulfilment, the director was careful not to overfulfil by too much since this would endanger fulfilment of subsequent plans. The 'ratchet effect', known in Eastern Europe as the 'base-year approach', means that this period's achievement is the starting point for next period's plan – 'planning from the achieved level', as it is also called.

A tendency to overindent for non-labour inputs and to hoard these as well as labour   Manpower was hoarded to meet unforeseen needs or the frequent changes in plans. Non-labour inputs too were hoarded, due, for example, to the horrendous supply problems associated with the materials allocation system and the fact that capital was a free factor to the enterprise. This led to such phenomena as *tolkachi* (expediters, unofficial supply agents, who barter with each other) and a powerful inducement to self-sufficiency in the supply of inputs.

Storming   This is the mad rush to fulfil plans at the end of the planning period (such as the month), explained by such factors as the bonus system and delays in receiving inputs from other enterprises.

Anti-innovation bias at the micro level   Innovation is the application of new ideas about products and techniques to the production process. While new priority large-scale technologies (in armaments, for example) are readily dealt with by command economies, vital, spontaneous, micro-level innovation is hindered in the traditional Soviet economic system by the following factors:

1. There is no competitive pressure to stay in business as in market economies.
2. The incentive system means jeopardizing short-term plan fulfilment and the prospect of 'ratchet effects'.
3. State-determined prices may mean adverse effects on value indicators.
4. There were the aforementioned problems of input supply.
5. R&D, traditionally taking place in specialized organizations within ministries, was separated from production (Berliner, 1976).
6. There is a frequent shifting around of managers to prevent 'familiness' (friendliness developing between the various individuals within an enterprise; coalitions could thwart the enterprise's superiors).

Thus it seems that the interests of enterprise, user and state often conflict in the command economy, but it is important to note (Nove, 1986) the impossibility of central planners generally knowing what is needed in precise, disaggregated detail. The price system is denied this informational role and this lies at the heart of the reform problem.

2. THE PRIVATE SECTOR

Private enterprise was severely limited in the traditional Soviet economic system as regards:

1. Area: Handicrafts, agriculture and certain consumer services were acceptable, but selling goods made by other people was not allowed.
2. Employment: The employment of another person outside the immediate family in the production of goods for sale was illegal.
3. Income: Direct taxes were heavier than in the state sector.

3. ECONOMIC REFORM IN THE SOVIET UNION AND EASTERN EUROPE

The severe microeconomic problems were accompanied by others. These included falling growth rates starting in the latter half of the 1950s, the growing complexity of economies (mathematical planning techniques not providing a panacea), the increasing scarcity of factors of production, and increasing foreign trade (with highlighted quality deficiencies relative to Western products). The result was a search for ways of improving the efficiency of planning without, in general, eliminating the command principle.

The Yugoslav self-management system and the Hungarian New Economic Mechanism (introduced en bloc on 1 January 1968) were and the Czechoslovak programme would have been (were it not for the 1968 Warsaw Pact invasion) radical departures from the traditional Soviet economic system. As far as the others were concerned, some generalizations are possible. There was a trend towards amalgamating enterprises into larger-scale production units (variously termed 'associations' and so on) in order to reap economies of scale, encourage technological progress (by linking R&D with production) and streamline the planning system by reducing the number of production units directly controlled by central planners. The number of enterprise success indicators was reduced and there were changes in emphasis; greater emphasis was placed on profit and sales. Some decentralization of decision making was involved, e.g. the details of production assortment. Improved incentives involved both retaining a greater proportion of enterprise net revenue (for personal bonuses, social–cultural activities and investment) and applying more stable rules and parameters (e.g. greater emphasis was placed on five-year plans in order to mitigate the effects of 'planning from the achieved level'). Increased importance was attached to indirect steering of the economy via 'economic levers', such as prices, the cost and availability of credit, and taxes. Prices changes were generally insignificant, although some improvements were made, e.g. raising wholesale prices (in order to reduce subsidies and cover new obligations such as capital charges) and introducing tiered prices (fixed, range and free categories).

The 1970s was a decade of retrenchment in general, contributory factors including the Prague Spring (snuffed out by the 1968 Warsaw Pact invasion of Czechoslovakia) and the 1974 OPEC oil price hike (which adversely affected the Western economies and, therefore, Comecon exports and led to gradual increases in the price of Soviet oil within Comecon). Domestically powerful vested interest groups (like branch ministries) did all they could to thwart the reforms, while piecemeal and modest changes proved inadequate to cure the old problems and even introduced new ones (such as hindering the old command elements). Consequently, the general mood of the 1970s was one in which emphasis was laid on making central planning more efficient. Planning techniques were improved (involving, for instance, integrated, computerized information and control systems to aid managerial-planning decisions), numerous experiments and a continuous series of administrative and indicator/incentive changes.

The 1980s saw further attempts at piecemeal reforms in general (Poland's reforms were Hungarian-like in essence but remained largely on paper). Gorbachev's accession to General Secretary of the CPSU in March 1985 heralded a new era in the broad sense, but failed to overcome the economic problems. Indeed, *perestroika* brought about increasing chaos as the Soviet system was left in limbo, neither traditional command planning nor market. It took the revolutions in 1989 to set course for a fundamental change. But the move from a command to a Western-type economic system had never been attempted before and gave policy makers brand new headaches to contend with.

4.   DEVELOPMENTS POST-1989

1989 was the year of revolution in Eastern Europe. The freeing of these countries brought universal rejoicing, but also a whole new galaxy of problems: how to tackle the transition to political democracy and a market economy. Economists have divided themselves into two rather fuzzy but essentially distinguishable camps: the advocates of a very rapid 'big bang' transition to a Western-type economic system and the 'sequentialists' who argue the pros and cons of various reform orderings. Aside from the intrinsic interest in industrial reform in various countries, it is hoped that some light may be shed on the complex issues of the transition by these empirical studies undertaken by some of the leading authorities in the world. McIntyre, for example, argues that even Zhivkov's Bulgaria undertook some successful partial industrial reforms; in a broader sense agricultural reform in China and Vietnam are notable examples of generally successful partial reform, although this cannot be discussed here. The East German experience, with the collapse of industry within the embrace of a wealthy 'twin', certainly gives advocates of the 'big bang' idea food for thought.

5. INDIVIDUAL COUNTRIES

Albania

Albania's revolution was self-made, Enver Hoxha exercising a Stalin-like control until his death in April 1985. His successor as first secretary of the Albanian Labour Party was Ramiz Alia. Relations were broken off in turn with Yugoslavia (1948), the Soviet Union (1961) and China (1978).

A centralized economy was only gradually introduced and traditional plan indicators did not operate until 1959 because of the lack of qualified personnel. There was a measure of decentralization in 1966, but not so much to enterprises (although there was a reduction in the number of plan targets) as to ministries and district councils; the enterprise and district councils sent up draft plans, based on the five-year plan, instead of the central plan starting off the process. Formerly all the indicators for each enterprise were approved by the Council of Ministers; after 1966 that body only approved plans annually rather than quarterly. Ministries disaggregated plans and passed them down to district councils for coordination and implementation. The role of the councils has varied over time, being reduced in 1977 and in-creased a decade later. A form of workers' control was introduced in 1966; advice could be offered to management when the enterprise plan was being drawn up (with the aim of disclosing hidden reserves and appeasing workers disappointed with the growth of consumption), but the idea soon lost signifi-cance. Until the mid-1960s there was a traditional set of wage and salary differentials, but then a drive for greater equality set in. The resulting loss of incentives led to bonuses and other benefits for plan fulfilment being intro-duced in the late 1970s. Experiments in selected enterprises (a reduction in the number of success indicators for instance) were conducted 1985–86. After that there was some recognition of the need for reform, but Soviet-type reforms were ruled out; *perestroika* was seen as the path to capitalism. The 1976 constitution banned loans or direct investment from capitalist coun-tries, while there was no (legal) private sector in industry.

The impact of the 1989 revolutions in Eastern Europe
The overthrow of Ceausescu in Romania was especially influential. The initial reaction was to blame the events in Eastern Europe not on socialism

as such, but on 'revisionist' forms. Political concessions were made during 1990, but things moved very quickly after the pro-democracy demonstrations by students, which began on 9 December 1990. On 11 December the Central Committee allowed independent political organizations; the very next day the Democratic Party was founded (by intellectuals and students), followed by others such as the Ecology and Christian Democratic parties. A free election was set for 10 February 1991 (later postponed to 31 March). Violent protests were contained by a combination of concessions and repression (arrests and imprisonment). A mass exodus (especially of the Greek minority at first) started in December 1990.

Recent economic reforms
In September 1989 Alia accepted the need for unemployment in the case of idlers and the irresponsible. The following month it was accepted that indirect rather than direct steering would characterize the new economic system. In January 1990 Alia proposed the election of enterprise managers by workers, a decentralization of decision making, wages linked with performance and market prices for some non-essential goods. In April he advocated greater self-financing for enterprises (long-term bank credits rather than grants being the exception rather than the rule) and concessions to the private sector; in July craftsmen and traders were allowed, although only family labour was to be employed (this restriction was subsequently removed), and direct foreign investment permitted. The 28 February 1991 decree allowed individual ownership of cars.

In May 1990 the then prime minister Adil Carcani outlined the new economic system, to take effect on 1 January 1991. Enterprises were put into three categories: those subject to physical output planning (e.g. oil and sugar); those allowed to determine above-plan output deliveries within their own districts in conjunction with the local authorities; and those free to determine their own output and prices. Certain enterprises are able to use up to 20 per cent of their capacities for self-determined above-plan output sold at market prices. Foreign trade has still to be conducted through state foreign trade corporations, although some foreign exchange can be used by the enterprises themselves for imports such as machinery.

Wholesale prices were to be based on the highest cost producers in order to reduce planned losses and, therefore, subsidies. Enterprises were to be self-financing as far as possible and 90 per cent of planned profit could be retained (85 percentage points for investment and five for bonuses). If an enterprise (or sub-unit) plans and succeeds in reaching targets for above-plan profits one-half goes to bonuses and the other half to investment. Penalties for a poorer-than-planned performance (not due to extraneous circumstances) include high interest rates, the sacking of managers and even plant closure. Workers could receive up to a quarter of pay in bonuses, but unplanned losses result in a pay reduction of 10 per cent. Only the total wage bill is planned, with the enterprise deciding on the distribution among workers. The total wage bill can be exceeded if the plan is overfulfilled. New workers can be taken on, but new jobs have to be found for those dismissed. Workers laid off through circumstances beyond their control receive 80 per cent of their normal wage, but those responsible for shortages receive only a half of their normal wages. Independent trade unions were formally legalized on 18 February 1991.

Schnytzer considers this sort of concern for the costs of the transition to a more market-orientated economy to be a positive feature of, by Albanian standards at least, a radical reform. Yet again the state has taken a pragmatic approach, Schnytzer argues, sacrificing economic ideology to the quest to stay in power.

The general election
The Party of Labour of Albania's (PLA) election manifesto included the following economic aspects: 'replacing the system of centralized direction and administration with the mechanisms of a market economy'; 'a balance between the state sector and free initiative'; 'the great state sector will vie and coordinate action with the cooperative and private sector'; state enterprises to be broken up into smaller units in order to increase competition; 'The fiscal system associated with the economic reform will ensure an equal distribution of income'; and investment priorities to be shifted away from heavy industry towards tourism, services and consumer goods.

The Democratic Party's election manifesto pledged the rapid introduction of a market economy based on private ownership.

The Spring 1991 election was won fairly comfortably by the PLA (more than two-thirds of the seats in the People's Assembly), although it had to rely heavily on the countryside; the larger towns proved to be strongholds of the Democratic Party. A general strike added to Albania's growing list of problems, however, and a coalition government was formed in June. New elections are due May–June 1992.

Bulgaria
There was a continuous stream of non-radical reforms in Bulgaria's socialist economy. In 1963 the horizontally integrated DSO (State Economic Organization) was authorized and this later became the basic production unit. The industrial structure became more concentrated over time: in 1965 9.6 per cent of enterprises employed more than 5 000 workers, but by 1987 the figure had risen to 41.4 per cent (Jones and Meurs, 1991, p. 316). The December 1965 'Theses' provided a blueprint for the New System of

Management. Aspects included a reduction in the number of enterprise success indicators, a measure of devolved decision making (over the details of production planning, for instance) and a declining importance attached to investment grants. One result of the 1968 Warsaw Pact invasion of Czechoslovakia was a recentralization. The term 'New Economic Mechanism' was used throughout the 1970s, but only the name resembled Hungary's system. The 1979 proposals and 1982-83 measures emphasized financial accountability and greater self-financing. The DSO had to fulfil five plan indicators and the wage fund was linked to productivity. Above-plan output could be sold and both the brigade and indirect steering of the economy by means of economic levers were given enhanced importance. The minimum wage was abolished and there were experiments linking managerial salaries to enterprise net income. There was a tiered system of prices.

McIntyre sees a genuine improvement in the 'small enterprise initiative'. This began in 1980–81 and involves state-owned, semi-autonomous, small and medium-sized units within DSOs having real flexibility to respond to changing market needs. The Bulgarian Industrial Association, set up in 1982, provides managerial and consultancy services and plays an entrepreneurial role in the setting up of new enterprises.

The June 1987 financial reforms saw the separation of the central and commercial banks. After the mid-1980s confusing changes took place, such as ministerial reorganization. Further reform proposals were put forward in 1987, with the aim of phasing them in after 1 January 1988. 'Strategic' matters were the prerogative of the centre. Enterprises faced mandatory 'state orders', but detailed decision making was enhanced. Prices were to move towards world levels. A three-tier system of enterprise, corporation and association was another element. The January 1989 decree called for the transformation of enterprises into 'firms'. Possible forms included joint stock and limited liability companies and provision was made for the distribution of shares to a firm's employees.

The private sector
This did not flourish, despite some mild encouragement in the 1980s. In January 1989 ten permanent employees were permitted (casual labour could be employed as well). The employment ceiling was not lifted until 23 March 1990 .

Joint ventures
There was little success in attracting Western capital despite the March 1980 legislation allowing majority foreign ownership and that of January 1989 allowing wholly foreign-owned companies.

Post-1989 developments

The Communist Party transformed itself into the Bulgarian Socialist Party and won 211 of the 400 seats in the Grand National Assembly in the June 1990 election. Political stalemate stymied most economic reforms for a long time, however (land reform was dealt with relatively early on). Prime Minister Lukanov resigned on 28 November 1990 and a coalition government was formed on 20 December under Dimitar Popov. New elections were planned for 1991. Circumstances have been difficult for Bulgaria. The Zhivkov regime was heavily dependent on Comecon (especially Soviet) trade, shortages and rationing have been prevalent, debt repayment is a major headache (on 18 April 1991 creditor governments agreed to a rescheduling), and Western aid has been slow in coming (the EC did not grant food aid until February 1991, for example).

Legislation passed in November 1990 aimed at demonopolizing the structure of industry. Enterprises have already started to be broken up, e.g. the four wine producers have become 33 (*Financial Times Survey*, 17 May 1991, p. 17). The Popov economic programme gained IMF approval and credits in February 1991. Some parts of the programme still need parliamentary approval, but it essentially consists of two elements:

1. *An austerity package*   The budget deficit was to be reduced from 13 per cent of GDP in 1990 to 3.5 per cent in 1991 (Judy Dempsey, *Financial Times Survey*, 17 May 1991, p. 16). There were to be reductions in expenditure on state administration, defence and subsidies. On 1 February 1991 subsidy reductions led to massive price increases averaging nearly 700 per cent, e.g. cheese 477 per cent, milk 500 per cent, meat 500 per cent, bread 611 per cent, electricity 713 per cent, public transport 1 100 per cent, and heating 1 650 per cent. The aim is to liberalize 80 per cent of prices. Interest rates have been raised substantially (inter-enterprise credit has kept enterprises going) and in January 1991 a 200-day 'social pact' was reached between the government, trade unions (now independent) and employees; this included a ban on strikes until July 1991 and partial (70 per cent) wage compensation for price rises.

2. *Liberalization of the economic mechanism*   This includes the prospect of legislation more favourable to foreign investment and a faster privatization programme. Privatization and property rights legislation was expected to be in place by the autumn of 1991. Ivan Pushkarov (the minister of industry, trade and services) is in favour of rapid privatization, although against a Polish-type voucher scheme. His goal is to privatize 20–30 per cent of state industry over three years (Judy Dempsey, *Financial Times Survey*, 17 May 1991, p. 18).

China

A history of industrial reform

There were early departures from the traditional Soviet-type system: enterprises lacked control over manpower allocation; virtually all profits were transferred to the state budget; the work unit was responsible for housing and welfare services such as pensions and sickness and disability benefits; and managerial bonuses were of limited importance because of relatively slack plans. Party influence on the enterprise has been greater, too, especially during the Cultural Revolution (1966–76); this influence has declined in recent years, but saw a resurgence after the Tiananmen Square massacre (June 1989).

The post-1978 period saw reforms, many of these still remaining despite Tiananmen. Some profit could be retained and above-plan output sold at market prices (this 'dual-price' system has been diminished to some extent recently due to such factors as illegal reselling for profit; there has still been no radical price reform in general). The 1981 'economic responsibility system' ('profit contract system') involved profit-sharing contracts. The 1983–84 'tax for profit' system involved the state benefiting from various taxes and charges, but not profit transfers. The 'contract responsibility system' involves a minimum amount of profits to be handed over to the state, with above-target profits either fully retained or at least more lightly taxed; in principle (but not necessarily in reality) failure to reach the contracted profit means payment of minimum tax obligations. By early 1990 more than 90 per cent of state industrial enterprises were on the system. The most recent experiment concerns the 'two-way (double) guarantee system', where essential inputs are guaranteed in return for guaranteed deliveries of output, taxes and profits. There has also been some limited experimenting with shares, but these are more like bonds with no ownership rights involved. As regards planning, the 1980s saw greater stress on 'guidance planning', where the state puts greater reliance on indirectly steering the economy via economic levers. The Chinese economy has always been more loosely planned than the Soviet economy, with greater stress on regional devolution (although this itself has varied in emphasis over time). Some tightening of control has been apparent post-Tiananmen.

Hsu argues that the relative importance of the planned state sector in the economy may increase in 1991–95, in spite of official proclamations to the contrary, due to the new importance attached to energy and basic materials and to the continuing recent favouring of large state enterprises.

Industrial structure
China differs from Eastern Europe in this regard. In 1982 small firms (5–33 employees) accounted for 59.2 per cent of industrial enterprises (compared with 6.6 per cent in Yugoslavia and 2.2 per cent in Hungary), while large firms (more than 243 employees) only accounted for 0.6 per cent of enterprises (compared with 33.5 per cent in Yugoslavia and 65.1 per cent in Hungary) (Wong, 1989, p. 38; Prybyla, 1989, p. 12). In 1987 large and medium-sized enterprises accounted for only 2 per cent of all industrial enterprises, but 50.0 per cent of the gross value of industrial output (Kueh, 1989, pp. 431–2). In his opening speech at the National People's Congress (25 March–9 April 1991) premier Li Peng stressed the need to promote enterprise groups that transcend regional and industrial lines in order to combat regional trade barriers.

Manpower
Enterprise bankruptcies have been few and far between. Urban unemployment was 2.7 per cent in 1989. Traditionally in China there has been no labour market, the 'iron rice bowl' mentality ensuring a job and a wage for life. There have been experiments with contract labour of late, however, and by the end of 1990 13 per cent of the workforce in state enterprises was affected.

The private sector
The 1980s has seen greater encouragement given to the sector, although the post-Tiananmen atmosphere has been chillier (e.g. the 'six evils' campaign of July 1989 against vices like gambling and pornography). The sector is currently seen as a tolerable supplement to the state sector. In 1989 the percentage distribution of industrial output by sector was as follows: state 56.1; collective 35.7 and private 4.8. The private sector accounted for 13 per cent of retail sales.

Foreign trade and capital
The yuan is not a fully convertible currency; there are foreign exchange auctions where enterprises earning or needing foreign currency can get together. Some large enterprises have been given direct trading rights. There is now greater emphasis on steering foreign trade indirectly via instruments such as the exchange rate and licensing.

In 1978 the 'open door' policy was announced. This involves the opening up of the economy to foreign trade, capital, technology and know-how. Special Economic Zones are a key feature. Foreigners are now allowed 100 per cent ownership. The door is still largely open, despite Tiananmen.

Cuba

A history of economic reform

The 1959 Cuban revolution was home-grown. In 1958 there were 2 000 enterprises in Cuban industry, mostly artisan workshops employing less than ten workers; the 162 sugar refineries and another 100 enterprises were the only ones with more than 100 workers (Figueras, 1991, p. 75). The industrial enterprise prior to 1976 was not on an economic accounting basis; instead it was financed through the state budget. The power of the political leadership was increased at the expense of the Central Planning Board in 1966 and even by the late 1960s there was no unified central planning system. In fact until the second half of the 1970s there existed no basic institutions of economic planning; the first five-year plan was 1976–80. The 'moral economy' stage, 1966–70, placed emphasis on moral as opposed to material incentives.

The System of Economic Management and Planning (SDPE) was adopted in 1976, although gradually introduced from the following year. The SDPE was heavily influenced by the 1965 Soviet reforms. For example, an increased emphasis was given to material incentives (a percentage of profits was retained and both this and wages were linked with performance), scope was given for above-plan output, and economic levers to steer the economy indirectly were given enhanced importance. In 1980 labour contracting was introduced, with managers able to dismiss workers under certain circumstances.

Some retrenchment took place after 1980, although there is some debate about the degree. In December 1984 the powers of the pro-SDPE Central Planning Board were reduced as a result of the setting up of the Central Group of party and state officials (the Central Group itself was replaced in September 1988 by the Executive Committee of the Council of Ministers). Factors such as the foreign exchange crisis and over-investment led to the so-called 'rectification campaign' in 1986. Aspects include the decreased stress on material incentives and the diminished role of the private sector. Some see the rectification process as a reform reversal, but Zimbalist argues that there has only been a slow-down in the decentralization trend. He notes the following developments in defence of his arguments: 'resource fairs' after 1979 allow enterprises to trade inputs directly; the encouragement given to above-plan output during the 1980s; the increased role of industrial associations; a decrease in the number of material balances drawn up centrally after 1988 and a decrease in the number of enterprise success indicators; the greater role played by enterprise brigades; 'continuous planning' (where enterprises start to work out their plans on the basis of the previous year's plan and an estimate of the next one before the arrival of the control figures); and the increasing application of Western management techniques. As the situation deteriorated in 1990 rationing became pervasive and Cuba entered 'a special period in a time of peace' to conserve resources.

Since the 1989 revolutions in Eastern Europe there has been increased emphasis on sectoral as opposed to global planning, due to supply disruptions resulting from the upheavals. Annual plans are now regarded as more hortatory than mandatory. Zimbalist sees the 1989–90 crisis as having led to tighter government controls over the economy, but there has been a controlled reform process designed to integrate Cuba into the world market. As regards foreign capital, the 1982 legislation allowed for 49 per cent foreign ownership of joint ventures, but that can now be exceeded. Corporations independent of the planning mechanism have been set up, e.g. *Cubanacan*, which promotes joint ventures.

Czechoslovakia
Czechoslovakia was already a democratic and advanced industrial state at the start of the socialist era. Perhaps it is not surprising, then, that the problems of command planning became visibly apparent at an early stage. A negative rate of growth of national income in 1962 caused considerable consternation.

A history of economic reform
Modest reforms were implemented in the late 1950s, involving, for example, associations and a measure of decentralization of decision making. The 1966–67 measures, however, were the most radical in the socialist world outside Yugoslavia. Directive planning was largely abandoned and enterprises were generally allowed to determine their own output and input mix in the light of maximizing net value added. Planning was mostly indirect via economic levers. Associations were amalgamated into trusts, workers' councils began to emerge in 1968 and there was a three-tier system of prices (fixed, limit and free). The August 1968 Warsaw Pact invasion put an end to the Prague Spring and traditional command planning was gradually and largely (though not entirely) restored.

The 1978 'complex experiment', involving 12 associations, led to the March 1980 'Set of Measures to Improve the System of Planned Management of the National Economy'. Industrial associations (VHJs) of various sorts became the basic production units, norms and plans became more stable, and the wage fund became more clearly linked to value added. Some enterprises were given direct trading rights.

Various experiments were conducted in 1987 and in December the principles for the 'restructuring of the economic mechanism' were adopted; these were designed to come fully into effect at the start of the 1991–95 plan period. The State Enterprise Act was implemented in June 1988. The old

VHJs were dissolved and replaced by 'state enterprises'. The role of the five-year plan was enhanced. Mandatory plan elements remained in such forms as 'state orders', but the main emphasis was placed on indirect steering and enterprises had increased scope for decision making (including investment). Enterprises were expected to become more self-sufficient financially and bankruptcy was a long-term possibility (after other measures such as direct administration and mergers had been tried). Enterprise managers were elected (although from a list drawn up by the founder who also had a veto) and workers' committees had some limited say in plan preparation. A reform of wholesale (but not retail) prices was set for the beginning of 1989, with account taken of costs, demand and world prices. A uniform commercial exchange rate for trade with non-socialist countries was introduced on 1 January 1989. Foreign exchange auctions began in July.

Joint equity ventures
The August 1985 decree fixed a 49 per cent maximum on foreign ownership, but at the beginning of 1989 the upper limit was removed. There was not a great deal of success, however.

The 'velvet revolution'
This began in November 1989. Vaclav Havel became president on 29 December 1989 (re-elected 5 July 1990) and Civic Forum/Public Against Violence won the free election of June 1990. The degree of Slovak sovereignty is a major problem; a referendum will determine whether the Czech and Slovak regions are to be independent. Vaclav Klaus became Finance Minister on 10 December 1989, an outspoken advocate of monetarism and of the market economy. He advocated an austerity programme and a phased but relatively rapid transition to the free market.

The banking system was transformed in January 1991, with the division into a Western-type central bank and commercial banks. An austerity programme involved, for example, a shift towards a budget surplus (there was a deficit in 1989) and a partial elimination of subsidies on goods such as food and petrol during 1990 (albeit with income compensation). The bulk of prices were liberalized at the start of 1991, when, after a drastic devaluation, the Czech crown became internally convertible (enterprises being able to buy hard currency from and sell it to the State Bank).

Central planning was phased out during 1990. The 1988 Enterprise Law was amended in April 1990. Committees were dissolved and replaced by a new two-tier system: the supervisory board is elected equally by the full-time employees and by the founder, while the director is appointed (and dismissed) by the founder in consultation with the board. The autonomy of the enterprise is stressed.

Privatization

The private sector was severely repressed in socialist Czechoslovakia, even by East European standards, although the 1980s had seen some let-up. The April 1990 privatization law gave equal recognition to private property. While the state is likely to retain control over strategic enterprises and public utilities, a privatization programme is now in operation. Competition has been encouraged by the splitting up of enterprises and by the passing of anti-trust legislation.

The Restitution Law (effective 1 April 1991) deals with the restitution of or compensation for non-agricultural property illegally expropriated after 25 February 1948 (Daniel Arbess, *Financial Times*, 7 March 1991, p. 33). If resident Czech citizens (or their resident heirs) are unwilling to pay for improvements made to properties subject to physical restitution, financial compensation only is available (in cash, up to a certain limit, plus shares in privatized enterprises up to a further limit). Most non-restitutable properties and businesses of local, 'non-public' character (e.g. shops, restaurants, small workshops and service enterprises) are being auctioned under the Small Privatization Law. Only citizen-residents are allowed to bid in the first round of any auctions; the first auctions actually started on 26 January 1991. The Major Privatization Law (passed 26 February 1991) applies to larger-scale enterprises and the programme was planned to start in the second half of 1991. The shares are to be held at first by a National Property Fund. The issuing of shares is to be accomplished by domestic and foreign flotations, controlled auctions to foreign investors, and 'investment points' distributed at a nominal price to adult Czech citizens exchangeable for shares.

East Germany

The German Democratic Republic (GDR: formally founded 7 October 1949) or East Germany (EG) had the highest standard of living among the socialist countries and, along with Czechoslovakia, was an advanced industrialized country before the socialist era. Economic policy was shaped by Soviet domination (especially in view of its position on the front line between East and West) and by the continual comparisons it suffered to West Germany (WG) rather than its poorer socialist neighbours (e.g. legitimacy was sought largely in rising living standards). *Glasnost* and *perestroika* in Gorbachev's Soviet Union unsettled the Honecker regime, while Gorbachev himself took an early interest in the EG industrial combine.

The speed at which the Honecker regime disintegrated in 1989, however, astonished everyone. Gorbachev's vision was an essential prerequisite. One of the other decisive elements was the flood of people to West Germany (343,854 in 1989 alone), sparked off by Hungary's decision to dismantle its border fence with Austria in May. On 9 November the borders between the two Germanies, including the Berlin Wall, were opened. Honecker was replaced as General Secretary of the Socialist Unity Party (renamed the Party of Democratic Socialism on 16 November) by Egon Krenz. The whole politburo and central committee resigned on 3 December and these two bodies were replaced by a new executive chaired by Gregor Gysi. Hans Modrow had been confirmed as prime minister on 13 November. In the 18 March 1990 free election there was a surprise win for the Alliance for Germany, comprising the Christian Democratic Union, the German Social Union and Democratic Awakening. Lothar de Maizière became prime minister. German economic and monetary union (GEMU) took place on 1 July 1990, political union took place on 3 October, and an all-German general election was held 2 December 1990 (won comfortably by Chancellor Helmut Kohl's CDU/CSU-DSU/FDP coalition).

Economic background
Hitler's defeat led to the division of Europe and left the two parts at the front line between socialism and capitalism. EG started off in generally worse shape than WG, the former suffering greater wartime destruction and paying heavy reparations to the Soviet Union. EG is also generally poorly endowed with raw materials, with important exceptions such as lignite and potash; this led to heavy dependence on imports of fuels and raw materials, especially from the Soviet Union. Sensitivity to price increases for these commodities led to attempts to substitute domestic ones whenever possible (e.g. lignite for oil) and at economic reform in order to raise the efficiency of usage. Labour was also an acutely scarce factor of production and this helps explain such policies as the drive for 'intensification' (output increases gained largely through raising the efficiency of input use), the building of the Berlin Wall in 1961 (to stem the flow of people to WG) and the concern to improve living standards as an incentive to work.

Industrial reform
Until its political disintegration EG always maintained a command economy. Nevertheless, a number of phases of industrial reform can be distinguished:

1. *The New Economic System (NES) 1963–71*   The NES was partly the result of a disappointing economic performance (the 1958 'main economic task' was a doomed attempt to catch up with and overtake WG in *per capita* production of major foodstuffs and consumer goods by 1961 and in labour productivity by 1965, itself aimed at staunching the flow of people westwards). It can also be seen as a laboratory needed by the Soviet Union to observe the effects of industrial reform. The NES was a very modest reform, although the most radical and comprehensive in Eastern Europe in the early

1960s (apart from Yugoslavia, of course). It should be seen as an attempt to achieve state goals more effectively by means of a combination of traditional command planning and the greatest use in pre-1989 EG of indirect steering of enterprises by economic levers. The number of enterprise success indicators was reduced and there was increased scope for decentralized decision making in areas such as investment, product and input mix, manpower allocation and foreign trade. A capital charge was introduced in 1967 and a modest price reform implemented. The VVB (association of nationally owned enterprises) was an essentially administrative (in contrast to operational production) intermediate body between ministry and enterprise. The VVB declined in importance during the 1970s and finally disappeared during the 1980s. A major amendment 1968–70 took the form of 'structure-determining tasks'; these were the result of decentralized investments departing markedly from the lines of development desired by the state and involved centrally planning certain key areas in precise detail. The resulting bottlenecks and shortages resulting from the neglect of the non-priority sectors, however, helped to bring the NES to an end.

2. *Recentralization 1971–79* While lacking a new theoretical basis, the period saw a distinct shift back to the pre-NES situation (although not entirely so). Attention was focused on improving the supply of consumer goods, 'intensification' and an active social policy (including a massive housing programme). EG's response to the 1973–74 oil shock was not to alter the economic system in any fundamental sense, but, for example, to bring domestic prices of fuels and raw materials closer to world levels, to increase the emphasis on exports, and to borrow from the West.

3. *The 1980s* The 1980s saw the GDR coping with severe foreign trade and payments problems, with the enhanced need for 'intensification' pursued by means of the combine (*Kombinat*) and the 'perfecting' (*Vervollkommnung*) of the economic mechanism. Radical economic reform was ruled out.

The combine became the basic production unit during the third wave of production unit during the third wave of formation 1978–80. In 1986 there were 127 combines in centrally directed industry and construction (varying in size from 2 000 to 80,000 employees, with an average of 25,000, and constituting 20–40 enterprises); there were also 94 combines in regionally directed industry, employing 2 000 on average. The combine is a horizontal and vertical amalgamation of enterprises, spanning the whole range of activities from R&D to marketing. The incorporation of leading supplier-enterprises was designed to ameliorate the endemic supply problems associated with command economies.

The 'perfecting' of the economic mechanism involved both improvements in both direct and indirect steering. As regards direct steering, for example, norms for material use were increased and tightened and the indicator system was amended to stress efficiency in the use of inputs. With respect to indirect steering, for example, enhanced stress was laid on credit policy and a 'contribution for social funds' (a payroll tax) was introduced in industry in 1984 in order to promote a more efficient use of manpower.

The reunification of the two Germanies

German economic and monetary union (GEMU) took place on 1 July 1990. The East Mark (EM) was replaced by the DM (at rates more generous than generally anticipated) and the *Bundesbank* took control of monetary policy, while 'economic' union essentially involves the adoption of WG's 'social market economy'. It can be argued that a slower pace of reunification was possible and even desirable. The effects on the EG economy have been varied. Inflationary pressures have been contained. But there has been a sharp decline in output (national income falling by perhaps 15 per cent in 1990) and a rapid increase in unemployment (836,000 or 9.5 per cent in April 1991, with a further 2 million on 'short time'). Important factors have been the rapid narrowing of the EG–WG wage differential and the inability of EG to devalue its currency because of monetary union. The short and medium-term forecasts for output and unemployment became steadily gloomier, with the recovery point for the EG economy shifted back from mid-1991 to later in the year or even 1992 (services and construction seem likely to lead the recovery). The long-run prospects for East Germany are generally considered to be excellent (they vary sectorally, of course), but some see the danger of a permanently relatively depressed region. The German government has been forced to adopt a more interventionist line as the situation deteriorated. EG is fortunate in having a wealthy 'twin' to help it through this stressful period: there is a lesson here for those who advocate 'big bang' and 'shock' therapies for isolated countries, especially in the absence of substantial Western aid.

Privatization

The fortunes of the private non-agricultural sector in the GDR fluctuated with the political climate, but were always subservient to the state sector. In 1979 the private sector contributed 3 per cent of Net Material Product (Åslund, 1985), while in 1985 the figures for industrial output alone reveal 2.3 per cent and for domestic trade 2.7 per cent (Brezinski, 1987, p. 86). There was an employment ceiling of 10.

The combines began to be split up and a trust body or holding company called the *Treuhandanstalt* (THA) (headed by Detlev Rohwedder until his assassination by the Red Army Faction on 1 April 1991; he was replaced by Birgit Breuel) was endowed with the ownership rights of around 8 000 'large enterprises', i.e. those with more than 250 employees (by February 1991 the number of enterprises had increased to 9 200). On 18 April 1991 it was announced that more than 1 261 enterprises had been privatized. The smaller enterprises quickly began to be returned to their former owners or sold off/leased.

Privatization in EG was slow at first: the process was not helped by the original decision to return property to former owners or their heirs. Initially physical restitution was stressed, but financial compensation has been given increasing emphasis because of the slow pace in settling claims. The March 1991 legislation gave priority to any investor offering the best job-sustaining and creating programme.

'Foreign' (including WG) investment is now welcomed in EG, although the amount has been disappointing to date. Deterrent factors include the restitution laws, EC regulations on monopolies, a poor infrastructure, environmental pollution and inherited corporate debt. This contrasts with the ban imposed by the Honecker and predecessor regimes, putting EG in the auspicious company of Albania in the whole of Eastern Europe. Hans Modrow accepted foreign investment in principle in a 17 November 1989 speech, while the January 1990 draft law stated that foreigners could even own more than 49 per cent of the equity if 'of interest to the economy' (e.g. new technology). On 1 March 1990 foreign companies were permitted to operate wholly-owned subsidiaries, while the July 1990 law conceded 100 per cent foreign ownership.

Hungary

A history of industrial reform

There were some earlier modest changes, but the overnight shift to the New Economic Mechanism (NEM) on 1 January 1968 represented a major departure from the traditional Soviet economic system. This was not market socialism, but direct planning was limited (for example, large investment projects, some centrally allocated inputs, Comecon obligations and defence). Enterprises did not generally face plan targets, but they were steered indirectly by a 'visible hand' of economic levers and informal pressures. Kornai (1986) sees the NEM as a combination of indirect bureaucratic control and elements of market coordination. 'Regulator bargaining' took the place of plan bargaining in the sense that enterprises were vertically dependent on the bureaucracy, e.g. negotiations over taxes and credits. There is a debate about the role played by profit; the profit tax, for example, reinforces profit incentives, while soft budget constraints and vertical dependence diminish them.

A four-tier pricing system was typical, namely fixed, ceiling, range and free. 'Competitive pricing' (abandoned by the end of the 1980s) was designed to act as a substitute for the lack of competitive pressures in the domestic economy; the prices of products such as energy and important raw materials were to approximate world levels.

The monopolistic structure of industry can be illustrated by the following figures. In 1975 the three largest producers accounted for more than two-thirds of production in 508 of the 637 industrial product aggregates (Roman, cited by Kornai, 1986, p. 1699). Since 1980 some trusts have been split up to increase competition. In the period 1980–85 the number of trusts declined from 24 to nine and more than 400 new and independent organizations were created out of this process and out of the division of enterprises (von Czege, 1987, p. 133).

The trend over time was towards greater refinement of the NEM, although there have been some setbacks, e.g. the 1972–78 retrenchment. After January 1982 'private work partnerships' ('work teams') were allowed in state enterprises, groups of workers being able to rent equipment after normal working hours. A managerial reform was started in January 1985 in which the workers in medium-sized and some large enterprises elected their directors (albeit subject to possible veto by the ministry or local authority); in small enterprises there was no veto).

Hungary under the NEM was a fully employed economy, where many people held two or even more jobs. On 1 January 1988 a (progressive) income tax system (and VAT) was introduced. Prior to this there was some form of tax on wage increases as an anti-inflation device. A bankruptcy law was introduced on 1 September 1986, but few enterprises were closed down due to factors such as the soft budget constraint.

A Western-type banking system was installed on 1 January 1987, with the National Bank becoming more like a conventional central bank controlling a number of commercial banks. Bonds have been issued since the early 1980s (enterprises being able to issue them after 1 January 1983) and shares since 1987.

Foreign trade and capital
Hungary had the most liberal trading regime in Comecon. Enterprises were allowed their own trading rights or to choose foreign trade corporation. After 1 January 1988 any state enterprise was able to trade with the West. In 1981 a single uniform exchange rate was introduced against hard currencies. The forint became 'internally convertible', with Hungarian enterprises being able to buy and sell hard currencies. Since 1 January 1991 Hungarian enterprises have been able to pay for imports with forints. By the end of the 1980s over 40 per cent of the value of hard currency imports were no longer

subject to controls; by the spring of 1991 about 90 per cent of imports needed no licenses.

A joint venture law was introduced in 1972. On 1 January 1989 100 per cent foreign ownership was granted.

Hare's conclusions are that the extensive reforms did not transform the Hungarian economy, because the authorities proved unwilling to enforce market disciplines and property rights were unchanged.

Since the free general election of March–April 1990 Hungary has continued with the IMF-inspired austerity programme and embarked on a relatively cautious transition to a Western-type economy. A more severe austerity programme and a speedier privatization programme were put forward towards the end of 1990. Most prices are now deregulated.

The private sector
The private sector was a relatively flourishing sector under the previous socialist regime. The following figures illustrate the importance of the so-called 'second economy' (comprising the formal, officially licensed, plus informal private sectors). In 1984 Net Material Product was accounted for by the following sectors (in per cent): state 65.2 and non-state 34.8 (cooperatives 20.6; household farming 2.8; auxiliary production of employees 5.9; and the formal private sector 5.5) (Kornai, 1986, p. 1692). Hare's figure for industrial output alone is less than 5 per cent for the private sector. On 1 January 1988 the employment limit for private activity was raised to 30.

Privatization
Early abuses were associated with 'wild' or 'spontaneous' privatization. Here managers benefited in the form of shares or well-paid positions in the new private firms as assets were sold off cheaply. The Hungarian Democratic Forum-led coalition government of prime minister Jozsef Antall adopted a cautious attitude at first. After much hesitation a three-year privatization programme was announced at the end of September 1990. This envisages half the state sector being affected, including all small businesses. A speedier privatization process is now in the offing. Hungary's policy is to avoid a large 'giveaway' of shares (perhaps 10–15 per cent may be sold at a discount to the workers of a particular enterprise) because of the need for budgetary revenue and to improve management. The compensation bill is still under discussion: the proposal is that the former owners are only to be partially compensated and in the form of vouchers exchangeable for shares in newly privatized enterprises. The degree of future state involvement in 'strategic industries' has also been the subject of considerable debate and the picture is still not clear.

Mongolia

The Mongolian People's Republic formally came into being in November 1924 (thus the second socialist country), although independence from China had been declared in December 1911 and again in July 1921. Opposition demonstrations in December 1989 started the political process which led to a free general election in July 1990, which the Mongolian People's Revolutionary Party won convincingly. In this sense Mongolia outpaced the Soviet Union, a country hitherto always faithfully followed in both economic and political matters (it was not until after the Second World War that any other country even recognized Mongolia).

Pre-socialist Mongolia was overwhelmingly agrarian (especially livestock). There were some initial attempts at drawing up a five-year plan for the period 1931–35, but the first formal one was for 1948–52. Annual plans, however, actually began in 1941 when the Planning Board was set up. In the early 1970s industrial associations along Soviet lines were established. In 1986 the commission for 'perfecting economic management and the economic mechanism' was formed and reforms along Soviet lines followed. Kaser uses the term 'Mongolian perestroika' to describe the 1984–89 period. For example, ministries were amalgamated and an experiment involving over 100 enterprises was conducted, in which greater financial autonomy was emphasized, decision making was decentralized somewhat (e.g. plan details), and pay and performance were linked. The Law on the State Enterprise came into operation on 1 January 1989, in which the principles of full cost accounting, self-financing and self-management were highlighted. 'State orders' were a feature, while self-management referred to the greater involvement of the workforce in enterprise decision making (including the election of the manager). Wholesale trade in producer goods was expanded substantially after late 1987. World prices were to be taken into account in the pricing of exportables and import substitutes and some prices were deregulated. Some enterprises were allowed direct foreign trading rights. The private sector was given greater encouragement.

Joint ventures

Those with the Soviet Union have a large history, and other socialist countries like Bulgaria and Czechoslovakia have also been partners. Joint ventures with Western companies were formally allowed (two already existed) under the March 1990 legislation (although not wholly foreign-owned companies).

Post-election Mongolia: privatization and the transition to the market

The formal start to the transition to the market was made in January 1991. A privatization programme has been outlined. The state is to retain control over key sectors like energy and mining, but the remaining enterprises are to become joint stock corporations; shares are to be distributed equally among Mongolian citizens of any age. Shops began to be auctioned in May 1991. The number and powers of economic ministries have been reduced. Macroeconomic stabilization measures have been taken, such as a doubling of fixed retail prices and wages. The intention is to liberalize 80 per cent of retail prices by the end of 1991, while wholesale prices were brought closer to world levels at the start of the year. Mongolia has been badly affected by the disruption of Comecon links and rationing and unemployment have both increased. Kaser argues that the transition to a mixed market economy will be especially difficult for a very poor country like Mongolia.

North Korea
Like the former German Democratic Republic, North Korea has suffered from the comparisons continually made to a successful capitalist 'twin'. It is no coincidence that the GDR had and North Korea still has an ultra conservative leadership and a command economy. Both Germany and Korea were divided after the Second World War, but, unlike East Germany, North Korea was then the more industrialized twin (especially regarding heavy industry). The Korean Workers' Party has been led by 'the great leader' Kim Il Sung since 1948, a president who practises a strong cult of personality and a policy of *'chuche'* or self-reliance (although greater attention has been paid to foreign trade and capital since the mid-1980s). This policy helped make North Korea into one of the most isolated of the socialist countries, this isolation increasing with the 'loss' of Eastern Europe. Not unpredictably, North Korea has reacted by stressing the value of socialism.

North Korea still has a rigid command economy, with economic plans containing very detailed output targets for each industrial enterprise. Rationing is far more pervasive than in traditional Soviet planning, there is a greater stress on moral incentives, and campaigns are common. Since 1961 the industrial enterprise has been run by a factory party committee rather than an individual manager, with managers, engineering staff and workers equally represented. Its executive board carries out day-to-day operations and is dominated by the party secretary and managers. The party secretary's decision is final.

Modest enterprise reforms began in late 1984 and involved the following: a greater emphasis on economic accounting; some devolved decision making (e.g. over the fixing of bonus rates, the share of profits going to investment and input allocation); and a greater role for material incentives (up to 50 per cent of excess profit can be used to increase output or benefits). Since 1975 there have been experiments with the 'associated enterprise system', linking geographically adjacent and related enterprises.

The private sector is small.

North Korea defaulted on its foreign debt in 1976 and has been considered a poor credit risk ever since. Joint ventures have been permitted since September 1984 (100 per cent foreign ownership has only recently been granted), but the limited number of foreign firms have been largely confined to Japanese citizens of Korean descent.

Poland

A history of industrial reform pre-1990
There were significant industrial reforms as early as 1956–57 (including the setting up of workers' councils), but recentralization set in as early as the next year. Between 1958 and 1972 there were relatively insignificant administrative changes and various experiments. The 1972 programme centred on 'large economic organizations' (WOGs), but the latter half of the 1970s witnessed a recentralization process due to deteriorating world and domestic conditions and to the excess demand caused by an ambitious growth strategy. This recentralization was part of a so-called 'economic manoeuvre', which started in 1976 and was designed to stabilize the economy. The industrial reform programme of 1 January 1982 was Hungarian-like in approach, one that put the greatest stress on indirect steering via economic levers and that was to be gradually introduced over a 3–5 year period. But factors such as severe input shortages ensured the dominance of administered allocation and confined the reform largely to paper. Martial law was in operation 13 December 1981–21 July 1983. The October 1987 'second stage' of the reform again hardly got beyond the paper stage, although there were some concrete results, e.g. the setting up of a single ministry for industry.

The 1990 'big bang'
Talks between the government and Solidarity began on 6 February 1989 and the so-called Roundtable Agreement was reached on 5 April (relegalizing Solidarity among other things). A partially free election was held in June 1989 and resulted in a Solidarity-led Government headed by Tadeusz Mazowiecki (his resignation was accepted on 14 December 1990, after coming a poor third to Lech Walesa in the presidential election). Poland was subjected to 'shock therapy' and the rapid introduction of a market-based economy. Macroeconomic stabilization involves strict fiscal (e.g. a balanced budget was aimed for), monetary (strict control of the money supply) and incomes policies (money wage increases over a centrally fixed norm were subject to a high and sharply progressive tax). The overriding aim was to tackle the near hyperinflation (640 per cent for the year to December 1989 and 244 per cent on average for the whole year). On 1 January 1990 most prices were liberalized and the zloty became internally convertible (citizens

and enterprises being able to exchange it for hard currency) and reduced to a single rate in line with the free market rate (the rate of 9 500 zloties to the US dollar held until 17 May 1991, when the zloty was devalued to 11,100 zloties to the US dollar in order to make exports more competitive; henceforth the zloty was to move against a trade-weighted basket of major currencies). Tariffs (now generally at low levels) largely replaced quotas. Industrial enterprises had to swim on their own in the new harsh financial waters, although there have been very few actual bankruptcies to date due to such factors as the growth of inter-firm credit, some redundancies, lower real wages and Comecon trading links (adversely affected by the January 1991 switch to hard currency trading). The reaction of enterprises was also disappointing during 1990 in the sense that there tended to be a greater stress on raising prices and reducing output rather than searching for ways to lower costs, increase efficiency and for new products and markets, although there was a remarkable surge in hard currency exports. One responsible factor is the highly monopolistic structure of industry. At the end of 1989 there were 6 008 industrial enterprises in the state sector with an average employment of 695. In 1988 the largest 113 enterprises, with an average employment of more than 5 000, accounted for 23 per cent of state industrial sales and 25.2 per cent of employment. The top 428 state enterprises provided 47.8 per cent of total industrial sales and 52 per cent of employment.

The rate of inflation fell dramatically (to 1.8 per cent in the month of August 1990, although rising again thereafter), but at the cost of increasing unemployment (from negligible proportions in 1989 to 1,124,753 or 8.3 per cent of the non-agricultural labour force at the end of December 1990), an initial fall in real incomes (the nominal figures for wages and prices show a 31.8 per cent fall in the 'real wage', but this is an exaggeration because of the increasing availability of goods), and declining output (for example, total industrial production fell by nearly 30 per cent in the first half of 1990 compared with the same period of 1989; *private* industrial output, it should be noted, actually rose by 2 per cent). These depressing figures partly explain the failure of Mazowiecki's campaign in the 26 November 1990 presidential election (Walesa won the 9 December run-off against the previously unknown Tyminski); he resigned the premiership too. Poland was rewarded in March 1991 with a 50 per cent reduction in the debts owed to Western governments.

The private sector

The nadir was reached in the mid-1950s, thereafter undergoing a cyclical recovery. On 1 January 1989 the private industrial sector was legally treated on a par with the other sectors. In 1989 the state sector accounted for 92.6

per cent of total industrial sales and the private sector 7.4 per cent (average employment per private enterprise was only 2.5).

Privatization is much in vogue, but the process has been slow and contentious. Early problems involved, for example, the so-called 'emancipation of the nomenklatura', where managers converted state enterprises into companies in which they held a controlling interest and where the shares were undervalued. Under the first privatization bill, eventually passed in July 1990, enterprises were to be transformed into joint stock companies; the shares are held by the Treasury which has to sell them off within two years. The normal limit for foreign investors is 10 per cent, and workers get 20 per cent of the shares in 'their' enterprise at a discount. Originally some 20 per cent of shares were to be freely distributed to the general public, but this figure is likely to increase due to a shortage of savings, i.e. free distribution (and direct sales) is (are) likely to increase at the expense of public offerings. In July 1990 about 40 large enterprises were said to be due for privatization over the following year. Five large enterprises were successfully privatized between the end of November 1990 and the middle of January 1991 (although it is reported that at least one ran into difficulties soon afterwards).

Small and medium-sized enterprises are being sold or leased directly. In the first half of 1990 10 per cent of urban shops were privatized. The new prime minister, Jan Krzystof Bielecki, was confirmed in office on 4 January 1991. He promised a more rapid privatization process, with increased emphasis on the distribution of free shares to the public. It is likely that former owners will be compensated only partially and in the form of vouchers exchangeable for shares in newly privatized enterprises.

Direct foreign investment
Foreign investment is actively sought and by the end of March 1990 there were 1 231 joint ventures (usually very small-scale). Wholly foreign owned enterprises have been allowed since 1 January 1989, but so-called 'Polonia' companies (owned by ex-Polish citizens) pre-dated this concession by 13 years. Further concessions were promised, e.g. all profits to be able to be repatriated instead of all hard currency profits plus 15 per cent of domestic zloty profits as at present.

Romania
Nikolai Ceausescu became First Secretary of the Communist Party in 1965 and introduced a form of family rule ('socialism in one family').

The pre-1967 industrial enterprise was even more centrally controlled than even its pre-1965 Soviet counterpart. The so-called 'Directives' were issued in 1967 and the first stage of the reform was implemented in 1969–

72. The *Central* was the basic production unit, typically a horizontally integrated amalgamation of enterprises. But there was still a higher degree of centralization than in the Soviet Union. Granick (1975) argues that there was little real decision making below the level of the ministry. Financial discipline was stressed, with an increased role for interest-bearing credits and penalties for non-fulfilment of the plan. One novelty was the formal replacement of 'one-man management' by 'collective management'. This involved a board of management at the enterprise level (called a 'workers' committee' after 1971) and an 'administrative council' (later called a 'council of the working people') at the level of the *Central*. But, in reality, the decision-making powers of these bodies were restricted.

During the second stage of implementation 1973–78 the following features are worth noting: a decrease in the number of *Centrals*; state approval for all investment was needed after 1973; and the number of centrally allocated products increased in 1974 despite the professed aim of reducing ministerial power.

The third stage of implementation was put into operation from the start of 1979. The New Economic-Financial Mechanism was theoretically based on the principle of workers' self-management and had as its main aim the imposition of financial discipline (increased financial accountability for decisions still largely made by the centre). There was a stress on self-financing and an increased emphasis on net output (to provide an incentive, along with price increases, to make a more efficient use of energy and raw materials). Large production units performed social functions such as the provision of housing and education.

Smith argues that Romanian self-management was not equivalent to its Yugoslav counterpart; workers were in a minority on so-called 'workers' committees' compared with management, party and trade union representatives. There nevertheless appeared to be a degree of real consultation in plan setting, the party seeing the committees as a means of achieving centrally determined goals by going over the heads of management.

Wages and salaries were to fluctuate with the degree plan fulfilment; the minimum wage was abolished in 1981 and September 1983 saw the end of both the guarantee of a monthly income equal to 80 per cent of an employee's regular pay and of the 20 per cent limit on extra income dependent on plan fulfilment. In November 1987 there were serious protests about economic conditions generally, including pay reductions due to non-plan fulfilment. In fact, unrest and strikes occurred throughout the 1980s, partly due to the austerity measures taken in order to pay off the foreign debt (achieved by the end of March 1989 according to Ceausescu). In October 1985 the military took control of thermal and hydroelectric power plants and two years later a state of emergency was declared in energy, thus militarizing the sector. After this the party took increasing control of the economy in an attempt to avoid radical reform.

The private sector under Ceausescu was practically non-existent and joint ventures were few despite an early law (1971: foreign ownership was limited to a maximum of 49 per cent).

Events after the 1989 revolution

The National Salvation Front took over the running of the country on 22 December 1989 and won the free election of the following May. Ceausescu and his wife Elena were executed on Christmas Day 1989. Smith argues that the destruction of 'civil society' under Ceausescu, plus the exceptionally broad industrial structure with its obsolete capital stock (partly the result of manic debt repayment), make for a particularly rough ride for Romania in its transition to a new society and economy.

The private sector

In March 1990 the law was relaxed to allow four categories of private ownership: small enterprises employing up to 20 people; cooperatives of up to ten; family businesses; and self-employment. In August, however, there was some retrogressive legislation aimed at controlling private retailing (specifically 'profiteering' and black market activities) via a ceiling 10 per cent margin on unprocessed goods bought from state or cooperative enterprises. In late July 1990 the privatization bill was passed: state control over 20 per cent of enterprises (including mines, the post, railways, armaments and energy); 80 per cent of state to be converted into joint stock 'commercial enterprises' before privatization; starting in the first quarter of 1991, 30 per cent of the value of the capital of these joint stock companies will be distributed to adult residents for free in the form of vouchers exchangeable for shares; a probable 30 per cent of the shares of a particular enterprise is to be offered to its employees in exchange for cash or vouchers; a block of shares is to be reserved for foreigners; sale of shares to the public expected to begin in the last quarter of 1991. A more rapid privatization of small industrial and service enterprises was envisaged, with the former restrictions removed.

Foreign borrowing was again made possible in January 1990 and 100 per cent foreign ownership of enterprises was to be allowed.

Planning quickly started to disintegrate, but in the absence of replacement market structures. The situation thus became rather chaotic. The financial situation also deteriorated as pay increased and working hours were reduced, independent trade unions playing a part in this. There were some price increases in July 1990; for example, for petrol, luxury goods and newspapers, but the proposed price reform of 1 January 1991 was postponed until 1 April (at first until 1 June).

The National Salvation Front's election manifesto was cautious on economic reform, aware of the social costs of transition. Roman's announcement (18 October 1990) of a 'leap towards a market economy' was the result of a deteriorating economic performance and the collapse of central planning. Quick measures included the following: a devaluation of the leu, with the aim of internal convertibility by 1992; the lifting of controls on prices (controls remained on domestic energy, bread, meat and housing rents); only a partial indexation of pensions and wages; and a wage inflation tax. A shift to a market-based economy is envisaged by June 1992. A progressive personal income tax system was introduced on 1 April 1991.

The Soviet Union
Schroeder's famous description of Soviet reform as one continuous 'treadmill', with a myriad of changes altering nothing in any substantial sense, is an evocative one. But with the power to enforce central commands perceptibly fading, the old administrative system is crumbling at a time when a market-orientated substitute is not in place. Enterprises and lower-level state authorities are increasingly engaged in barter these days.

A history of industrial reform
The Liberman article in Pravda of September 1962 sparked off the first really open and broad economic debate since the 1920s. Experiments led to the so-called Kosygin reforms of 1965, which were planned to be gradually applied to industry by 1968. The branch ministerial system was restored (in 1957 regional economic councils had been set up); the number of enterprise success indicators reduced to eight; there was supposed to be a move towards wholesale trade; a capital charge was introduced; and there was to be a greater emphasis on long-term credits rather than grants. Even this modest reform, however, was chipped away in the post-1968 Czech invasion atmosphere. During the 1970s recentralization there was an emphasis on improving management and planning by means of integrated, computerized information and control systems, while the number of enterprise success indicators was increased. Decentralized investment was abandoned altogether in 1976. Earlier, in 1973, a decree pronounced the production association to be the main production unit in order to streamline the planning process, reap economies of scale and stimulate technical progress. In 1971 'counter plans' were introduced in order to induce the adaptation of plans more ambitious than those set out in the five-year plan. There was increasing attention paid to net output to encourage a more efficient use of inputs; after 1979 'normative' net output was given greater emphasis (the sum of *required* wage costs, social insurance and profit). Continuous attempts were made to increase the importance of five-year plans (more stable norms and so on). The

'comprehensive (programme) goal' approach to planning and management dealt with technical innovation and/or regions (e.g. the territorial production complex). Within the enterprise brigades have become more popular: these set their own work schedules to carry out assigned tasks, with the aim of increasing incentives and discipline.

Little was achieved during Andropov's brief secretarial term (November 1982–February 1984). He stressed order and discipline, decentralized investment was resuscitated, and the 1 January 1984 experiments highlighted contractual deliveries as an enterprise indicator. Chernenko (February 1984–March 1985) cautiously continued the Andropov line.

The Gorbachev era

Gorbachev became General Secretary on 11 March 1985, bringing in his wake *perestroika* (restructuring or economic and social reform), *glasnost* (openness) and democratization. Acceleration of growth was an early priority, but then gave way to a stress on economic reform. The discipline campaign (e.g. against alcohol) faded in time too. At first democratization involved fairly modest policies, such as separating party and state and giving a greater role to the latter. But political reform began to race ahead of economic reform, with the emergence of independent parties at the level of the republic or below. The threat to the very existence of the union by nationalist movements led to a reversal of the policy of liberalization in late 1990. Presidential powers have been increased and force used on occasion (e.g. in the Baltic Republics).

Industrial policy has involved a number of elements: decreasing the power of ministries, while enhancing both the strategic control of the centre and the decision-making powers exercised by the enterprise; a greater role for regional decision making (e.g. experiments in 'territorial self-financing'; strengthening the link between pay and performance/skill (note that independent trade unions have now emerged); and stressing the importance of quality of production (the State Quality Commission assumed only a temporary importance, however).

Industrial reform has been varied. There have been ministerial amalgamations. Various experiments have involved, for example, the VAZ (Volga Car Plant) and the Frunze machine tool enterprise at Sumy, followed (on 1 January 1987) by five industrial ministries and 37 enterprises being placed on a 'full economic accounting' basis (all expenditures, including investment, have to be covered by revenue earned or credits borrowed, and ministries are not allowed to transfer profits from solvent to loss-making enterprises).

The June 1987 Law on the State Enterprise (Association) had to be applied generally and gradually. Gosplan is seen as an 'economic headquarters' dealing with 'strategic' matters, while ministries are weakened. Primary reliance is on economic management rather than administrative methods. The banking system is to move towards more of a Western pattern of central and commercial banks. Enterprises are to be the subject of further amalgamation, but in the meantime the association is the basic production unit following the principles of:

1. 'Self-management': the workforce has a more active involvement in plan formation and in the election of management (the choice always had to be confirmed by superiors, but the experiment was scrapped in its entirety in December 1989).
2. 'Full economic accounting' and 'self-financing': all costs, including investment, are to be covered from revenue earned or from repayable credits.

Norms are to be stable for at least a five-year period. 'State orders' are not to take up the entire capacity of an enterprise and are not meant to be compulsory in the traditional sense (in reality they have been mandatory and the bulk of capacity has been taken up). Wholesale trade is meant to become dominant and there is to be an increasing conversion from defence to civilian production. Radical price reform was continuously delayed.

In the realm of foreign trade and capital there has been considerable movement. An increasing number of enterprises have been allowed to engage directly in foreign trade, and since 1 April 1989 any state or cooperative enterprise can be involved provided the product is competitive in world markets. Hard currency auctions are now organized. Since 1 January 1987 foreign ventures with Western companies have been possible. Initially 49 per cent was the maximum foreign ownership, but in December 1988 this was lifted and on 28 October 1990 100 per cent foreign ownership was approved.

The private sector
In 1987 there was a considerable relaxation of the laws relating to private and voluntary cooperatives. In March 1990 it was decreed that all forms of property are to be treated equally and private businesses are permitted to hire labour.

Economic reform by decree
The increasing chaos in the economic system described earlier led the Supreme Soviet to approve, in September 1990, the implementation of economic reform by presidential decree until 31 March 1992. The 27 September decree ordered contractual deliveries to be upheld until the end of 1991 by

both enterprises and local authorities. The 4 October decree gave enterprises the right to negotiate wholesale prices except for products such as oil, gas, coal and electricity; on 1 January 1991 many wholesale prices were raised substantially (e.g. oil 133 per cent and gas 100 per cent) and on 2 April 1991 retail prices were increased by about 60 per cent on average (there were wide variations, e.g. meat and meat products up to 200 per cent, and vodka zero). On 14 December 1990 republics and enterprises were forbidden to conclude deals with domestic and foreign enterprises that prejudiced existing economic links. Of course the problem with decrees is ensuring that they are actually implemented at a time when central authority is crumbling.

The transition to a market-based economy

There has been much debate and a number of programmes put forward, but, as yet, little action. In November 1989 Abalkin suggested a diversity of ownership forms, macroeconomic stabilization and phased moves towards a competitive market-based economy. The four phases are as follows:

1.   1990: legal preparations and macroeconomic stabilization measures;
2.   1991–92: implementation of the reform measures;
3.   1993–95: 'fine tuning' the economic mechanism. By 1995 80–90 per cent of output should be market determined and the budget deficit reduced to 3–4 per cent of GNP. Abalkin rules out a Polish-style 'shock treatment', because he considers that the Soviet government does not enjoy the required level of trust by the population.
4.   1996–2000: the firm establishment and development of the new economic mechanism.

In December 1989 the then prime minister Ryzhkov adopted on the whole a cautious attitude. He emphasized the need to increase the production of consumer goods. The budget deficit should be decreased from 10 per cent to 2–2.5 per cent of GNP by 1993, but price reform should be delayed (for agricultural purchase prices from 1990 to 1991; new wholesale and purchase prices should be set in 1991 and retail price changes should be completed in 1992). Ryzhkov proposed the following transition to a market-based system:

1.   1990–92: because of the need to saturate the consumer goods market, state orders for consumer goods should be given in the first two years of the five-year plan. In sectors such as fuel, chemicals, timber, metallurgy and most building materials state orders should be reduced to 90 per cent of capacity.
2.   From 1993 onwards: economic methods are to go into force to the maximum extent. By 1995 the share of property relations should be

state enterprises 65 per cent, shareholding companies 15 per cent, and leased enterprises 20 per cent.

In May 1990 Ryzhkov spelt out his programme for the gradual move towards a 'regulated' market economy, with the aim of controlling inflation but preventing a sharp contraction of output. The republics would be given more power, but the central authorities would decide how much. The stages are as follows:

1. 1990: laying the legal foundations of a market economy.
2. 1991–92: major steps to be taken towards the market, e.g. price reform.
3. 1993–95: the further reduction in administrative restrictions. State orders (starting in 1991) should be gradually limited to defence needs, public education, scientific and technical programmes, market stocks for the population, and the creation of state reserves of materials and equipment. State orders will account for no more than 40 per cent of the total output of the means of production.

Some of Ryzhkov's proposals for price reform proved to be controversial and politically unacceptable. The proposal to triple the price of bread on 1 July 1990, for example, led to panic buying. Partial income compensation for price rises was envisaged. The more radical economists also claim that administrative price increases without strict austerity measures are a recipe for high inflation.

In July 1990 came the so-called Yeltsin '*500-day confidence mandate*'. (The principal author was actually Grigori Yavlinsky.) The emphasis is on privatization (partly as a means of achieving macroeconomic stabilization via sales proceeds) and the postponement of price liberalization. Yeltsin also favours a genuinely free union of sovereign republics. The sequence runs as follows: first 100 days legislation; next 150 days stress on privatization and anti-monopoly laws; next 150 days stress on market prices and competition; final 100 days stress on 'aggressive stabilization'.

The programme which emerged on 11 September 1990 was more on the lines of the Ryzhkov–Abalkin proposals than the expected compromise. Macroeconomic stabilization would come first, including a series of state controlled price increases; the budget deficit was to fall to 2.5–3 per cent of GNP in 1991. A market-based economy would be established by the end of 1995.

The Shatalin programme
Although Ryzhkov argued that the Shatalin programme would lead to a large rise in unemployment and inflation, Gorbachev seemed to sympathize largely

with Shatalin at first ('I am more impressed by the Shatalin programme'), but then became concerned, especially with the power given to republics. It has also been criticized for being too ambitious time-wise, especially with regard to destatization and privatization.

There are a number of principles and a 500-day schedule:

1.   *The principles*   Austerity measures (stabilization) should come before price liberalization, otherwise inflation will result. The prices of up to 150 essential goods and services are to be frozen until the end of 1991, with wage indexation generally only covering essential goods and services. The republics would generally decide the balance of powers *vis-à-vis* the centre, in a voluntary economic union of sovereign republics (those opting out could take observer or associate status) although there should be a single currency, market, customs and banking system. A market economy is the aim and there should be equality in the treatment of ownership forms. A rapid process of 'destatization' and privatization is envisaged (the former is a broader concept involving leasing, employee ownership, cooperative ownership, and joint stock companies whose shares could be held, at least at first, by state-holding companies). Sectors such as defence, oil and gas, power, railways, the post office and long-distance communications, however, should remain in state hands.

2.   *The 500-day schedule*   This can be described as a rapid sequential programme and runs as follows:

   1.   First 100 days, starting 1 October 1990: stabilization measures, with the budget deficit reduced to 5 billion roubles by the end of 1990 and zero by the end of 1991 (spending to decrease, and revenue increased by some initial privatizations).
   2.   Days 100–250: the republican authorities will continue to issue state orders (although on a voluntary basis and at negotiated prices) in order to prevent a sharp fall in output. Further privatizations take place.
   3.   Days 250–400: 'stabilization of the market' phase, when the rouble becomes internally convertible and privatization progresses (to account for 40 per cent of manufacturing, 50 per cent of construction and transport, and 60 per cent of retail trade and services by the end of the period). Between 70 and 80 per cent of prices are to be deregulated, leaving fixed ones for essentials like oil, gas, steel, bread, meat, dairy products, sugar and basic medicines.

4. Days 400–500: the 'beginning of recovery' stage. Privatization to account for at least 70 per cent of industry and 80–90 per cent of construction, transport, retail trade and services.

Gorbachev's initial enthusiasm for the Shatalin scheme, however, declined as the political situation deteriorated. The powers given to the republics is one reason why the radical Shatalin programme was not adopted, but others include the failure of the West to grant large-scale aid (Jeffrey Sachs, *International Herald Tribune*, 15 May 1991, p. 8).

'Basic directions for the stabilization of the economy and the changeover to the market'
This programme was approved by the Supreme Soviet on 19 October 1990. This involved greater concessions to Ryzhkov–Abalkin than expected. The term 'basic directions' suggests a vaguer scheme, e.g. the republics can interpret the directions and work out the details. The existing economic links and agreements between enterprises and the state are to remain in force until the end of 1991. The (unified) market (with a single currency) will eventually rule (except in sectors like defence, health, education, and science and technology), although the state will regulate the market to combat inflation, unemployment, and excessive wealth and regional differentials. Indexation linked to a basket of consumer goods will vary: 100 per cent for pensions, stipends and subsidies, and up to 70 per cent for fixed income groups like doctors and teachers. All forms of ownership are to be treated equally. Destatization and privatization will take place 'over a long period'; initially the emphasis will be on sectors such as trade and services and on small enterprises in general. The centre will control defence, foreign policy, space research and environmental standards.

Four stages are envisaged, although no firm timetable is attached. The movement from one stage to the next is conditional on achieving the goals set. One time scale mentioned related to the 'foundations' of a market being perhaps laid in eighteen months to two years.

1. *Stage 1* emergency measures; stabilization, with the budget deficit reduced to 25–30 billion roubles in 1991 (i.e. not exceeding 2.5–3 per cent of GNP). The state will retain control of the prices of products such as fuel, raw materials, construction materials and basic consumer goods. Price controls should generally last through 1992, by which time only the prices of bread, meat, dairy products, transport fares, medicines and a few other staples would remain fixed. A start is to be made to destatization and privatization.

2.   *Stage 2*   severe financial restrictions and a flexible price system. Small businesses to be privatized and a market infrastructure is to be established. The retail prices of many consumer goods would be gradually liberalized.

3.   *Stage 3*   the formation of the market. The market infrastructure continues to evolve, and destatization and privatization gather pace. A housing market would develop.

4.   *Stage 4*   Completion of stabilization. Stabilization of the market and the financial system, with the budget balanced and an ample supply of goods and services assured. Destatization and the establishment of a competitive market are pushed along, especially in the light and food industries, agriculture and services. The preconditions will be created for a move to the internal convertibility of the rouble (with enterprises in the Soviet Union allowed to buy and sell currencies at the market rate).

With the very existence of the country under threat, however, economic reform took a back seat to preserving the union in the autumn of 1990. Gorbachev saw a greater degree of central control in general as a prerequisite for a shift towards a market-based economy. In the referendum of 17 March 1991 (the Baltic republics, Armenia, Georgia and Moldavia did not take part) the total turnout was 80 per cent and an overall 76 per cent 'yes' vote was given to preserving '... a renewed federation of equal sovereign republics...'.

The economic situation further deteriorated in 1991. Strikes escalated, led by the coal miners from 1 March. The miners' demands comprised political as well as economic ones (e.g. Gorbachev's resignation), but the May agreement included substantial wage increases and a transfer of control from federal to republican authorities (the former levying a tax).

On 23 April the Supreme Soviet approved prime minister Pavlov's 'anti-crisis' programme: a moratorium on strikes until the end of 1991; the enforcement of planned contracts; 'emergency regimes' in key sectors such as power and transport; an emergency system for the distribution of foodstuffs; austerity measures, such as controls on investment spending; encouragement given to foreign investment and private agricultural activity; and the speeding up of destatization/privatization (especially in small-scale service activities) and of price liberalization. On the same day, Gorbachev signalled a swing back to the centre ground of politics by signing an agreement with nine republican leaders, including Russia's Boris Yeltsin (the Baltic Republics, Georgia, Armenia and Moldavia did not take part). Essentially, the 'anti-crisis' programme was supported, although concessions were made: a new union treaty (of 'sovereign' states) was to be signed, which would involve a 'radical' increase in the role of the republics and allow them 'independently to decide on the question of accession to the union treaty' (those republics choosing not to sign the new treaty would have to pay world prices and in hard currency for energy and raw materials); there were to be fresh elections for 'organs of Soviet power' (a more broadly-based federal government is likely in the meantime); and concessions were to be made on (already announced) price increases and sales tax increases and on wage indexation. There is much controversy about the so-called 'Grand Bargain', the possibility of large-scale Western aid being provided in return for a radical economic reform programme.

Vietnam

A history of economic reform

Attracted by Maoist thought, the 1958–59 period saw increasing emphasis on mass mobilization methods such as socialist emulation and political exhortation/consciousness raising. The October 1958 new system of management had its slogan 'cadres take part in work, workers take part in management'. But doubts set in by the end of the next year and the 1960s witnessed a shift towards the Soviet model. During the 1970s there was a general movement towards plan coordination at the provincial level. Beresford makes the point that the imposition of the North's model on the South after 1975 caused such problems that economic reforms became necessary; the South is now the 'engine of growth'. The September 1979 reforms culminated in the January 1981 implementation of the 'three-plan system' for the industrial enterprise: planned output (produced with state-supplied inputs); above-plan output (produced with own-procured inputs); and unplanned secondary output (including by-products). Output outside the plan can be sold on the free market if the state is not interested.

In order to widen wage differentials (and thus to increase incentives), a piece rate system of wage remuneration began to be introduced in 1980 (although not very successfully) and there were also bonuses for improving product quality and savings in the use of raw materials. In the 1982–85 period criticism of command planning mounted and there was increasing recognition of the need for a decentralization of decision making. The Sixth Congress of December 1986 (confirmed by the Central Committee plenum of the following August) set the priorities as agriculture, consumer goods and exports, and called for 'renovation'. Renovation involved the elimination of the 'subsidy-based bureaucratic centralism mechanism' and its replacement by a planning mechanism based on 'socialist cost accounting' ('self-financing' as far as possible). Most enterprises today face only one indicator called 'contribution to the state budget', but 'key' enterprises (e.g. in coal, electric power and rail transport) also have output targets to fulfil.

Wages are linked to performance, although there is a minimum wage; management has a choice of piece or time rates. There is still interference (from local authorities for instance), but the reform is still radical with the economy steered mainly indirectly via economic levers.

Financial reform
In September 1985 a new Dong replaced the old at a ratio of 1 to 10, although limits per family were placed on immediate exchange in order to penalize free market traders. Unfortunately, state enterprises were adversely affected as well since they needed cash to purchase scarce inputs; this exacerbated goods shortages and, ultimately, inflation when the state rescued enterprises with credit injections. Subsidized ration certificates were replaced by pay increases to compensate for price rises, although rationing had to be reintroduced in January 1986. Inflation was over 700 per cent in early 1987. There was a shift to a Western-style banking system and an austerity programme was implemented. Expenditure cuts (e.g. subsidies) were made and the Dong moved towards the free market rate. Inflation plunged to 34 per cent in 1989 (although the rate started to rise once again in the second half of the year), but unemployment increased (officially over 9 per cent in the towns).

The private sector
Encouragement has been given to the private sector since 1986, but a mass privatization programme along present-day Eastern European lines is not Vietnamese policy. In mid-1989 the employment limit on private enterprises was lifted. In 1988 the private sector accounted for 19.6 per cent of industrial output and more than 50 per cent of retail trade. The new Law on Private Enterprise, effective from 15 April 1991, recognizes the equality of private business before the law, although strict state control is exercised over the licensing of sensitive activities (e.g. the media, explosives and precious metals) and those in state administration and serving army officers are debarred in order to combat corruption. But the private sector is still seen as playing a subordinate role.

Joint ventures
The 1977 legislation fixed a 49 per cent ceiling on foreign ownership, but 100 per cent was allowed after 1 January 1988.

Reaction to the revolutions in Eastern Europe
Vietnam's leaders draw a clear distinction between political and economic liberalization. Multi-party democracy has been ruled out and political reform has followed the line of separating party and state, ending abuses such

as special privileges and corruption, and forging closer links with the people. As in China, stability is considered a prerequisite for successful economic reform and recently there has been a tightening of political control. The Draft Platform for the Building of Socialism in the Transition Period emerged from the November 1990 session of the Central Committee in preparation for June 1991 Seventh Party Congress. The economic reforms are to proceed, policy being 'To build a planned commodity economy, to put into operation a market economy with state management'.

Yugoslavia

Ever since its birth in 1918, Yugoslavia has been plagued by ethnic strife. The country will not survive in its historical form and may not survive at all with, for example, Slovenia and Croatia in particular striving for at least a loose confederation. The country has come close to civil war, notably in the spring of 1991 over the question of the Serbian minority in Croatia.

After Tito's quarrel with Stalin over who was boss, traditional command planning (voluntarily adopted) soon gave way to a unique form of market socialism. After 1950 there developed a system based on 'self-management' of the 'socially owned' industrial enterprise via an elected workers' council. Enterprises do not have state targets imposed upon them, but the state steers the economy indirectly by means of economic levers (although fiscal policy has been weakened by federal weakness and monetary policy by a soft budget constraint and enterprise influence over banks) and more directly by, for example, temporary wage and price freezes. Large industrial enterprises predominated, resulting in a highly imperfectly competitive economic structure. By 1973 only 4 per cent of industrial enterprises in the social sector employed fewer than 125 workers, while 57 per cent employed more than 1 000. This caused concern that self-management would be compromised by the power of management and state administration and is one reason why in the 1970s the Basic Organization of Associated Labour (BOAL) replaced the enterprise as the basic legal and economic unit. Each BOAL represented a stage in the production process, the smallest unit producing a marketed product. There has been controversy surrounding the balance of decision-making powers between the workers' council and the manager (the latter's real power is greater than on paper because of a higher level of technical expertise, one argument goes) and over exactly what the enterprise prime maximand is ('net income', the sum of wages and profits, or net income per employee). Prices have suffered considerable interference, although the trend over time has been towards market determination.

Several sub-periods have been variously categorized: 1952–65 has been termed the 'visible hand' period (when, for example, the state exercised tight control over investment and foreign trade); 1965–74 is called the 'market self-management' period (involving, for example, a significant liberalization of prices, trade and investment); while the next one to around 1982 is the 'social planning' period. The latter resulted from a compromise between centralism and decentralism and involved 'social compacts' and 'self-management agreements'. Contractual planning, which acts with the market, involves information exchange and agreements between government authorities, trade unions and 'economic chambers' (representing enterprises). Social compacts are not legally binding; they mainly cover broad policy objectives such as prices and pay at a republican and inter-republican level, and are concluded between territorial authorities, economic chambers, trade unions and the party. Self-management agreements are legally binding contracts dealing with investment and the delivery of goods and so on between economic agents such as enterprises and BOALS. After 1983 increasing emphasis was placed on the market, 'social planning' suffering from problems such as collusion (rather than competition) and the difficulty of actually enforcing contracts (Ben-Ner and Neuberger, 1990, pp. 786–7).

The December 1988 Enterprise Law reinstated the 'enterprise' as the basic production unit, with profit maximization the goal and freedom to establish any sort of enterprise.

Joint ventures
The original legislation was passed in 1967, but majority foreign ownership was allowed in November 1984 and 100 per cent permitted in 1989.

The private sector
In 1946 the employment maximum (including family members) was fixed at a mere five for handicrafts. Greater encouragement to the sector over time has meant concessions; in 1987 the (regionally varying) ceiling was raised to ten in Slovenia and later on to 20. In 1986 the private sector accounted for 5.7 per cent of production.

The Markovic programme
The first phase concerned a (further) IMF-inspired austerity programme introduced in December 1989. Hyperinflation was to be combatted by restrictive fiscal and monetary policies and wage controls. Prices and foreign trade were largely liberalized. Banks are now private, limited liability joint stock companies. On 1 January 1990 the new dinar was fixed at a rate equal to $DM^1/_7$ (until 30 June at first, but the dinar was not in fact devalued to $DM^1/_9$ until 1 January 1991).

The December 1988 Enterprise Law replaced the 1976 Law on Associated Labour: the stress was on freedom to establish any type of enterprise, with all forms of ownership treated equally. The decision-making authority of managers was increased *vis-à-vis* the self-management bodies (which became advisory in principle). The second phase was unveiled on 29 June 1990, the main emphasis being on the transition to a more Western-type market economy. The August 1990 Law on Social Capital saw the transformation of enterprises into share-holding companies. The current federal emphasis is on worker share ownership (sold at a discount proportionate to years of service). The problem, as explained by Estrin and Takla, is that there is no general agreement on the precise sort of reform that is required either within the central government or between republics. Slovenia, for example, wants a rapid transfer to a Western-style market economy, whereas Serbia is far less enamoured with markets and privatization. The political turmoil and the threat to the very existence of the country is hardly conducive to the introduction of federal economic reforms.

An update to this chapter is given in the Postscript, page 278.

REFERENCES

Aslund, A. (1985) *Private Enterprise in Eastern Europe*, London: Macmillan.
Ben-Ner, A. and Neuberger, E. (1990) 'The feasibility of planned market systems: the Yugoslav visible hand and negotiated planning', *Journal of Comparative Economics*, vol. 14, no. 4.
Berliner, J. (1976) *The Innovation Decision in Soviet Industry*, Cambridge, MA: MIT Press.
Brezinski, H. (1987) 'The second economy in the GDR – pragmatism is gaining ground', *Studies in Comparative Communism*, vol. XX, no. 1.
Figueras, M. (1991) 'Structural changes in the Cuban economy', *Latin American Perspectives*, vol. 18, no. 2.
Granick, D. (1975) *Enterprise Guidance in Eastern Europe*, Princeton: Princeton University Press.
Jones, D. and Meurs, M. (1991) 'On entry of new firms in socialist economies: evidence from Bulgaria', *Soviet Studies*, vol. 43, no. 2.
Kornai, J. (1986) 'The Hungarian reform process: visions, hopes and reality', *Journal of Economic Literature*, vol. XXIX (December).
Kueh, Y. (1989) 'The Maoist legacy and China's new industrialization strategy', *China Quarterly*, no. 119.
Prybyla, J. (1989) 'Why China's economic reforms fail', *Asian Survey*, vol. XXIX, no. 11.
Von Czege, A. (1987) 'Hungary's New Economic Mechanism: upheaval or continuity', in Gey, P., Kosta, J. and Quaisser, W., *Crisis and Reform in Socialist Economies*, London: Westview Press.
Wong, C. (1989) 'Between plan and market: the role of the local sector in post-Mao reforms in China', in Gomulka, S., Yong-Chool Ha and Cae-One Kim (eds), *Economic Reforms in the Socialist World*, London: Macmillan.

2 Albania: The purge of Stalinist economic ideology

Adi Schnytzer

1. INTRODUCTION[1]

In 1989 the Warsaw Pact member countries of Eastern Europe experienced popular revolutions which led to a dismantling of communist dictatorship and calls for economic reform leading to a restoration of capitalism. In Albania, on the other hand, a monopoly of political power remained in the hands of the Party of Labour of Albania (PLA) until December 1990 (*New York Times* and *Chicago Tribune*, 13 December 1990). From the latter part of 1989 through 1990, the Albanian leadership attempted to maintain its hold on political office by dismantling its economic ideology and instituting an economic revolution from above. In this chapter the industrial reform of 1990 is analysed as a response, on the part of the Albanian leadership, to the threat to their political survival generated by events elsewhere in Eastern Europe. Also discussed are some of the broader conceptual implications for economic reform implementation arising from the Albanian experience.

Between 1945 and 1978,[2] the Albanian leadership adopted an economic strategy which may be understood as a literal application of that set out in Stalin's last published work, *Economic Problems of Socialism in the USSR*. In an earlier work (Schnytzer, 1982), I argued that adherence to Stalinist economic principles was subject to the constraint that the PLA remain in power and, more specifically, the adopted development strategy needed to generate sufficient economic growth to ensure a steady increase in the standard of living, itself a formal requirement of the Stalinist system. Until 1978 the Albanian government was assisted by a steady stream of foreign aid (Schnytzer, 1978).[3]

During the 1980s the Albanian economy was without foreign aid for the first time in its modern history and the overall level of performance declined (for a survey of this period, see Kaser, 1986 and Sjöberg, 1990). This gave rise to a shift in emphasis from heavy industry to consumer goods and agricultural reform was also stressed. Such deviation from the Stalinist development strategy is consistent with the political pragmatism of the Albanian leadership already noted.

On the nature of the rules governing the functioning of the industrial enterprise, however, the PLA leadership remained consistent until the crisis hit Eastern Europe in 1989. That is, the allocation of resources must be determined on the basis of command planning and state ownership of the means of production. It is the central empirical thesis of this chapter that, as throughout its history, when the PLA leadership has been faced with a choice between political self-interest and stated economic ideology, the former has emerged victorious.[4] Thus, in 1990 a virtually unchanged political leadership[5] presented and implemented economic reforms which, for the first time, granted scope for private economic activity outside agriculture and a role for the market in determining the allocation of resources by state-owned industrial enterprises. A theoretical analysis of the failure of a conciliatory approach to political crisis in communist dictatorships is presented in Schnytzer (1990).

A summary of the official economic ideology of the PLA in the period immediately prior to 1989 and the initial Albanian response to the collapse of communism elsewhere in Eastern Europe in 1989 are presented in section 2. The economic reforms introduced in 1990 are described in section 3, while in section 4 Coase's transactions cost theory of the firm is used to derive some lessons from the PLA's economic reform.

2. THE ALBANIAN LEADERSHIP QUA ECONOMIC STALINIST

The importance of command planning for the Albanian economy was well put in an editorial entitled 'He who violates the plan violates the law' in the PLA daily *Zëri i popullit* (23 January 1986):

> Our economy is a planned economy. The economic policy of the party is synthesized in our plans. They constitute an integral unity with correct proportions and coordinated tasks, in accordance with the requirements of the law, and the party's line and policy, in close connection with the concrete internal and external conditions and circumstances in which we live, build and defend our socialist order. Our plan is a direct function of the construction of socialist society and a synthesis of the creative thought of the masses, who are interested directly in the full realization of the tasks constituted by the plan. The party has never placed, and does not place, anything above the interests of the masses. Therefore, the execution of plan tasks in every link and by every individual, sector, enterprise, agricultural cooperative, district and ministry is a great patriotic duty, a party and state duty.

The *Weltanschaung* upon which the above quotation is based leaves no room for the operation of the free market in production.[6] In virtually all communist societies throughout most of their history, a free market has been tolerated in the agricultural produce of private plots. In Albania in the 1980s attempts were made to eradicate even this vestige of capitalism. Perhaps nowhere was PLA leader Ramiz Alia's professed attitude towards the market more clearly expressed than in the following remarks made during a speech to the Third PLA Central Committee Plenum on food supply in 1987 (Tirana Domestic Service, 24 April 1987):

> According to existing regulations, agricultural cooperatives must sell their products to the state trade ... organs. It is not infrequent, however, for village state stores to reject some produce ... due to quality or because more has been produced than has been planned. In these cases a proportion of production is lost, rotting in the field ... Meanwhile, cooperative members, taking a basket of figs, a handful of parsley or a dozen eggs, go to town. Is this in the interests of socialism, of the people, and of group property? Obviously not, because when the trade sector fails to collect cooperative output, on the one hand the social labour to produce this output is lost, and on the other hand, when the individual goes to market or sells his product to some middleman, he loses time *and the private market is stimulated*. [Emphasis added.]

Alia went on to point out that the sole purpose of the private plot in agriculture was to provide cooperative farm members with food for their own needs. In the case of excess supply, output was to be sold to the state or the cooperative. By 1989 the failure of attempted complete socialization of agriculture had apparently convinced the Albanian authorities to embark on a reform in that sector (Sjöberg, 1990). On the other hand, with respect to industry, decentralization of economic decision-making power to enterprises was contemplated only in the context of condemnation of reform elsewhere in Eastern Europe and the Soviet Union. A brief summary of this aspect of PLA ideology before the latter half of 1989 serves to reinforce the contemporaneous picture of anti-market and anti-democratic sentiment (if such reinforcement is necessary!) among Albanian leaders.

One of the criticisms levied by Albania at the Soviet Union when diplomatic relations between the countries were ruptured in 1961 was that the Soviets and their East European allies had turned their backs on Marxism–Leninism and that, in consequence, the road to a return to capitalism was open (Griffiths, 1963). This rhetoric continued unabated until the latter part of 1989, when politbureau member Lenka Çuko could report to the Eighth Central Committee Plenum that a prophesy had been fulfilled (*Zëri i popullit*, 27 September 1989):

> The modern revisionists have launched a savage campaign to revise and even deny the teachings of Marxism–Leninism on the party and socialism. Having marketed the 'theory' of the party's transformation into a 'purely ideological

factor' and having replaced [it] with the theory of 'the party of all the people', the revisionists have now come to the point of adopting outright bourgeois theses on political and ideological pluralism, as is happening in the Soviet Union, Poland, Hungary and elsewhere. 'Theories' about power-sharing with other parties, about relinquishing the leadership of the state in the economy ... and so forth, have all become the present foundation of antisocialism ... Our party and Comrade Enver Hoxha long ago foresaw and warned of the consequences of following the road of treason to Marxism–Leninism.

Thus, state leadership of the economy and a one-party political system emerge as essentials of Marxist–Leninist thought.[7] On the other hand, Çuko made it clear that the Albanian leadership must respond to events abroad and thereby made explicit some of the faults of the existing system. She laid stress on the need to democratize the PLA, pointed out that there were party members who use their position for personal gain, acknowledged the existence of widespread shortages of consumer goods and asked whether reforms in agriculture might not prove amenable to adaptation elsewhere in the economy.

Çuko went on to argue, the first time a politbureau member had done so publicly, that party membership need not be a prerequisite for the holding of important administrative or managerial posts. PLA First Secretary, Ramiz Alia, began his speech to the Plenum with, not surprisingly, a full endorsement of Çuko's views and explicitly acknowledged the impact of external events on Albania (*Zëri i popullit*, 29 September 1989):

In my contribution here, I would like to draw attention to some problems that have arisen at the present stage of socialist construction in our country or resulting from current international developments, and particularly those that have emerged in the countries of the East.[8]

Alia went on to defend socialism and insisted that economic Stalinism remained the ideology of the party (*Zëri i popullit*, 29 September 1989):

We will never permit the weakening of common socialist property. We will never permit that the way be opened to the return to private property and capitalist exploitation. We will never permit the weakening of the dictatorship of the proletariat, in the same way that we have never and will never share power with any antipopular force. We will never relinquish and never permit the weakening of the leadership role of our Marxist–Leninist party for the sake of the so-called pluralism dished out by the bourgeoisie.

And yet, towards the end of the speech, there came a dramatic shift of emphasis. Alia pointed out that under capitalism 'competition, the threat of bankruptcy and insecurity exercise powerful pressure on both the worker and his employer'. Under socialism this 'blind and pitiless' economic mechanism is absent. In other words, the design of incentive-compatible mechanisms is difficult and the role of the individual suddenly becomes important: 'Harmonizing the general interests of society and those of the individual is one of the most difficult problems of socialism' (*ibid*).[9] According to Alia, the failure to achieve such harmonization led to the downfall of socialism in Eastern Europe. Putting it another way, economic Stalinism had failed and the PLA would have a chance to remain in power only if it were prepared to change its strategy. The first socialist holy cow to be destroyed in the wake of this confession was full employment. Alia argued that if workers were lazy or absented themselves from work for no good reason, then they should find themselves without a job (*ibid*):

> Among us the view prevails that the state does not leave people unemployed. However, for the sake of socialism, sluggards, the careless and the irresponsible must not be allowed to profit. In my view, these people can be left without work.

Economic Stalinism in Albania was dead. It remained to be seen what would take its place.

3. THE ALBANIAN ROAD TO CAPITALISM

The Eighth Plenum of the PLA Central Committee had been one of ideas. Radical shifts in ideology mandated the design of a new economic system which would lessen political pressure on the communist regime. In the closing months of 1989 Albanian leaders explored in public some of the possibilities. In a speech in the Tropojë region in October (*Bashkimi*, 6 October 1989) Alia pointed out that indirect rather than direct steering would characterize the new system, while noting that Albania would never be induced 'to embark on the road of concessions'. Three days later, in the Pukë region, Alia raised a difficult agency problem in the issue of property rights, but failed to explain the solution (*Bashkimi*, 9 October 1989):

> Let no-one think that, since the forests are state property, the state cannot fine itself for damage caused by its enterprises. As you see, these problems are also related to the Eighth PLA Plenum: Is the economy to be guided by economic methods or administrative commands?

On the occasion of the 77th anniversary of Albanian independence and the 45th anniversary of the country's liberation, Prime Minister Adil Çarçani stressed that the Albanian concept of socialism had never been rigid, adaptation to change being one of its strengths (*Zëri i popullit*, 29 November 1989). In December, Ramiz Alia suggested the heresy that the PLA may no longer know what the masses felt about the economy (Tirana Domestic Service, 12 December 1989):

> The party needs to know as well as possible what the workers are thinking about socialist property and what measures need to be taken to strengthen it. The same applies to production relations, pay, prices, services, public order, administrative activity, law enforcement, and so on.

The first specific reform legislation emerged as a Decision of the Ninth PLA Central Committee Plenum.[10] Henceforth, virtually all party meetings at the local level would be open to non-party members and there would be two or three candidates for each constituency for the People's Assembly (albeit chosen by the Democratic Front). Enterprise directors would be elected, apparently freely, by the workers, who would also have the right to dismiss them (in the past the PLA had always appointed enterprise directors). Jobs in the administrative hierarchy would be obtained by the victors of competitions rather than as a consequence of political patronage and the mandate of elected party functionaries would be limited to four or five years, depending on the specific position. On directly economic matters, the following decisions were taken:

1. There must be a decentralization of economic decision-making power from the centre to the base, along the lines of the reforms in agriculture;
2. District Executive Committees are to have sources of income other than the state budget, and are henceforth to be free to engage in investment activity. One new source of income is to be 'excess savings' by enterprises within their district;
3. Enterprises should be sub-divided into small units[11] and material incentives such as piece work and specific task contracting be used wherever feasible;
4. Enterprises should be financially independent, with long-term bank credit replacing state subsidies. The latter are to be used only where 'absolutely essential';
5. Wages are to be based not only on plan fulfilment, but also on enterprise profits;
6. Wholesale price reform is necessary to improve enterprise efficiency;
7. Agricultural procurement prices are to rise;
8. Retail prices of 'primary necessities' are to remain fixed at previous levels, but the prices of luxuries are to change in accordance with '*supply and demand*';
9. Citizens may undertake *private* building-activities for their own use. Individuals and groups may contract among themselves and/or with

the state to build. In this way housing shortages may be alleviated. Furthermore, the state would sell some apartments to their occupants;

10.   The increase in industrial food processing is to be a major priority and agricultural cooperatives may now sell food in the towns at prices they themselves determine.

The above decisions are insufficiently detailed to permit a complete picture of the 'new economic mechanism', as it came to be called, to be drawn. More decisions were soon to be forthcoming, although even at this early stage the radical nature of reform was clear.[12] The invocation of supply and demand as factors determining the price of anything was hitherto unheard of in communist Albania. On the decentralization of economic decision-making power to industrial enterprises, it was recommended that the party leadership examine concrete proposals (as yet unspecified) more closely. Alia's justification for this important change in principle represents a victory for his powers of logic (*ibid*):

> Comrade Enver often stressed that the masses must feel themselves to be a creative factor ... under all circumstances of social activity. This is achieved if they join in the drafting and execution of plans, but finds full expression when the principle that the working class takes the leading role in society is applied ... and this can be achieved only if worker control is given omnipotent power over everything everywhere, *as was conceived when it was first introduced*.[13]
> Power is in the hands of those who have the right to make decisions. *There is no power without authority*. If the working class is given the right only to suggest and propose, it will be toppled from power. [Emphases added.]

Thus, the notion of a communist party as the vanguard of the proletariat and the sole instrument for the dictatorship of that proletariat (arguably the fundamental concept underlying Marxism–Leninism) lay in ruins. From this point on, the phrase 'Marxism–Leninism', as used by PLA leaders, would be pure window dressing. The concept of democratic centralism and the role of the law of value under socialism were soon provided with concomitant reinterpretation by Adil Çarçani (*Zëri i popullit*, 17 February 1990). Command planning must now be understood as excessive centralism, while enterprises should 'engage in their own planning'. This will prove beneficial for socialism (*ibid*):

> Democratic centralism will thus not be affected, only excessive centralism – which must be checked – and the line of the masses in the economy would be applied better, both at the planning and implementation stage, and the relationship between supply and demand would be improved on the basis of the law of value, which operates also under socialism.[14]

It had long been axiomatic in Albanian writings that inflation was an evil associated with capitalism, its existence in the Albanian economy never having been acknowledged. On the 17 March 1990, the daily *Bashkimi* provided a textbook account of the way in which repressed inflation manifested itself in the Elbasan district. Thus, in 1989 many agricultural cooperatives in the district overfulfilled their plans. Members, in consequence, received extra incomes which they attempted to spend on non-existent consumer goods. Under these circumstances 'equilibrium is upset' and 'inflation "rears its head" and enters the monetary sphere'. The obvious solution to the problem was an increase in the supply of consumer goods. The article did not speculate on the possibility of an increase in prices to reduce excess demand, but the next stage of the reform (discussed below) incorporated this option also.

In his report to the Tenth Plenum of the PLA Central Committee (Tirana ATA in English, 19 April 1990), Ramiz Alia noted that, in consequence of the Decision of the Ninth Plenum, there had been a significant turnover of enterprise directors and other officials. He observed that fully 67 per cent of central government employees were now non-party members, but provided no earlier figures as a basis for comparison.

Alia also discussed resistance to the reform. Its major source was reported to be administrative employees who were unwilling (or unable) to meet new job specifications. 'It is easier to do a job you have been used to for dozens of years than to master a new method of management.' That the leadership would adopt a hard line against resistance was implied by Alia's assertion that the class struggle was being waged in reform implementation.

As has been noted, the package of measures introduced at the Ninth Plenum was, in spite of its relatively radical nature, somewhat vague. The full details of the reform were presented to the Seventh Session of the Peoples' Assembly by Prime Minister Çarçani (Tirana ATA in English, 8 May 1990). They may be summarized as follows.

With respect to plan indicators, the reform divided enterprises into three categories. First, enterprises producing 'important' commodities, such as 'oil, chrome, copper, coal, electrical energy, textiles, sugar, flour, and edible oils', would remain subject to the physical planning of output. Second, enterprises producing consumer goods made of 'metal, wood, ceramics, terra cotta, etc.' would be free to determine their own levels of output and prices. Finally, all other enterprises would receive from the central authorities a global sales target and output targets for export and commodities to be delivered outside their own districts. For goods to be sold within the enterprise's own district, planned output would be determined by the enterprise in conjunction with the Executive Committee of the local People's Council.

In addition to planned output (regardless of the level at which planning took place) enterprises would be free to use up to 20 per cent of their productive capacity to produce either for export or the domestic market.[15] In the domestic market they would do their own selling and set prices in accordance with supply and demand. Enterprises could use unplanned export earnings to acquire unplanned imports. In the case of above-plan exports, foreign trade would continue to be conducted through state foreign trade enterprises.

With respect to non-labour inputs, the principle used was that the planner of output would be responsible for the provision of inputs. Centralized distribution would continue where there was central planning of output, while inputs for the production of goods destined for the market would be provided by the market. Transactions in the extant capital stock of an enterprise are not discussed in Çarçani's presentation and it seems reasonable to assume that, in the short term,[16] the firm could not dispose of its capital stock.

A more radical change was envisaged in the case of labour allocation. Henceforth, only the total wage bill would be determined centrally and enterprises would be free to determine the distribution of the wage bill among workers. Çarçani explained (ATA in English, 8 May 1990):

> Within the planned wage bill, the enterprise will have the right to employ as many workers as it deems necessary to fulfil the production plan. It will no longer be forced to employ workers beyond its real need, but neither can it reduce the existing number of workers without guaranteeing them, in cooperation with the Executive Committee of the district people's council, work within or outside the enterprise. As up to now, the latter will enjoy the right to exceed the planned wage bill when it exceeds its production plan.

The reform envisages also a decentralization of investment decision-making power. Thus, whereas previously all planned enterprise profits were paid into the state budget, the latter would henceforth receive only 10 per cent of enterprise profits. Enterprises would be required by law to reinvest 85 per cent of their profits in whatever manner they deemed appropriate, while the remaining 5 per cent could be allocated towards incentive payments. Where enterprises prove unable to meet their investment needs out of profits and the amortization fund, they could apply for short- or long-term bank financing.

The central (and only) bank[17] would now be free to decide whether or not to grant investment credit and would be required to supervise projects to ensure that money was being spent in accordance with the original terms of the loan. Finally, the 'bank will follow and control the process ... down to the complete payback of the credit'.

It was anticipated that financing of enterprises out of the state budget would virtually cease and a clear distinction was drawn between planned and unplanned losses. In the case of planned losses, due to circumstances outside the enterprise's control, the state would provide a unit subsidy to give 'the enterprise the necessary income for its reproduction'. On the other hand, unplanned losses (*ibid*):

> ... owing to bad management, cost increases, impaired quality of output, unjustifiable changes in the structure of production or the nonfulfilment of plans will not be compensated. They will be included in the economic–financial results of the enterprise in the coming year and ... the bank will grant credits at higher interest rates. If these losses ... are again incurred in the following year, sanctions will be applied ... beginning with dismissal of the leading administrative staff of the enterprise, the dissolution and transfer down to the suspension of its production activity. In such a case, the state will undertake the employment of workers.

As an added incentive to avoid unplanned losses, it was decided to fine all employees up to 10 per cent of their wages in the event of unplanned losses. However, the proposed reform did not restrict changes in the incentive structure to penalties only. For accounting purposes, enterprises would be divided into smaller units in order to facilitate financial control and bonus payments were to be tied directly to the profits of the relevant unit. In the event that an enterprise planned an above-plan increase in profit and fulfilled or overfulfilled its plan, half the extra profit would go to investment and half would be paid out in bonuses. Where this plan target was not met, workers could nonetheless obtain a bonus if they overfulfilled their own targets.[18] Workers could supplement their incomes by bonuses to the extent of up to the equivalent of three months' wages, regardless of how the bonus was earned.

The increased scope for market activity implied by the reform brought with it a need for a new legal framework to facilitate voluntary exchange. The PLA leadership seemed well aware of the difficulties posed by this requirement (ATA in English, 8 May 1990):

> Selling and purchasing relations among enterprises will be coordinated through contracts. In order to increase their role in working out and fulfilling the plans, it is thought that they should contain new elements of mutual obligation [including clauses mandating up to full compensation for damages caused] as well as strict measures in case the buyer does not pay his obligations on time, or when one of the parties violates contract discipline ... The Council of Ministers has studied further measures ... to strengthen the role of state arbitration in solving the civil and judicial disagreements created among enterprises, institutions and agricultural cooperatives.

A rationalization of the price system completed the range of proposals for substantial reform of the Albanian economic system at this time. Retail prices of basic necessities were either to remain unchanged or be subject to a one-off increase (in the case of compotes and jams, wines, shoes and textiles), whereas, as has already been noted, retail prices of other consumer goods would be determined by the market. The issue of monopoly was not addressed, although it is unlikely to have been a problem. The area in which totally decentralized pricing would take place was, in practice, restricted to the handicrafts sector, which is composed of many small enterprises.

Wholesale prices were to be changed to provide enterprises with greater starting profits or reduce planned losses facing the introduction of the reform. Thus, instead of being based on branch-average costs of production, wholesale prices would be based on the costs of the highest-cost producer in the branch. This shift towards marginal cost pricing would reduce the number of enterprises with planned losses and, thereby, reduce the extent of enterprise subsidization by the state.

Prior to an evaluation of the lessons to be learned from the reform, the remaining important reform measures taken in 1990 should be noted. At the beginning of July the Eleventh Plenum of the PLA Central Committee decided, *inter alia*,[19] to permit private activity in the area of handicrafts and retail services (*Zëri i popullit*, 13 and 14 July 1990). However, private enterprises were restricted to the employment of family members only.[20] Introducing this latest change, Ramiz Alia stated the PLA's political position well: 'There is no time left for lectures and propaganda. We must all act fast' (*Report on Eastern Europe*, Radio Free Europe, 10 August 1990, no. 32). And act fast they evidently did, for throughout July, the Albanian press was full of articles hailing the privatization and documenting growing numbers of new businesses.

The final important economic reform measure introduced by the PLA leadership in 1990 was taken by the Presidium of the People's Assembly, under the chairmanship of Ramiz Alia, on 31 July. A decree was passed on the 'protection of foreign investments' in Albania whereby (Tirana Domestic Service, 31 July 1990):

... investments and economic activity may take place on the territory of the People's Socialist Republic of Albania involving the work of enterprises, firms, foreign persons or Albanians resident abroad, in accordance with the legislation governing this activity.

The decree envisaged that foreign investors would be safe from the threat of arbitrary nationalization, would be compensated for losses incurred owing to war, a state of emergency or natural disasters on the same basis as domestic enterprises (which presumably receive complete compensation). The range of economic activities in which foreigners would engage was defined very broadly. A second decree on joint ventures indicated the scope of their activity (*Gazeta zyrtare*, 1990, no. 6, p. 189):

These enterprises ... are to modernize existing plants or build new plants with advanced technology. They will be based on the extraction and processing of the country's raw materials and will aim at increasing exports or reducing imports, expanding the range of consumer goods, creating new jobs, introducing new and modern methods of organization and management in production and services, and so forth.

Foreign enterprises would finance themselves as regards both domestic and foreign currency via accounts in the Albanian State Bank and would be permitted to repatriate profits in whatever currency they might be earned. The decrees did not restrict foreign investments to joint ventures.[21]

Insufficient time has elapsed to permit an evaluation of the success of the reform (although see the postscript for additional remarks). However, that implementation of the latest measures was not proceeding smoothly (as had been the case with the earlier measures) was pointed out by Alia in September (Tirana ATA in English, 7 September 1990). He argued that the steps taken during the previous six months had been too advanced for the 'personal development,..., experience and psychological training' of the Albanian people. He was also critical of, on the one hand, the bureaucratic 'routine and tranquillity' of those managers who and state agencies which obstructed reform and, on the other hand, of liberals who would disband cooperatives and privatize the whole economy. Alia noted the damage done to the economy by a drought which had begun in 1988 and whose full effects were felt in 1990 and promised that further measures would be taken to improve the supply of consumer goods.

One immediate consequence of the reform and/or the drought (there is no sound basis for an accurate attribution) was the appearance of open unemployment in the summer of 1990.[22] The 25 July issue of *Zëri i popullit* promised that all unemployed workers in Tirana would have jobs again by the end of August, while the 25 August edition of the same newspaper claimed that the drought had led to a drop in electrical output worth $20 million and that concomitant losses in industry amounted to $60 million.[23] Plant closures were a reported consequence of the drought, and although workers had been guaranteed 80 per cent of their previous salaries, there were complaints that some of these payments had not been forthcoming.

Finally, some perverse consequences of the new economic mechanism relating to incentives should be noted. On 1 August 1990 Albanian radio reported a meeting of the Council of Ministers. The stated purpose of the meeting was to make certain adjustments to the reform package in the light of some unanticipated outcomes. Since bonus payments were now to be tied to planned increases in profits, a considerable number of enterprises, Executive Committees of People's Councils and even ministries had set themselves lower output targets in the draft plan for 1991 than had been set (from above) for 1990 and in some instances, targets were below even expected actual levels of output for 1990. The Council of Ministers (perhaps confusing profit maximization with output maximization) argued that 'the essence of the new economic mechanism had not been understood'.

Another difficulty (possibly arising from the belief that state subsidization of enterprises would continue and from the understanding that unplanned losses would be penalized) was that some firms apparently planned losses for themselves for 1990. The government's response to this dysfunction was straightforward: the law was amended so that firms were forbidden to plan losses, only the state could do so. The Council of Minister's response to reduced output targets was less comprehensible (Tirana Domestic Service, 1 August 1990):

> The mechanism demands that an enterprise plans for a net income in a coming year which will be greater than its net income in the previous year, by way of increased production, greater efficiency, the enterprise's profits, and its workers' pay.

Unless net income is interpreted as revenue, the above quote makes no sense. If, on the other hand, an increase in planned sales is intended, there is a problem of incentive compatibility since maximization of profit growth, which the bonus scheme implies, need not imply an increase in sales.

It was the Albanian government's intention that economic reform would be implemented in all enterprises on 1 January 1991. According to Professor N. C. Pano, who visited Albania in December 1990, it was clear that implementation was proceeding according to plan (personal communication).

4. THERE IS NO SUCH THING AS A FREE MARKET

At the time of writing (February 1991) it is unclear whether the PLA will remain in power long enough to implement fully its economic reform or whether, if a new political party takes power, reform will continue along the lines already introduced.[24] Election platform documents for the PLA (*Albanian Telegraphic Agency*, 1 January 1991) and the newly formed Democratic Party ('Platform of the Democratic Party', Tirana, 12 December 1990) provide few specific details. The opposition party appears to favour more rapid reforms, but differs unambiguously from the PLA position only in arguing for the privatization of agriculture. The PLA document argues for the independence of cooperatives from state control, but against privatization on the grounds of economies of scale. It further promises freedom of economic emigration and justifies the breakdown of enterprises into smaller units 'to attenuate and avoid the monopoly position in the market and the price fixing

... to open the way to competition for economic efficiency and quality' (p. 6). The document provides no evidence to suggest that the PLA would not proceed with economic reform as described above. Consequently, it seems more useful to discuss a number of conceptual issues of wider relevance arising from the reform than to attempt a more detailed evaluation of its specifics.

In a seminal article on the nature of the firm, Coase (1937) considered the role of market and non-market resource allocation in a capitalist economy. His essential contribution lay in the realization that market transactions are not costless. In a competitive economy, the firm arises as an organization within which resources are allocated by central direction (Coase, 1988, p. 53):

> To determine the size of the firm, we have to consider the marketing costs (that is, the costs of using the price mechanism) and the costs of organizing of different entrepreneurs, and then we can determine how many products will be produced by each firm and how much of each it will produce.

Coase shows that an efficient equilibrium emerges in a competitive economy in consequence of the profit maximizing behaviour of firms.[25] He refers to central planning in a fascinating footnote (Coase, 1988, p. 37):

> It is easy to see when the state takes over the direction of an industry that, in planning it, it is doing something which was previously done by the price mechanism. What is usually not realized is that any business man, in organizing the relations among his departments, is also doing something which could be organized through the price mechanism. There is, therefore, point in [the argument that] the problems involved in economic planning [are] the same problems that have to be solved by businessmen in the competitive system ... The important difference between these two cases is that economic planning is imposed on industry, while firms arise voluntarily because they represent a more efficient method of organizing production. In a competitive system, there is an 'optimum' amount of planning!

The important thing to note about this quote is its starting point: a competitive economy with an output mix and industry-specific capital stock generated on the basis of consumer preferences is set upon by a planner. By implementing a degree of planning beyond that which has already emerged via the market, the planners generate inefficiency. Consider now the application of this model to reform in an economy which has been centrally planned for several decades. Owing to planners' preferences, the output mix differs from that in a market economy; in particular, there are fewer consumer goods than would be produced if resources were allocated on the basis of consumer preferences. On the other hand, regardless of the type of reform introduced, the industry-specific capital stock which is in place cannot be redirected to increase significantly the output of consumer goods. Hence economic reform implies *transition costs* and such a reform will be efficient only if it minimizes such costs.

The PLA's economic reform may be interpreted as an attempt to allow *the market* to determine the optimal output mix while minimizing the costs of transition. Thus, in contrast to the 1968 New Economic Mechanism in Hungary, for example, the decentralization of economic decision making with respect to output was not formally complete, nor was the freeing up of prices restricted to specific sectors.[26] By permitting enterprises to use up to 20 per cent of productive capacity as they wished and by tying bonus payments to profits (albeit perhaps not optimally)[27] the PLA facilitated a redirection in output subject to the specificity of capital constraint.

Production above and beyond the centrally planned level will be taken to the point at which price equals marginal cost. Nonetheless, inefficiency persists whenever the centrally planned quantity of output exceeds total demand. Such an outcome is, however, readily observable and plan targets may be lowered in the subsequent plan period. Hence, it might be anticipated that over time the extent of decentralized planning would be increased. The attempt to create a genuine labour market, the privatization of handicrafts, small-scale retail services and a portion of agriculture and the legislation on foreign investment also suggest an intention to let the market determine its own extent.[28]

In a number of its components, the reform implies concern for the costs of transition not apparent in, for example, the January 1990 reform in Poland. First, there is the requirement that workers made redundant be found alternative employment. While such a regulation might imply high organization costs in a large economy, it is possibly workable in Albania, whose population is around 3.3 million and is divided among 26 districts. Second, there is the continued mandatory planning, in physical units, of basic commodities. A significant economic consequence of the fall of communism in Eastern Europe has been uncertainty substituting for rigid planning at the level of the enterprise even in the absence of a fully articulated reform programme. An efficient market has not replaced planning, because the legal and institutional framework necessary to reduce marketing and information costs and to provide appropriate incentives is not in place. By insisting that a given quantity of certain commodities be produced (and maintaining the more or less appropriate incentive structure) the PLA has reduced the uncertainty which is generated by both 'big bang' reforms and an economic policy vacuum.

The efficient replacement of planners' preferences by consumer preferences in determining the allocation of resources requires the development of a capital market. It is not surprising that most attempted reforms of a social-ist economy have failed to cope adequately with this problem, since it is the capital market whose institutional framework is the most complex and has taken the longest time to develop under capitalism. To the extent that threat-ened closures of loss-making enterprises are carried out, a reform which permits firms to start with a positive level of profits (via wholesale price reform) and which grants them some scope to function on the market and to determine their own investment policy may succeed in generating the appro-priate capital structure *in time*. The centralized closure of enterprises which make losses when confronted by irrational prices in a centrally planned environment is not parallel, in its efficiency implications, to the bankruptcy of inefficient firms in a competitive economy.

In its desire to implement reform, the PLA leadership has had the advan-tage over other governments in Eastern Europe by maintaining, until very recently, a monopoly of political power. Given the inevitable resistance to economic reform brought about by the consequent income redistribution, it is ironic that a democratic government, by virtue of its very nature, is least well equipped to overcome the resistance while most keen to implement changes. It may possibly be a historical curiosity that the PLA leadership showed itself so determined in the implementation of economic reform in 1990.

The foregoing arguments are summarized simply. If the market best de-termines its own extent in a competitive economy, there is no reason to believe that it cannot also find its own optimal level out of central planning. But markets operate on margins and therefore require time to bring about significant structural adjustments. The PLA, once the most doctrinaire Stalinist regime in the world, may yet leave it with a lesson for the transition to capitalism which its own leaders could scarcely have contemplated a mere two years ago.

An update to this chapter is given in the Postscript, page 279.

NOTES

1. I wish to thank Professor N. C. Pano for critical comments on an earlier draft and for the provision of primary source material.
2. The official break in relations between Albania and China took place in July 1978 although the precise date at which Chinese foreign aid to Albania ceased is unclear.
3. On the difficulties imposed by a change in aid donors, see Hillman and Schnytzer (forthcoming).
4. On political self-interest models as applied to capitalist economies, see Stigler (1988) and Mueller (1989).

5. It should be noted that five full and two candidate members of the politbureau were dismissed on 11 December. However, unlike the case in other East European governments, the First Secretary and Prime Minister remained in power.
6. Elements of the market have always been present in the Albanian economy in that there has been consumer choice and a limited labour market.
7. In keeping with the Albanian practice of the time, in this chapter I use the terms 'Stalinist' and 'Marxist–Leninist' interchangeably. However, it should be noted that Stalinism has now been renounced by the PLA.
8. 'The East' refers to the Soviet Union and Eastern Europe.
9. This formulation represents a genuine innovation in Marxist–Leninist thought.
10. See Alia's speech in *Zëri i popullit*, 25 January 1990. The decision was broadcast by the Tirana Domestic Service, 3 February 1990.
11. It is not clear whether the small units were to be brigades or departments.
12. Of course, the reforms were radical only in the Albanian context.
13. See Schnytzer (1982) on the original conception of worker control.
14. It had been a basic tenet of Albanian political economy (following Stalin) that the law of value played a very restricted role under socialism. See Schnytzer (1982).
15. Agricultural cooperatives would be free to use all of their capacity as they saw fit.
16. Long-run changes in capital allocation are considered below.
17. However, on 26 December 1990, the joint venture Illyria Bank was formed. In May 1990 there was only one bank in Albania.
18. It will be recalled that the Decision of the Ninth Plenum had envisaged the introduction of individual-specific remuneration schemes.
19. The plenum had been convened on 6 July in response to a student demonstration on 2 July and the attempted exodus of thousands of Albanians via foreign embassies. Another decree was passed granting the right of assembly.
20. This restriction no longer applies (*Chicago Tribune*, 2 January 1991).
21. The Albanian government has apparently offered to sell land to a US oil company for purposes of exploration.
22. While it may be that there had been open unemployment in Albania before this time, there is no evidence to support this view.
23. Most of the energy needs of Albanian industry are met from hydroelectric sources.
24. Parliamentary elections were originally scheduled to take place on 10 February 1991 with the new Democratic Party fielding candidates (*Chicago Tribune*, 15 December 1990). They are now to take place in March.
25. For an elaboration of the marketing, or as it is now known, transactions cost theory of the firm and a survey of the extensive research to which it has given rise, see Demsetz (1988), particularly Chapter 9.
26. In the Hungarian case, commodities were divided into three groups. For one group, central authorities would continue to set prices, for a second, enterprises would be free to set prices within centrally determined limits, while for the final group enterprises would set prices according to supply and demand.
27. I ignore here the problem of property rights, which has been subjected to considerable a priori theorizing but, in the context of a socialist economy, virtually no empirical scrutiny.
28. Free access for foreign firms may alleviate the problems of monopoly associated with reform. On this difficulty see Schnytzer (1991).

REFERENCES

Coase, R. (1937) 'The nature of the firm', *Economica*, no. 4. Reprinted in Coase, R. (1988) *The Firm, the Market and the Law*, Chicago: University of Chicago Press.

Demsetz, H. (1988) *Ownership, Control and the Firm: The Organization of Economic Activity*, vol. 1, Oxford: Basil Blackwell.

Griffiths, W. (1963) *Albania and the Sino-Soviet Rift*, Cambridge, Mass.: MIT Press.

Hillman, A. and Schnytzer, A. (forthcoming) 'Creating the dependent reform-resistant economy: socialist comparative advantage, enterprise incentives and the CMEA', in Hillman, A. and Milanovic, B. (eds) *The Transition from Socialism in Eastern Europe: Domestic Restructuring and Foreign Trade*, Washington: World Bank.

Kaser, M. (1986) 'Albania under and after Enver Hoxha', in US Congress Joint Economic Committee, *East European Economies: Slow Growth in the 1980s*, vol. 3, Washington: US Government Printing Office.

Mueller, D. (1989) *Public Choice II*, London: Cambridge University Press.

Schnytzer, A. (1978) 'China and the Soviet Union as major trading partners: the impact of aid on Albanian industrial development', in US Congress Joint Economic Committee, *Compendium on the Chinese Economy*, Washington: US Government Printing office.

Schnytzer, A. (1982) *Stalinist Economic Strategy in Practice*, London: Oxford University Press.

Schnytzer, A. (1990) 'An economic model of regime change: freedom as a collective good' (mimeo).

Schnytzer, A. (1991) 'Socialism in less than one country', in Hillman, A. (Ed.) *Politicians and Markets*, Boston: Kluwer Academic Publishers.

Sjöberg, Ö. (1990) 'The Albanian economy in the 1980s: the nature of a low-performing system', Stockholm Institute of Soviet and East European Economics, working paper no. 10.

Stigler, G. (Ed.) (1988) *Chicago Studies in Political Economy*, Chicago: University of Chicago Press.

3   Innovation with an unchanging core: No path to the market in Bulgaria?

Robert J. McIntyre

Western scholarly opinion tends either to accept a monochromatic picture of an unchanging Soviet-type economy model or notice only developments which seem to portend greater use of markets as coordinating devices. This chapter calls attention to institutional–structural developments in Bulgaria during the period up until 1989 which suggest that retention of Soviet-type core institutions is consistent with qualitatively significant incremental economic reform. This experience supports a larger argument (McIntyre, 1989a, b), drawn from a variety of European socialist cases, that a wide range of variation is possible in the institutions developed around and in the presence of Soviet-type command planning. What this portends for the future is unclear in light of the simultaneous assertion that central planning is a thing of the past and the failure everywhere in Eastern Europe to create viable alternative institutional forms. If shock therapy approaches to rapid marketization and privatization fail, this conceptual argument contradicting the conventionally assumed immutability of societies organized around Soviet-type economic institutions then raises the possibility of multiple feasible systems types in coming years.

Bulgaria started from a particularly low material and cultural level, as well as unfavourable resource and energy endowments, but achieved relatively dynamic and successful initial modernization within Soviet forms. Comprehensive state ownership and physical central planning characterized the rapidly expanding urban, industrial core. The rural economy was collectivized and rapidly mechanized in a manner that led to high rural incomes and generally good results, aided by effective integration of the family garden plots with the collective sector. Bulgaria sustained rapid and qualitatively significant growth over the 1970–85 period in the continued presence of the crucial core institutions of Soviet-type planning and economic coordination. The simultaneous 'standard of living' programme produced a steady and relatively rapid rise in the range and quality of goods and services available to the consumer sector and achieved this result in part by finding ways of expanding the role of small-scale enterprises and integrating them with the large-enterprise state sector.

Fast structural transformation, rapid growth in incomes and improvement in the quality and quantity of consumer goods available during the 1945–

1975 period, produced a widespread view that the country was well governed and little pressure for economic or political reform. Less satisfactory economic results in the following decade, and severe problems beginning in 1983–85, were accompanied by rising political discontent. Bulgaria was deeply committed to the CMEA bilateral trade patterns. Especially important was the Soviet Union, which provided the major market for manufactured and agricultural output and the principal source of raw materials. The decay of this trade relationship, beginning in the Andropov period, sharply depressed overall Bulgarian economic performance. Soviet trade retrenchment after 1986 compounded the problem and led Bulgaria to begin borrowing heavily abroad.

While the political effects of *perestroika* and *glasnost* were late arriving in Bulgaria, they struck with particular force, since the collapse of the coordinating function of the Bulgarian Communist Party (BCP) parallel hierarchy occurred in the context of these already existing economic difficulties. The absence of historical anti-Soviet feeling and the successful creation of a CPSU-like political order contributed to the lack of an experienced and coherent opposition. A political crisis developed and by the Autumn of 1989 resulted in the abrupt resignation of Todor Zhivkov after 35 years in power. This left Bulgaria with a leadership vacuum when no alternative structures of coordination and control emerged. In an atmosphere of growing chaos in March 1990, both principal and interest payments on the foreign debt were suspended. From a position of relative prosperity and seemingly successful development, Bulgaria suddenly faced the possibility of real deprivation at the same time that creation of entirely new forms of economic organization were required.

1. RECURRENT EARLIER STRUCTURAL AND PLANNING SYSTEM REFORM

The Bulgarian experience with economic reform dates from the time of the *sovnarkhozy* (regional economic councils) reform in the Soviet Union in 1957 (which was followed in 1959 by a similar Bulgarian economic regionalization) and intensified at the time of the Liberman discussions in the Soviet Union in 1962–65. Since then the Bulgarian economic and planning system has gone through a typical cycle of changes, reversals and revival. The relatively good performance of the Bulgarian economy prevented serious criticism prior to the early 1980s and thereby prevented the movement for conventional economic reform from ever gathering real momentum. The combination of factors that emerged toward the end of the 1981–85 plan (persistent weather problems adversely affecting both agriculture and industry, energy stress heightened by damaged economic relationships with the Soviet Union, and problems in adjusting to rising quality standards in both Western and CMEA markets) briefly pushed conventional economic reform to the top of the political agenda. Yet when the Thirteenth Party Congress ended in April 1986, the reform agenda remained much the same as what was described in the Central Committee Theses of late 1965 (Jackson, 1986, pp. 47–9). Bulgarian reform developments of these two intervening decades echo familiar themes, seeking greater enterprise flexibility, autonomy, and responsiveness to both world and domestic market conditions, while asserting the need for strict economic accounting (*stopanska smetka*) within the centrally planned environment.

Despite the nearly constant discussion of reform since the late 1950s and the steady and self-conscious use for the last decade of the term New Economic Mechanism, with its Hungarian overtones, nothing similar happened in the large enterprise sector of the Bulgarian economy. Even in those small service and trade categories where Hungary (and the erstwhile GDR) encouraged a modest and tightly controlled expansion of the private sector, no such Bulgarian policies or actions could be discerned until the autumn of 1987. Within the large enterprise sector there were recurrent reform and reorganization measures which were often contradictory or temporary in their effects. Despite nearly constant talk of 'reform of the economic mechanism', there appears to have been very little impact on the management and planning system as it affects the daily behaviour of the large socialist organizations, unless the sharp increase in scale resulting from the formation of the *Durshaven stopanstvo organizatsia* (DSO: the Bulgarian version of the economic association) is treated as a decentralizing reform. The DSOs were originally formed after 1964 and assumed first the operational prerogatives of and then full ownership rights over their previously autonomous subunits. Prior to the more radical measures of the mid- and late 1980s, this issue of economic reform centred on the detail of the control of DSO behaviour by planning and ministerial hierarchies.

While new types of peripheral economic institutions were created over the last decade, very little was done to alter the functioning of the large state organizations or to deal with the dysfunctional behaviour and incentive patterns of the classical Soviet-type industrial enterprise. Thus economic changes in Bulgaria up until 1989 can best be described as 'institutional innovations in the absence of reform' (McIntyre, 1988a, 1989a, b). (For a more detailed treatment of the Bulgarian reforms see Lampe, 1986; McIntyre, 1988c; Jeffries, 1990; Jackson, 1990.)

2. ALTERNATIVES TO CONVENTIONAL ECONOMIC REFORM: THE 'SMALL ENTERPRISE INITIATIVE'

Conventional 'economic reform' thus had little effect on the behaviour of the core institutions of the Bulgarian socialist economy. The relatively sharp favourable changes in consumer living standards observed over the 1970–85 period occurred principally as a result of the foundation and effective performance of relatively autonomous small and medium-sized units (generally located within existing larger state enterprises) and the great improvement in food supply under the new form of integration between the Agro-Industrial Complexes (AIC) and the personal plots (the latter are considered in detail in McIntyre, 1989b). These two changes in economic practice are in a sense outside the realm of conventional reform, but the 'small enterprise' and 'small-scale agricultural' initiatives developed their own momentum and had major effects on the way the Bulgarian system actually functioned.

3. THE BIA, BANKING AND THE 'SMALL ENTERPRISE INITIATIVE'

The organization of the Bulgarian financial system is part familiar and part unusual. The bulk of credit extension and the monitoring of transactions between enterprises are carried out by the Bulgarian National Bank (BNB) which functions much like Gosbank in the classical Soviet model. Long-term investment financing for projects included in the annual plan is thus administered by the BNB, which also makes short-term working capital loans. In addition to the functions of central banking and currency control, the BNB has acted like the Soviet State Bank (Gosbank) in monitoring the financial aspects of plan fulfilment and the financing of investments included in the plan. In 1986 it was decided to separate the central banking and investment functions, creating a new Investment Bank to handle the latter. A similar separation was introduced in the 1960s and then reversed.

There is another source of credit to enterprises that is less familiar, and while not free of connections to the BNB, can be viewed as coming from a separate financial decision-making centre. The Mineral Bank-Bank for Economic Initiatives (MB-BEI) plays a major role in financing credit for two quite different categories of projects: (1) above-plan projects of large enterprises that help to achieve the plan more effectively; and (2) foundation or expansion loans for small and medium-sized enterprises. The Mineral Bank is a joint stock company owned 50 per cent by 'other banking institutions' (meaning the BNB) and 50 per cent by some 200 large economic organizations. It is closely linked to the BNB (the chair of the MB is the first deputy chair of the BNB) and to the Bulgarian Industrial Economic Association (the chair of the BIA is chair of the 'expert council', which appraises individual applications for credit to the Mineral Bank). The functions of the BIA and MB were not affected in any clear way by the reorganization of the banking system introduced in June 1987, although the MB is instructed to take on the attributes of a 'commercial bank' (Daviddi, 1987b). What happened to these financial channels after November 1989 is unclear.

The Bulgarian Industrial Association was founded in 1982 as a 'voluntary membership organization'. In addition to trade promotion, it engaged in a unique set of activities which range from provision of management and technological consulting services to the foundation of new enterprises. The BIA both directly stimulates enterprise formation in areas where its studies have discovered gaps in the domestic or export market and provides a kind of venture capital support to new projects developed by existing enterprises (Mishev, 1985, 1986; Puchev, 1986 and 1990b). In some ways it operates like a national 'Ministry of New Methods and Products' (McIntyre, 1988b), despite having no such statutory standing. Its power and latitude for independent action seemed to be very great, and it was able to work outside (or easily transcend) traditional organizational channels. The special role of the BIA in stimulating the foundation of new small-scale production units is one of the intriguing features of the New Economic Mechanism period, which could have implications for developments in the 1990s. These new enterprises have played a major role in the rapid improvement in the quality and supply of a large range of clothing, small appliance and speciality food products. The link between the BIA and the Mineral Bank was strong to the point where the Mineral Bank was referred to as 'the bank of the BIA', although that seems to be something of an exaggeration.

The lending policies of the Mineral Bank are different for its two different categories of borrowers. Quarterly competitions are held for funds to be distributed through the small enterprise programme. Applications are reviewed, ranked and funded by an outside expert council (made up predominantly of economists and strongly influenced by the BIA) until the allocated funds are exhausted. As of the beginning of 1986, 60 projects had been put into operation, 400 more had been approved and were in the process of construction, and a total of 1500 such small plants were planned to be in use by the end of the ninth five-year plan in 1990 (Mishev, 1986). About 5 per cent of total capital investment is to be allocated in this fashion. Despite the use of the term 'competition', this is not formally equivalent to the late lamented Yugoslav investment auction (Neuberger, 1959), since in the Bulgarian case the interest rate is determined by the bank after the loan is approved and is not itself an element in the bidding. Projects are ranked on the basis of their effectiveness (apparently their payback period) modified by any special characteristics, such as high energy saving or large foreign currency generating potential. The interest rate on these loans is generally 4 per cent (2–15 per cent) with a repayment period of up to 36 months.

Loans to established enterprises for above-plan investment projects (projects designed to facilitate achievement of the planned results in most cases, but in ways not foreseen in the plan) are handled in an entirely different manner. Appraisal of projects is done on a year-round basis by the professional staff of the bank and approved projects are normally charged interest rates around 4 per cent, but the bank has the authority to lower rates as far as 2 per cent when there is a special desire to stimulate the sector or the investor has a particularly good credit history. Rates as high as 15 per cent may be charged to investors with a bad credit history or whose work on a current project (initially funded at a lower interest rate) has been unacceptably prolonged. The MB may also request that the BNB impose salary penalties up to a maximum of 20 per cent in cases where long delays in completing investment projects are due to managerial incompetence or inattention. As much as 5 per cent of the loan may be assigned to cover start-up costs and raw materials for up to 72 hours of testing, but additional working capital must be borrowed from the BNB (Boichev, 1985). A number of Bulgarian economists have supported increasing the share of investment funds allocated through the MB-BEI, especially through the small and medium-sized enterprise programme.

4. SMALL AND MEDIUM-SIZE ENTERPRISES

It is important to be clear about the character of the BIA small enterprise programme, which has been erroneously cited as an example of movement toward private ownership. These units were not private in any respect and reflected a management experiment within the general pattern of state ownership. They are best viewed as semi-autonomous divisions of existing larger enterprises which remained responsible for coordination and general supervision of the small enterprise activities. Still, the managerial staff of the small enterprises appeared to have much more autonomy and room for independent action at all levels of business behaviour, including product design, production methods and practices, marketing and pricing. The divisions often had a separate brand name and sometimes had tied retail outlets operating under that name and selling only their own output.

Units producing a wide range of consumer goods have been introduced, e.g. mayonnaise and Italian ice-cream, rubber sports shoes, various clothing and small appliance items, and injection-moulded polymer furniture. The last product is the output of the firm IPOMA, which is located on the edge of

Sofia and is a particularly interesting example of several institutional innovations which are mentioned as goals in Bulgaria. While derided as pipe-dreams by some Western commentators, these practices were established business facts in this case. In addition to a highly disciplined work environment (clean, orderly and obviously well organized) with modern injection moulding equipment, IPOMA operates with the following features: a fully worked out brigade system (which is, in effect, a group piece rate, applied on top of a wage structure that embodies standard skill differentials starting from the legal minimum income); financial autonomy as regards industrial ministries, with direct dealings with the Finance Ministry and banks; hiring practices which are highly selective (long probationary periods and acceptance by an elected brigade council are required for permanent employment); dependence on contractual relationships for sales and acquisition of inputs; and an overall environment which amounts to enterprise autonomy or self-management. This enterprise received extensive press attention and was clearly an example of the best rather than the typical achievement. It also used methods that cannot easily be transferred to large state organizations.

After initial concentration on consumer good products, the BIA shifted attention to research and technology applications on the one hand and computer services on the other. Some of the most advanced computer system and robotics projects undertaken during the 1980s seem to have been partially financed through the small enterprise programme. The BIA has stimulated formation of the first Bulgarian science parks in conjunction with university research facilities (three parks were planned, the first scheduled to open in 1987). Separate organizations to develop and/or produce small batches of newly developed speciality products were to be established under the personal direction of the chiefs of university research sections.

The BIA has also stimulated the formation of several consulting and technical service enterprises. One example of the surprising developments under this programme is provided by IKO, described as an 'information and consulting complex' and consisting of nine small enterprises that have grown up around the leading Bulgarian management journal *IKO*. This is in effect a consortium of nine distinct computer consulting and information service units operating (in a 'California-style' building with separate meeting rooms for normal business and creative sessions, and a glass-covered central courtyard shared by all units) under a single general manager, but with separate financial accounts. This development occurred under the direction of the editor of the management journal (founded in 1970), apparently in response to requests from readers for assistance in applying the techniques described in its pages. This enterprise is also said to be run in a brigade fashion, but combines the efforts of a 150-person staff with the freelance services of nearly a thousand management and technical consultants and translators. In addition to the journal, the sub-sections are: Express, Consult, Service, Programme, Inform, Patent, Contact, Merkur, Technology, Invest and Design. An additional organization, Iko-Intellect, was founded in 1986 as a management training school.

The small enterprise programme was an important and authentically innovative form of decentralizing reform. It was a move 'closer to the market' in the limited sense that the small enterprises were set up as a result of research or observation suggesting their usefulness in the light of market conditions. They were much freer to respond to small shifts in consumer preferences and able to do so more rapidly, had somewhat stronger performance bonus and reward arrangements for their managers, and appear to have some small price setting latitude. The small enterprises tended to apply the brigade method more fully and enforce more stringent hiring standards than elsewhere in the Bulgarian economy. They were nonetheless state enterprises in a system where the role of classical command planning, materials allocation and price formation had changed very little. For an interpretation which denies that the small enterprises represented a net favourable addition to the Bulgarian economic system see Winiecki (1988, p. 33, as cited by Jeffries, 1990, p. 95).

The small enterprises reflect an effort to improve the supply of services and simple consumer goods outside the existing large enterprise channels, so it is useful to compare them with measures adopted in other Eastern European countries having the same purpose. The approach taken in the German Democratic Republic, involving pure private operation of small service and production facilities under centralized price control and in a generally cooperative relationship with large state organizations, is discussed in McIntyre (1989a, b). In Hungary the existing structure of very small private retail outlets (basically booths rather than stores) and services has been augmented by a programme of renting out state-owned premises (small restaurants in particular) to the highest bidder for five-year periods. During the term of the lease the winning bidder operates the premises much like a private small business in a capitalist system, but with the state receiving a considerable share of the profits. Although Western visitors often confused small well-stocked branches of state retail organizations with these private units and thereby exaggerated their role, they had become an important element in the Hungarian service sector before the explicit privatization programme begun in 1989.

5.   THE NEW ECONOMIC-LEGAL CODE OF 1989 AND LAST REFORM EFFORTS

One-person (no hired labour) repair, tailoring and personal service shops have always existed in Bulgaria, although they did not bulk large in the overall service sector of the economy. Experiments with purely private small-scale service units were carried out in 1985 in remote corners of Sofia and in 1987 a reform legalizing and encouraging such efforts was announced. As part of the comprehensive new economic-legal code adopted in January 1989, a new employment ceiling of ten employees was established for purely private business, with provision for additional seasonal employees (*FBIS*, 25 January 1989, p. 13). This limit was eliminated in March 1990.

Clearly the small enterprises played a role in testing some of the economic accounting and financial discipline provisions of proposed general reforms, and the BIA appears to have been actively involved in the process of 'reform design'. With the intensified emphasis on technological change after the February 1986 plenum of the Bulgarian Communist Party, the BIA also played a role in the distribution of the new fund for adoption of especially efficient or high quality processes (Tonkov, 1986). In addition, the BIA advocated a competition philosophy, which while not running in the direction of adoption of a full market system, seeks to increase the extent of competition between socialist units. The BIA also advocates systematic revitalization of poorly managed or equipped enterprises by a two-stage process in which after consulting and evaluation firms are either revitalized under their existing management or are (in something colourfully called 'socialist bankruptcy') put in the hands of another group or organization which wishes to take them over.

The comprehensive set of economic and legal arrangements announced in the 'Decree on Economic Activity' of January 1989 (*FBIS*, 25 January 1989, pp. 6–21) were striking in their acceptance of all types of state, cooperative and purely private productive property and apparent rejection of the persistence of a central controlling function for classical central planning. The minister in charge of planning and economics asserted that this set of measures marked the development of a 'new model of socialism in Bulgaria' and 'definitely destroys the command-administrative structures' (*FBIS*, 25 January 1989, pp. 21–2). There was no time to test the viability of this set of reform arrangements or to see what institutional forms and accommodations emerged in practice. This set of complex and apparently carefully worked out measures is evidence of significant political flexibility and institutional creativity, nearly a year before the collapse of the BCP government. The 1959 territorial reorganization (revised again in 1987) and the ensuing decentralization of control over municipal affairs, adds another interesting dimension to the current situation.

Some real decentralization of economic and social planning had thus already been built into the Bulgarian governmental fabric before the collapse of the old system and without any particular free-market trappings.

The strong showing of the renamed Bulgarian Socialist Party (BSP) in the June 1990 parliamentary elections and the lack of a coherent programme by the 16-party United Democratic Front, suggest little support for a complete recasting of the system regardless of what happens elsewhere in Eastern Europe. While pressures for smaller scale and decentralization are strong, they are not necessarily consistent with Western understandings of privatization. After a six-month political impasse, a coalition government was formed in late December 1990 which is dominated by the BSP and the Agrarians (eight and two ministers, respectively). The coalition government is headed by an unaffiliated prime minister Dimitar Popov, and includes three UDF and four independent members.

In the period before the October 1991 Parliamentary elections the government passed several significant legislative acts, e.g. allowing (but not carrying out) the privatization of agriculture and sharply raising consumer prices, designed to curry favour with the IMF and so return to good debtor status. At the time this chapter is being written in the spring of 1991 there is no new world to analyse. The old order has collapsed and nothing has risen to replace it. The relevance of the recent past is unclear until the context of future Bulgarian economic life is clarified.

6. IMPLICATIONS FOR OTHER COMMAND ECONOMIES

The most important conclusion to be drawn from this truncated experience is that the BIA 'small enterprise' initiative offers an important alternative for various Soviet-type economies wishing to capture some of the dynamic potential of the Hungarian NEM reforms, but hoping to avoid such large and potentially threatening changes in the core economic institutions. These measures had produced strong quantitative and qualitative results in their early years, prior to the Russian shock and its delayed unravelling effects in Bulgaria. The physical standard of life in Bulgaria rose relatively rapidly and steadily over most of the post-war period, but especially in the period after 1965. The sharp changes in the stock of major consumer goods and diet are detailed in McIntyre (1988c, pp. 124–9). The range and availability of domestically produced consumer goods expanded, with clear improvements in quality and style. Imported consumer goods appeared on a significant scale, although mostly from other Eastern European countries. These elaborations of consumer standards were not much noticed in the West, partly because of the geo-political filter applied with opposite effect to countries perceived to be close to (as opposed to moving away from) Soviet forms of organization. When comparisons are explicitly or implicitly made between Bulgaria and countries such as Hungary or Czechoslovakia, it is important to note that very large differences in living standards existed prior to the socialist period. By the early 1980s, rapid Bulgarian progress had closed much, but far from all, of this historical and cultural gap. Because of its heavy dependence on the Soviet Union in particular and CMEA trade more generally, Bulgaria suffered a more abrupt and extreme disruption from the transformation of these relationships during 1989, 1990 and 1991.

The developments considered here were not economic reforms in the conventional sense of the words. They did not redesign the incentive arrangements or organizational structure of the large state enterprises. For that reason they appear to have largely escaped the attention of students of comparative economic systems in the West. I argue that they nonetheless produced a fundamental change in the performance and character of the economic system (in the broadest sense of the words). It provides evidence that diverse economic tactics can prove successful, if supported with correct parallel policies and resource commitments. It also shows evidence of some considerable degree of success in generating increased attention to improvement in the range and quality of consumer goods produced internally, prior to the development of strong market forces of the conventional type. This experience may prove useful in predicting and analysing the future evolution of the Soviet economic system. It provides evidence of successful incremental reforms, in the absence of predominantly large-scale state institutions and of market-like responsiveness in the absence of markets *per se*, a currently unfashionable idea, but one whose time may come again.

An update to this chapter is given in the Postscript, page 286.

REFERENCES

Boichev, V. (1985) Interviews on 29 November and 16 December 1985.

Bornstein, M. (1985) 'Improving the Soviet economic mechanism', *Soviet Studies*, vol. 37, no. 1.

Choleva, S. (1986) Interview on 11 July 1986 (production manager, IPOMA, Science and Production Centre for Polymer Articles).

Daviddi, R. (1987a) 'Bulgaria: domestic economic performance and foreign economic relations in the 1980s', in Joseph, P. (Ed.) *The Economies of Eastern Europe and Their Foreign Economic Relations*, Brussels: NATO Economics Directorate.

Daviddi, R. (1987b) 'Monetary reforms in Bulgaria' (paper presented at the Workshop on Financial Reform in Socialist Economies), Florence: European University Institute.

Foreign Broadcast Information Service, Eastern Europe Series (*FBIS/EE*), Washington, DC: US Government.

Jackson, M. (1981) 'Bulgaria's economy in the 1970s: adjusting productivity to structure', in Joint Economic Committee of the US Congress, *East European Economic Assessment, Part 1, Country Studies*, Washington: US Government Printing Office.

Jackson, M. (1986) 'Recent economic performance and policy in Bulgaria', in Joint Economic Committee of the US Congress, *Eastern European Economies: Slow Growth in the 1980s, vol. 3, Country Studies on Eastern Europe and Yugoslavia*, Washington: US Government Printing Office.

Jackson, M. (1990) 'The Bulgarian case: The dangers of procrastination in the transition from socialism to capitalism' (paper presented at the American Economic Association, Washington, DC).

Jeffries, I. (1990) *A Guide to the Socialist Economies*, London: Routledge.

Kaser, M. (1981) 'The industrial enterprise in Bulgaria', in Jeffries, I. (Ed.) *The Industrial Enterprise in Eastern Europe*, New York: Praeger.

Lampe, J. (1986) *The Bulgarian Economy in the Twentieth Century*, London: Croom Helm.

McIntyre, R. (1988a) 'The small enterprise and agriculture initiatives in Bulgaria: institutional invention without reform', *Soviet Studies*, vol. 40, no. 4.

McIntyre, R. (1988b) 'The ministry of new products and processes in a collectivist state' (manuscript).

McIntyre, R. (1988c) *Bulgaria: Politics, Economics and Society*, London: Frances Pinter.

McIntyre, R. (1989a) 'Economic change in Eastern Europe: other paths to socialist construction', *Science and Society*, vol. 53, no. 1.

McIntyre, R. (1989b) 'Economic changes without conventional reform: small-scale industrial and service development in Bulgaria and the GDR', in Weichhardt, R. (Ed.) *The Economies of Eastern Europe Under Gorbachev's Influence*, Brussels: NATO Economics Directorate.

Mishev, S. (1985) Interviews on 1 November and 27 November 1985 (vice president, BIA).

Mishev, S. (1986) Interview on 4 July 1986.

Neuberger, E. (1959) 'The Yugoslav investment auction', *Quarterly Journal of Economics*, vol. 73, no 1.

Puchev, P. (1986) Interview on 9 July 1986.

Puchev, P. (1990a) Interview on 23 July 1990.

Puchev, P. (1990b) 'A note on government policy and the new "intrapreneurship" in Bulgaria', *Small Business Economics*, vol. 2, no. 1.

Tonkov, V. (1986). Interview on 14 July 1986.

Wallimann, I. and Stojanov (1988) 'Workplace democracy in Bulgaria: from subordination to partnership in industrial relations', *Industrial Relations Journal*, vol. 19, no. 4.

Wallimann, I. and Stojanov (1989) 'Social and economic reform in Bulgaria: economic democracy and problems of change in industrial relations', *Economic and Industrial Democracy*, vol. 10, no. 3.

Wiedemann, P. (1980) 'Economic reform in Bulgaria', *Forschungsberichte 62*, Wien: Wiener Institut für Internationale Wirtschaftsvergleiche.

Winiecki, J. (1988) *The Distorted World of Soviet-type Economies*, London: Croom Helm.

Wiles, P. (1977) *Economic Institutions Compared*, Oxford: Basil Blackwell.

Zwass, A. (1984) *The Economies of Eastern Europe in a Time of Change*, Armonk, New York: M.E. Sharpe.

4 Industrial reform in China

Robert C. Hsu

Since late 1978, when its leaders launched their modernization drive, China
has experimented with many reforms to increase its industrial efficiency and
vitality. Although the reforms have been slowed down since 1989, they have
already made profound and irreversible changes in the Chinese economy
and society.

The focus of the industrial reforms is the state-owned industrial enterprise, which has been rigidly controlled by state planners and bureaucrats.
Thus it is useful at the outset to explain briefly the nature of China's state-
owned industrial enterprises and the state agents who control them.

State-owned industrial enterprises are but one of the three categories of
industrial enterprises in China in terms of ownership. The other two categories
are collectively-owned enterprises and private enterprises.[1] State-owned
enterprises are small in number compared with non-state enterprises, but are
very important in terms of their share in total industrial output (although this
share has declined steadily in the 1980s). In 1988 they constituted only 1.2 per
cent of the number of industrial enterprises, but produced about 57 per cent of
total industrial output (see Table 4.1). They are typically much larger in size
and more concentrated in heavy industry than the other types of enterprises. In
1988 they produced 47 per cent of light industrial output and 62 per cent of
heavy industrial output (State Statistical Bureau, 1989, p. 261).

State-owned enterprises are administratively supervised and controlled
by authorities at one of the three levels of government in China (the central
government, the provincial, municipal or regional government, and the city
or county government), depending on the nature of the enterprise. Because
of China's large size and regional diversity, the intermediate and lower-level
governments have an important role in industrial administration that is unique
among the socialist countries. Besides those directly under their control,
these various levels of government also have some influence over other state
enterprises that are located in their areas but not directly under their administration. For example, local governments may supply electricity and water
to centrally controlled enterprises and apply their own regulations such as
requiring a certain amount of output for the locality. As a result, there are
considerable regional variations among state-owned enterprises in terms of
operational rules. In addition, Chinese leaders have adopted alternative policies for pricing, planning, investment and so forth for different industries.

Table 4.1   Categories of industrial enterprises

	State-owned	Collectively-owned	Private
Number (in 1000)			
1985	94	1 742	3 348
1986	97	1 823	4 785
1987	98	1 819	5 553
1988	99	1 853	6 148
1989	102	1 747	6 124
Share of output* (%)			
1980	76.0	23.5	0.0
1985	64.9	32.1	1.9
1986	62.3	33.5	2.8
1987	59.7	34.6	3.6
1988	56.8	36.2	4.3
1989	56.1	35.7	4.8
Employment (in million)**			
1980	33.3	14.3	
1985	38.2	17.1	
1986	39.6	17.8	
1987	40.9	18.3	
1988	42.3	18.5	
1989	42.7	18.5	

*These figures do not add up to 100 per cent because the share of 'other enterprises', such as joint enterprises, is not included.
**Figures for collectively-owned enterprises include those in cities and towns only.

Sources: State Statistical Bureau (1989), Tables 6-44 and 6-10; State Statistical Bureau (1990), pp. 16, 68, 69.

Hence, what is true of enterprises in one region or industry may not be true of enterprises in other regions or industries.

In 1988 about 73 per cent of state-owned enterprises and 19 per cent of collectively-owned enterprises were officially classified as 'independent accounting enterprises' (*duli hesuan qiye; Zhongguo Tongji Nianjian*, 1989, p. 271). This means that they are responsible, in theory, for their own profits and losses, have their own accounts with banks, and have the legal authority to sign contracts with other enterprises. They are, therefore, the most important enterprises in the economy to implement industrial reforms. The size distribution of these enterprises in terms of employment in 1987 is given in Table 4.2. Enterprises without independent accounting were established by other organizations such as large enterprises, government units, schools, research institutes and even military units, and remain dependent on them administratively and financially.

Table 4.2   Size distribution of industrial enterprises* (1987)

No. of employees	No. of enterprises
Below 10	57,618
10–50	155,236
50–100	73,310
100–500	107,078
500–1 000	15,157
1 000–3 000	7,717
3 000–5 000	903
5 000–10 000	583
Above 10,000	302
Total	417,904

*This table includes only state-owned and collectively-owned industrial enterprises with independent accounting status.

Source: State Statistical Bureau (1988), p. 293.

1.   FINANCIAL AND PLANNING REFORMS

Between late 1978 and 1984 China's industrial reforms were mainly concerned with giving enterprises greater financial incentives and managerial autonomy. These included financial reform, changes in the scope of planning and plan targets, and changes in state materials allocation.

Financial reform was implemented in stages through trial and error. In 1978–80 enterprises were permitted to retain part of their profits if they fulfilled their plan targets. This system of 'profit retention' led to excessive fiscal deficits for the state, and so the 'profit contract system' was introduced in 1981–82. In this system enterprises were permitted to retain a certain percentage of the profits over and above a certain base figure, which was negotiated with the local (provincial, city or county) government. However, this system gave local governments too much financial authority over the enterprises located in their areas; in addition, there was rarely any penalty to the enterprise for failing to reach the base profit (Naughton, 1985, p. 236). Consequently, it was replaced by a 'tax for profit' system, which was introduced in two stages over the period 1983–84. Under this system enterprises were required to pay sales tax, income tax, capital charges and rental charge ('adjustment tax'), but they were not required to remit profits to the state. In this way, it was expected that enterprises would become more motivated and accountable for their own profits and losses, while government interference with management would be reduced. It was also expected that the new taxes would give the government a new 'economic lever' in implementing 'guidance planning' as discussed below. However, as Riskin (1987, p. 346) notes, the state in reality continued to claim a share of the after-tax profits under various guises.

In addition to financial reforms, China's reformist leaders have also taken steps to reduce direct state planning of enterprises in order to give them more flexibility to respond to market demand. Chinese reformers have envisaged a 'socialist mixed economy' in which two types of planning, mandatory and guidance planning, coexist with the market mechanism. *Mandatory planning* is the orthodox type of socialist planning with compulsory targets for enterprises. By the early 1980s many Chinese planners and economists had concluded that excessive mandatory planning produced rigidity and disincentives for the enterprises and should, therefore, be limited to essential products and the key enterprises that produce them. For most products Chinese reformers recommend *guidance planning*, which involves merely suggested targets to enterprises. These targets are not binding and the enterprises can adjust them in accordance with changes in the market or in supply conditions. The state relies on indirect 'economic levers' (price regulations, taxes, credit, interest rate, state purchase orders and so forth) to induce enterprises to behave in the desired manner.[2] Minor products that are not subject to either mandatory or guidance planning are to be regulated entirely by the market.

In accordance with this reformist view on planning and the market, the scope of mandatory planning in Chinese industry has been greatly reduced and that of guidance planning and the market expanded. In 1979 188 manufactured consumer goods were subject to mandatory planning and allocation. This number was reduced to about 60 by 1985 and 23 in 1987 (*Renmin Ribao*, 13 April 1985, p. 2; *Guangming Ribao*, 10 March 1990, p. 3).

The number of industrial materials subject to mandatory planning by the State Planning Commission was reduced from 256 in 1984 to 65 in 1985, 26 by the end of 1987 and to 17 in 1989 (*Renmin Ribao*, 13 April 1985, p. 2; 9 November 1987, p. 1; *Jingji Ribao*, 16 October 1989, p. 1). Industrial materials produced under mandatory planning are centrally allocated by the State Materials Supply Bureau. Any excess output is to be marketed by the producers themselves. Thus, with the decline in mandatory planning, the portion of major industrial materials allocated by the state has substantially declined over time, as can be seen in Table 4.3.

Table 4.3   State supply of materials (%)

	Steel	Coal	Lumber	Cement
1980	74.3	57.9	80.9	35.0
1987	41.1	47.2	27.6	15.5
1989	42.6	45.2	26.5	12.2

Sources: *Guangming Ribao*, 10 March 1990, p. 3 for 1980 and 1987; *Jingji Ribao*, 24 October 1989, p. 2 for 1989.

These statistics have to be read with an important qualification. The decline in mandatory planning and state allocation of materials does not mean that all the unplanned output is thereby fully available in the market. Economists at the Institute of Finance and Trade Economics (1989, p. 6) have pointed out that goods and materials in shortage that are not centrally allocated tend to be 'intercepted' and controlled by local governments or by the so-called 'administrative corporations', which are former government departments nominally incorporated to evade the transfer of power to enterprises. Consequently, there is no corresponding expansion in the scope of the market for these products.

The number of plan targets has also declined, but the trend here is less clear-cut and consistent. In 1978 there were eight mandatory targets: output of the major product, output assortment, quality, cost, profit, rate of raw material consumption, labour productivity and use of working capital. In 1980, they were changed to output, quality, profit and product delivery as the criteria for profit retention. In 1986 as the government felt that it was losing control of enterprises, new targets such as technical innovation, new product development, and labour productivity were added (Xi and Du, 1989, p. 60). Since 1989 the main targets are generally output, assortment and quality, although they vary with industries and regions; lower-level governments sometimes add to the level of a particular target or add additional targets.

Plan targets are generally not considered to be taut. A World Bank study has found overfulfilment by sample enterprises in 1983 (Granick, 1987, pp. 120–3). Although there was widespread and growing underfulfilment of plan targets in the late 1980s,[3] this should not be taken as an indication of increasing plan tautness. Rather, it is a sign of the growing ineffectiveness of planners' control over enterprises as the latter became increasingly preoccupied with profit maximization in a chaotic economic environment. In 1989 China's industrial enterprises self-marketed about 30 per cent of their output (Institute of Finance and Trade Economics, 1989, p. 4). This does not suggest that enterprises are hard pressed to fulfil their plan targets.

The pro-democracy movement of 1989 and the general chaos of the Chinese economy in 1988–89 prompted Chinese leaders to reassess their market-orientated reforms. In November 1989 the Central Committee of the Chinese Communist Party decided to increase the central control of the economy by strengthening mandatory planning and by stressing the leading role of large state-owned enterprises. In early 1990 an experimental 'double guarantee' system was introduced for 234 key industrial enterprises. Under the system, the state guarantees the supply of energy and essential materials to these enterprises, and the latter in turn guarantee certain contracted levels of profits, taxes and products (Swaine, 1990, p. 30). Chinese authors have also used the term to mean the state's guarantee of both funds and materials to these enterprises. In mid-1990, as the Chinese economy remained sluggish and these key enterprises continued to experience slow sales and financial difficulties, the authorities decided to provide supplementary funds to them to ensure the fulfilment of their plan targets (*Jingji Ribao*, 2 August 1990, p. 1). These developments are significant as they represent partial reversal of China's decade-long planning reform.

2. PRICE REFORM PROBLEMS

Chinese reformers have long recognized that China's price system is irrational, many prices being set by the state at levels that are related neither to their costs of production nor to demand. They have, therefore, advocated a price reform in which most prices would be determined by supply and demand (Hsu, 1991, Chapter 5). However, the fear of inflation has discouraged Chinese leaders from implementing such a price reform. Thus in 1979–83 only individual price adjustments were made. In May 1984, as a transitional measure to pave the way for a price reform, a two-tier or 'dual-track' price system was adopted for many industrial materials and producer goods. It consists of low state-determined prices for planned output and higher market prices for above-plan output. The purpose of the system is to safeguard planned production while giving enterprises the flexibility and incentive to produce more for the market.

This dual-track price system, still in existence as of late 1990, applies to energy (petroleum, coal, electricity) and basic materials such as steel, pig iron, timber, cement and chemicals. For output within mandatory planning targets, the lower planned prices apply; above-plan output is to be sold by the producers at market prices. For enterprises that use these materials for their planned production, the state allocates a certain amount of them (about 60 per cent of what was needed in 1989: Institute of Finance and Trade Economics, 1989, p. 4) to help fulfil their plan targets. The materials for above-plan output are to be purchased in the market at market prices.

The two-tier prices are inherently incompatible, however, and this has given rise to many problems. First, the possibility of selling part of their output at higher market prices gives producers an incentive to circumvent their plan quotas. This, in turn, makes it difficult for the state to supply materials needed by other enterprises to fulfil their plan targets. As a result, there was growing underfulfilment of plan targets in the late 1980s, as mentioned above. Second, the system is abused by many corrupt officials and well-connected people who have privileged access to low-priced materials allocated by the state. They have enriched themselves by reselling them at higher prices. Popular resentment against this type of corruption played an important role in the pro-democracy movement of 1989. Third, the continuing low planned prices of energy and industrial materials have discouraged production and encouraged waste. This has contributed greatly to China's chronic shortages in energy and industrial materials.

Because of rising inflation, the Communist Party leadership decided, in September 1988, to delay the price reform for two years in order to 'stabilize the economic environment'. However, because the dual-track price system has contributed greatly to official profiteering and popular discontent, the leadership decided in November 1989 to reform it in 1990–91. The plan is to reduce the number of industrial materials that have dual prices. For products that continue to have dual prices, the price differentials will be reduced (*Jingji Ribao*, 17 January 1990, p. 2). Thus there will be another round of individual price adjustments without a genuine price reform. In 1990, state price control of four types of fabricated steel plates was eliminated (*Jingji Ribao*, 16 July 1990) and the planned price of coal has been raised. China's eighth five-year plan (1991–95), as ratified by the Seventh National People's Congress on 9 April 1991, confirms that the dual-track price system will be gradually eliminated through the narrowing of price differentials by raising state-set prices for essential materials (*Renmin Ribao*, 16 April 1991).

3.   OWNERSHIP REFORM

Reform of the ownership system consists of the introduction of shareholding and private ownership and the expansion of collective ownership.

Shareholding has been advocated by many reformist economists since 1985 as the best way to invigorate the enterprise by utilizing idle funds for investment and by motivating workers. It is also believed that state interference in enterprise management will be checked because the government has to exercise its 'ownership right' through the board of directors. Opponents, however, question both the compatibility of stock ownership with socialism and the feasibility of absorbing large amounts of idle funds (Hsu, 1991, Chapter 3).

In spite of these reservations, the reformist government of Zhao Ziyang decided to experiment with shareholding ownership. In 1984–88, it permitted some 6 000 enterprises to issue shares for sales (*Jingji Ribao*, 9 May 1989, p. 3). Eligible buyers were enterprise employees, other enterprises and state authorities; the general public was permitted to buy only in a small number of enterprises on an experimental basis.

China's experiment with shareholding, however, has not been successful. Many enterprises have abused the system and used it merely as a guise for giving their workers bonuses. Shares are sold to employees at artificially low prices. Individual shareholders receive not only dividends but also a very high rate of interest, whereas the state as a shareholder is paid a lower rate of return. Dividends and interests are counted as part of the costs of production in order to reduce taxes. Finally, shareholders do not bear risks because their shares can be sold back to the companies at the original price (*Jingji Ribao*, 17 Feb. 1989, p. 3; 21 February 1989, p. 1; 25 March 1989, p. 2).

These problems are not surprising. They reflect the distortions that are bound to arise when fragments of the market system are introduced into a socialist economy in a piecemeal and superficial manner without complementary and coordinated reforms. Thus in the absence of a genuine stock market, it is impossible for investors to assess objectively the worth and profitability of an enterprise and the value of its shares. Although China has security markets, they deal primarily in treasury bonds.

The use of shares as disguised bonuses to employees helped to fuel China's inflation as well. Consequently, in early 1989, following its decision to postpone price reform in order to fight inflation, the party leadership also decided to put a two-year freeze on the sale of shares of state-owned enterprises.

There are indications that the experiment with shareholding ownership will be resumed in the near future once the government has drafted new regulations to check current abuses. The main objective is to absorb idle funds in the economy. Reportedly, there will be stricter regulations concerning the issuing of stocks and the type of funds that can be used to purchase them; dividends will be paid after and not before taxes are paid; there will be ceilings (about 15–20 per cent) on interest and dividends (*Jingji Ribao*, 17

February 1989, p. 3). Also, the authorities will emphasize shareholding by other enterprises rather than by enterprise employees (*Jingji Ribao*, 13 June 1990, p. 1).

Outside the state sector, both collective and private industrial enterprises have grown in terms of both number and output shares during the 1980s; the private ones in particular enjoyed very rapid growth (see Table 4.1). Most of these collective and private enterprises are the so-called village–township enterprises. The collective ones, which include rural cooperatives, were either reorganized from the collective enterprises run by the former rural brigades or communes, or established and run by villages and townships. Private enterprises are also the product of China's rural reform. In 1979-80, peasant households were first permitted to engage in non-farming activities such as making handicrafts for the market. They have found their new pursuits to be much more profitable than farming and their number has multiplied. After 1984 small private businesses were also officially permitted in the cities, although a small number of them had existed previously. Currently, of all private businesses engaged in small-scale manufacturing, more than 90 per cent are located in rural areas.

Private industrial enterprises are typically household establishments with few employees.[4] They make minor, relatively low-quality consumer goods by using labour-intensive methods of production. As these products are not produced or used by the state-owned enterprises, private enterprises do not compete with the latter for market or rely on them for sub-contracts. On the other hand, collective enterprises are typically larger than the private ones. They use relatively capital-intensive and technically advanced methods of production to produce higher quality products, ranging from consumer goods to tools and small machines. Many of them are located in villages and townships that are close to large cities, and they have taken advantage of their location to supply parts to state-owned enterprises in the cities. Other collective enterprises may produce products that state enterprises do not want to produce or cannot produce in sufficient quantities to satisfy the market (Dong, 1988, pp. 176–87). In some areas where local employment opportunities are limited, large and medium-size state enterprises have helped their workers to set up collective enterprises in order to employ the workers' children (Lo, 1990). These collective enterprises tend to produce products that are needed by the parent enterprise.

Some collective enterprises such as small tobacco plants, wineries, textile plants, sugar factories and canneries, which process locally produced agricultural materials, compete intensely with state-owned enterprises, usually with the help of local protection. They thus divert raw materials from state plants, thereby adversely affecting the latter's planned production. Some private businesses also compete with state enterprises for materials by paying higher prices for them. They are able to do so partly because the prices of their products are not controlled by the government and partly because they have more flexible management.

After the suppression of the pro-democracy movement in June 1989, the market system in general has been under attack and private businesses have been criticized for being unscrupulous in money-making, including evading taxes. The austerity policy adopted since late 1988 has seriously damaged private businesses. Tighter government regulations, including new tax regulations, have also been adopted to control private businesses. Consequently, their number declined in 1989 (see Table 4.1). As for collective enterprises, they do not face political or ideological problems. However, the lack of credit and materials also forced some of them to close down in 1989. In addition, as discussed above the state's new 'double guarantee' system gives top priority in the supply of energy and materials to 234 key enterprises. To implement that system, the state has closed down some collective enterprises that are inefficient in the use of energy and materials.

4. THE CONTRACT RESPONSIBILITY SYSTEM

In 1984 Chinese leaders decided to experiment with two reform measures in enterprise management, the 'contract responsibility system' (CRS) and the 'director responsibility system', as part of their efforts to deepen industrial reform. The first measure is discussed in this section, while the second one will be discussed in the next section.

The inspiration for the CRS came from China's agriculture. A rural household responsibility system was first implemented in China's agriculture in 1979 with impressive results. Peasant households are responsible for delivering a given amount of agricultural output to their teams in return for their use of land, and they are free to keep any excess output. In early 1981 the government started to introduce the CRS into medium and large state-owned industrial enterprises on a trial basis. As the initial results were favourable, the leadership decided in 1984 to popularize it. By 1987 about 75 per cent of state industrial enterprises had adopted it (*Renmin Ribao*, 28 January 1988, p. 1). Since then it has become the focus of China's industrial reform. In early 1990, more than 90 per cent of state-owned industrial enterprises were on the system (*Jingji Guanli*, No. 5, 1990, p. 14).

The basic philosophy of the CRS is the belief that state-owned enterprises can become autonomous and motivated without ownership reform if the 'ownership right' of the state is separated from the 'management right' of the enterprise ('separation of the two rights'). It is believed that this can be accomplished through the CRS, under which enterprise directors or managers sign a contract with state authorities to deliver a specified amount of taxes and profits to the state in return for management autonomy and profits incentives during a given period of time (normally three years).[5] Depending on the terms of contract negotiated, all or part of excess profits above the base figure will be kept by the enterprise to be used for reinvestment, collective welfare and bonuses, whereas any deficiency in profits will be made good by the enterprise. Also, there may be additional criteria for evaluating enterprise performance.[6]

One of the first enterprises to adopt the CRS in 1981 was Capital Steel of Beijing. It has often been cited as a showcase for the CRS because of its success in various areas: a high growth rate of profits (an average annual growth of about 20 per cent over the period 1981–89), a high growth rate of profit remittance to the state (7.2 per cent), and a high rate of investment (60 per cent of retained profits) (*Guangming Ribao*, 19 March 1990, p. 3). Koo (1990, pp. 799–811) shows that Capital Steel has indeed performed well and has been cost-effective. He identifies the following factors as the causes of its success: a direct link between profits and workers' benefits; a merit-based wage and promotion system; long-term investment in workers' education; and an open and adaptive management style. These factors are clearly enterprise-specific (i.e. they are related to the quality and strategy of a specific enterprise's management) and cannot be brought about by the CRS alone. Naturally, without the broad managerial autonomy permitted by the CRS, these factors cannot flourish. Thus it is fair to say that, given the state ownership of enterprises, the CRS is a necessary but not sufficient condition for innovative management and efficient production.

In practice, a high percentage (at least as high as 20 per cent in 1989) of enterprises under the CRS have not performed well. In 1989 only 80 per cent of all enterprises under the CRS fulfilled their contracts (*Renmin Ribao*, 2 July 1990, p. 2). One operational problem with the CRS is that the calculation of expected costs and profits for a multi-year contract period assumes a stable economic environment, including stable taxes and prices, which China lacked throughout much of the 1980s. Another problem is that the contracts are individually negotiated between enterprise directors and state officials, thus permitting much bureaucratic discretion. The contractor or director is in theory selected by state officials in an open bidding from any interested individual or group of workers. In reality, officials tend to 'select their own people and exclude those who disagree with them' (Liu, 1990, p. 22). In other words, former state-appointed plant directors are usually selected.[7]

A fiscal problem has also resulted from the operation of the CRS. Because the base figure for profits to be turned over to the state is pre-determined in the contract for the contract period, the state's share of profits tends to be rigid in an upwards direction if enterprise profits increase more rapidly than expected. On the other hand, when enterprises make unexpectedly low profits or even losses, enterprise directors are usually able to renegotiate the base figures with state officials. The rationale is that unexpected losses or low profits can occur due to circumstances beyond the contractors' control, such as tax or input price increases. In this way, the contractors bear little risk and enterprises continue to operate with a soft budget constraint, with the state bearing the fiscal consequences.

Thus, the efficacy of the contract responsibility system is inherently limited. It is necessarily a second-best reform measure because it assumes that the directors and workers would behave as if they owned the property. In addition, in a broader context, as long as China's price system remains irrational, improved microefficiency cannot add up to economy-wide allocative efficiency. However, as a transitional reform measure, it is arguably superior to the earlier financial incentive schemes implemented in the early 1980s.

Recent government pronouncements indicate that the 'development and perfection' of the CRS will be the focus of China's industrial reform in the near future. One change to be adopted is to alter the way the contract profit for the state is calculated (from the current pre-tax basis to a post-tax basis) so that the government's tax base will not be reduced by the CRS. This was confirmed in the eighth five-year plan ratified by the Seventh National People's Congress in April 1991 (*Renmin Ribao*, 16 April 1991).

5.   ENTERPRISE LEADERSHIP AND MANAGEMENT

An important aspect of enterprise leadership is the selection of the enterprise director (manager). Here the practice varies, depending on whether the enterprise is on the CRS or on the traditional planning/control system. For enterprises on the CRS, the successful contractor serves as the director. Theoretically, any individual or group of workers with the requisite abilities and security deposit can bid for the contract to manage the enterprise. If a group of workers are awarded the contract, the workers themselves elect the director. In most cases, however, it is the former state-appointed director who is given the contract, as mentioned above. For enterprises that remain under the traditional state planning/control system, most directors are still appointed by state authorities. The rest are elected by the enterprise's congress of workers and staff, subject to state approval. Directors generally serve a four-year renewable term.

Another important issue in enterprise leadership concerns the relationship between the director and the party committee secretary, and the latter's role in the enterprise. In May 1984 the Chinese leadership introduced in a few cities (2 913 enterprises) the 'director responsibility system' to replace the former 'system of director responsibility under the leadership of the party committee'. In September 1986 the decision was made to popularize the system and more than 23,000 enterprises adopted it in the same year (*Zhongguo Jingji Nianjian*, 1985, p. II-2 and 1987, p. IV-1). By the end of 1988, most state enterprises had officially made the change. According to the 1986 regulations on directors of state-owned industrial enterprises, the director under the new system has the overall responsibility for the enterprise and is in charge of production and management. The party committee, which previously assumed overall enterprise leadership, is in charge of ideological–political work and supervision.

In practice, however, this has not always been the case. Many party committee secretaries have resisted the change and have continued to interfere with the directors' work. Generally speaking, an overlapping 'dual-track system' in enterprise leadership prevails, in which the director is responsible for production whereas the secretary is responsible for more than ideological–political work. In matters of personnel and workers' discipline, the director often shares power with the secretary even though these matters are production-related. In fact, many party committee secretaries are involved in directing production because they serve concurrently as deputy directors. In an unknown number of cases, party secretaries serve concurrently as directors (*Jingji Guanli*, No. 5, 1990, p. 24). Since the Tiananmen tragedy of June 1989, the role of the party has presumably increased, although there has been no new legislation to that effect.

Despite the fact that enterprises have more autonomy to produce for the market, the scope of managerial decision making remains limited because of various policy constraints imposed by the government. First, as discussed above, the prices of industrial materials produced for mandatory plans are set at low levels under the dual-track price system; only the excess self-marketed output is priced by the enterprises themselves. As for consumer goods, as of 1990 the prices of nine categories of goods such as cigarettes, bicycles and televisions are set by the government; the prices of 30 categories of products, such as refrigerators, washing machines, light bulbs and textile products, may fluctuate within a certain range set by the government (Li, 1990, pp. 240–1). The other consumer goods are priced by the enterprises themselves.

Nor can enterprises freely engage in foreign trade, according to new regulations adopted in 1988. With the exception of designated trading companies, enterprises have to obtain export or import certificates in order to export or import specific products. Alternatively, they have to rely on the trading companies for such purposes. Should foreign investors become interested in joint ventures, local or central authorities have to screen and approve any such proposals.

Finally, in terms of employment decisions, enterprise management does not have much flexibility in hiring or firing. Local labour departments, which are responsible for local employment provision, impose labour quotas on state enterprises irrespective of other plan targets (Chen, 1987, p. 164). Formerly all industrial workers in state-owned enterprises were permanent workers. As part of reform, a contract labour system has been introduced. Within the labour quotas, contract workers can be hired for 3–5 years after which their employment may be terminated or renewed. In 1987 contract workers constituted 52 per cent of the new hires (*Zhongguo Jingji Nianjian*, 1988, p. IV-46). At the end of 1990 13.5 million workers (about 13 per cent of all workers in state enterprises) were on contract (*Renmin Ribao*, 1 March 1991, p. 2). There is also a new category of temporary worker who can be fired at any time. Workers who were hired before the reform continue to enjoy permanent employment. When they retire, it is customary for their children to be hired to fill their quotas (Byrd and Tidrick, 1987, p. 70).

To motivate the workers, enterprises rely on material incentives primarily in the form of a time-rate wage system plus generous bonuses. A wage reform was introduced in 1988, which ties the total wage fund of an enterprise to its performance. In 1988 about 30 per cent of all state-owned enterprises were on the system. Given the total wage fund, enterprises have the power to decide how it should be distributed. As a result, the wage system varies greatly between enterprises, the range including fixed wage, floating wage and piece-rate systems.[8] Enterprises also have much leeway in giving bonuses and wage supplements in spite of government efforts to limit bonuses. In 1978 these bonuses and wage supplements amounted to 15 per cent of basic wages; in 1987 the figure was 45.7 per cent (*Zhongguo Jingji Nianjian*, 1989, p. III-10).

The Chinese socialist doctrine holds that workers' 'socialist enthusiasm' can be increased and their sense of being the 'masters of the workplace' enhanced through their participation in 'democratic management'. Workers' organizations are the vehicles for this participation, including the workers' congress and its standing body, the trade unions. However, except for a brief period in 1979-80 when workers' self-management was advocated by a few reformist economists, workers' participation in management has not been the focus of China's industrial reform in theory or practice (Hsu, 1989, pp. 506–8). In some cases, the workers' congress does elect the plant director, subject to government approval. The official functions of unions are typically perfunctory and political; they include workers' education, transmitting and implementing party policies, and supporting enterprise administration.

6.   CONCLUSION

Since 1979 China has introduced many reform measures to spur industrial productivity. The reform was accelerated in 1984, but has slowed down since the suppression of the pro-democracy movement in June 1989. No one single reform measure has been particularly successful. Although Chinese enterprises have gained much autonomy to produce for the market, the scope of their managerial decision making is restricted and the operation of the market is distorted by various policy constraints. Thus Chinese industry remains by-and-large inefficient. In 1989 16 per cent of state-owned industrial enterprises incurred losses (*Jingji Ribao*, 28 February 1990, p. 1). A study of some 400 enterprises conducted by the Institute of Economics of the Chinese Academy of Social Sciences concludes that total factor productivity in these enterprises did not increase at all during 1980–87; in fact, it declined in 1983–84 and 1985–87 (Du *et al.*, 1990, pp. 4–5).

One cause of this lacklustre performance is the piecemeal and myopic nature of China's reform, 'groping for the stones while crossing the river', as the Chinese themselves have attempted to justify it. This has led to the creation of a disjointed dualistic economy, as exemplified by the dual-track price system, in which an emaciated planned sector and a distorted market sector coexist. Neither sector works well, and they both work against each other to create all sorts of frictions, distortions and abuses.

This dualistic system has also spawned vast vested interests in the bureaucracy and the economy who have benefited from its existence. They may constitute a major obstacle to further reform in the future, along with party conservatives who oppose genuine market-orientated reform in order to forestall future demand for political liberalization.

POSTSCRIPT

China's eighth five-year plan (1991–95) and a broader ten-year development programme (1991–2000), which were first adopted by the Central Committee of the Chinese Communist Party on 30 December 1990, were ratified by the Seventh National People's Congress on 9 April 1991. According to premier Li Peng's report to the Congress and the latter's own plan outlines (*Renmin Ribao*, 11 April 1991 and 16 April 1991), the average annual growth rate of the economy during the plan period 1991–95 is envisioned to be 6 per cent, with 3.5 per cent for agricultural growth and 6.5 per cent for industrial growth. In the ten-year period 1991–2000, agriculture, energy, transportation, posts and telecommunications, and basic raw materials are to receive state priority. Manufacturing industries are to be modernized through upgrading in technology, including reductions in the consumption of energy and raw materials (*Renmin Ribao*, 25 April 1991, p. 1).

This new ranking of sectors seems appropriate, as investment in agriculture, energy and basic materials was relatively neglected in the 1980s and bottle-necks and imbalances in the economy appeared. It is essential, however, not to go to the other extreme and create a shortage of manufactured goods lest the inflationary pressure be aggravated and export earnings jeopardized. Also, the financing of large state investments may be problematic. High export earnings and a great deal of foreign capital will be needed for the import of capital goods needed for the investment projects.

No new reform initiatives are offered in the documents. The eighth five-year plan merely affirms China's intention to continue the reforms that have been adopted. These include continuing price adjustments and the contract responsibility system discussed above as well as a further decline in the scope of mandatory planning and expansion in that of guidance planning. However, given the new importance of energy and basic materials, it is doubtful that mandatory planning in these sectors will be reduced. China will also continue the recent policy of favouring large state-owned enter-prises, especially those in the new priority industries. Thus, the relative importance of the planned state sector in the economy may expand in the 1991–95 period in spite of official proclamations to the contrary.

Li Peng's report also stresses the promotion of enterprise groups that cut across different regions and industrial branches. Given the existence of trade barriers set up by local governments to protect local industries, inter-regional enterprise groupings should facilitate the inter-regional division of labour. It is doubtful, however, that many enterprises in different regions will have the incentive to collaborate, given the lack of competitive pressure on and the soft budget constraint of many state-owned enterprises.

ACKNOWLEDGEMENT

The author is grateful to Mr Ma Changshan of the Institute of Economics, the Chinese Academy of Social Sciences, for the clarification of several points discussed in this chapter. The author alone is responsible for any remaining errors.

NOTES

1. As used in China, the term collectively-owned enterprises, or collective enterprises for short, is a very broad category that includes not only cooperatives set up by peasants and

workers themselves, but also public or semi-public enterprises organized under the auspices of township and village governments. Some state-owned enterprises have also set up collective enterprises to employ their workers' children (more on this below).

2. Guidance planning is similar to the Western indicative planning in its reliance on economic incentives for implementation. It differs from the latter in that it gives plan targets to individual enterprises.

3. For example, in 1988 the plan fulfilment rate was 91.9 per cent for coal, 88.9 per cent for coke, 86.1 per cent for pig iron, 90.4 per cent for cement and 96.2 per cent for steel (*Jingji Ribao*, 24 Oct. 1989, p. 2).

4. For example, in Wenzhou, Zhejiang province, where private enterprises have flourished, the average number of employees in household-based businesses was three in 1985. In businesses jointly run by a number of peasants, the number of employees ranged from 30 to 50 (Dong, 1988, pp. 179–80). However, in a small number of commercial and service businesses with branches in different areas, the number of employees has been as high as a few hundred.

5. In the Chinese usage, the term 'director' is used in the case of a plant, whereas 'manager' is used in the case of a multi-plant enterprise.

6. For example, the Changchun Water Pump Factory in Changchun has the following criteria for evaluation in its contract: upgrade the enterprise; improve technology; develop new products; raise the quality of products; increase the value of assets; utilize raw materials and energy efficiently; uphold the quality of output; and maintain safety (Koo, 1990, p. 799).

7. Mr Ma Changshan of the Institute of Economics of the Chinese Academy of Social Sciences pointed this out to me.

8. In a floating wage system, workers' wages vary with enterprise performance and workers' productivity. The precise arrangement varies with the enterprise.

REFERENCES

Byrd, W. and Tidrick, G. (1987) 'Factor allocation and enterprise incentives', in Tidrick and Chen (eds) (1987).

Chen, J. (1987) 'The planning system', in Tidrick and Chen (eds) (1987).

Dong, F. (1988) *Jingji Fazhan Zhanlue Yanjiu*, Beijing: Jingji Kexue Chubanshe.

Du, H. *et al.* (1990) in *Jingji Yanjiu*, 1990, no. 1.

Granick, D. (1987) 'The industrial environment in China and the CMEA countries', in Tidrick and Chen (eds) (1987).

Guangming Ribao, various issues.

Hsu, R. (1989) 'Changing conceptions of the socialist enterprise in China, 1979–1988', *Modern China*, vol. 15, no. 4.

Hsu, R. (1991) *Economic Theories in China, 1979–1988*, New York: Cambridge University Press.

Institute of Finance and Trade Economics (1989) in *Caimao Jingji*, no. 10.

Jingji Guanli, various issues.

Jingji Ribao, various issues.

Koo, A. (1990) 'Contract responsibility system: A bridge of transition from a planned economy to market economy', *Economic Development and Cultural Change*, vol. 38, no. 4.

Li, H. (1990) *Dalu Jingji*, Taipei: Shangye zhoukan.

Liu, S. (1990) in *Caimao Jingji*, no. 1.

Lo, W. (1990) in *Jingji Guanli*, no. 5.

Naughton, B. (1985) 'False starts and second wind: financial reforms in China's industrial system', in E. Perry and C. Wong (eds), *The Political Economy of Reform in Post-Mao China*, Cambridge: Harvard University Press.

Renmin Ribao, various issues.

Riskin, C. (1987) *China's Political Economy*, New York: Oxford University Press.
State Statistical Bureau (1988) *Zhongguo Gongye Jingji Nianjian*, Beijing: Zhongguo Tongji
    Chubanshe.
State Statistical Bureau (1989) *Zhongguo Tongji Nianjian*, Beijing: Zhongguo Tongji
    Chubanshe.
State Statistical Bureau (1990) *Zhongguo Tongji Zhaiyao*, Beijing: Zhongguo Tongji Chubanshe.
Swaine, M. (1990) 'China faces the 1990s: A system in crisis', *Problems of Communism*, vol.
    39, no. 3.
Tidrick, G. and Chen, J. (1987) *China's Industrial Reform*, New York: Oxford University Press.
Wu, J. and Zhao, R. (1987) 'The dual pricing system in China's industry', *Journal of Com-
    parative Economics*, vol. 11, no. 3.
Xi, W. and Du, H. (1989), in *Jingji Yanjiu*, 1989, no. 11.
Zhongguo Jingji Nianjian, various years, Beijing: Jingji Guanli Chubanshe.

5 Industrial reform and the Cuban economy

Andrew Zimbalist

Few would contest that the Cuban revolution faced its most difficult crisis in 1990. Cuba's economic and political world crumbled around it and the CMEA market, which had rescued the revolution from the US embargo, disintegrated. Coming on the heels of four years of economic stagnation and the Ochoa crisis of 1989,[1] many believed the revolution was in a struggle for its very survival. Some members of the Cuban exile community in Miami, for instance, promoted bumper-stickers anticipating Christmas celebrations in Havana while others opened up real estate businesses with pretensions of commercializing properties in their homeland. Yet the Castro government did not fall in 1990 and, indeed, at this writing (January 1991), shows few signs that it will in the near future.

The crisis of 1989-90 led to tighter government control over the economy as well as over independent political activity. The government's economic strategy is two-pronged: first, to guarantee the basic nutrition and livelihood of the population during the critical transition period; second, to design and implement wide-ranging reforms that will enable the economy to become an effective participant in the world market. The latter goal necessarily consists of both domestic and international components intended to introduce greater efficiency and flexibility into the economic mechanism. Yet, the problematic experiences with reform in Eastern Europe and the Soviet Union, *inter alia,* have reinforced Castro's own disposition to maintain close control over the step-by-step reform process. This essay will discuss that process in the context of the ongoing rectification campaign (*campaña de rectificación*) and the Cuban historical experience with economic reform.

1. THE CUBAN REFORM DYNAMIC

In contrast to the experiences of most of Eastern Europe, Cuban socialism was home-grown and, in contrast to the Soviet Union, the revolutionary government in Cuba enjoyed the support and enthusiasm of the vast majority of the population at the time of the revolution. Given these circumstances, it is not surprising that throughout the 1960s the Castro government essentially sought to define its own, unique institutions of socialist political economy. It is further noteworthy that at precisely the moment the Cubans were moving toward the moral economy projected by Che Guevara, the Soviets were putting in place 'materialistic' reforms influenced by the Liberman proposals. Cuba's effort at a moral economy foundered, among other things, due to excessive idealism. As more pragmatic policies were adopted during the 1970s, the idealism of the 1960s receded but did not disappear.

Cuba did not have stable institutions of economic planning until the latter half of the 1970s. Indeed, Cuba's first five-year plan did not come until 1976–80. The gradual introduction of Cuba's new planning system, the SDPE (*Sistema de Dirección y Planificación de la Economía*) was begun in 1977.[2] The SDPE was basically modelled after the 1965 Soviet reforms. It sought to: (1) put enterprises on an economic accounting basis; (2) introduce a profitability criterion with its corresponding incentives; and (3) promote decentralization, organizational coherence and efficiency. As with the earlier Soviet reform, it met with the obstacles of bureaucratic resistance, pervasive shortages and an irrational price structure. Possibilities for decentralized decision making in Cuba have also been constrained by the inadequate supply of skilled managerial and technical labour. Moreover, Cuba confronted additional difficulties in adapting the Soviet-styled reform to Cuban political culture. The Cubans began tinkering with their new system almost from the outset.[3]

A central theme of the SDPE was decentralization. By putting enterprises on an economic accounting scheme and introducing profit sharing, enterprises were supposed to be exercising increasing autonomy from the centre. This, in turn, was to promote efficiency. Nominal economic accounting and profit sharing by themselves, however, did little, if anything, to enhance the scope of enterprise decision making. In the context of centrally fixed prices, centrally determined investments and extensive input shortages these mechanisms did not alter the basic mode of operation of Cuban planning. With prices centrally set every five or more years, they were not a reliably rational guide to production or allocation choices; nor could they systematically identify through a profitability index well-managed enterprises. With shortages commonplace, otherwise efficient enterprises were often thwarted in their production efforts because of non-delivery, untimely delivery, or delivery of improperly specified, poor quality inputs. Bottlenecks and planning imperfections, in turn, necessitated amendments to the plan after the beginning of the year, often raising an enterprise's output target without increasing its supply of raw materials (see, among others, Ayala Castro and Ferrer, 1989).

Enterprises, behaving rationally in this environment, hoarded inputs, thereby aggravating the shortage and supply problem. Since the behaviour of profits was fickle because of these and other factors, the planning authorities were compelled on equity grounds to limit the extent of profit retention and distribution, thus weakening the incentive effect. And since profits thrived in certain enterprises despite the absence of properly specified, high quality production, the planners devised new administrative regulations to control this behaviour. In the end the profitability algorithm became hopelessly complicated and the incentive mechanism debilitated. Since the centre decided what investment projects were to be undertaken, the fact that enterprises paid for increasing shares of investment costs out of their bank funds rather than state budget funds (the share of enterprise financed investments in total investment financing in Cuba rose from 1 per cent in 1981 to 30 per cent in 1985: Banco Nacional de Cuba, 1986, p. 6) did not imply a substantive decentralization of capital allocation.

To be sure, in at least one important respect the SDPE represented further centralization of the planning system. Prior to 1976 the system of material supplies was carried out by consolidated enterprises;[4] subsequently, most material balances came to be implemented by the Central Planning Board (Juceplan) or the Central State Committee on Technical-material Supplies (Ceatm).

The SDPE, then, like the 1965 Soviet economic reforms, did not bring a significant change in the underlying centralization of decision making in the economic mechanism. There were, however, peripheral changes which accompanied the SDPE, many introduced in an effort to adapt the Soviet centralized model to Cuban conditions, that did increase the flexibility of the system and allow for some decentralization of decision making. Among these new policies was the post-1976 system of popular power which controlled the management of locally orientated service and production enterprises. In the mid-1980s such enterprises amounted to 34 per cent of all Cuban enterprises.[5] The local budgets of popular power grew from 21 per cent of the total state budget in 1978, to 26 per cent in 1980, to 30 percent in 1982 and 33 per cent in 1984. The local budget share in the Soviet Union in 1980 was 17.1 per cent (Mata, 1986, p. 56).

Another policy allowed for enterprises to make their own contracts for products that were not centrally balanced. There has also been encouragement for the development of 'secondary' (above-plan) production. Further, the realization that there were growing stocks of unused inputs within enterprises led to the practice of 'resource fairs' where enterprises traded freely and directly with each other. These fairs were first organized by the Ceatm in 1979. The fairs of 1979 and 1980 witnessed the sale of 40 million pesos of inputs. Inventory sales of production inputs by enterprises have continued to grow. In October of 1982 the President of Juceplan reported that some 500 million pesos of such resources had already been identified.[6] In May 1985, at the conclusion of the Fourth Plenary on the SDPE, the judgement was reached that the Ceatm was still allocating too many products and the number should be significantly reduced, allowing enterprises to contract directly with each other for these products (Juceplan, *Dictámenes de la IV Plenaria*, 1985, p. 25). In fact, the degree of centralization contemplated in the Soviet-designed system was never approached in Cuba, as it was resisted by sectoral and provincial planning bodies.

Other measures of decentralization included the strengthening of the Cuban Institute of Internal Demand, the introduction of free labour contracting in 1980,[7] and an increasing acceptance of private productive and service activity (most notably housing construction cooperatives and free farmers' markets). There was also some light manufacturing by artisans, and enterprises were permitted to use up to 30 per cent of their profits to make input purchases from the private sector.

Free farmers' markets were opened in 1980. Sales of fresh vegetables and fruits grew rapidly until the February 1982 government crackdown on 'abuses' (exorbitant prices, excessive middleperson profits and resource diversion from the state sector). Sales began to grow again after the promulgation of new regulations in May 1983 (20 per cent sales tax, progressive income tax on private farmer income from 5 to 20 per cent, and the expansion of the state-controlled parallel market to compete with the farmers' markets). However, new abuses, more serious diversion of resources from state uses, and reported incomes above 50,000 pesos for truckers, wholesalers and some farmers led to the indefinite closing of these markets in May 1986. Although such free market sales of produce were permitted in the other socialist countries pre-*perestroika*, private plots tended to be no larger than one-quarter or one-half a hectare (except in Poland and Yugoslavia, where private farming was predominant). In Cuba such plots typically range from 20 to over 60 hectares. Although private farmers are required to deliver a share of their output to the state, actual deliveries are often modest relative to output, leaving substantial produce to be consumed locally or marketed independently. Castro, for instance, charged that some private farmers delivered no more than 10 per cent of their output to the state (Mesa-Lago, 1988, p. 71). Thus, the potential for economic and political disruption emerging from the private agricultural sector in Cuba *prima facie* was greater than elsewhere in the CMEA.

Nevertheless, these decentralizing measures taken together did not alter the key dynamic of Cuban planning. Prior to the beginning of the rectification campaign in April 1986,[8] it was apparent from various government documents and speeches that the need for further decentralization and greater worker participation was clearly perceived. The documents of the May 1985 Fourth Plenary evaluating the SDPE, in particular, laid out a series of decentralizing measures that the Cubans intended to carry out. With the severe foreign exchange difficulties that Cuba began to experience around that time, along with the growing excess of incomplete investments projects, however, resources became too scarce to sustain the momentum toward decentralization, and the state tightened its grip on the economy in order to economize on the use of foreign exchange as well as to bring existing investment projects to successful completion.

Unintended or profligate use of resources in both the private and public spheres came under increasing scrutiny, as did the lack of coordination among sectoral ministries of the economy and among state planning institutions (e.g. the State Committee on Finances, the State Price Committee, the National Bank and Juceplan). Together with the difficulties of increasing labour indiscipline (exacerbated by shortages of inputs and consumer goods), enterprise overstaffing, corruption among officials and ideological concerns, these problems brought on the rectification campaign in early 1986. Market-orientated decentralization was put on hold, although efforts at administrative decentralization were continued.

2. CHARACTERIZING THE RECTIFICATION CAMPAIGN

There is no question but that the rectification campaign brought a halt to the previous trend toward both liberalization and increased emphasis on material incentives. Many prominent interpreters of Cuban reality, however, have exaggerated the nature and meaning of this shift, either by misapprehending the substance of the SDPE or by misconstruing the new policies. Both Jorge Pérez-López (1986, p. 34) and Jorge Domínguez (1988, p. 6), for instance, claimed that the SDPE itself represented market socialism and the trimestral publication of Radio Martí (1986, p. 13) declared the dissolution of the SDPE with the rectification campaign.[9] Pérez-López (1986, p. 16) also charged that Cuba had suspended worker productivity bonuses. Mesa-Lago (1988, pp. 74–80) wrote that most urban private sector activity had been eliminated. Pérez-López, Domínguez, Mesa-Lago and others have compared the rectification campaign to the late 1960s, a period when there were no individual bonuses, no overtime pay, no unified central plan, no cost accounting, no national budget and little record keeping.[10]

The reality is different. As we have noted, the SDPE did not approach market socialism and its basic structure, with modifications, is still intact. Worker productivity bonuses were never as prominent in Cuba as elsewhere in the CMEA, yet they are still very much in evidence. Urban private sector activity has come under increasing regulation but is still permitted. None of the salient characteristics of the late 1960s economy are present in the rectification campaign, although one can readily observe the strong hand of Fidel Castro in each period.

The rectification campaign is more usefully understood as a phase in the typical reform cycle of a centrally planned economy (CPE). Periods of liberalization in CPEs, prompted by the quest for greater efficiency, inevitably generate economic, political and social tensions as well as outcomes that are antithetical to the stated goals of socialist society, e.g. growing income differentials, inflation, investment diverging from plan and increased corruption. It is natural, if not inevitable, that liberalization policies provoke periods of reassessment and retrenchment, as experienced in Hungary and China. Of course, the nature, timing and intensity of the cycle depends on factors peculiar to each country and to the international political and economic climate. Further, in Cuba's case the emphasis on moral incentives reflects the home-grown revolutionary process and the consequent ideological formation of the leadership.

3. THE POLICIES OF RECTIFICATION

Balancing material and moral incentives

Material incentives are problematic in centrally planned, shortage-type economies. Not only are there ideological concerns with inequality and attitude, but there are limits to motivating workers and managers with more money if there are not desirable goods available for purchase. These limits are more severe for CPEs with lower levels of economic development, especially during times of severe foreign exchange constraints. Another difficulty with material incentives at the workplace affects market and planned economies alike: measuring individual contribution to the quantity and quality of output is never straightforward. Each of these problems was pertinent to the Cuban situation in the mid-1980s.

Three types of material incentives for workers are used in Cuba: *normas* (piece rates); *primas* (bonuses); and *premios* (profit-sharing). The details of their operation are peripheral to my main concern (Zimbalist, 1989). It is, however, relevant to note the following. *Normas* were applied to 1.2 million workers (37.2 per cent of the labour force) at the end of 1985. Three-quarters of the *normas* were 'elementary', i.e. not determined by a time-and-motion study. Income paid for overfulfilment of *normas* grew from 121.7 million pesos (3.9 per cent of worker income on average in 1980) to 274.5 million pesos (6.0 per cent of worker income in 1985). *Primas* were introduced experimentally in 1979 and then gradually applied throughout the economy the following year. Varieties of *primas* abound in Cuba, but most involve giving a bonus to a group of workers for increasing exports, saving raw materials or energy, overfulfilling quality or quantity targets, or developing new products. The value of *primas* paid out grew steadily from 14 million pesos in 1980 to 90.7 million pesos in 1985, the latter figure still only representing 1.9 per cent of the basic wage. *Premios* were introduced experimentally in 1979. By 1985 total *premio* payments amounted to 71.1 million pesos or 1.6 per cent of the basic wage. Among other things, the extension of *premios* was frustrated by Cuba's system of administered prices, making the meaning of profit or any financial indicator dubious. Taken together the three material incentives grew rapidly during the early 1980s, but still only accounted for 10.6 per cent on average of the basic wage in 1985, considerably below elsewhere in the CMEA.[11]

In addition to the problems discussed above, it was discovered that often the three incentives overlapped, paying the worker twice or thrice for the same work, e.g. sugar mill workers paid for exceeding their *norma,* working overtime and increasing exports. To avoid this duplication, many *primas,* especially those related to export production, have been curtailed. In other cases, incentives were applied that had little justification, such as mechanics paid five times for repairing the same piece of machinery or radio announcers working on piece rates. In yet other cases, elementary *normas,* set with the

Table 5.1   *Application of material incentives, 1985–90 (in millions of pesos)*

year	(a) total wages	(b) norm overfulfil.	(c) primas	(b)/(a) (%)	(c)/(a) (%)	(d)* (%)	(e)** (%)
1985	7139	275	91	3.85	1.27	11.2	67.0
1986	7359	251	88	3.40	1.19	11.1	68.0
1987	7290	188	52	2.58	0.72	10.9	68.3
1988	7641	186	45	2.44	0.59	11.9	67.5
1989	7971	188	47	2.36	0.59	12.3[+]	66.9[+]
1990[++]	2058	45	10	2.18	0.50	na	na

* absenteeism
** index of worker efficiency (*aprovechamiento en hombres días*)
[+] January through September only
[++] January through March only

Source: Comité Estatal de Estadísticas, *Boletín Estadístico* (June 1990), pp. 120–1; Zimbalist, A. and Brundenius, C. (1989) *The Cuban Economy: Measurement and Analysis of Socialist Performance*, Baltimore: Johns Hopkins University Press, pp. 131–8.

participation of the affected workers, were too low. In 1986 more than one-third of all workers with *normas* produced over 130 per cent of their rate.[12] In these instances, the designs of certain incentives and output goals were re-evaluated.

As shown in Table 5.1 above, rectification brought a gradual reduction in the application of both *normas* and *primas*. No data were available to the author on the use of the *premio* after 1985, but interviews with enterprise directors confirm that there has also been a move away from this incentive.

The last two columns in Table 5.1 support the case *prima facie* that the diminished use of material incentives after 1985 did not have a deleterious effect on worker effort. In particular, one can detect very little, if any, significant change in the rates of worker absenteeism and worker efficiency between 1985 and 1989. Indeed, effort seemed to have improved between 1985 and 1987 and then deteriorated between 1987 and 1989. One might attribute the latter period decline to: (1) moral incentives wearing thin over time; (2) workers taking more time off for shopping and waiting on lines; and/or (3) increased shortage of raw materials for production and a corre-sponding increase in absenteeism or decrease in efficiency. In any event, considering the entire four-year period, it does not appear that the effort to rebalance moral and material incentives had a direct, discernible impact on productivity.

Reducing the scope of private sector activity

The most important policy of rectification regarding private activity was the abolition of the free peasant markets on 15 May 1986. As noted above, the leadership perceive a plethora of threats from these markets. Private farmers were enriching themselves, among other things, dispiriting the membership on the newly formed cooperative farms. Castro gave examples of a farmer who made 50,000 pesos from planting a hectare of garlic and of another who hired four workers and owned two trucks and earned 150,000 pesos, or roughly 65 times the average yearly wage. Castro claimed that it was virtu-ally impossible to collect taxes effectively on these high peasant incomes. Urban workers and consumers supposedly were not only demoralized by the easy money made by private farmers, but also indignant at the astronomical prices they were obliged to pay for fresh produce on these markets. More significantly, the operation of these markets entailed a substantial diversion of resources away from the state plan and toward the private sector, such as the private use of state trucks, shirking at work or leaving early, and pilfer-ing of items like gasoline and insecticides. They also prompted farmers to reduce deliveries to the state of exportable produce in order to sell it at higher prices on the free markets. With rectification, the state has attempted to replace these markets, which accounted for less than 5 per cent of food sales according to official figures, by expanding the state-run parallel markets. Also, a new distribution enterprise (*Frutas Selectas*) was set up and farmers were offered higher prices for sales to the state. To say the least, this new arrangement has created considerable inconvenience for large numbers of consumers who have been forced to locate new sources of supply for many food items.

Another significant measure was to regulate the sale of private housing. The 1984 housing law provided for converting all tenants into home owners within 20 years (it was already the case that over 60 per cent of dwellers owned their homes). The state had already sanctioned private home construction and greatly eased private access to building materials. The result was twofold: a construction boom with private construction accounting for one-third of new houses in the 1980s and a speculation boom with skyrocketing prices for real estate. To curb the latter and its beneficiaries, the state decreed that all housing sales would have to pass through a state agency that would regulate prices. The 1984 housing law itself was left intact.

Other private sector activity has come under tighter state regulation and, thus, the scope of some activities has been reduced. The principal new restriction since 1986 is that private service workers (such as plumbers, electricians and mechanics), artisans, street vendors, taxi drivers and so on must be licensed and must receive all materials through a state-issued certificate. That is, the state still recognizes that many services can be provided more efficiently by the private sector, but it does not want the success of this sector to be at the expense of diverted resources and pilfered materials. In the spring of 1989 the private advertising section in the popular magazine *Opina*, which had been curtailed, was reopened. The number of private wage workers and workers for their own account fell from 52,100 in 1985 to 43,200 in 1987 as private non-farm income fell from 102.5 million pesos to 67.8 million pesos, but private non-farm income began to recover in 1988 rising to 80.7 million pesos.[13] Thus, urban private sector activity has been reduced, but it has hardly been obliterated.

Despite the closing of the peasant markets, private farm income (officially reported) actually increased from 495.6 million pesos in 1985 to 528.9 million pesos in 1988. Within the private agricultural sector, incomes of workers in producer cooperatives fell from 161.8 million pesos in 1985 to 152.5 million in 1988, while the incomes of individual private farmers expanded from 333.8 million pesos to 376.4 million.[14] The greatest difficulty, however, has been with respect to the wholesale and retail distribution of this output, not the production itself. The shortage of trucks and the inadequacy of storage, refrigeration and packaging facilities, as well as the poor internal organization of the state distribution network, often leads to the wastage of 25 to 35 per cent of certain crops such as potatoes, tomatoes and onions.

As of November 1990 the Castro government remained opposed to reopening the farmers' markets in the conditions then prevailing, but it began to discuss openly the importance of an expanded private service sector. The campaign to reduce excess staff in enterprises and government offices would necessitate a redeployment of personnel to other jobs. Some would go to agriculture to work on the newly colonized plots, but others would join the growing ranks of workers for their own account. In the government's conception, not only would this alleviate unemployment problems, but it would also attenuate the strains and inconveniences of everyday life in Cuba. The new private service workers, for instance, could work as carpenters, painters, plumbers, electricians, mechanics and thus help to prolong the useful life of a badly dilapidated housing stock. The state would need to expand its materials supply network to provide these new private workers with inputs and to experiment once again with introducing an effective system of individual income taxation. As these systems developed, government officials envision the possibility of a subsequent expansion of the sector to include private service and retail cooperatives (e.g. restaurants). According to the vision described to this author in November 1990, private farmers' markets could only be contemplated after these new policies and institutions were in place and successfully functioning.[15]

Efforts at administrative decentralization
Although market-orientated decentralization has (for the moment at least) been eschewed, the Cuban government has actively pursued policies aimed at administrative decentralization. Even though the main architect of the 1975–85 liberalization policies, Humberto Pérez, was replaced in early 1985 as head of the Central Planning Board, the perception of a torpid, overcentralized system remained and was widespread amongst government economic functionaries and managers. The momentum toward decentralization, although slowed and redirected, has not been broken.

Several ongoing efforts, such as the formation of production brigades in agricultural and industrial enterprises as well as the formation of and transfer of planning functions to *uniones de empresas* (industrial associations), have continued. Production brigades are sub-units of an enterprise that perform a distinct productive function. While they remain part of the enterprise, in theory they also begin to operate as a separate accounting unit. Enterprises contract out a production plan to the brigade and the brigade receives bonuses according to its performance. Eventually, it is expected that brigades will also be self-financing and will form their own stimulation funds. Brigades are allowed to organize their own work as well as hire (after suggestion from above) and fire their own brigade chief.[16] By making the productive unit smaller and the incentive more immediate, it is hoped that this organizational change will promote greater worker participation and productivity. The brigades began experimentally in agriculture in 1981 and in industry in 1983. By 1986 there were 2 500 brigades in some 300 enterprises, 120 state farms and 180 enterprises outside agriculture. Agricultural brigades average approximately 75 workers each.[17]

Another potential way by which enterprise flexibility or autonomy can be increased is through amalgamation. Since 1977 Cuban enterprises have been joined together with other horizontally or vertically related enterprises to form *uniones de empresas* (Díaz Martínez, 1983). By bringing units at the base together it is hoped that the new larger units will be able to carry out more functions (e.g. research and development, materials supply, maintenance and repair) and become less dependent on the centre. As of 31 December 1985 there were 42 *uniones* in industry (involving some 390 of the 800 industrial enterprises) and 61 economy-wide (involving almost 500 of the 2 240 enterprises on the island). There is not enough evidence at this time to assert that the *uniones* have facilitated the intended decentralization, but several planning administrators have argued this to be true for certain sectors and the planning reforms proposed by the *Comisión Nacional del Sistema de Dirección de la Economía* in 1988 called for further amalgamation of enterprises into *uniones* as part of the ongoing thrust toward plan simplification and procedural decentralization.

A recent article from the journal of Juceplan details the ongoing amalgamation of industrial enterprises into *uniones*. The number of economic units (either enterprises or *uniones)* directed by the ministries of transport, food, basic industry, metallurgy and light industry was reduced from 155 in 1988 to 88 in 1989, a reduction of 43.2 per cent. This apparently simplified the tasks of management sufficiently to allow for the reduction of administrative personnel in these ministries from 5 600 to 3 636 (or by 37.3 per cent).[18]

The brigade might appear to work in the opposite direction to the *union,* one enlarging the administrative unit and the other diminishing it. This is true, but the purposes are different and their effects on participation operate in distinct and potentially complementary ways. The *union,* which can be but usually is not an accounting unit, allows more activities to take place at local initiative, free of central tutelage. The brigade reduces the size of the decision-making and incentive unit related to direct production matters.

Other initiatives are new. In 1988, following the recommendations of a special commission to study the SDPE, several new procedures were adopted in the planning process.[19] The number of commodities and commodity groups subject to central planning was to be drastically reduced from 2 300 to 800 (vol. 1, p. 8). The number of directive indicators to the enterprise was to be cut from an average of 28 to 18 (vol. 1, p. 9). The system of material balances was to be decentralized by 'extending direct ties in order to eliminate intermediaries in the process of elaborating and executing the plan of material and technical supplies' (author's translation, vol. 1, p. 7). Concretely, the number of material balances drawn up by Ceatm (the central state material supply committee) was to be reduced by 382 (31 per cent) and passed down to the level of the industrial association or the enterprise (vol. 1, p. 35). Further, according to a February 1989 report of the *Comisión Nacional del Sistema de Dirección de la Economía*, direct supplies contracting was established between enterprises for 518 different products during 1988.[20]

Experiments are also being carried out in central planning methods. In 1988 experimentation was begun in 33 enterprises in 'continuous planning'. This method calls upon the enterprise to draw up a production and input plan, based on last year's levels and its expectations for the coming year, prior to receiving the plan control figures from the national ministry. That is, the enterprise is supposed to begin annual planning before it receives instructions from the planning hierarchy. Under traditional procedures plan control figures often arrived at the enterprise too late for a serious discussion or for any meaningful amendments to the plan to occur (Ayala and Ferrer, 1989). In its conception continuous planning avoids the last-minute rush syndrome and it allows for some greater initiative at the enterprise level. It does this, of course, at the expense of a possible loss of coordination, but, given the failure of the planning authorities to produce a realistic, balanced comprehensive plan in the past, it is not clear what if anything is lost by the new method. At present continuous planning is still in the experimental stage, but as of mid-1990 it had been extended to approximately one-third of Cuba's productive enterprises.

Experiments with pricing policy are also under way. Some foreign trade enterprises are using international prices. Other enterprises, which are the sole producers of a given product, are being allowed to set the product's price, subject to issued guidelines and subsequent review by the State Price Committee.

The planning process itself, of course, has been radically altered in practice by the supply disruptions and transformations originating in Eastern Europe and the Soviet Union since 1989. Although annual plans continue to be produced, they are regarded more as hortatory than mandatory. The central government itself seems to have admitted indirectly the impossibility of global planning in the present context by changing its top-level planning organization and by placing clear focus on priority sectoral as opposed to global plans.[21]

The greater latitude permitted by this new planning environment has facilitated some of the reforms occurring in enterprise management. The initiative for serious changes in Cuba's enterprise management system came from the Ministry of the Armed Forces. In July 1987 the decision was taken to begin sweeping experiments in the management of a number of military enterprises. The experiments involved a variety of modern Western management techniques, such as management by consensus, group work, quality control circles, job rotation and participatory decision making. The experimentation began in the machine shop of the Che Guevara military products factory during September and October of 1987. Over the next production period quality indicators rose by 20 to 60 per cent despite a reduction in quality control personnel of 33 per cent.[22]

The success of these experiments led to the decision to generalize the techniques throughout the economy. A national management training system (SUPSCER) was set up in 1988 to help introduce and disseminate these methods. Western experts have been called upon to help design course modules, give specialized seminars to enterprise directors and union leaders, build a curriculum for a new masters' programme in management and engage directly in enterprise consulting. Over 1 000 administrators have already taken short courses and several industrial sectors have successfully introduced management reforms.

More than a dozen enterprises under the Ministry of Basic Industry have introduced Japanese-style quality control circles. Initial reports suggest impressive quality and productivity gains. It appears that one of the important reasons for these gains is the absence of a rigid quantity plan. That is, the new planning environment liberates ministries and enterprises from the quantity fetishism of conventional central planning. The more rational and democratic methods are being applied because of the space created by aberrant conditions in the macroeconomy. One interesting result of these reforms is that a larger constituency is being built at the base for greater decentralization in the economic mechanism.

International opening
Since the 1985–86 foreign exchange crisis precipitated by the depreciating dollar, falling petroleum prices, drying up of hard currency credits, low sugar prices, Hurricane Kate and the tightening US embargo, Cuba has pursued both import substitution and export promotion with great vigour. The commitment to generating hard currency earnings and integrating into the world market economy became even stronger during the collapse of the CMEA in 1989–90.[23]

Beginning in 1988, the Cubans introduced new trade policies and structures intended to decentralize and dynamize the foreign sector. An agreement was signed with the Soviet Union to allow direct economic relations between certain Cuban and Soviet enterprises, contemplating 65 separate projects. *Cubanacán,* a Cuban corporation not subject to and unencumbered by the state planning apparatus, was created in 1988 to promote joint ventures in tourism and other sectors. The 1982 joint venture law has been made more flexible, allowing foreign enterprises more than 49 per cent ownership, and applied successfully by *Cubanacán* to start up a total of 12 joint ventures by November 1990, nine of which were in tourism. *Cubanacán* has reinvested some of its profits in sectors such as biotechnology, marketing and nickel. *Cubanacán's* mission is to maximize profit, so that by investing in new sectors it brings the pressure of the world market to bear on the targeted enterprises. Further, by sharing its accumulating experience in international finance and marketing, *Cubanacán* is also able to promote success in other export projects.

Other corporations (e.g. *Gaviota, Cubalse, Uneca* and *Cimex*), also independent of the central planning apparatus, have been established. In 1990 a new mechanism to enlist foreign cooperation was introduced, namely *producción cooperada.* The idea here is to induce foreign companies to supply missing inputs (e.g. raw materials, technology, packaging and marketing) in the Cuban production process and, in return, assign them a portion of the revenue generated. There are already more than a dozen projects of this genre, with several involved in basic industrial production.

The government has also assigned an increasing priority to the medical products branch, which exports pharmaceuticals, biotechnological and genetic engineering products and medical equipment. The *Centro de Ingenería Genética y Biotecnología* (CIGB) has commercialized 11 products, including vaccines for meningitis B and hepatitis B, a dermal growth factor, a drug to lower cholesterol and blood pressure levels, an HIV1 test and various reagents. The value of the centre's exports has grown from zero in 1988 to some 300 million pesos in 1989 and a projected 800 million pesos in 1990. The development of this branch as well as the electronics branch has been reinforced by a 21.7 per cent increase in the government's 1990 budget allocation to scientific research and development; in contrast, there has been a reduction of 10.4 per cent in spending on state administration as well as cuts in most other budgetary areas. Several other export products hold significant promise, including sugar derivatives, nickel/cobalt, fish products, zeolite and citrus fruits. Overall, Cuba's hard currency commodity exports grew by $273 million in 1989, 24.5 per cent above 1988. Despite the shutdown of the Moa nickel plant for energy efficiency reasons in September 1990, hard currency exports of goods registered appreciable growth again in 1990.

Cuba's service exports are also on the upswing, as investments in tourism are paying off nicely. The number of tourists to Cuba has grown from 208,000 in 1987 to 326,000 in 1989, and is projected to reach 600,000 by the mid-1990s. In 1989 95.9 per cent of Cuba's tourist income was in hard currency.

Despite important gains from these new efforts, the massive trade disruption from the former CMEA economies, with whom Cuba conducted 83–87 per cent of its trade in recent years, cannot be replaced in the short run. The official plan for 1990 called for a real output growth (in gross social product) of 1 to 2 per cent. According to official figures, through June of 1990 'mercantile production' in agriculture was up 2.9 per cent over the first six months of 1989, in construction the increase was 4.5 per cent and in industry there was a drop of 1.1 per cent.[24] This suggests an overall upward trend, but several points should be noted. First, these figures are measured in current, not constant, prices. Second, mercantile production is gross, not net. Third, mercantile production includes the sale (decrease) of inventories. When adjustments are made for the sale in 1990 of goods produced in 1989, it is clear that the downward trend in industry is much sharper than is suggested by the fall of 1.1 per cent. Fourth, Cuban officials acknowledge that the economy took its biggest hit in August following the Iraqi invasion of Kuwait and the initial sharp increase in world oil prices.

In any case, the ongoing deterioration in trade with Eastern Europe and the deepening economic depression and political instability in the Soviet Union make it extremely likely that matters will get substantially worse for the Cuban economy before they get better. It is reasonable to expect a drop in real national income in Cuba of five per cent or more for 1990.

4.   CONCLUSION

The Cubans have always attempted to keep their distance from the Soviet model, but in the absence of a clear alternative they adopted most of the model's basic features during the 1970s (Zimbalist and Smith, 1990). The disillusionment with central planning in the Soviet Union and Eastern Europe has led the Cuban leadership to reassert their longstanding scepticism of the Soviet model and to acknowledge the need to return to the drawing board of socialist economics.

Although thus far the actual steps of economic reform in Cuba have been modest, it is clear that a momentum and a constituency for greater decentralization is building. Presently, there are three brakes on further decentralization:

1.   The leadership believes it has learned a lesson from the CMEA reform experiences, namely decentralizing control and mixing plan with market elements can be highly destabilizing both economically and politically. Hence, the current plan is to reform slowly, step-by-step and with clear government control over the process.

2. The foreign exchange crisis allows little leeway in the use of resources. Given the small size of Cuba's economy and its great dependence on foreign trade, practically all economic activity is either directly or indirectly connected to importing and exporting. The consequent perception of a need to assert tight central control over foreign exchange thwarts the liberalization process.

3. The ongoing US embargo and aggression have reinforced the existing centripetal tendencies. Should the United States begin a normalization of its relations with Cuba, then the Cuban government will lose its primary justification for tight political controls and repression. Normalization would also ameliorate Cuba's foreign exchange crisis and permit tens of thousands of US tourists and dozens of US businesses to nourish the forces of reform and liberalization within the country.

The ultimate extent and success of reform efforts in Cuba, then, will depend largely on political forces. The present reforms, particularly those regarding foreign trade, offer interesting promise for the future. The first challenge for the Castro government, however, will be to negotiate the economic hardships and political imbroglios of the initial transition period from the protected CMEA to the world market.

An update to this chapter is given in the Postscript, page 285.

NOTES

1. Arnaldo Ochoa was the commander of Cuban troops in Angola and a leading officer in the Cuban Armed Forces. He was arrested, tried and executed for corruption and narcotics trading. His week-long trial was broadcast on national television and included extensive testimony from Fidel Castro and other leaders. Other key political figures were charged along with Ochoa. Questions arose as to why Raul Castro, Fidel's brother and head of the Armed Forces, did not know about Ochoa's dealings or, if he did know, why he did nothing about it. Some speculated that Ochoa, as a rising political star, represented a challenge to Castro and was executed for this reason.

2. The adoption of the SDPE occurred in 1976, but this year was designated as a year of study and preparation. The gradual implementation of the system began in 1977. Since mid-1986 it has been more commonly referred to as simply the SDE.

3. In the mid- and late 1970s, as Cuba was introducing the Soviet-styled SDPE, the model came under continual criticism in Cuba for being too centralized. At the time, Cuba pioneered in establishing its system of Popular Power (with contested local elections) and in turning over the management of local enterprises to the newly elected municipal bodies. Miguel Figueras, Vice President of the State Planning Board (Juceplan) at the time, commented to the author that between 1977 and 1981 the Cubans 'were decentralizing 15 per cent' of the Soviet-style planning institutions each year.

4. The Cuban phrase is *empresas consolidadas*. They were an earlier and generally smaller incarnation of the later *union de empresas* or association.

5. The share contributed to output by local enterprises was, of course, considerably less than 34 per cent, since these enterprises were generally quite small.
6. *Granma* (5 October 1982, p. 2). Additional data through 1984 and analysis is provided in U-Echevarría, O. *et al.* (1986), in *Cuba: Economía Planificada*, vol. 1, no. 2, pp. 110–39.
7. This system was actually begun on an experimental basis in 1979 in the province of Pinar del Rio, but was not implemented until 1986 in Havana. The Soviet Union, of course, has had this system for many years. In the Soviet Union, as in Cuba, free contracting denoted the right to hire freely within plan stipulated limits, but not to fire.
8. The rectification campaign is the name given to the current period of re-evaluating the balance of material and moral incentives, redressing the perceived excesses connected to materials incentives and private sector activity, and addressing other problems of economic and political management.
9. Also see the essay by Rabkin (1988), who asserts that there was 'managerial autonomy' prior to the rectification campaign (p. 35).
10. See also, inter alia, Domínguez, J. (1985) and Treaster, J. (1987).
11. In the mid-1970s, for instance, the variable part of the basic wage ranged from 15.2 per cent in Hungary to 55.2 per cent in the German Democratic Republic, with Bulgaria at 39.8 per cent, Poland at 31.7 per cent, the USSR at 36.4 per cent, and Czechoslovakia at 43.8 per cent (Acosta, 1982, p. 291).
12. *Granma*, 14 January 1987, p. 5. The ratchet effect further complicated the productive use of *normas*.
13. Indications are that it continued to increase in the first half of 1989, when total private sector incomes increased 4.7 per cent (*Anuario Estadístico de Cuba, 1987*, p. 193; Comité Estatal de Estadísticas, *Balance de Ingresos y Egresos Monetarios de la Población*, July 1989, p. 21 and August 1989, p. 3).
14. *Ibid.*, July 1989, p. 21.
15. This paragraph is based on interviews with Carlos Aldana and Roberto Robaina of the politbureau (Robaina is an alternate member). Castro also alluded to a prospective expansion in workers for their own account in public speeches during October and November 1990.
16. The practice of brigade members selecting their own chief has developed unevenly. Without the custom of exercizing such authority, it often takes time before worker attitudes and behaviour adapt to their new, augmented prerogatives. In early 1987, for instance, it appears that most brigade chiefs in agriculture were still appointed by the state farm administration and approved by the Ministry of Agriculture (communication from Mieke Meurs). On the internal structure of the brigades, see Ghai *et al.* (1986, h. 4.1).
17. According to early indications, the brigades were stimulating both increased worker involvement in decision-making and increased productivity. See Kay (1987), Meurs (1988) and Codina (1987). It is also supported in the case of non-sugar agriculture by two detailed studies of the Cuban Ministry of Agriculture *Evaluación de la experiencia sobre la introducción de la brigada permanente de producción y el cálculo económico interno en las empresas del Ministerio de la Agricultura*, Havana, November 1985 and *Informe: resultados económicos de las empresas constituídas en BPP*, Havana, 1986. In 1990 brigades organized by task (e.g. hoeing a field) were reorganized to permit evaluation and reward on the basis of final output rather than task. This change was intended to avoid the incentive to fulfil an intermediate quantity target at the expense of final output or quality.
18. Comisión Nacional de Perfeccionamiento de SDE (1989) in *Cuba: Economía Planificada* no. 4, July–September. Also see Comisión Nacional del SDE (1989), *Balance de las tareas para el perfeccionamiento del sistema de dirección de la economía*, febrero 1988–enero 1989, Havana (February).
19. The new planning procedures are published in two volumes, entitled *Decisiones Adoptadas Sobre Algunos Elementos del Sistema de Dirección de la Economía*, Havana: Juceplan, March 1988. An abridged version is published in *Cuba: Economía Planificada* (the journal of Juceplan), 1988, vol. 3, no. 3, and 1989, vol. 4, no. 1.

20. *Balance de las tareas para el perfeccionamiento del sistema de dirección de la economía* (p. 10). Also see U-Echevarría and Trueba (1990) and Hernández and Riveron (1989).
21. Since September 1988 the Central Group (*Grupo Central*) has been replaced by a smaller body, the Executive Committee of the Council of Ministers, as the primary state organ responsible for orientating the economic plan. It is not apparent what, if any, influence this has had on the degree of centralization or decentralization in the planning process. The Executive Committee reports meeting bi-weekly to discuss a broad range of sectoral and administrative issues, usually with representatives from enterprises or administrative bodies in the affected areas (*Granma*, 25 September 1989, pp. 2–5).
22. Grupo de Perfeccionamiento de las Organizaciones Empresariales e Instituciones del MINFAR (1989) *Bases Generales del Perfeccionamiento en el MINFAR*. Havana, September, p. 198.
23. The main issue for Cuba will not be the shift to hard currency trade *per se*, but the relative prices at which Cuba's trade takes place. Unlike the pattern in Eastern Europe, most of Cuba's exports are basically homogeneous commodities (e.g. sugar, nickel, tobacco and citrus), not manufactured goods. Cuba can find a market for virtually all of its goods and service exports. The question is, at what price? As of this writing (January 1991), the relative prices of oil and sugar in Cuba–Soviet trade (roughly 1 tonne of sugar equals 1.9 tonnes of petroleum) approach those that would prevail were Cuba selling sugar to and buying petroleum from the United States. At present preferential raw sugar prices in the United States are around 22 cents per pound, while the residual world market price for sugar is just under 10 cents per pound.
24. 'Mercantile production' is roughly defined as the value in current prices of finished or semi-finished goods destined for the market (Comité Estatal de Estadísticas, *Boletín estadístico de Cuba*, enero–junio 1990).

REFERENCES

Acosta, J. (1982) *Teoría y práctica de los mecanismos de dirección de la economía*, Havana: Editioral de Ciencias Sociales.
Anuario Estadístico de Cuba (1987).
Ayala Castro, H. and Ferrer, P. (1989) in *Economía y Desarrollo*, no. 3.
Balance de las tareas para el perfeccionamiento del sistema de dirección de la economía.
Banco Nacional de Cuba (1986) *Informe Económico*, March.
Codina, A. (1987) 'Worker incentives in Cuba', *World Development*, January.
Comisión Nacional del SDE (1989) *Balance de las tareas para el perfeccionamiento del sistema de dirección de la economía*, febrero 1988–enero 1989, Havana, February.
Comisión Nacional de Perfeccionamiento de SDE (1989) in *Cuba: Economía Planificada*, no. 4 (July–September).
Comité Estatal de Estadísticas (1989) *Balance de Ingresos y Egresos Monetarios de la Población*, July and August.
Comité Estatal de Estadísticas (1990) *Boletín estadístico de Cuba*, enero–junio.
Cuba: Economía Planificada (1988) vol. 3, no. 3 and (1989) vol. 4, no. 1.
Cuban Ministry of Agriculture (1985) *Evaluación de la experiencia sobre la introducción de la brigada permanente de producción y el cálculo económico interno en las empresas del Ministerio de la Agricultura*, Havana, November.
Díaz Martínez, G. (1983) in *Cuba Socialista*, no. 8 (September–November).
Domínguez, J. (1985) 'Cuba: charismatic communism', *Problems of Communism* (Sept–Oct).
Domínguez, J. (1988) 'Blaming itself, not himself: Cuba's political regime after the Third Party Congress' in Roca (Ed.) (1988).
Ghai, D. *et al.* (1986) *Labor and Development in Rural Cuba*, London: Macmillan.
Granma, 5 October 1982; 14 January 1987; 25 September 1989.
Grupo de Perfeccionamiento de las Organizaciones Empresariales e Instituciones del MINFAR (1989) *Bases Generales del Perfeccionamiento en el MINFAR*, Havana, September.

Hernández, A. and Riveron, N. (1989) in *Economía y Desarrollo*, no. 2.

Juceplan (1985) *Dictámenes de la IV Plenaria*, Havana.

Juceplan (1988) *Decisiones Adoptadas sobre Algunos Elementos del Sistema de Dirección de la Economía*, Havana, March.

Kay, C. (1987) 'New Developments in Cuban Agriculture: Economic Reforms and Collectivization.' Occasional paper no. 1, Centre for Development Studies, University of Glasgow.

Kim, I. and Zacek, J. (eds) (1990) *Reform in Communist Systems: Comparative Perspectives*, Washington, D.C.: The Washington Institute.

Mata, N. (1986) in *Finanzas y Crédito*, no. 5.

Mesa-Lago, C. (1988) 'The Cuban economy in the 1980s' in Roca (Ed.) (1988).

Meurs, M. (1988) 'Planning, Participation and Incentives in Socialism: The Case of Cuban Agriculture', Ph.D. thesis, University of Massachusetts, Amherst.

Ministerio de Agricultura (1986) *Informe: resultados económicos de las empresas constituídas en BPP*, Havana.

Pérez-López, J. (1986) 'Cuban economy in the 1980s', *Problems of Communism* (Sept–Oct).

Rabkin, R. (1988) 'Cuba: the aging of a revolution' in Roca (Ed.).

Roca, S. (Ed.) (1988) *Socialist Cuba: Past Interpretations and Future Challenges*, Boulder: Westview Press .

Staff of Radio José Martí (1986) *Cuba Quarterly Situation Report*, vol. 3, no. 3, section III.

Treaster, J. (1987) 'Castro recoils at a hint of wealth', *New York Times*, 8 February.

U-Echevarría, O. *et al.* (1986) *Cuba: Economía Planificada*, vol. 1, no. 2.

U-Echevarría, O. and Gerardo Trueba, G. (1990) in *Cuba: Economía Planificada*, no. 5 (January–March).

Zimbalist, A. (1989) 'Incentives and Planning in Cuba', *Latin American Research Review*, vol. 24, no. 1.

Zimbalist, A. and Brundenius, C. (1989) *The Cuban Economy: Measurement and Analysis of Socialist Performance*, Baltimore: Johns Hopkins University Press.

Zimbalist, A. and Smith, W. (1990) 'Reform in Cuba', in Kim and Zacek (eds) (1990).

6 Industrial reform in Czechoslovakia

Ludek Rychetnik

1. INTRODUCTION

The August 1968 invasion of the Warsaw Pact forces halted the economic reform process associated with the political liberalization of Prague Spring. Although the financial system retained some of its importance, directive central planning and control were largely re-established in the 1970s. Worsening external conditions in the second half of the 1970s and pressing domestic economic and ecological problems, however, required some new corrective reform measures.

In 1958 enterprises began to be amalgamated into industrial associations (the *VHJ*, *výrobní hospodářské jednotky*), the administrative 'branch directorates' (*hlavní správy, glavki*) having been abolished (see Vácha, 1978, for a description of the *VHJ*). Changes in the planning mechanism in 1979 (described in Rychetnik, 1981) were aimed at separating long-term strategic management at the level of an industrial branch (for which industrial ministries were responsible) from operational and strategic management at the level of the *VHJ*. The *VHJs* were the subject of taxation and payments to the state budget and the bearer of the central plan targets. They were made responsible for technical and economic development within their sphere of production and were to be given all the necessary power to carry out and responsibility for their technical, economic and social functions. But the fulfilment of plan targets remained the first priority, even though some of them were expressed in terms of value added and efficiency 'ratios'. Moreover, industrial associations continued to operate in a highly distorted, monopolistic market and manipulated the state plan targets and prices, using their virtual informational monopoly and network of connections in the political and planning hierarchy (for a detailed and witty analysis see Mlčoch (1980–83).

These timid adjustments of the planning mechanism could not and did not prevent the further deterioration of Czechoslovak economic performance. This was reflected in a growing technological gap *vis-à-vis* advanced Western countries (and the consequent worsening foreign trade situation) and in growing ecological damage. However, the international and domestic political atmosphere was not favourable to another market-orientated reform attempt until the late 1980s.

2. THE 1987–89 REFORM

In January 1987 a joint document ('Zásady...', 1987) was issued by the presidium of the Communist Party and the federal government. It announced a 'fundamental restructuring' of the economic mechanism. Two subsequent documents specifying further details were published in 1987 and 1988, and a series of legislative acts plus some cautious market liberalization measures followed.

Experiments with elements of the new mechanism started immediately in 1987. Selected associations and enterprises were placed on a self-financing basis and were given greater autonomy as regards foreign trade. The scope of the experiment was gradually expanded in 1988–89; further industrial enterprises, trade as a whole, services, and agricultural and food production became involved. The old *VHJ*s were dissolved and independent 'state enterprises' established. Wholesale prices were reformed and in foreign trade the system of multiple exchange rates was simplified and the commercial exchange rate devalued in January 1989.

Although the main thrust of the reform was directed towards institutional reconstruction, the government's economic policy continued to aim at stabilizing the economy throughout the period. However, fiscal policy in 1987 and 1988 (as in 1986) managed to balance the budget only formally with the help of the state reserves created in previous years; the situation deteriorated in 1989, when current receipts may have exceeded current expenditures by as much as 10 billion Koruna (about 1.6 per cent of NMP). The main cause was a 5 per cent shortfall in budgeted incomes, although expenditure economies partially mitigated its impact. The restrictive credit policy was also formally maintained, short-term bank credit to enterprises being cut by 15.2 billion Koruna in 1989 and investment credit increased by only 2.2 billion Koruna. But this did not represent a real credit restriction. During the organizational reform state enterprises were provided with their own working capital of 15.5 billion Koruna in total from state resources (Analýza vývoje..., 1990).

By January 1990 the economy as a whole was to enter a one-year transitional period of the new mechanism. Popular explosion and the 'velvet revolution' in November 1989 ended this reform stage and cleared the way for a more fundamental systemic reform, including the establishment of private property rights in capital and the liberalization of prices and foreign trade. The developments in 1990 will be dealt with in section 3.

Organizational structure
Before their dissolution, the old associations took three forms (in decreasing order of centralization):

1. 'Branch national enterprises', possibly with smaller ones attached.
2. 'Concerns' associating national enterprises, research institutes and other business service organizations under a concern's 'general directorate'.
3. 'Trusts', consisting of national enterprises and other service organizations, coordinated by a trust's 'general directorate'.

The branch national enterprises and concerns, being legal persons, were elements of a two-stage management hierarchy: ministry – national enterprise/concern. The trusts did not have the status of a legal person; they represented a middle layer of a three-stage hierarchy: ministry – trust – national enterprise (Decree No. 91/1974, Vácha, 1978 and Chalupa *et al.*, 1985).

The Czechoslovak industrial structure was highly concentrated in comparison with any Western market economy. An average centrally controlled national enterprise had 2 064 employees in industry and over 2 400 employees in construction in 1988. Table 6.1 shows the distribution of industrial national enterprises by size.

Table 6.1   Industrial national enterprises by number of workers in 1988

Workers	National enterprises
1 – 500	91
501 – 1 000	196
1 001 – 2 500	390
2 501 – 5 000	160
5 001 +	53
Total	890

Source: Czechoslovak Statistical Yearbook, 1989.

Enterprises controlled by the local councils (*národní výbory*) were somewhat smaller; they employed 239,267 workers in 322 units in 1988 (743 workers on average), apart from 16,829 workers working in 3 084 local workshops (5.46 workers on average). Also industrial cooperatives were relatively large; 395 industrial cooperatives had 180,133 members and workers in 1988 (456 workers on average) (Czechoslovak Statistical Yearbook, 1989).

The 1988 Law of the State Enterprise (no. 88) established the state enterprise as an independent legal person, which was to operate in a relatively autonomous manner in a 'guided' but increasingly more competitive market. The amended Economic Statute (no. 98, 1988) recognized and protected property rights (also including intangible assets) and the right of 'stewardship' by the state enterprise of an entrusted segment of national capital. The true owner, the state, was represented by the founder, either the central or local government body. The manager was formally appointed by the founder after having been elected by the employees from a list of candidates prepared by the founder. An employee-elected council had supervisory powers and limited entrepreneurial powers in strategic decision making.

The new state enterprises were created out of 1 714 'national enterprises' or other organizations of similar type in four phases in the period between July 1988 and July 1989. Thus 412 new state enterprises were established out of some 650 national enterprises on 1 July 1988, other conversions following on 1 January, 1 April and 1 July 1989 (Matějka, 1988). An organization which would not be viable as an independent enterprise was merged with another state enterprise. This explains the reduction in the number of units by more than a third. Another decree (no. 185, 1989) allowed state enterprises to create (voluntary) associations while maintaining their legal status. Theoretically, this was to open the way to efficiency-driven concentration processes in the economy. In the absence of competitive pressure, however, this possibility could be used to save the old *VHJ* apparatus. It can be concluded that the highly concentrated industrial structure was not changed by the 1988 reform.

The economic mechanism
The new 'reconstructed' mechanism retained the principle of a centrally planned economy; the state national economic plan remained the main tool of management. But central planning and management would concentrate on economic policy, adjustments and development of the economic mechanism (the published version was not considered as the final model but rather a transitional stage 'for the 1990s'), i.e. on directing the most important technological development programmes, and on monetary, financial, wage, labour and price policies. Hence, the role of industrial ministries would change; they would not draw up their individual plans or create and use financial reserves, and their staff would be cut. As the founder of the state enterprises, the relevant ministry would also decide on liquidation of loss-making units, after correction measures had failed (imposed 'consolidation regime', direct administration by the centre for up to three years and merger or division).

The state enterprises would operate and compete in a market environment with a great deal of autonomy in selecting their production programmes and choosing outlets and suppliers. In elaborating their plan, the enterprises had to respect only the binding parameters of the state plan and did not have to submit the plan for approval to any supervisory body. But the ministry could impose production targets ('state orders') and limits for raw materials in short supply and for hard currency. Furthermore, it could still impose an obligation on the state enterprise to make a contract or abrogate a contractual obligation, but only under specified exceptional circumstances (such as defence requirements and international obligations or the protection of life, health and the environment). The enterprise, in turn, was entitled to compensation for losses incurred. The law on the State Economic Tribunal (no. 99, 1988) was amended accordingly, but primarily the state would 'guide' enterprises with the help of economic levers. The state enterprise was obliged to form the following specialized funds (profit allocation being regulated by long term 'normative' ratios):

1. The development fund was fed from depreciation allowances, profit and costs, in order to finance R&D programmes and the modernization and expansion of fixed capital assets. The former technical development fund was merged with the former investment fund. With greater independence in investment given to state enterprises, the development fund assumed key importance in financial management of the enterprise in the new mechanism.
2. The bonus fund was fed from profit and used for personal and team rewards.
3. The cultural and social fund was also fed from profit. It was used to pay for recreation, sport and other social purposes.
4. The reserve fund was fed from profit and used as a general reserve.

Other capital funds represented the sources used to finance fixed and current assets. The two most important were the fixed capital and working capital funds (Podnik..., 1989).

Taxes and payments
The state enterprise paid the following taxes and transfers (*odvody*) to the state budget:

1. The wage fund charge was paid as a percentage (50 per cent in 1989) of the wage bill.
2. The capital charge was to be calculated as a percentage of the sum of the fixed capital fund and the working capital fund (net worth or 'shareholders fund'). It was experimented with but not actually introduced in 1990, partly because of the difficulties in obtaining a realistic estimate of the fixed capital value. Instead, the enterprise had to pay the profit tax (below), not less than 2 per cent of its 'shareholders fund'.
3. Payment out of the residual profit (profit tax): the rate was not uniform for all industries, the most common being 50 per cent in 1989 and 55 per cent in 1990.

4.   The depreciation charge was paid individually, but only by enterprises included in a 'run down' (divestiture) programme.
5.   The environmental charge was paid as a tax for water or air pollution, and for the occupancy of agricultural land.

The wage fund charge and the capital charge were designed as 'criterion charges' to stimulate efficient use of scarce resources and to be paid regardless of the amount of profit created by the enterprise. Capital efficiency, nevertheless, remained one of the weaker points of the reform.

Prices

A wholesale price reform was prepared in 1987–88 and the new wholesale prices were introduced on 1 January 1989. The purpose was to bring the centrally controlled prices nearer to 'social costs', including the 50 per cent wage fund charge (to stimulate manpower economies) and a uniform 4.5 per cent profit rate (related to the book value of fixed capital). The reform was to prepare the ground for continuous adjustment of prices (considering the market, the use value of the product and foreign prices of comparable products) and, eventually, gradual price liberalization. The state was to continue to control most prices until 1991. The prices of new products were set according to the rules of price formation and had to be approved by the ministry, with large enterprises exercising considerable influence on this process. The reform did not affect retail prices. They remained centrally fixed on the whole, and separated from wholesale prices by the turnover tax with highly differentiated rates.

Wages

In the pre-reform wage system, the industrial wage consisted of two components: the basic wage and the incentive component. The basic wage was determined by national tariff scales, subject to the total wage bill limit set at the level of the *VHJ* or enterprise. The wage bill limit was related to the planned volume of value added by coefficients individualized by enterprises, with further adjustments for under- and overfulfilment. The incentive component (about 10 per cent of the wage packet) consisted of several categories of rewards, bonuses and premiums, some paid from savings on wages and others paid from the rewards fund.

Labour productivity increased faster than average wages in industry (Table 6.2), but the planned relation between the growth of labour productivity and average wages was not achieved.

The reform did not represent a radical change in the wage system. It envisaged a modernization of the tariffs, unification of the wage bill coefficients, possibly with a transition to an incremental form, and a greater role

Table 6.2 *Industrial labour productivity (in terms of net material product in constant prices) and average industrial wage growth rates.*

Year	Labour productivity	Average wage (growth rate %)	Difference
1984	4.3	2.2	2.1
1985	2.8	1.7	1.1
1986	2.6	1.6	1.0
1987	3.9	1.7	2.2
1988	3.3	2.1	1.2

Source: Czechoslovak Statistical Yearbook 1989

for that part of the wage related to the profitability of the enterprise. The experimenting enterprises tested different variants, but none of them turned out to be fully satisfactory (Polák, Kubišta and Čápová, 1988). In the absence of rational market-determined prices, no indicator could express the real contribution of the worker or enterprise (Mühl and Zvolenský, 1986). No improvements in the wage system could eliminate the persistent inflationary pressure caused by widespread inefficiencies and systemic rigidities in the entire economy.

Investment and banking
In the pre-reform mechanism several categories of investment were recognized and financed either from the investment fund (centrally initiated, more important projects) or the technical development fund, but all projects had to be planned ahead and approved by higher management bodies.

The reform documents announced a fundamental change of a systemic nature. The state would continue to finance or subsidize investment projects of strategic national importance, but there would be no binding central limits on investment construction carried out by state enterprises and no reallocation of investment capital between them. The former technical development fund, as already noted, was merged with the former investment fund into a single development fund, which was to be the source of all investment and development expenditures by the enterprise. Hence, investment construction would be within the power and responsibility of the enterprise, subject to the availability of financial resources, either from retained profit or from commercial credit. Other sources of capital were not mentioned at that stage.

The role of banks, as the only financial intermediaries at that stage, would become crucial in the new mechanism. The new banking laws (December 1989) set up a system consisting of the new Czechoslovak State Bank, independent commercial banks and savings banks. The State Bank was created from the old state 'monobank' by separating its commercial banking departments. It would act as an issue bank and lender of last resort for the commercial and savings banks. It would be relatively independent and have the character of a federal state body charged with statutory responsibility for the stability of the currency. It would also be responsible for the stability and strengthening of the exchange rate. It would not automatically guarantee the financial obligations of the government. It would supervise the issue of banknotes and coins, and as lender of last resort it would set the base rate of interest. It would issue licences for the establishment of commercial and saving banks. Gradually, as the money market develops, the State Bank would guide it in collaboration with the Ministry of Finance, reflecting the monetary point of view.

Three new banks were formed to take over and develop the commercial activities of the old monobank: the Commercial Bank in Prague, the General Credit Bank in Bratislava, and the Investment Bank in Prague. The former two banks inherited the old state bank branches in major towns, while the Investment Bank started to build its network (Salzman, 1989). Apart from these three banks, there were two old commercial banks which survived from the prewar times: the Czechoslovak Trade Bank and the *Živnobanka*. They were strictly confined to foreign currency operations. These constraints on their activity have been lifted and they are gradually to expand into general banking.

The investment and capital functions constituted the weakest point of the 1987 reform. Although state enterprises had the right of stewardship over the assets they operated with, these assets remained state owned and no physical person or group of persons bore ultimate responsibility for them. The economic mechanism did not create a direct material interest in maximizing capital efficiency. Hence, it generated a permanent pressure from the enterprises to expand through investment construction, financed from any possible funds, be it from retained profit, credit or state subsidy. In this respect, the new mechanism was similarly flawed as the prereform one; a chronic inflationary tendency was built into it.

Exchange rates, foreign trade and joint ventures
In the pre-reform mechanism, foreign trade was carried out primarily by specialized organizations which isolated domestic producers from the world market. The system of exchange rates was highly complex, consisting of fixed, differentiated (non/commercial, tourist) and multi-component (including unofficial internal 'corrective' coefficients) rates. The system of exchange rates was reformed in January 1989. The commercial exchange rate was devalued by 173 per cent and the internal corrective coefficients abolished.

The experimenting enterprises tested a new system of foreign exchange 'normative coefficients' determining the respective shares of the central fund and the exporting enterprise in hard currency receipts. The 'normative coefficients' were constant but individualized by enterprises in the first stage. The intention was to introduce a uniform coefficient in the future (a 60 per cent share for the central fund was proposed).

The new Law on Exchange Control (December 1989) established the right to open an interest-bearing external bank account and keep hard currency in it for any legal or physical person. The latter were allowed to hold foreign exchange in cash up to the limit of 500 ('Tuzex' valuta) Koruna. Legal persons (enterprises) were obliged to offer their earned foreign exchange for sale to the Bank but only up to the limit set by the state plan. Experimental auctions of foreign exchange have been organized since July 1989; the going rate exceeded the official rate 6–7 fold (they continued throughout 1990 until internal convertibility of Koruna was introduced in January 1991).

The few joint ventures established before the reform were regulated by a government decree of August 1985. This limited the share of the foreign partner to 49 per cent of equity and subjected joint ventures to other existing laws (the Czechoslovak Chamber of Commerce listed ten laws, two decrees and nine other official documents). The first Law on Joint Ventures was passed in November 1988. It abolished the 51–49 per cent rule and stated that central bodies would support joint ventures in broadly specified cases and industries and provide legal guarantees to foreign firms. Joint ventures would not be subject to the state plan or any interference, but operate according to contracts. Profit transfer abroad was guaranteed.

Analysis of the 1987–89 reforms
The new economic mechanism was designed by reform-minded economists working in the government. It was not intended as a definitive model but rather as a stage in the transition to another more efficient variant. Although the market was to be gradually liberalized and play an increasing role in stimulating initiative independent of the state, many restrictive rules and measures severely curtailed market forces. In these measures the old idea of the state as the supreme entrepreneur and administrator of social wealth found its expression.

Theoretical economists of the Academy of Sciences and higher schools submitted the published rules to open and severe criticism. They did not attack the gradualistic approach of the reform, on which point there was considerable consensus at that time. They argued that the system of planning and management based on long-term 'normative ratios' was inherently unstable, because it would not prevent the continuation of chronic disequilibrating tendencies and was, indeed, likely to generate new ones. They also pointed out inconsistencies in the rules between the supposedly market environment within which the enterprises were to operate and the methods of state guidance and control of the enterprises (Klusoň *et al.*, 1988; Zieleniec *et al.*, 1988).

Later in 1988, after four years of government sponsored research, the Forecasting Institute of the Academy of Sciences completed a long-term prognosis of economic and social development, which convincingly showed that the established trends and existing long-term plans would result in economic and ecological crisis. What was needed, they argued, was a radical turnaround to a free market economy, convertibility of the currency and integration into advanced Western markets. Although the report in its entirety had to be made confidential, a series of papers based on it was published. They only confirmed what had been the overwhelming public opinion for many years and prepared the intellectual ground for the 'velvet revolution' in November 1989, which removed personal and political obstacles to such a turnaround. Three economists of the Forecasting Institute (including its director) took economic posts in the new caretaker coalition government. This government and the next, formed after democratic elections in June 1990, took as their primary task to elaborate and implement a coherent programme of transition to a free market economy based on private property rights.

3.   ECONOMIC REFORM IN 1990 AND EARLY 1991

Originally the state plan, which still included some physical targets, was prepared for 1990 under the old government, but traditional central planning fizzled out during the year. The main points of the new government's reform strategy were as follows (Čalfa, 1990; *Scénář ekonomické reformy*, 1990):

1.   The creation of a non-inflationary environment through tight fiscal and credit policies: The provisional budget for the first quarter of 1990 and the subsequent regular budget aimed at a surplus. Credits were cut and a partial ban on new investment projects was imposed. A single bank (minimum lending) rate was established and set at 4 per cent in January 1990, when the new State Bank started to operate. The bank rate was subsequently raised to 5 per cent in April, 7 per cent in October and 8.5 per cent in November, when the commercial banks were permitted to raise their rate to 22.5 per cent to more than match inflation and thus keep the real interest rate positive. A further increase of the bank rate to 10 per cent followed in January 1991.

2.   Support was given to the emerging private sector and preparatory steps were taken to privatize the state sector. Following an amendment to the Constitutional Law which proclaimed equality of private ownership with all other ownership forms, a Law on Private Businesses was passed in April 1990. It established the right of all citizens to engage in any business activity except those designated to remain a state monopoly. It liberalized entry by replacing the old inflexible licensing procedure by simple registration. It provided necessary legal guarantees for entrepreneurial activity. Two categories of businesses were distinguished: sole trader and entrepreneur listed in the enterprise register. Apart from a difference in taxation and book-keeping duties, the enterprise could engage in exporting and importing, after registering with the Ministry of Foreign Trade, but in spite of government support, private businesses still encountered administrative and other obstacles at the local level.

The 1988 Law of the State Enterprise was amended in April 1990. The employees' self-management bodies were dissolved (without much protest). The new governing bodies were given an embryonic two-tier structure consisting of a supervisory board (*dozorčí rada*) and the director. The 'work collective', consisting of full-time employees, elects half of the members of the supervisory board, the other half being appointed by the founder. The latter also appoints the director in a competition, after consulting the supervisory board which, in turn, has the right to recommend to the founder the dismissal of the director. The amended law emphasized the independence and economic autonomy of the state enterprise. Public utilities formed a special type of enterprise with enhanced rights for the founder: no supervisory board is created. In a drive to stimulate competition, many new enterprises were created by allowing the constituent units to go independent and by dissolving the former industrial associations.

A new Company Law was also passed in April 1990. The company's founder can be a legal person or a physical person. The minimum capital is 100,000 Koruna. The minimal nominal value of a share is 1,000 Koruna. A share can be freely tradable (ordinary or so-called 'holder share') or registered with the company on the owner's name (private company share or 'owner share'). Foreigners may purchase the latter type only. Preference shares may be issued on up to 50 per cent of the company's nominal capital. Special employee 'owner shares' may be distributed for free or at a discounted price; they confer undiminished rights on the owner. The general meeting of shareholders elects a management board (*představenstvo*), supervisory board and at least one auditor. A meeting of employees elects one-third of the members of the supervisory board if the company employs more than 200 employees.

As a temporary measure, the law allows for the foundation of a company by a single legal person. In this, it prepares conditions for the state enterprises to be transformed into state companies, where the state originally holds all the shares, and eventually to be privatized.

3.   As regards price liberalization, initial steps were taken in 1990. The scope for contractual prices was extended and food subsidies were replaced by a wage supplement in June. But chronic suppressed inflation was coming into the open even in the more regulated retail price sector (Table 6.3). With the exception (agreed with the IMF) of a few commodities (such as grain, water, coal, oil, electricity and essential food and other items), prices were deregulated in January 1991.

Table 6.3   Retail price indices 1990 (comparable quarter 1989 = 100)

First quarter	103.4
Second quarter	103.9
Third quarter	114.1

Source: Federal Ministry of Finance Report, *Hospodářské noviny* (daily), no. 132, 22 Nov 1990.

The growth of prices accelerated in the last quarter of 1990 and especially in January and February of 1991 after liberalization, when a widespread misuse of its monopoly position by the State Trade Enterprise was suspected.

A new Law on Protection of Economic Competition was passed in January 1991 and became effective on 1 March 1991. It provided for setting up new federal and republican competition offices, which are entitled to step in and investigate mergers of enterprises if their combined market share exceeds the 30 per cent threshold. It was made subject to special permission by the respective office cartel agreements with a market share greater than 5 per cent of the national market or 30 per cent of the local market.

4.   Industrial policy continued to support selected development programmes (such as environmental protection projects and tourist infrastructure, including transport) and to run down mining and (recently) arms production. Directive management of the state enterprises was substantially cut down in the first half of 1990, but state-owned enterprises were slow to adapt to the new conditions. The economic situation was aggravated by declining oil supplies from the Soviet Union and by the Gulf crisis in the autumn.

Industrial production and construction activity declined on the whole in accordance with the aims of central structural policy (by 3.8 per cent in the extractive industries, 2.5 per cent in manufacturing and 5.7 per cent in construction in the first half of the year compared with the same period in 1989). However, expectations of improved efficiency and profitability, on which the state budget was based, were not fulfilled. The financial position of state-owned enterprises deteriorated and the overall level of insolvency increased. Unemployment made an appearance and started to increase.

A serious threat to economic stability came from fast growing wages. Nominal industrial wages increased (by 2.2 per cent in the first half of 1990), while labour productivity declined (by minus 0.9 per cent). The Koruna devaluation increased the incentive to export and caused domestic shortages of materials and intermediate products.

5.   Reintegration into the world trade is also an aim. An amended Law on Foreign Trade abolished the state monopoly by opening foreign trade to physical persons listed in the enterprise register and registered by the Ministry of Foreign Trade. The Czechoslovak Koruna was devalued several times bringing the commercial exchange rate near to the tourist rate (commercial rate: December 1989 $1=14.30 Koruna; January 1990 16.75; October 1990 24.00). In January 1991 the Koruna was made internally convertible after another devaluation to a single fixed exchange rate (unifying the tourist and commercial rates) of 28.00 Koruna per dollar. The rules of internal convertibility stipulate that for the time being the Koruna remains an internal currency valid only on Czechoslovak territory, but any physical person is entitled to a purchase of foreign currency up to 5 000 Koruna equivalent per annum, and any legal person registered with the ministry of foreign trade can import goods and services and pay for them in Czechoslovak Koruna. The registration condition was subsequently abolished for all but a few special items. However, only licensed firms can have a foreign currency account. The foreign trade licensing system was lifted, but a ban on the export of essential commodities and a 20 per cent import tax on basic consumer goods were introduced (as temporary measures taken in agreement with the International Monetary Fund).

The EC brought Czechoslovakia into its system of favourable trade terms. Negotiations about entry into the IMF started immediately in January 1990 and were successfully completed in October. Membership of the World Bank was renewed in September.

The law on joint ventures was amended in April; the licensing procedure was simplified and a wider choice of legal form for the venture was made available. Subsequently, a series of bilateral international agreements provided guarantees to foreign investors.

A joint venture that was set up between the Skoda car factory and Volkswagen and agreed to by the owner (the Czech government) in December 1990 became the best known example. Volkswagen took an initial 25 per cent stake in return for a DM500 million equity investment, to be increased in the future up to 70 per cent.

These measures, together with the February 1991 Major Privatization Law, paved the way to an easy entry of foreign capital investment (for a clear summary see 'Czechoslovakia opens for business' by Arbess, 1991). Also special federal and republican agencies to aid foreign investors were established in February.

In 1990 a major intellectual effort went into the clarification and identification of systemic reform steps, establishing the basic legal framework for private property rights and a free market economy. It was a year of laying foundations. All experience indicated that the transition would be more difficult than envisaged. In particular, only preliminary steps to the key process of privatization of state enterprises could have been taken in 1990. In legal terms privatization is framed in four acts, two of them being passed in 1990:

1. The Restitution Law was passed in October 1990. It applies to property confiscated in the 1955–59 period, mainly residential houses, restaurants, hotels and workshops, and entitles the original owners, their (last will) heirs or direct family members to apply for restitution. This will happen either in physical form, if possible, or as financial reimbursement (at the price at the confiscation date plus 3 per cent per annum).

2. The Minor Privatization Law was passed in the same month (October 1990). Under this law, minor businesses have been sold in public auctions for cash since January 1991. Anybody can propose a business unit for privatization under this law, if it was state- or local government-owned on 1 November 1990. The privatization commission in each district will include it only if it has a chance of being sold in a public auction, that is if there is a potential buyer. Excluded are units subject to physical restitution under the Restitution Law, or owned by social organizations, joint stock companies, cooperatives, joint ventures, or in legal use by a foreign business. The buyer must be a physical person, not an enterprise or a cooperative, and a Czechoslovak citizen (foreign buyers will be admitted in the second round of auctions). It has been estimated that privatizations under this law will include some 130,000 units and will take more than a year to complete.

The first two auctions took place in Prague on 26 and 27 January 1991 (reports by Leslie Colitt in *Financial Times*, 25 and 29 January). The list of the businesses was published two weeks before. It included 20 units, the most attractive and biggest being the restaurant Moskva at *Příkopy* in the Centre of Prague with a calling price of 22.5 million Koruna. It had to be withdrawn in the end, together with two other units, because the original owners applied for restitution under the Restitution Law. Seventeen shops were auctioned eventually, but one sale had to be declared null and void because the buyer turned out to represent a cooperative. But the first auctions were considered a success. The selling price exceeded the calling price more than ten times on average (from 2.1 to 22 million Koruna).

3. The Bill on Extrajudicial Rehabilitation was passed in February 1991. It opens the way for the return of non-agricultural property confiscated by the communist government after the 1948 takeover and not covered by the October 1990 Restitution Law. The exact scope and form of redress, as well as the Bill's linkages to privatization, were the subject of a prolonged controversy in the Federal Assembly. Economic, political and moral aspects were considered. The moral aspects referred to the natural right of a citizen to his/her original property and a deputy pointed to the relevant clause of the recently passed constitutional law on civil rights. The political aspect included the at least partial revival of the old middle class, which used to be the social basis of the prewar democratic regime. Economic arguments were given in favour of compensation rather than physical restitution, since the former would allow privatizations to proceed without any delay.

    The Law as passed stipulates that the original owner or other 'qualifying person' (heir, child or spouse, parent or sibling, in this order), a Czechoslovak citizen permanently residing in the country, has to file for restitution by 30 September 1991. The 'obliged (physical or legal) person' holding the property has to keep it in good condition and, if the claim is proven, hand over possession by 31 October 1991. 'Substantial' increases in the value of the real estate must be reimbursed by the qualifying person. In cases (categorized in the Law) where physical restitution is not desired by the latter, or is not possible, the qualifying person is entitled to compensation (up to 30,000 Koruna in cash and a further 30,000 Koruna in securities).

4. The Major Privatization Bill ('On Conditions for the Transfer of State Property to Other Persons') was passed five days after the Bill on Extrajudicial Rehabilitation, but its preparation actually started in early 1990. It had to overcome serious financial, institutional and cultural obstacles.

These included the scarcity of domestic capital, absence of a capital market infrastructure, lack of experience with capital ownership among the population and, lately, insolvency of many enterprises in question.

The property transfer proceeds according to a 'privatization project', usually elaborated by the enterprise or, alternatively, by its founder. Nevertheless, the latter bears responsibility for the privatization project in all cases. This document describes aspects such as the designated property, the manner in which the state acquired it, valuation of the assets, the proposed method and timetable of the transfer (including any settlement with the qualifying person under the Extrajudicial Rehabilitation Law, and further details on potential buyers), the present and expected market position of the enterprise, and the number and qualification of the employees.

Once the privatization project has been approved by the federal Ministry of Finance or a republican government body, it is published and the enterprise is transferred to a newly established federal or republican National Assets Fund (NAF). In accordance with the privatization project, the property is subsequently used to form a limited or other company, sold fully or partially, or transferred to a municipality or a pension fund. The federal NAF will be registered as an enterprise and governed by a presidium whose nine members will be elected by the Federal Assembly for five years. The presidium appoints a nine-member professional executive committee. The Federal Assembly also elects a five-member supervisory board to oversee the NAF's activity.

The privatization project can choose a suitable mixture from a number of methods of disposal of the issued shares, including domestic and foreign flotation, public auction (as under the Minor Privatization Law) or a special auction where the participants would bid with 'investment coupons'. Every Czechoslovak citizen over the age of 18 will be entitled to purchase the investment coupons at a not-yet-specified nominal price and use them in these auctions either directly or through investment funds. These auctions are expected to provide a rough market valuation of the assets and turn into an embryonic capital market. Clearly, asset valuation is one of the critical issues of the privatization programme and, in the case of major enterprises, Western accountancy firms have been invited to carry out the assessment.

4.   FUTURE PLANS

The reform entered into its critical stage in January 1991 when prices were liberalized and internal convertibility of Koruna was introduced. Inflation was expected to reach some 30 per cent per annum. The restructuration and privatization of large enterprises was expected to start. This would bring about a further increase in unemployment for which a 'social net' of unemployment benefits and retraining facilities has been prepared. The capital market made its first appearance in 1990 when two investment trusts were formed and started to sell their shares. The opening of a stock exchange was under preparation, scheduled for the end of the year. Another step in the gradual build-up of market economy institutions is a fundamental tax reform. The work on it started in 1990 and the actual tax reform is expected to be implemented in 1993.

The Czechoslovak reform started as a response to a long run political and economic malaise rather than to a single external shock or an acute internal crisis. It also has a clear general long-term aim: the transformation into an efficient market economy based on private property. But its immediate success would be judged in terms of four criteria (Klaus, 1990): the rate of economic growth, rate of inflation and rate of unemployment, and foreign debt. These indicators will be watched carefully in the future and will affect the future political development of the country.

In organizational and political terms the centre of the reform initiative definitely shifted during 1990 to the federal Ministry of Finance and the newly established Ministries for Administration and Privatization of National Property of the Czech and Slovak Republics. At the same time, the amended Law on the Federation ('Law on Competences') passed in December 1990 devolved further important powers to the republican governments. But powerful voices continued to call for Slovak national sovereignty and greater Moravian and Silesian regional autonomy, and the preservation of Czechoslovakia as a unitary state was in doubt at the time of writing in March 1991.

An update to this chapter is given in the Postscript, page 280.

REFERENCES

Analýza vývoje čs. národního hospodářství (1990) in *Hospodářské noviny*, no. 24, 13 June.

Arbess, D. (1991) in *Financial Times*, 7 March.

Čalfa, M. (1990) Programme of the new Federal Government (in Slovak), *Hospodářské noviny* (daily), no. 33, 4 July.

Chalupa, R. *et al.* (1985) *Slovník ekonomických pojmů plánovitého řízení*, Praha: Práce.

Klaus, V (1990) Address to Trade Union representatives, in *Hospodářské noviny* (daily), no. 107, 18 October.

Klusoň, V. *et al.* (1988) *Teoretické problémy fungování, hospodářského mechanismu*, Praha: Ekonomický ústav ČSAV.

Matějka, J. (1988) in *Hospodářské noviny*, no. 26, 1 July.

Mlčoch, L. (1980–83) *Chování československé podnikové sféry* (internal print). Reprinted 1990: Praha: Ekonomicky ústav ČSAV.

Mühl, R. and Zvolenský, V. (1986) in *Hospodářské noviny*, no. 47, 21 November.

Podnik v novém hospodářském mechanismu (1989), Praha: SNTL.

Polák, J., Kubišta, M. and Čápová, M. (1988) in *Hospodářské noviny*, no. 34, 26 August.

Rychetnik, L. (1981) 'The industrial enterprise in Czechoslovakia' in Jeffries, I. (Ed.) *The Industrial Enterprise in Eastern Europe*, Eastbourne: Praeger.

Salzman, R. (1989) in *Hospodářské noviny*, no. 47, 24 November.

Scénář ekonomické reformy (1990) in *Hospodářské noviny*, no. 75, 4 August.

Směrnice k zabezpečení komplexní přestavby hospodářského mechanismu (1988) in *Hospodářské noviny*, no. 8, 26 February.

Vácha, V. (1978) *Koncepční řízení VHJ*, Praha: SNTL.

Zásady přestavby hospodářského mechanismu ČSSR (1987) in *Hospodářské noviny*, no. 5, 30 January.

Zieleniec, J. *et al.* (1988) *Socialistický podnik a plánovité řízení*, Praha: Ekonomický ústav ČSAV.

7   East Germany

Ian Jeffries

1.   INTRODUCTION

East Germany (or perhaps more aptly now Eastern Germany, henceforth EG) was an advanced industrialized country before the socialist era. The German Democratic Republic (GDR) was formally founded on 7 October 1949, but sprang from Hitler's defeat in the Second World War and the subsequent division of Germany. The country was literally on the front line between East and West and economic policy was shaped by Soviet domination and the continual comparisons it suffered with prosperous West Germany (WG) rather than its poorer socialist neighbours. Legitimacy, for example, was sought largely in rising living standards. Gorbachev's appearance on the scene unsettled the conservative Honecker regime, although the new Soviet leader's aim was not to cause political instability and, indeed, he took an early interest in the EG industrial combine.

The Honecker regime collapsed like a pack of cards in 1989, decisive elements including Gorbachev's unwillingness to use Soviet troops to preserve the old order and the flood of people to WG sparked off by Hungary's decision to dismantle its border fence with Austria in May. The borders between the two Germanies, including the infamous Berlin Wall, were reopened on 9 November. Honecker was replaced as General Secretary of the Socialist Unity Party by Egon Krenz. On 3 December the whole politburo and central committee resigned, Hans Modrow having been confirmed as prime minister on 13 November. In the 18 March 1990 free election there was a surprise win for the Alliance for Germany, the leader of the largest party in the coalition (the Christian Democratic Union), Lothar de Maizière, becoming prime minister. German economic and monetary union (GEMU) took place on 1 July 1990, political union took place on 3 October, and an all-German election was held on 2 December 1990 (won comfortably by Chancellor Helmut Kohl's coalition).

2.   INDUSTRIAL REFORM IN THE HONECKER ERA

EG is poorly endowed with raw materials, with important exceptions such as lignite. This led to heavy dependence on imports of fuels and raw materials, especially from the Soviet Union. Price increases for and shortages of these commodities led to attempts to substitute domestic ones whenever possible (e.g. lignite for oil) and at economic reform to raise the efficiency of usage. Labour was also an acutely scarce factor of production and this helps explain such policies as the drive for 'intensification' (output increases gained largely through raising the efficiency of input use), the building of the Berlin Wall in 1961 and the concern to improve living standards as an incentive to work.

Until its sudden political disintegration EG always maintained a command economy. Nevertheless, a number of phases of industrial reform can be distinguished. These have already been described in the introductory chapter: the New Economic System 1963–71, a modest reform, yet the most radical and comprehensive in Eastern Europe in the early 1960s (apart from Yugoslavia, of course); recentralization 1971–79; and the 1980s.

The 1980s saw EG coping with severe foreign trade and payments problems (the EG *Staatsbank* estimated that EG's net foreign debt was $18.5 billion at the end of 1989), with the enhanced need for 'intensification' pursued by means of the combine (*Kombinat*) and the 'perfecting' (*Vervollkommnung*) of the economic mechanism. Radical economic reform was not on the agenda.

The combine
Combines were not around in significant numbers until 1968–69 (Melzer, 1981; Bryson and Melzer, 1987; Stahnke, 1987; Jeffries, 1990). Acceleration during the third wave of combine formation (1978–80), however, saw it established as the basic production unit. By 1981 combine formation was essentially completed, with 133 in centrally directed industry and construction. These combines varied in size from 2 000 to 80,000 employees, with an average of 25,000, and constituted 20–40 enterprises. By 1986 the number had fallen to 127; there were also 94 combines in regionally directed industry, with an average of some 2 000 employees and producing mainly consumer goods.

The combine was a horizontal and vertical amalgamation of enterprises, under the unified control of a director general. The 'parent enterprise' (*Stammbetrieb*: enterprises under the direction of a dominant parent enterprise) was increasingly the most important organizational type and was destined to be the sole one. Other types included enterprises under the direction of an independent management body; management carried out by a group of the leading enterprises in various product groups; and a single large enterprise.

The activities of a combine spanned the whole range from R&D (in order to encourage innovation) to marketing (so as to improve quality). The vertical element involved the incorporation of the most important supplier enter-prises, with the aim of improving the acute supply problems that afflict command economies. The combine was seen as a means of streamlining the command economy, rather than replacing it, by, for example, reducing the number of production units to be centrally directed and allowing central bodies and ministries to concentrate on 'strategic' matters. For example, the director-general had to report each investment of more than 5 million EG Marks (EM), without a maximum value in the case of certain projects, to the State Planning Commission (SPC), which also specified the contractors (Tröder, 1987, p. 88). Major investment projects of national importance were in large measure centrally planned and major percentages of their finances were covered by budgetary grants (Parsons, 1986, p. 33). Further advantages were seen in the following:

1. improving information relating to actual production processes, the combines having to submit their plan drafts not only to the competent minister, but also to the SPC, the Ministry of Finance, and the State Bank;
2. the reaping of economies of scale;
3. concentrating production;
4. making a more rational use of materials;
5. encouraging innovation and the modernization of assets by the in-house manufacture of rationalization equipment and parts;
6. improving the supply of consumer goods by the combines ultimately having to devote at least 5 per cent of output to consumer goods;
7. improving foreign trade decision making; and
8. aiding labour redeployment and retraining.

The broad targets passed down by ministries allowed room for manoeuvre, but monitoring bodies kept a close and frequent check on plan fulfilment.

Over the period 1981–82, in order to encourage exports and to improve knowledge about international markets, 24 foreign trade enterprises were placed under the joint jurisdiction of the Ministry of Foreign Trade (MFT) and the particular combine whose production profile matched that of the exports. Twenty with export ranges dissimilar to those of any combine were subject to the joint jurisdiction of the MFT and an appropriate industrial ministry. The situation in 1986 was that 64 foreign trade enterprises were divided into five groupings: 23 subject to the dual authority of the MFT and the particular combine; 12 subject to the dual authority of the MFT and the appropriate industrial ministry; 12 also subject to the dual authority of the MFT and the industrial ministry, but whose enterprises were reorganized into 61 foreign trade units, without legal rights of their own, which were supposed to cooperate with combines; seven enterprises and combines empowered to engage directly in foreign trade transactions; and ten still subject to the direct and sole authority of the MFT. Note that although this arrangement eroded the strict separation of production and foreign trade, which was a feature of the traditional Soviet model, all foreign trade enterprises were still ultimately supervised by the MFT (Jacobsen, 1987; Klein, 1987).

The director-general of the combine was responsible for disaggregating the plan tasks received via the ministry to its own enterprises. The decision-making rights of the combine increased with respect to both latter organizations. Although the enterprise remained a legally independent unit and was able to draw up contracts with other enterprises both within and without the combine, the director-general of the combine was authorised to transfer tasks, functions and plant from one enterprise to another, to hire and fire enterprise managers, and to create new enterprise divisions.

Possible disadvantages of combine formation were: (1) the adverse effects on innovation of monopolies and the diminution of cross-branch cooperation; and (2) related to enterprise decision-making rights: the division of authority between enterprise and combine was not always clear, but the former certainly lost out significantly; there was always the danger of a parent enterprise appropriating advantageous portions of a programme to itself.

A more recent experiment involved 16 major combines, which were granted increased decision-making authority (including the use of export earnings). The aim was to include all combines by 1991.

The 'perfecting' of the economic mechanism

The 'perfecting' of the economic mechanism involved improvements in both direct and indirect steering (Melzer, 1987). As regard direct steering, for example, norms for materials use were increased and tightened and the indicator system was amended to stress efficiency in the use of inputs (after 1983 'net production', 'net profit', 'products and services for the population', and 'exports' were the main indicators). With respect to indirect steering, for example, enhanced stress was laid on credit policy (Buck, 1987) and a 'contribution for social funds' (a payroll tax) was introduced in 1984 in order to promote a more efficient use of manpower.

The recent 'perfecting' strategy was clearly not based on any new theoretical blueprint, but judgements on its results have been varied. Hamel and Leipold (1987), following Höhmann, succinctly lay out the opposing 'Popperian' and 'Krylov' theses. The Popperian thesis, following Karl Popper's reform strategy of piecemeal social engineering, holds that step-by-step improvements are possible in command economies. The Krylov thesis is based on the Russian poet's fable of four animal musicians who kept swapping seats but in vain as far as musical harmony was concerned. This doubts the possibility of an economically efficient amendment of a command economy. It is rather like Gertrude Schroeder's view of Soviet economic changes as a `treadmill' of reform, unable to solve basic problems because the system itself remains basically unchanged (Schroeder, 1986).

3.   THE ECONOMIC POLICIES OF THE MODROW REGIME

The EG government after November 1989 was in a dilemma. On the one hand, the more radical economic reform was, the more similar would be the two economic systems and, therefore, the greater the pressure for unification (this would be aggravated by the increased flow of people westwards as unemployment rose in EG). On the other hand, the less radical economic reform was, the greater the impulse to migrate. It was the EG prime minister Hans Modrow who first mooted the idea of a 'treaty-based community' (*Vertragsgemeinschaft*). This notion, temporarily taken up by Chancellor Kohl, involved tackling economic and social problems of common concern in the framework of 'confederative structures'.

The EG government certainly intended moving towards a more market-orientated system; Modrow talked about a 'market-orientated planned economy'. In his November speech to the *Volkskammer* (People's Chamber) he said that there should be 'no planning without the market, but no unplanned market economy ... This does not mean that central planning will be abolished, but a real socialist planned economy needs the market'. He spoke against party interference and the 'arbitrary ordering around of the economy to its detriment'. Prices should reflect costs, and prices of basic commodities should reflect 'economic reality'. 'Idiotic' subsidies should be abolished. In a December speech to managers, he talked about the need for a decentralization of decision making, a new management training institution and an independent central bank.

On 21 November 1989 came the announcement that more than half of the state-decreed plans for individual branches of the economy and also 10-day and monthly targets for enterprises were to be abolished. Local authorities were to have greater independence as regards spending.

On 3 January 1990 Christa Luft (the then minister for the economy) suggested that EG must begin 'The transition to an efficient market economy, although account had to be taken of social and environmental concerns'. On 11 January it was announced that the State Planning Commission was to be replaced by an Economic Committee (comprising directors, economists and political groups). The combines were to be split up and a trust body

(*Treuhandanstalt*) was set up in March 1990 to deal with restructuring, liquidation, credit guarantees and privatization.

With regard to ownership, the Modrow government believed that, while the state sector should be dominant in sectors such as energy, heavy industry and transport, the private sector should be encouraged. Hans Modrow himself, as early as 18 November 1989, talked about the possibility of it taking over small firms (especially those producing consumer goods). Christa Luft mentioned the possibility of widespread privatization, while Christian Meyer (the then Deputy Minister for Foreign Trade) envisaged a 'tidal wave' of small and medium-sized enterprises. A 300 employment ceiling was mooted. The smaller enterprises nationalized in 1972 would be offered back to the original owners. The Association of Small and Medium-Sized Firms was set up in December 1989 and this was followed the next month by the Private Employers' Federation.

On 25 January 1990 it was announced that price controls were to be removed in stages by 1992. The huge annual sum spent on subsidies (around EM 51 billion) was to be reduced in three stages. As a first step, it was announced (on 15 January 1990) that the subsidies on items like children's clothes and shoes would be reduced by EM 1.2 billion. The corresponding price rises would be compensated by an additional monthly allowance of EM 45 for each child up to 12 years of age and EM 65 for each child aged 13 and over.

On 1 April 1990 the *Staatsbank* became an independent central bank, losing its commercial operations to *Deutsche Kreditbank*, which was formerly part of the state bank and which now provides finance for industry and banking services for the population. The Foreign Trade Bank (*Aussenhandelsbank*) lost its monopoly of foreign exchange and credit activity. Both EG enterprises and foreign companies were to be able to buy shares in EG commercial banks, while these banks, in turn, were to be able to buy shares in enterprises.

At its 1–2 January 1990 conference, the Free German Trade Union Federation proclaimed its independence from party and state.

No direct foreign investment (including WG as 'foreign') was allowed under the Honecker and predecessor regimes, putting the GDR in the auspicious company of Albania in the whole of Eastern Europe. In a 17 November 1989 speech to the *Volkskammer*, Hans Modrow made the ideological breakthrough: 'The GDR is open to suggestions by our capitalist partners that were earlier treated cautiously or ignored ... Joint ventures, direct investment, profit transfers, pilot projects to preserve the environment are no longer foreign words to us'. A 49 per cent maximum stake in a joint venture by a 'foreign' (including WG) partner was suggested at first, but on 12 January 1990 the *Volkskammer* agreed to a higher percentage when this was 'of interest to the economy' (e.g. new technology). The draft law presented two weeks later stipulated this condition when the enterprises involved were small. Christa Luft said that small WG companies would be able to start up fully-owned subsidiaries. On 1 March 1990 foreign companies were permitted to operate wholly-owned subsidiaries, while the July 1990 law conceded 100 per cent foreign ownership.

While German reunification is to be welcomed wholeheartedly, it is worth noting that there was nothing inevitable about the extremely rapid pace. Even GEMU could have been slowed up by the granting of substantial aid to the Modrow regime (on 4 February 1990 Chancellor Kohl stated that such aid was necessary before the EG election, but this was not forthcoming) and by the earlier ending of the special financial inducements granted to migrants. It just happened that 2 December 1990 was the date of the next general election in WG, thus subjecting events to short-term political expediency. Later on EG's economic collapse became the dominant consideration, but the extent of this collapse after GEMU gave further weight to the argument that a slower process of reunification would have been desirable. The president of the Bundesbank, Karl-Otto Pöhl, was forced to accept the rapid speed of monetary union by political pressure; he saw the prior need for structural change before monetary union, e.g. the setting up of a competitive market economy and the adoption of a conventional monetary policy. The Bundesbank had recommended EM 1 : DM 1 for personal savings up to EM 2 000 and EM 2 : DM 1 for everything else (although Pöhl conceded that the actual, overall EM 1.8 : DM 1 came close to his proposal) and Pöhl was not even consulted when the then WG Economics Minister, Helmut Haussman, unexpectedly announced on 6 February 1990 that GEMU was to take place. On 19 March 1991 Pöhl restoked the controversy when he said that 'We introduced the DM with practically no preparation or possibility of adjustment, and, I would add, at the wrong exchange rate ... So the result is a disaster, as you can see'. (On 16 May 1991 Pöhl announced his resignation as of the following October, although he stressed personal reasons.) It could be argued, therefore, that EG's interests in general would have been better served and the positive features of its identity better preserved by a less rapid process of fusion.

4. GERMAN ECONOMIC AND MONETARY UNION

The WG government estimated that the EG economy was about one-tenth the size of WG's at the time of union (in the second half of 1990, according to the Federal Statistics Office, EG's GNP was 8.3 per cent of WG's). Monetary 'union' is rather an inapt term because the EM has simply been *replaced* by the DM, with the Bundesbank in control of monetary policy. Monetary union is also usually seen as the *final* stage, exchange rate adjustments being used to ease the transitional stage of uniting two unequal economies. Against this sort of advantage, speedy union does bring benefits in such forms as the assurance of a sound, convertible currency. Although there are obvious differences in circumstances (the early postwar economy was not a command one), the June 1948 currency reform, coupled with the abolition of most price controls and rationing, was the prelude to the WG 'economic miracle' (*Wirtschaftswunder*). This experience seemed initially to set a happy precedent.

Economic 'union' essentially involves the adoption of WG's 'social market economy'. Even here, however, some phasing was inevitable. Some prices (e.g. housing rents and property leases, public transport and energy tariffs) continued to receive temporary subsidies. WG income and corporate taxes were introduced in January 1991. The general achievement of WG environmental standards was set for the year 2000 (although this varies: for example, emission standards for new investment projects applied from the beginning of July 1990, while existing lignite power stations have to adapt by 1996). Privatization will, of course, take time.

The EM was replaced by the DM at rates more generous than generally anticipated: individual savings 1 : 1 for people aged 60 and over for savings up to EM 6 000, aged 15–59 up to EM 4 000, and aged below 15 up to EM 2 000; wages and pensions 1 : 1; and corporate debt 2 : 1. The term 'debt' is a little odd since it is owned internally, the result of enterprises having formerly to transfer most net revenue to the state budget and, therefore, forced to borrow from the banks. Thus there is no clear relationship between the debt owed by and the viability of individual enterprises, and the prospect of viable enterprises being needlessly bankrupted provided a powerful argument for writing it off; present German government policy is to consider debt relief on a case-by-case basis.

The effects of GEMU on unemployment and inflation
There is some dispute about the long-run prospects for EG. They are generally seen as excellent, but the most pessimistic observers fear a South Italy (*Mezzogiorno*) scenario where the area remains permanently less developed, experiencing relatively high unemployment and a sustained migration of younger people. There is, however, general agreement that the short to medium term is and will be extremely difficult given the relatively obsolete capital stock and uncompetitive enterprises in many sectors of the economy. Labour productivity in EG pre-GEMU was well below that of WG, estimates varying from 30 per cent (Theo Waigel, the WG Finance Minister) to 50 per cent on average, the picture varying substantially between sectors (produc-

tivity growth in the future depends on factors such as improved incentives due to payment in a sound, convertible currency, retraining, the new technology embodied in WG and foreign capital assets, and the growth of the private sector). Unemployment has substantially increased, while output has fallen. Honecker's EG was a fully employed economy (in 1989 there were 8.7 million employees and apprentices plus a further 1 million self-employed and cooperative members). In contrast, 836,900 (9.5 per cent) were unemployed in April 1991 (272,017 in July 1990) and a further 2 million were on 'short time' (*Kurzarbeit*) (656,277 in July 1990). The WG unemployment rate in 1990 was 7.2 per cent. For some 'short time' means no time; on average short-time workers are employed for only half their normal working time (DIW *Economic Bulletin*, 1990, vol. 27, no. 10, p. 5). A significant increase in open unemployment was forecast after 30 June 1991 as certain employment protection schemes come to an end (although other forms of aid, such as retraining, are available). Note, however, that some 1 million new jobs and 300,000 new enterprises have been created since the beginning of 1990 (*The Economist*, 6 April 1991, p. 10).

There has been considerable industrial unrest in EG (there were large demonstrations against unemployment in March 1991) and a rapid narrowing of the EG–WG wage differential (nominal wages in EG rose by more than a third in 1990: Holger Schmiedling, *Financial Times*, 25 February 1991, p. 17; since the start of 1990 wages have risen by almost half: George Akerlof *et al.*, *Financial Times*, 21 May 1991, p. 16; EG pay is now 60 per cent of the WG level: Karl-Otto Pöhl, *International Herald Tribune*, 3 July 1991, p. 13). The merging of WG and EG trade unions is one factor in this process. Note that the nominal wage ratio pre-GEMU was not out of line with the productivity ratio: a typical EG industrial worker, in terms of EM, earned about one-third the DM wage of his WG counterpart (in the second half of 1990, according to the Federal Statistics Office, the average gross monthly wage was 37 per cent of the WG level, while productivity was only 28.5 per cent). In terms of the measured competitiveness of EG exports to the West, however, the picture was much more bleak: Holger Schmiedling argues that on this basis the EM was worth only DM 0.23 (*Financial Times*, 25 February 1991, p. 17) and Akerlof *et al.* make a similar point (preview of forthcoming article in *Brookings Papers on Economic Activity*, 1991, no. 1, in *The Economist*, 11 May 1991, p. 89). Temporary wage subsidization is one solution recommended (e.g. *Financial Times*, 21 March 1991, p. 22; *The Economist*, 6 April 1991, p. 77; and Akerlof *et al.*, *Financial Times*, 21 May 1991, p. 16); the real wage would be lowered to employers, while migration to WG would be deterred (Richard Portes, *Financial Times*, 25 March 1991, p. 21; and David Begg and Richard Portes, *International Herald Tribune*, 19 June 1991, p. 4). Akerlof *et al.* estimate that at current wages EG enterprises employing only 8 per cent of industrial manpower can sell their output at prices high enough to cover their operating costs; they argue that higher wages will cause more migration by increasing unemployment than they will deter by closing the wage gap, since most easterners want to stay in EG as long as work is available even at current pay levels roughly half those in WG (*Financial Times*, 21 May 1991, p. 16). Those sceptical of wage subsidies include Samuel Brittan (*Financial Times*, 30 May 1991, p. 23). He argues that there is the danger of subsidies becoming permanent and that a tax-based incomes policy is preferable. Across-the-board wage subsidies also hinder the adjustment process.

The forecasts about output and employment, in consequence, became gloomier, aided by the massive switch in EG expenditure towards WG goods (which boosted the WG economy: 4.5 per cent growth in 1990) and the dramatic collapse of Comecon and other trade. EG is unable to devalue its currency in order to remain competitive because of monetary union. The most pessimistic observers predicted a peak unemployment rate of 4 million, in contrast to the relatively optimistic official forecast of an average unemployment level of 1.1–1.4 million in 1991 peaking at 1.6–1.9 million by year end (German government's annual economic report published 8 March 1991). The EG turning point was originally forecast to be in mid-1991, but this has shifted to later in the year or even 1992. In 1990 EG national income fell steeply (by perhaps 15 per cent). In the six months after the 1948 currency reform in WG industrial production rose by more than 50 per cent, whereas in EG July–December 1990 it fell by more than 50 per cent despite substantial subsidization (Holger Schmiedling, *Financial Times*, 25 February 1991, p. 17). Industrial production in EG in 1990 fell by almost 30 per cent (*Deutsche Bank Bulletin*, July 1991, p. 9).

A more favourable scenario is to be found on the inflation front. The 1990 WG inflation rate was actually lower (2.7 per cent) than in 1989 (2.8 per cent) despite larger and larger aid to EG as the economy collapsed. Greater concern was shown for the prospects for inflation in 1991, however. A new ten-point three-year plan was announced on 12 February 1991 to help EG to the tune of an extra DM 10 billion a year, including extra expenditure on the infrastructure and retraining and a one-year extension to the 12 per cent of investment grants for investors in EG. On 8 March 1991 the government agreed an extra DM 12 billion for both 1991 and 1992. It was announced on 27 March 1991 that government-backed bank loans to enterprises, due to be repaid by 31 March, were to be postponed indefinitely. The government formally conceded in February 1991 that its election promise of no tax increases could not be kept, although the Gulf crisis and aid to Eastern Europe were also cited as contributory factors. In late June 1991 Karl-Otto

Pöhl estimated that DM 150 billion would be transferred from WG to EG in the course of the year.

The privatization programme

The combines began to be split up. A trust body or holding company (*Treuhandanstalt*, henceforth THA) was set up in March 1990; this deals not only with privatization, but also with restructuring, liquidation and credit guarantees (to provide temporary protection to enterprises). Detlev Rohwedder (head of the WG company Hoesch) was chairman of the executive board until his assassination by the Red Army Faction on 1 April 1991. He was replaced by Birgit Breuel, who was formerly in charge of the 15 regional offices.

The THA was endowed with the ownership rights of around 8 000 'large' enterprises (those with more than 250 employees), but as the combines continued to be split up the number increased to 9 200 by February 1991. Enterprises were instructed to draw up DM balance sheets, becoming publicly-quoted (AG) or limited companies (Gmbh) in readiness for privatization. The actual process of privatization was slow at first, but speeded up later. In mid-January 1991 the THA reported that more than 450 enterprises had been privatized, raising DM 2.5 billion in sales (*International Herald Tribune*, 15 January 1991, p. 11). The THA reported on 18 April 1991 that 1 261 industrial enterprises had been privatized, 403 in the last quarter of 1990 and 858 in the first quarter of 1991. WG Companies purchased 90 per cent of them, foreigners 5 per cent and the remaining 5 per cent were management buy-outs (an 'especially generous' attitude would henceforth be taken to management buy-outs). The percentage sectoral breakdown was as follows: capital goods and motors 40; food and drink 30; electronics and scientific instruments 17; and chemicals and rubber 12. A more recent figure for privatization is 2 200 (544 enterprises in May alone), with foreigners accounting for 81 (David Goodhart, *Financial Times*, 1 July 1991, p. 6). As far as closure is concerned, 333 enterprises either have been or are in the process of being liquidated; 87,292 jobs were involved (David Goodhart, *Financial Times*, 19 April 1991, p. 3 and David Gow, *The Guardian*, 19 April 1991, p. 15).

Note, in contrast, that the smaller enterprises nationalized in 1972 quickly started to be returned to their former owners. Service establishments such as restaurants and cafes are being sold off or leased. More than 70 per cent of shops are now privatized (David Goodhart and Andrew Fisher, *Financial Times*, 7 February 1991, p. 4); 25,000 shops and other service enterprises have been privatized (David Goodhart, *Financial Times*, 5 April 1991, p. 18).

One of the major reasons for the initially disappointingly slow privatization programme was the original decision to return physical property, as far as possible, to the original owners or their heirs. The 15 June 1990 agreement between the EG and WG governments stated that those who left after 1949 (or their heirs) had the right to reclaim the assets left behind, property being returned 'as far as this is possible, taking into account the social and economic realities that have developed over the last 40 years' (the German Constitutional Court confirmed, on 23 April 1991, that this did not apply to the period 1945–49, although some partial compensation was recommended). This meant, for example, that buildings converted for 'general or commercial use' and for community use, or firms which had become part of larger units would not be affected. The deterrent effect on sales to domestic and foreign investors led to a revised property claims agreement (David Goodhart and Leslie Colitt, *Financial Times*, 12 September 1990, p. 4). Claims on small businesses had to be submitted before 16 September 1990 and all other claims before 13 October 1990. The vast majority of claimants would not be able to reclaim the property itself; property needed for urgent business reasons (such as employment-creating investment) could be sold. Monetary compensation would be paid to claimants based on what the property was worth when taken over plus 1 per cent annual interest payments on that sum. New rules were again issued on 6 February 1991 due to the continuing deterrence of the huge number of claims (about 1.2 million claims on property and 10,000 on enterprises); another factor was the wish of THA to find investors offering long-term business programmes and the prospects of preserving employment levels. It is now easier for new investors to take over EG property, with the claimants being compensated financially once their cases have been approved. Claimants wishing to take back physical property have four weeks to agree to do so, have to accept the entire property, and must pay for any improvements made. On 7 March 1991 the THA announced that it was to sign deals with more than 50 international banks and management consultancies to arrange sales; each will be offered a package of around ten enterprises and be paid both a daily allowance to cover costs and a fee for every sale.

On 12 March 1991 the government agreed to a further relaxation of the legislation. The THA now has the authority, until the end of 1992, to give priority to any investor promising the best job-sustaining and creating programme (Richard Smith, *International Herald Tribune*, 13 March 1991, pp. 11–13). Rapid construction is sought. A former owner would at least have to match any other offer. The THA has also now to confer with the five EG *Länder* (states) over large plant closures (David Goodhart, *The Financial Times*, 22 March 1991, p. 2). Restructuring is to be given greater emphasis. The new policy covers the Nazi property confiscations of 1933–45 as well as the post-1949 socialist ones (1945–49 is unaffected because of the reunification treaties agreed with the Soviet Union).

Foreign trade and capital

In the mid-1980s, according to official GDR statistics, something like 65 per cent of EG's foreign trade was with Comecon (nearly 40 per cent with the Soviet Union alone). EG was a major supplier of capital goods to Comecon and heavily dependent on imports of fuels and raw materials. The GDR enjoyed considerable trade concessions with the European Community (EC): EG exports to WG were allowed in free of tariffs and levies, although there were still quotas on agricultural products and manufactures like steel and textiles. The EC (excluding WG) accounted for 5 per cent of EG's foreign trade in 1988 (DIW *Economic Bulletin*, 1990, vol. 27, no. 3, pp. 1–4). There are varying estimates of the impact of a united Germany on the EC. David Marsh and David Goodhart (*Financial Times*, 10 December 1990, p. 9) put a united GNP at 27.8 per cent (the share of population goes up from 19 per cent to 23 per cent), while Theo Sommer (*European Affairs*, February–March 1991, p. 41) reports a united figure of 31 per cent of EC GDP (compared with 26.7 per cent for WG alone).

EG as part of a united Germany is now naturally a full member of the EC. Transitional concessions have, however, been agreed, e.g. the phasing in of non-nuclear safety and environmental standards (those relating to air and water by 1996 for instance); industrial subsidies; and Comecon agreements to continue until the end of 1991 as far as the area of EG alone is concerned (renewable for a year). Despite German government credit guarantees and other help, however, Comecon trade has collapsed at an unexpectedly rapid rate. This has aggravated the unemployment problem, as mentioned above. The East Berlin Institute for Applied Economic Research has estimated that in 1988 260,000 workers were directly employed in industrial exports to the Soviet Union alone and 220,000 indirectly; the 480,000 total accounted for 15 per cent of total employment in EG industry (DIW *Economic Bulletin*, 1990, vol. 27, no. 6, pp. 14–15).

As regards 'foreign' capital (including WG), there has been some disappointment. EG now has the enormous advantage of being supported by a wealthy twin within the EC and it has a sound, convertible currency (profit repatriation, therefore, is no problem). Many inducements also prevail, e.g. a 12 per cent investment grant was originally applicable from 1 July 1990 to 30 June 1991, when the rate was to be reduced to 8 per cent for another year, but the 12 per cent rate has now been extended for another 12 months. Foreign Minister Hans-Dietrich Genscher has said that an investor putting DM 100 million into EG would receive up to DM 57.3 million in forms such as grants, subsidies, tax write-offs and special depreciation rates (*International Herald Tribune*, 4 May 1991, p. 11). He also said that only 5 per cent of all investment in EG had come from outside Germany as a whole (*The Times*, 4

May 1991, p. 23). There are, however, a number of obstacles to private investment flows into EG, such as:

1. The restitution claims of former owners and the confusing changes in legislation have not helped;
2. The European Commission has been unhappy at the monopolistic implications of some mergers e.g. in banking, electricity, insurance and airlines (*Interflug* was closed down by the end of April 1991, *Lufthansa's* initial offer having been rejected on monopoly grounds; other airlines, such as British Airways, also showed early interest);
3. A generally poor infrastructure and environmental pollution;
4. Inherited corporate debt (the German government considers debt relief on a case-by-case basis).

CONCLUSION

The long-run prospects for EG within a united Germany are generally considered to be excellent, although some see the danger of a permanently relatively depressed region. The official government view, as put by Chancellor Kohl on 10 April 1991, is that '... we shall solve the economic problems and we shall need five years ... but I fear that after 45 years' experience it will take longer than three, four, five years before we are able to celebrate full unification'. As we have seen, the short and medium term is and will be very difficult ones for EG, more difficult than first imagined. EG and WG are natural partners, sharing a common language, history, culture and industrial tradition. The industrial structures are similar, e.g. both are strong in engineering. WG capital, technology and know-how can be combined with relatively cheap (at least initially, although the speed at which the EG–WG wage differential is closing is causing alarm) and skilled labour and management. EG provides a significant market (for consumer durables, for instance), a trained labour force, good trade connections with Eastern Europe and a services network. EG, however, has limited natural resources, its infrastructure (e.g. telephone system) is generally poor, and there are severe pollution problems (especially due to its heavy reliance on lignite as a primary energy source: 71 per cent in 1984).

The picture varies across the board, of course. The more favourable prospects are to be found in sectors such as textile machinery, printing presses, petrochemicals, machine tools, measuring and control equipment, optical instruments (although the markets for precision and optical machinery are currently depressed), computers and software, glass, services (including retail trade) and tourism. The construction industry could boom, but was initially depressed because local authorities have been starved of funds (there were signs of recovery in early 1991). Services and construction seem likely to lead the recovery. A less rosy outlook characterizes such sectors as lignite and lignite-based chemicals, mining equipment, plastics, consumer electronics, shipbuilding (this sector did show some growth in 1990 despite being badly affected by declining Soviet orders, but the 1991 prospects look bleak), heavy engineering and transport equipment (although railway wagons are better placed), textiles and clothing, footwear, confectionery, coffee, consumer electronics and agriculture (there were signs of recovery in food production in early 1991). But an injection of foreign capital, technology and know-how can often work wonders, as can be seen in the motor car industry (e.g. the Trabant has now been phased out altogether and replaced by VW models).

The German government itself has been forced to take a more interventionist attitude towards the EG economy as the situation deteriorated. The 1948 experience has proved to be not so appropriate as hoped, since it did not deal with the problems of the transition from command to market economy. The old *Ordnungspolitik* was geared to creating the right environment for the private sector to flourish, such as the provision of a basic infrastructure, a sound currency and a competitive environment (Richard Smith, *International Herald Tribune*, 4 March 1991, p. 9). This has not proved to be adequate. Kenneth Parris goes as far as to recommend an updated version of Roosevelt's New Deal, with large retraining programmes and infrastructural job-creation schemes (*International Herald Tribune*, 12 April 1991, p. 4). On 12 April 1991 the government decided to set up two joint committees with the opposition Social Democrats, one dealing with property rights and administration and the other with employment and retraining.

The EG experience has enormous implications for the countries of Eastern Europe facing the transition to market economies. The exposure of EG to the harsh realities of international competition, even in the embrace of a wealthy twin, has been traumatic. The Eastern European countries may lose confidence in current policies as they see EG struggling despite massive WG support within a reunited country (although they are able to adjust their exchange rates, of course). Those who advocate a 'big bang' approach coupled with a harsh 'shock' therapy, particularly in the absence of substantial Western aid, are surely risking Eastern European faith in political democracy and market economies.

An update to this chapter is given in the Postscript, page 281.

REFERENCES

Akerloff, G., Rose, A., Yellen, J. and Hessenius, H. (1991) 'East Germany in from the cold: the economic aftermath of currency union', *Brookings Papers on Economic Activity*, no. 1.

Bryson, P. and Melzer, M. (1987) 'The Kombinat in GDR economic organization', in Jeffries, Melzer and Breuning (eds) (1987).

Buck, H.-F. (1987) 'The GDR financial system', in Jeffries, Melzer and Breuning (eds) (1987).

Hamel, H. and Leipold, H. (1987) 'Economic reform in the GDR: causes and effects', in Jeffries, Melzer and Breuning (eds) (1987).

Jacobsen, H.-D. (1987) 'The foreign trade and payments of the GDR', in Jeffries, Melzer and Breuning (eds) (1987).

Jeffries, I. (Ed.) (1981) *The Industrial Enterprise in Eastern Europe*, New York: Praeger.

Jeffries, I., Melzer, M. (eds) and Breuning, E. (advisory Ed.) (1987) *The East German Economy*, London: Croom Helm.

Jeffries, I. (1990) *A Guide to the Socialist Economies*, London: Routledge (Chapter 7).

Klein, W. (1987) 'The role of the GDR in Comecon: some economic aspects', in Jeffries, Melzer and Breuning (eds) (1987).

Melzer, M. (1981) 'Combine formation and the role of the enterprise in East German Industry', in Jeffries (Ed.) (1981).

Melzer, M. (1987) 'The perfecting of the planning and steering mechanisms', in Jeffries, Melzer and Breuning (eds) (1987).

Parsons, J. (1986) 'Credit contracts in the GDR: decentralized investment decisions in a planned economy', *Economics of Planning*, vol. 20, no. 1.

Schroeder, G. (1986) *The System versus Progress: Soviet Economic Problems*, London: The Centre for Research into Communist Economies.

Stahnke, A. (1987) 'Kombinate as the key structural element in the GDR intensification', *Studies in Comparative Communism*, vol. XX, no. 1.

Tröder, M. (1987) 'The 1981–5 Order of Planning', in Jeffries, Melzer and Breuning (eds) (1987).

8 Hungary

Paul Hare

1. INTRODUCTION[1]

From 1948 until the general election of 1990 (with rounds in March and April), Hungary was under Communist Party control. Especially in the early 1950s, the country's economic policy, as well as the detailed economic arrangements in most sectors of production, were completely dominated by the Soviet model. This meant that the great majority of production units was nationalized, and Soviet-type central planning was rapidly instituted, along with the usual Soviet priorities for rapid industrialization with an emphasis on heavy industry. In addition, the Cold War atmosphere of the time resulted in a reorientation of Hungary's trade towards the Soviet Union and other Eastern Bloc partners.

By the mid-1950s, the combination of political repression and excessive rates of accumulation had created an explosive situation, which the then Communist Party was unable to control despite a (short-lived) leadership change and some economic concessions which allowed living standards to recover somewhat. Demonstrations in Budapest in October 1956, to which the security police reacted with a degree of violence reflecting their very real fears about the situation, soon gave way to a full-blown popular uprising. Communist control was only restored after a large-scale Soviet intervention put down the revolt and installed Janos Kadar as the new party leader. At the time the West did almost nothing to assist Hungary's freedom fighters, being pre-occupied with the Suez crisis; subsequently, however, Western countries did allow entry to many Hungarian refugees, perhaps as many as 200,000.

Following this major crisis, the old Communist Party virtually collapsed, many collective farms were abandoned or returned to former owners, and production slumped. Kadar's first task was to rebuild the party under a new name – the Hungarian Socialist Workers' Party (HSWP). At the same time, he made clear his commitment to improving living standards, and sought support from all social groups in developing the economy. By the early 1960s he felt sufficiently secure to resume the collectivization of agriculture and this time most of the sector was successfully transformed. Moreover, by a sensitive treatment of the private sector in agriculture, Hungary was able to create a reasonably productive agriculture capable both of feeding the population and providing substantial exports. Not only did this provide a secure base for reforms in industry, but reforms in agriculture also offered models which could be applied elsewhere (Swain, 1986).

Pressure for industrial reform was already apparent in the mid-1950s, as the inefficiencies associated with the extremes of Stalinist centralization were increasingly recognized. One of the first, and still among the best, of the early critical studies of centralization was Kornai's book, on the problems of Hungarian light industry (Kornai, 1959). A striking feature of Kornai's analysis is that he was able to combine detailed comment on the specific institutional and management arrangements in light industry with an awareness of certain general properties of the Soviet model. For instance, he drew attention to the ineffectiveness of partial reforms, because of the inherent tendencies in the system to reinstate controls that had been relaxed; this is a theme we return to below.

Despite Kornai's warnings, serious reform in Hungary's industrial sectors had to await the introduction of the so-called New Economic Mechanism in 1968, although a number of partial reforms were introduced earlier in the 1960s. These included the combination of enterprises into trusts or associations, a process that also occurred in the rest of Eastern Europe. The objective was to improve the efficiency of planning by reducing the number of units to which instructions had to be issued, and by allowing somewhat greater managerial autonomy. Other reforms sought to simplify the set of plan indicators or to improve enterprise incentives. In line with the general discussion of Eastern European economic reforms in Hare (1987), all these early reforms could be categorized as cautious.

In contrast, the reforms of 1968, the New Economic Mechanism, were certainly radical by the standards of the time. Our detailed analysis, therefore, begins with this reform package and traces the subsequent developments in Hungary's approach to industry, concluding with some speculation about likely developments under the new government emerging from the 1990 election, the first democratic one in Hungary since the 1940s. To give some background to this examination of Hungarian policies, section 2 outlines the country's economic organization and structure paying particular attention to industry; a few tables are also provided here to indicate the main trends of development relevant to the later discussion. Section 3 focuses on Hungary's economic management arrangements, while section 4 deals with the increasingly urgent issue of revitalizing an economy that has now stagnated for nearly a decade, and the emerging problems of transition to a market-type model.

2.   ECONOMIC ORGANIZATION AND STRUCTURE

During the period of communist rule, Hungary's industry (and much of the remainder of the economy) was organized hierarchically. Thus the Council of Ministers was at the highest level, supervising the work of branch ministries,[2] functional ministries[3] and a variety of other high-level state agencies or offices.[4] At the lowest level of the system were the basic producing units themselves, namely the state enterprises (including large enterprises, associations and trusts), cooperatives, and small private producers. In parallel to this 'government' structure was the corresponding 'party' structure: the Politburo and Central Committee; regional and district party committees; and party committees in all socialist sector workplaces (i.e. state enterprises, cooperatives, and the state management organs) throughout the country. Through this extensive network, as well as through its control over senior appointments (the so-called *nomenklatura* system), the HSWP was able to dominate decision-making processes in all areas of economic life.

By the early 1960s the number of producing units in Hungarian industry had fallen to an extremely low level, as a result of efforts to concentrate production through mergers and associations of enterprises. Despite several attempts to break up large units into their constituent parts, there was little change in the situation even through the 1980s, except that many small,

Table 8.1   Organizational structure of industry, 1987

Organization\Item	Gross output %	Average employment	Number of units
State enterprises	90.44	1 206	1 043
Cooperatives	6.85	141	1 392
Industrial and service cooperative		32	846
	0.68		
Enterprise working group		13	12 484
Private artisans	1.64	1.3	44 101
Other economic associations	0.37	6.1	3 590

Note: Column 1 shows the percentages of gross industrial output produced by the different types of unit; column 2 shows the average employment in each type of unit.

Source: Iparstatisztikai Evkönyv 1988, p. 14; (Budapest: KSH, 1989)

private or semi-private units were started up. But in terms of shares in output and employment, state enterprises remained predominant, as indicated clearly in Table 8.1. Moreover, if industry is decomposed into its separate branches, many of them turn out to contain only a few firms. For instance, in 1988 there were only two state enterprises making domestic chemicals, and barely a dozen in many branches of light industry and food processing. Moreover, even in branches with more enterprises (like engineering), it was very common for firms to divide up the relevant product group into segments in which they specialized (up to 1982 such profile controls were imposed by the centre). Hence, in reforming the Hungarian economy, the question of monopoly power has to be addressed, as we shall see later on (Hare, 1990).

Within the economy as a whole, industry plays a very important part, as is shown in Table 8.2. The table indicates the share of industry in GDP since the early 1960s, together with growth rates of GDP and some of the major industrial branches. The dominant position of engineering is quite clear. It can also be seen that some quite substantial structural change has occurred since 1960, particularly with the relative decline in mining and light industry, and the expansion of chemicals and electricity generation. Finally, the stagnation of the 1980s is very evident and constitutes one of the strongest factors pushing Hungary towards further and increasingly radical economic reforms.

Since Hungary is such an open economy,[5] it is also important to provide some background information on the role of industry in Hungary's international trade. The procedures for conducting trade are very different in Hungary's two main market areas. Formally, for most of the period we are covering here, foreign trade has been a state monopoly, although since the 1960s an increasing number of trading organizations and even individual enterprises have been given independent foreign trading rights. Even so, both imports and exports have been subject to a variety of controls, and most transactions have been subject to a wide range of distorting taxes and subsidies (Hare *et al.*, 1990).

From Hungary's point of view, Comecon trade, especially with the Soviet Union, has provided much of the country's energy requirements (often at prices below world market levels), as well as an outlet for relatively low quality production which could not have been exported to the West. On the other hand, the presence of the guaranteed CMEA market has undoubtedly distorted a good deal of Hungary's industrial investment. Hungary's hard (or convertible) currency trade comprises its trade with Western economies (e.g. the OECD countries), most developing countries, as well as some of its trade with CMEA partners. Although this trade has sometimes been conducted on barter lines (counter trade), most of it has followed normal market principles. However, imports into Hungary have always required import licences

Table 8.2   Industry in the Hungarian economy

(a)   *Shares* (%, using 1986 prices)

Item\Year	1960	1970	1980	1988	1989
Industry in GDP	34.3	36.6	37.2	36.5	35.2
Structure of industry[1]:					
(Socialist sector)					
Mining	13.4	11.1	8.1	6.6	5.7
Electricity	4.0	4.7	5.7	6.0	6.2
Metallurgy	12.3	10.6	9.1	8.5	10.5
Engineering	19.5	22.7	23.6	25.8	24.8
Building materials	4.3	3.6	3.5	3.4	3.1
Chemicals	9.0	13.5	18.6	19.6	18.5
Light industry	17.5	15.1	13.7	12.9	12.4
Other industry	0.7	0.9	1.0	0.8	0.8
Food industry	19.3	17.8	16.7	16.4	17.8

[1]   percentage of gross output, neglecting industrial output produced in other sectors (amounting to 5.3% of the totals reported above, in 1980). The private sector produced under 5% of total industrial output in Hungary until privatization got underway in 1989; on this, see sections 4 and 5.

(b)   *Growth rates* (constant prices; all data refers to value added)

Item\Period	1960–65	1965–70	1970–75	1975–80	1980–85	1985-88
National Income[1]	4.1	6.8	6.2	2.8	1.3	0.8
Industry	7.1	7.3	7.7	4.0	3.0	1.1
Individual branches[2]:						
(Socialist sector)						
Mining	5.4	3.7	2.1	0.5	0.0	–1.4
Electricity	8.8	8.2	7.6	5.9	2.9	2.2
Metallurgy	5.4	5.5	5.0	1.6	0.0	2.7
Engineering	9.7	7.7	7.8	3.2	3.4	2.8
Building materials	6.5	5.2	5.1	4.3	0.0	3.6
Chemicals	13.8	11.6	10.5	6.4	2.3	2.9
Light industry	6.4	4.4	5.7	2.1	1.1	1.4
Food industry	7.4	4.7	4.7	3.3	2.0	0.6

Note: all growth rates are expressed in average annual terms.
[1]   This is the MPS aggregate measure of economic activity, not the SNA measure (which is GDP).
[2]   Growth rates of gross output.

Sources: Statisztikai Evkönyv 1988 and 1989, various tables (Budapest: KSH, 1989 and 1990) in the postwar period, although restrictions were eased on many imports from the late-1980s onwards as the country began to open up to the West. Some Western exports to Hungary, mainly high technology items with actual or potential defence connections, have also been controlled through COCOM. Finally, the European Community and some individual member states have imposed quotas and other restraints on some of Hungary's output. These principally affect agricultural products, but some limits apply to such industrial products as footwear; it is expected that the bulk of these EC restrictions will be lifted by 1995.

Table 8.3 presents some data on the main components of Hungary's trade both in transferable roubles and in convertible currencies, focusing on industrial products. In its structure, Hungary's trade is relatively backward for its level of development, in that its exports are mostly not very sophisticated products, and the weights accorded to agriculture and the food industry, as well as to basic materials and engineering, are surprisingly high. The pattern of imports basically reflects the country's resource endowments, and the usual inability of a small country to produce the full range of goods and services desired by households and industrial users. Note also that the patterns of hard currency and rouble trade are somewhat different, the latter accounting for a higher proportion both of imports of materials and energy, and exports of technically complex goods.

Table 8.3   Hungary's foreign trade in 1988

Branch\Trade	Transferable roubles		Convertible currencies	
	Exports	Imports	Exports	Imports
Energy sources	0.8	55.8	11.4	6.2
Raw materials	4.8	26.2	35.7	37.1
Semi-finished goods	19.8	29.2	78.1	91.2
Spare parts	21.3	16.9	11.7	39.7
Machinery, etc.	98.6	42.4	37.1	36.9
Industrial consumer goods	34.5	27.7	45.9	27.5
Agricultural goods	8.1	1.0	29.5	9.9
Food industry	19.9	4.4	46.8	20.4
TOTAL	207.9	203.5	296.2	268.9

Note: All data in the above table are in billion Forints. As a rough approximation, the figures can be converted to 1990 pounds by dividing by 100.

Source: *Statistical Yearbook of Foreign Trade 1988*, Budapest, 1989, tables 14 and 15

But all trade between Hungary and its former CMEA partners was to be conducted in hard currency terms at world market prices from the start of 1991. This implies very considerable terms of trade losses for Hungary at 1989 trade volumes. However, actual trade with the East, especially with the Soviet Union, has been falling sharply over the last few years, and this will certainly continue. Hungarian firms have actually proved more successful than expected in redirecting trade to Western markets in the past year. This, together with a more restrictive policy on individual access to hard currency for travel purposes, has resulted in a huge improvement in Hungary's current account in 1990 (expected to exceed $1 500 million), despite a continuation of the policy of relaxing controls over imports, as well as a severe drought affecting agricultural exports.

Trade, of course, not only provides goods and services for immediate use but also contributes to the innovation process, mainly through the import of modern capital goods. In the Hungarian case, Western economic links have contributed to technological change mainly through the joint venture and licensing mechanisms, while Eastern links placed more emphasis on the distribution of productive capacity within given product groups. The transfer of Western technology to Hungary was investigated very thoroughly in Marer (1986), with some important general issues to do with such transfers surveyed in Wienert and Slater (1986).

Unfortunately, although Hungary has participated more actively in these East–West links than several other Eastern European countries, its rate of technological development has still been much slower than one might expect for a country at its level of development. This is despite the existence of a long-established institutional structure in Hungary intended to promote the introduction of new technology (Balázs *et al.*, 1990), and despite high levels of spending on R&D and investment (especially in the 1970s as regards the latter). The reasons for this unsatisfactory outcome are explored fully in the next section.

3. ECONOMIC MANAGEMENT

Hungary's system of economic management has undergone several stages of transformation since the early 1960s, as a result of which it has shifted away from the traditional Soviet-type model towards a more market-like system. However, even by the late 1980s the reformed system was not yet functioning like a Western market economy. It remains to be seen whether the political reforms of 1989–90 are sufficient to provide the required stimulus to complete the shift to a market economy. There are grounds for optimism, for reasons that should become clear below.

The first major shift away from the Soviet model occurred with the introduction of the New Economic Mechanism in 1968, which recognized the deficiencies of overcentralized planning and set out to build on successes already achieved in agriculture (Swain, 1986). This reform, seen as quite path-breaking at the time, ended the traditional practice of breaking down the national plan into compulsory plans for each separate production unit. Economic management by direct planning was replaced with management by financial regulators, a range of taxes, subsidies and other price-type instruments which influenced the financial conditions under which enterprises could operate without involving direct instructions (except in connection with CMEA trade commitments and some defence-related production). Rather than creating the environment of an efficient market economy, however, these reforms replaced the old plan bargaining system with a system of 'regulator bargaining', in which firms were able to negotiate about their financial conditions (Antal, 1985). In addition, entry and exit of firms was extremely restricted in most branches (due to the need for ministerial permission to start a new firm and 'responsibility to supply', which prevented the exit even of loss-making firms).

The New Economic Mechanism reformed prices into something approximating two-channel prices (in which there are different mark-up rates on capital and labour inputs), relaxed the rules of price formation/adjustment (by creating categories of free, limited and fixed prices) (Hare, 1976), liberalized credit and investment rules, and partially decentralized foreign trade by fixing uniform dollar and rouble exchange rates and granting independent foreign trading rights to many firms.

Most important of all, though, this reform introduced profits taxation and sought to re-establish enterprise-level incentives based on profit[6], to replace the previous system based on the fulfilment of certain plan targets (usually gross output) (Hare *et al.*, 1981). Under the traditional system, enterprises were allowed to retain some profits for specified purposes, such as the payment of bonuses, but above-plan profits were normally remitted to higher levels of the economy; this amounted, in effect, to a marginal tax rate on profits of 100 per cent, which was not very effective as a stimulant to greater enterprise efficiency. Under the reforms, a more reasonable general profit rate was established whereby enterprises would have an interest in increasing profits. Post-tax profit was then split into two funds, a development fund (to finance decentralized investments) and a sharing fund (for wage increases and bonuses). Contributions to the development fund were subject to further proportional taxation, while disbursements from the sharing fund were subject to progressive taxation. The object of the latter was to discourage enterprises from paying out large wage increases: thus the tax on wage increases was set at higher rates than that on bonuses (in each case the tax payable was a proportion of the proposed increment in the wage bill, the rate varying from zero to several hundred per cent).

The complexity of the New Economic Mechanism was considered to require a range of so-called financial 'bridges' to ease the transition between the old system and the new. These bridges were highly differentiated taxes and subsidies on imports, exports and production, intended to be temporary, and intended roughly to equalize the initial conditions of different enterprises. They represented a compromise between those who wanted to bring about the conditions of a market-type economy very quickly, and those in Hungary's leadership reluctant to see any serious reform at all. Although such a compromise might have been necessary to get any significant reforms accepted, it soon became evident that the 'temporary' bridges would not be removed and the whole reform package was quickly undermined from within. For all the rhetoric, no one was prepared to enforce market discipline on Hungary's enterprises, with consequences that remain with us into the early 1990s.

What remained of national planning after 1968 was a continued commitment to prepare medium-term (five-year) plans, which became guides to the government and central agencies, mainly influencing the structure of investment. Enterprises were supposed to prepare plans in the light of their own judgements about the markets in which they operated, and about technological opportunities and developments. Ministries were expected to prepare medium- and long-term forecasts about the prospects for various branches, and encourage enterprises to develop in the light of these forecasts. In principle, this could have been a form of indicative planning, or it could have operated via the kinds of sectoral study prepared in the UK either by the National Economic Development Office (NEDO) or by the Scottish Development Agency (SDA). In practice, the behaviour of the system failed to change as much as had been expected.[7] Let us now consider why.

The reasons for failure can be traced to three key factors: macroeconomic balance (persistent shortage), enterprise expectations, and the failure to reform certain aspects of Hungary's economic arrangements essential for the creation of a well-functioning market system.

Like the other East European countries, the Hungarian economy has experienced persistent and widespread shortage conditions since soon after the introduction of central planning. While in consumer goods markets the most severe shortages have been confined to housing, telephones and cars (so that Hungary has not recently experienced the queues and rationing of everyday items seen elsewhere), intermediate inputs have been in short supply and the labour market has been very tight. Several explanations have been offered for the phenomenon of shortage: these include the state's overriding commitment to the maintenance of full employment (Granick, 1975, especially Chapters 8 and 10); the establishment of 'incorrect' relative prices which distort the pattern of demand without implying overall, macroeconomic disequilibrium (Portes, 1989), and the institutionalization of a 'normal' intensity of shortage (Kornai, 1980). Although there is continuing controversy about these explanations, and much empirical testing, the effect for many enterprises has been to make a high proportion of their output readily saleable. There has been little need for a serious marketing effort, nor much incentive to engage in risky innovation.

Added to this was the belief by many enterprise managers (confirmed to a large extent by subsequent events) either that the reforms would not endure, or at least that market forces would not be allowed to result in enterprise closures or other 'unpleasant' adjustments. This expectation led enterprises to cultivate relationships with their ministerial superiors and to seek 'advice' about what they should be doing, often in preference to developing horizontal, market-orientated links (Bauer, 1975). Aside from their understandable uncertainty about the future or effectiveness of the reforms, there were other reasons for managers to behave in this way. Thus central agencies disposed of certain resources (such as investment funds and foreign exchange) which enterprises needed, and the *nomenklatura* system conferred on ministries and the higher party bodies a decisive influence over senior appointments. In these important respects, the old system was untouched by the reforms.

Finally, the 1968 reform package (or, more accurately, reform compromise) did not include certain areas now seen as extremely crucial, at least in part because it was based on an incorrect 'theory of reforms'. It was widely believed that price reforms and decentralization which mainly affected the markets for goods and services in Hungary would be sufficient to bring about a rapid and substantial improvement in economic performance. We now know that this view is wrong, not only for Hungary but also more generally. For what is also required, it seems, is the restoration of markets for capital, land and foreign exchange; the development of institutions and a suitable legal framework to support (and to some extent regulate) these markets; and an effective separation of productive units from the political superstructure. Of the principal factor markets, only the labour market already functioned to some degree as a market. But even there, the wage structure within the socialist sector (state enterprises and cooperatives) was highly regulated, and provided poor incentives for the accumulation of skills or for high quality work (Falus-Szikra, 1985). Many of the economic developments in Hungary since the 1968 reforms can be seen in the light of an understanding of these issues (Brada and Dobozi, 1990).

However, the understanding was slow in coming. During the 1970s, for instance, there was some recentralization of controls over about 50 of the very largest enterprises, increased central restrictions both on price formation and on the differentiation of wages. At the same time investment enjoyed boom conditions, with some state-sponsored (and in some instances ill-judged) central development programmes forcing the pace of development in selected sectors, but enterprise investment also taking off. Through an unfortunate conjunction of circumstances, just as the Hungarian leadership were embarking on their ambitious growth programme, seen by many observers as a substitute for further reforms, as in Poland, the Western world's financial markets were awash with petro-dollars seeking somewhere to invest, following the first oil crisis of 1973. Hence it proved easy for the Hungarians to fund much of their investment programme from external sources. As a result, living standards continued to rise rapidly in parallel with the investment boom, while the country accumulated external debt.

In theory, of course, the new investments should have led to increased hard currency exports sufficient to service, and ultimately repay the accumulated debt. Supported by special credits favouring investments expected to increase hard currency exports, this did happen to some extent. But several factors were operating against Hungary by the end of the decade, and in the early 1980s. The first was the second oil crisis of 1979,[8] which led to Western recession and a reduced demand for Hungary's exports. The second was the rise of the so-called NICs (newly industrializing countries, such as Taiwan, Singapore and South Korea) which were raising their technological level, and their ability to produce and market sophisticated products in the West, at an astonishing rate; some of these countries quickly established positions in markets which the Hungarians had planned to enter or develop. The third factor was the inefficiency of Hungary's own investment process, with projects often delayed and costing far more than planned, using outmoded technology, and unable to produce output of the quality required for successful sales in Western markets. The result was increasing difficulty in servicing the debt, and a realization by Western bankers and governments that the Hungarians were becoming over-extended.

Gradually, therefore, it became apparent to all that the growth strategy was not succeeding; this realization also discredited the approach of partial reforms within Hungary's modified Soviet-type system, but it was too soon, politically, to overthrow it (Brezhnev was, after all, still in power in the Kremlin). The outcome, therefore, was renewal of the momentum behind economic reforms, the beginnings of a reform process that extended through the 1980s, and a gradual introduction of the policies and institutions needed for a functioning market-type economy. These steps were accompanied by cut-backs in investment and a sharp slow-down in the growth of consumption, as Hungary's macroeconomic policy adapted to the requirements of improving the external balance. Hence the 1980s became a decade of economic stagnation, despite which the gross external debt continued to rise, reaching $20.6 billion by the end of 1989, the highest per capita debt in the region. Hungary's debt service ratio (interest and amortization on medium- and long-term debt as a percentage of one year's exports) reached a peak of 65 per cent in 1986, before falling back to about 45 per cent in 1989; even the latter figure, however, remains uncomfortably high.

Focusing on industry, to which most of the reforms were directed, the 1980s began with a further attempt to break up certain trusts (four were broken up in 1980–81, creating about 50 new firms; 19 trusts remained, incorporating nearly 300 enterprises) and large enterprises into their con-stituent units, a new price reform which introduced 'competitive' prices (an administrative device to bring the domestic prices of exported goods into line with external prices) and a revival of small-scale economic activity.[9] The latter was especially important because it effectively legalized a lot of the economic activity that had previously taken place semi-officially or even illegally, as part of the 'second' economy (Galasi and Sziráczki, 1985). But it also created new categories of small enterprise and cooperative which, although formally still part of the socialist sector, were not to be subject to all the detailed and complex regulations applied to the larger firms. In addition, various forms of association and economic partnership were legal-ized, including some which involved renting existing enterprise assets to some of an enterprise's workforce to deliver services to the firm on a more commercial basis than previously (the so-called economic working groups). Within a very short time several thousand of these new types of organization had come into being, undoubtedly a most promising development, though one which would inevitably generate pressures for further change in the same direction.

Aside from learning to live with the new pricing rules (which was some-times quite problematic, as the rules sometimes *discouraged* hard currency exports), much of the socialist sector was unaffected by these reforms, except to the extent that firms began to believe the government's renewed reform rhetoric and talk about 'the market'. However, most firms had good reason to be quite cynical about the government's reform intentions, and it is doubtful whether many felt obliged to change their economic behaviour at this stage.

Certainly the 1979–80 package of measures failed to address what were seen as the main problems facing Hungary: high and increasing hard cur-rency debt, the slow development of hard currency exports to the West, technological backwardness, continuing shortage in some markets, and eco-nomic stagnation, the latter resulting from a half-hearted attempt to apply macroeconomic policy to restrain demand. Indeed some measures actually contributed to the problems. In particular the government's insistence on allowing living standards (consumption) to rise, albeit more slowly, during most of the 1980s required a decline in investment and still resulted in adverse hard currency balances. Similarly, the failure to impose financial discipline on enterprises (i.e. the maintenance of what Kornai calls the 'soft budget constraint') permitted inefficient firms not only to survive, but in some cases even to expand, and undoubtedly slowed down much-needed structural change.

Fortunately, in the mid- and late 1980s, further measures were introduced which, while not especially effective in themselves, laid the foundations for real 'marketization' of the economy in the early 1990s. These included a banking reform, the introduction of a bond market and initial preparations for a stock market, decentralization of foreign trading rights, liberalization of imports and domestic prices, tax reform (personal income tax and the VAT), decentralization of enterprise management and important legal reforms (bankruptcy law, enterprise law). Most of these measures applied to the whole economy, but they were intended to have particular significance for industry, which was widely recognized to be functioning badly in many branches.

The banking reform of 1986 had the aim of separating commercial bank functions from those of the central bank (the latter's functions including monetary policy, financing the government, and managing both foreign exchange reserves and the exchange rate). Thus the Hungarian National Bank remained as the central bank, but five new banks were hived off from it, to become the new second-tier, commercial banks. Initially, enterprise accounts were assigned to particular banks, but after a year they were allowed to shift their accounts and the banks were allowed to compete for business. In addition to these banks, several other new banks emerged: some were joint ventures with Western banks, others were specialized, small banks to promote particular sorts of enterprise involving the introduction of new technology. In practice competition among the banks was limited because the small banks were often merely administering funds supplied by the ministries, while the larger ones were constrained to go on lending to poorly performing enterprises (to avoid bankruptcy). Nevertheless, the institutional framework for a modern, competitive credit system based mainly on profitability is now established in Hungary (Bácskai, 1989).

The bond market started in 1982, but it remains small in terms of the share of investment finance that it raises. Some bonds are only issued for purchase by enterprises, while others, offering lower interest rates, can be bought by the general population. More recently preparations began for a stock market, as a result of the reform of enterprise law referred to below. This started operation in 1990. Again, these are important institutional changes, although their significance will depend on how the government finances its operations in the future, and on the rapidity of privatization (see next section). So far the markets for financial securities have been very thin.

Step by cautious step, Hungary's previous leaders allowed more organizations to conduct foreign trade independently, so that the formal state monopoly over foreign trade became decreasingly relevant. Imports were gradually liberalized so that by the end of the 1980s over 40 per cent of the volume of hard currency imports was in commodity groups no longer subject to controls; this proportion rose considerably further in 1990 and was expected to exceed 80 per cent by 1991. As this liberalization was taking place, the so called 'competitive' price system was abandoned and prices, too, were gradually liberalized (although on the remaining constraints: see Swaan, 1989).

The year 1988 began with a tax reform intended to bring Hungary's tax structure more into line with the systems more usual in Western countries. Thus a VAT system was introduced, as was a personal income tax system. On the former, the new structure allowed for four standard rates of tax: zero, 6 per cent, 11 per cent and 22 per cent (and higher rates for some 'luxury' items), and provided an opportunity to remove or reduce the extent of differentiated taxes applied to production. However, a wide range of 'special' taxes and subsidies remains in the tax structure, most of which are gradually being reduced in line with the government's plans.

As regards the personal income tax, since the state both planned production and, to a large extent determined incomes, there was no need for a comprehensive income tax under Hungary's traditional planning system, or even in the years following the 1968 reforms. Only certain high incomes earned outside the socialist sector were taxed at that time, and even there one has to question the extent to which the incomes in question were effectively taxed. Thus the introduction of income tax in 1988 was a major innovation. The new system taxes individuals (rather than couples, as in the UK up to April 1990), includes all sources of income (although there is a separate arrangement for interest income, taxed at a flat rate of 20 per cent), and is quite steeply progressive with a rate structure ranging from zero on low incomes, through various intermediate bands, up to a top rate of 56 per cent (in 1989) (Newbery, 1990). For earnings from the socialist sector, wages were 'grossed up' so that for most people after-tax income was little changed; this obviously raised the cost of labour to enterprises which, given the general shortage of labour, was not unwelcome from an efficiency point of view. It also changed the relative returns of second economy and 'official' work, since wages for the former were not 'grossed up' in the same way.

In the mid-1980s an important reform of enterprise management structures took place across the whole economy. This established enterprise councils in most enterprises (excluding some of the largest, concerned with defence-related production or production for major CMEA orders; these remained under ministerial supervision), initiating an important process of decentralization, and distancing enterprise activities from ministerial influence. The councils had the responsibility to determine and approve enterprise business plans, and to supervise the work of the enterprise director. In small and medium enterprises, the councils could also appoint the director and determine the terms and conditions of his or her employment. In larger enterprises, it was more common for the ministry itself to propose candidates for the post of director, which the enterprise council could accept or reject.

Around the same time there was a new bankruptcy law which sought to put pressure on ailing firms to reorganize themselves or go into liquidation; in the event, however, the authorities were unwilling to allow major businesses to go under, confirming the continuing inter-penetration of economic (business) and political considerations in Hungary. But the existence and strength of business pressures resisting these traditional links became clear after the passage of the 1988 enterprise law.

5. PROBLEMS OF TRANSITION TO A MARKET-TYPE ECONOMY

The reforms outlined above amount to a very extensive list, but they remained unable to transform the Hungarian economy largely because property rights were unchanged, the authorities proved unwilling to enforce market-type disciplines, and because political considerations overrode sound economic arguments far too often. Thus the political changes of 1989–90, which have resulted in the end of the communist monopoly of power and the election of Hungary's first non-communist government for over 40 years, provide an opportunity for much more substantial change, with marketization, structural change and privatization all very high on the policy agenda.

It is insufficient merely to create new institutional forms; they must be made to work in specific ways if Hungary's economic performance is to improve at all rapidly. This is evident in the case of industry, since decades of poor investment decisions (sometimes influenced by external factors such as the requirement to trade with the Soviet Union in certain products) have resulted in an industry which is badly structured, mostly of a relatively low technological level, and not strongly orientated towards successful and rapidly expanding trade in hard currencies. Thus a central priority for industry must be to devise suitable mechanisms and institutions to generate improved investment decisions to enable the economy to move towards a better, more competitive structure as rapidly as possible. This is partly a matter of reforming the financial system, which was referred to in the last section, but mainly a question of making it fulfil its tasks effectively: that is, the tasks of project selection, rapid correction of previous errors (if necessary through bankruptcy and/or management changes), and the accumulation of funds for investment. Up to the present, none of these has been done well.

However, measures taken by the outgoing communist government, as well as the early measures of the new coalition government led by the Hungarian Democratic Forum, indicate that there is a will to address the problems very seriously. At the microeconomic level, the main point is to get markets functioning well through liberalization and measures to stimulate competition, and also to push privatization as rapidly as possible. The on-going liberalization involves the gradual relaxation of direct controls over imports (licensing), relaxation or removal of remaining price controls and constraints on trade. It will also involve, at some stage, making the Forint convertible, although the timing and precise form of this is not yet clear, and is still hotly debated within Hungary, both within the new government and among academic experts.

In 1989, using some of the provisions of the 1988 enterprise law,[10] some companies had already started to privatize themselves. To do so, they had to take advantage of the mid-1980s devolution of power to enterprise councils which was deemed also to have devolved property rights over enterprise assets to the enterprises themselves. Hence firms could and did seek new owners, to whom they sold shares in the business. As one can imagine, such a decentralized approach to privatization (so called 'wild' privatization) was open to serious abuse, since there was no control over the valuation placed on the enterprise's assets or over the identity of the new owners (who could include some of the managers); nor did the state receive any income from the sale of a company corresponding to its accumulated investment over the years.

Towards the end of 1989 the public outcry over these arrangements forced the parliament to act. It did so by establishing a State Property Agency to supervise the privatization process. The Agency holds and manages government shareholdings, is deemed to be the effective 'owner' of all state assets (this was regarded as a form of 're-nationalization'), and establishes the rules of the game for privatization. In particular, valuation is compulsory and can be vetoed by the Agency if considered too low, and much of the revenue from privatization must be channelled to the state budget. The budget also gains from a capital charge related to the assets contributed by the state in those enterprises not yet privatized. Since this is quite properly regarded as a form of public dividend, once an enterprise is privatized it no longer has to pay this charge; instead, however, it would be expected to pay dividends to the new shareholders. In practice most firms will still privatize themselves under the new arrangements, but in an environment where the procedures are much more effectively defined and enforced than in 1989.

On specific goals, there has been some discussion about sectors which may or may not be privatized. For instance, some of the commercial banks are likely to remain in state hands (at least for a time) and the state will retain a majority stake in insurance companies, some of the mass media (e.g. the TV), and national resources such as mining (much of which is, in any case, loss-making). The government initially announced a target of 70 per cent of industry to be privatized within 5 years, with the process expected to accelerate rapidly from late 1990 onwards. In services, about 40,000 small firms, mainly supplying services to the population and often organized as cooperatives or state enterprises, are to be privatized very rapidly; this is the so-called 'pre-privatization' in Hungary. After months of hesitation, the government announced in late 1990 a three-year privatization programme envisaging the privatization of about half the state sector, including all small businesses (such as shops). This programme is expected to accelerate rapidly in 1991 (Grosfeld and Hare, 1991).

To support the restructuring of the economy, the 1986 bankruptcy law was being invoked in autumn 1990 against a number of large enterprises and by the end of the year agreement had been reached on a much needed strengthening of the law. Initially, there were plans to force about 40 companies into bankruptcy, but the Ministry of Industry and Trade is currently targeting only seven, of which only two are large enterprises. The financial position of all enterprises under the ministry has been reviewed, and at least 50 (out of over 600) have very high outstanding debts and are currently making losses. The seven targeted enterprises are all judged to have a hopeless market position, and liabilities already in excess of assets; others with better longer-term prospects may be helped. The overall aim here, obviously, is to convince enterprise managers that they can no longer rely on state subsidies to keep them in business. At the same time the ministry would like other creditors to use their legal powers to force other loss-making firms to close; it remains to be seen how much this actually happens, although the new bankruptcy law will help.

In the field of macroeconomic policy, the present situation in Hungary and the likely impact of policy on industry are both rather complex. According to ERI (1990), industrial output should have declined by 4–5 per cent in 1990, largely due to the fall in rouble exports and an accompanying decline in investment. There was a roughly 3–4 per cent decline in real incomes in 1990, and over 5 per cent more is expected in 1991. This is a far less dramatic decline in living standards than experienced in Poland, but could still pose a political threat to the government. For the economy as a whole, unemployment was rising, with those claiming benefit reaching about 1 per cent of the labour force by the end of 1990 (i.e. just over 50,000 workers) and many others actively seeking new jobs.

Inflation in consumer prices was almost 30 per cent in 1990 (and was expected to be nearer 40 per cent in 1991), creating strong pressure for high wage settlements. A good deal of this inflation results from the government's programme to cut subsidies and reduce the government deficit, in line with its agreement with the IMF. The same agreement also envisaged that domestic demand will be restrained to permit about 4 per cent of the GDP to be used to service outstanding debt and reach the international payments position desired by the IMF. Fortunately, as indicated above, hard currency trade in 1990 developed more strongly than expected, as firms managed to shift some rouble exports into the Western markets. Nevertheless, it is clear that the servicing of hard currency debt remains a serious burden on the Hungarian economy at present, and will be for the foreseeable future.

Given all the changes going on in Hungarian industry in the early 1990s, what are its medium- and longer-term prospects? In making a judgement about this, I shall assume that all CMEA trade takes place in hard currencies by the start of 1991, and that Hungary is on course to join the European Community by the late 1990s. Even with these assumptions, the short-term prospects for Hungarian industry are clearly poor, with several branches having to decline sharply or even close down altogether, with corresponding increases in unemployment and derelict industrial sites. On the other hand, some branches, including some like food processing which are currently not very profitable or efficient, have enormous potential in the European market. With better design, packaging and marketing, and the removal of EC restrictions on Hungary's exports of food products, parts of the sector could grow very rapidly. Similarly, Hungary has great strength in parts of engineering; again, better design, management and marketing could enable the country to carve out significant markets in the West within a few years. Hence over a period of five years or more, I would take a rather favourable view of Hungary's prospects, provided that certain conditions are satisfied.

These conditions include the external ones already mentioned, to do with access to EC markets on suitable terms. But I would also add conditions to do with Hungary's internal political stability, and the continued commitment of the government to push through the reform programme, in order to ensure that firms and other important economic agents are convinced that the marketization process will not be abandoned, and hence change their economic behaviour to take advantage of the new situation (rather than continuing to resist change, as so often in the past). On the question of political stability, it must be said that the transition from one party state to a democratic political system proceeded remarkably smoothly in 1989 and 1990. However, the new system obviously needs some time to consolidate itself and gain confidence. No-one can yet be quite sure whether it will succeed, or whether Hungary's current economic problems and the complexity of the transformation process will prove to be overwhelming.

In this context, Western countries can play a very valuable, confidence-building role. At EC level, or through actions by individual governments, various forms of aid can be supplied to the new government in Hungary to support desirable economic reforms. Individual Western firms are already demonstrating some commitment to the 'new' Hungary by entering into joint venture agreements and other forms of economic association with Hungarian firms. So far, as indicated above, the amounts of capital involved have not been large, but there is no doubt that an expansion of this sort of activity can quickly change the climate within which business is conducted in Hungary, and hence increase the chance that the whole reform package might succeed. Let us hope that this is what happens.

ACKNOWLEDGEMENTS

I am grateful to the editor of this volume for helpful comments and suggestions which enabled me to improve this chapter considerably; Anna Canning also provided some much appreciated research assistance. Remaining errors and omissions are my own.

NOTES

1. For a detailed analysis of the background to Hungary's postwar economic development, and analysis of the main events and trends, see Berend and Ránki (1985), Pető and Szakács (1985), and Berend (1990).
2. The number of industrial branch ministries varied from time to time. Thus after 1968 there were three (concerned with heavy industry, light industry, and metallurgy and engineering), but at the beginning of 1981 these were merged into a single industry ministry (Hare, 1983). In addition, the food industry is supervised by the ministry of agriculture.
3. The most important functional ministry is the ministry of finance; but there are also the ministries of domestic and foreign trade, recently merged to form a single trade ministry. There was also a ministry of labour, but this became an office for labour and wages in the early 1980s, only to return to ministry status at the end of the decade.
4. These agencies include the planning office (currently being incorporated into the ministry of finance), the price office (likely to become an agency concerned with monopoly and competition), the national office for technical development. During the 1980s it also became increasingly important to recognize the role of the Hungarian National Bank in economic management.
5. Thus in 1988 Hungarian exports amounted to about 37.6 per cent of GDP, and its imports came to 34.8 per cent. Of the total trade (exports plus imports), about 42.1 per cent was conducted in transferable roubles and the remaining 57.9 per cent in convertible currencies (including 16.1 per cent of Hungary's trade with socialist countries). Source: *Statistical Yearbook 1988* (in Hungarian), Budapest: KSH, 1989, various pages.

6. Not surprisingly, in all the socialist countries the use of profit in this way was regarded with great suspicion by traditional Marxists. However, the limitations of more narrowly-based indicators of enterprise activity, such as costs and gross output, were increasingly recognized, especially in Hungary, after 1956, where dogma was less entrenched. For a detailed analysis of the increasing role of profit in Eastern Europe and bureaucratic efforts to undermine it, see Asselain (1984).
7. Nevertheless, it is generally accepted that the reform did give rise to improvements in the quality and range of consumer goods available in Hungary. It also undoubtedly improved the economy's flexibility, an important factor, especially in hard currency export markets. However, it did not stimulate any dramatic improvement either in innovative performance or in the rate of productivity growth in Hungary.
8. It should be noted here that both the oil crises of 1973 and 1979 imposed direct costs on Hungary, though with some delay because of the under-pricing of Soviet oil after 1973 and again after 1979. During the 1970s, Hungary's terms of trade worsened by about 15–20 per cent which, for given import volumes, required the volume of exports to rise by a corresponding percentage merely to maintain a given trade balance, let alone to improve it.
9. There were also some changes in the central administration, notably the merger of three branch ministries noted earlier. For details of the 1979–80 reforms, see Hare (1983).
10. Act VI of 1988, which came into effect on 1 January 1989. This Act provided for joint stock companies, limited liability companies and various forms of economic association. Other related legislation introduced in 1988 and 1989 facilitated the transformation of existing state enterprises into one of the new forms, as a step on the way to privatization.

REFERENCES

Antal, L. (1985) *Gazdaságirányitási és Pénzügyi Rendszerünk a Reform Utján*, Budapest: Közgazdasági és Jogi Könyvkiadó.

Asselain, J.-C. (1984) *Planning and Profits in Socialist Economies*, London: Routledge and Kegan Paul.

Bácskai, T. (1989) 'The reorganization of the banking system in Hungary', in C. Kessides, T. King, M. Nuti and C. Sokil (eds), *Financial Reform in Socialist Economies*, Washington, D.C.: The World Bank.

Balázs, K., Hare, P. and Oakey, R. (1990) 'The management of R&D in Hungary at the end of the 1990s', *Soviet Studies*, vol. 42, no. 4.

Bauer, T. (1975) in *Közgazdasági Szemle*, vol. 22, no. 6.

Berend, I. (1990) *The Hungarian Economic Reforms 1953–1988*, Cambridge: CUP.

Berend, I. and Ránki Gy. (1985) *The Hungarian Economy in the Twentieth Century*, London: Croom Helm.

Brada, J. and Dobozi, I. (eds) (1990) *Money, Incentives and Efficiency in the Hungarian Economic Reform*, Armonk, NY: M.E. Sharpe.

Davis, C. and Charemza, W. (1989) *Models of Disequilibrium and Shortage in Centrally Planned Economies*, London: Chapman and Hall.

ERI (1990) *Economic Trends in Hungary 1990*, Budapest: Economic Research Institute.

Falus-Szikra, K. (1985) *The System of Incomes and Incentives in Hungary*, Budapest: Akademiai Kiado.

Galasi, P. and Sziráczki, Gy. (1985) *Labour Market and Second Economy in Hungary*, Frankfurt: Campus Verlag.

Granick, D. (1975) *Enterprise Guidance in Eastern Europe*, Princeton, NJ: Princeton University Press.

Grosfeld, I and Hare, P. (1991) 'Privatisation in Hungary, Poland and Czechoslovakia', paper prepared for the PHARE programme, Commission of the European Communities (DGII), *European Economy* (July).

Hare, P. (1976) 'Industrial prices in Hungary', *Soviet Studies*, vol. 28, nos 2 and 3.

Hare, P. (1983) 'The beginnings of institutional reform in Hungary', *Soviet Studies*, vol. 35, no. 3.

Hare, P. (1987) 'Economic reform in Eastern Europe', *Journal of Economic Surveys*, vol. 1, no. 1.

Hare, P. (1990) 'Reform of enterprise regulation in Hungary – from 'tutelage' to market', paper prepared for the PHARE programme, Commission of the European Communities (DGII), *European Economy*, March.

Hare, P., Radice, H. and Swain, N. (eds) (1981) *Hungary: A Decade of Economic Reform*, London: Allen and Unwin.

Hare, P., Révész, T. and Zalai, E. (1990) 'Trade distortions in the Hungarian economy', paper prepared for the PHARE programme, Commission of the European Communities (DGII), mimeo.

Kornai, J. (1959) *Overcentralisation in Economic Administration*, Oxford: OUP.

Kornai, J. (1980) *The Economics of Shortage*, Amsterdam: North Holland.

Marer, P. (1986) *East–West Technology Transfer: Study of Hungary 1968–1984*, Paris: OECD.

Newbery, D. (1990) 'Tax reform, industrial restructuring and trade liberalisation in Hungary', paper prepared for the PHARE programme, Commission of the European Communities (DGII), *European Economy*, March.

Pető, I. and Szakács, S. (1985) *A Hazai Gazdaság Négy Évtizedének Története, 1945–1985*, vol. 1, Budapest: Közgazdasági és Jogi Könyvkiadó.

Portes, R. (1989) 'The theory and measurement of macroeconomic disequilibrium and shortage in centrally planned economies', in Davis and Charemza (1989).

Swaan, W. (1989) 'Price regulation in Hungary: indirect but comprehensive bureaucratic control', *Comparative Economic Studies*, vol. 31, no. 4.

Swain, N. (1986) *Collective Farms which Work?*, Cambridge: CUP.

Wienert, H. and Slater, J. (1986) *East–West Technology Transfer: The Trade and Economic Aspects*, Paris: OECD.

9   Mongolia
Michael Kaser

1.   THE VOLTE-FACE OF 1990

The Asian states with the longest experience of a communist political monopoly are the Union and Autonomous Republics of the USSR and Mongolia. Throughout the territory north and east of China once ruled by Genghis
(Chingis) Khan, communist party exclusivity was established during the
1920s, followed by the command economy. The remainder of the early 13th
century Empire came under the same dispensation by the end of the 1940s
with the attachment of Eastern Europe and of China to the 'Sino-Soviet
bloc'. It was with good reason that Hicks's prototype 'command economy'
was the Mongol Empire (Hicks, 1969, p. 21), but seven centuries then
ensued of economic torpor, the last three under a fatalistic theocracy; it
cannot be denied that the modern command economy transformed Mongolia
in the space of seven decades (Sanders, 1987).

In 1990, nevertheless, Mongolia became the first Asian communist state
to abandon the 'mono-archy' (Brus and Laski, 1989, p. 39) of a centralized
fusing of political and economic power. A mere seven months elapsed between the first anti-government demonstrations of December 1989 and the
free elections of July 1990 and the same haste was evident when Dambiyn
Dorligjav, a deputy prime minister in the new administration, said on 2
November 1990 that 'We have no time to lose to transfer to a market
economy'.

The systemic turnaround concurrently taking place in Eastern Europe is
mostly without non-communist participation in the government, but the
Mongolian elections, like those of Albania and Bulgaria, gave a majority to
the ruling Communist Party. The Mongolian People's Revolutionary Party
(MPRP), which took office after those elections, is not yet thoroughly reformist (as the discussion in section 3 of this chapter shows), but in coalition
with the other main parties committed itself to marketization. President
Punsalmaagiyn Ochirbat is on the reform side of the MPRP; the vice-presi-
dent and chairman of the Little Hural is an opposition deputy, the Social
Democrat leader Radnaasümbereliyn Gonchigdorj. Prime Minister Dashiyn
Byambasüren (an economist) is on the same side of the MPRP and has as
deputies representatives of two other parties, namely Davaadorjiyn Ganbold
of the National Progress Party (which campaigned on a programme of a free

enterprise market economy with a mixture of public and private ownership) as his first deputy, and Dambiyn Dorligjav of the Mongolian Democratic Party; Choyjilsurengiyn Purevdorj of the MPRP is a third deputy premier. Individual ministers will patently change with the passage of time and the evolution of policies, but coalition government has replaced the autocracy of the past.

Institutionally, consensus has been fostered by changes in both legislature and executive. The Great Hural (now 430 seats), until 1990 usually convened once a year and then only for short sessions to rubber-stamp the government's propositions, has now been opened to multi-party elections, but will continue to have few sessions (only four in its five-year life). The crucial change is that it appoints a Little Hural (a newly-revived chamber) of 50 members (plus chairman, vice-chairman and secretary) selected by proportional representation on the votes cast in the general election, which is in much longer session (two sessions a year of up to 80 days each). In turn the Little Hural appoints a government of 16 members, the prime minister, his three deputies, 11 ministers and a State Committee chairman. The formal parallels with the contemporary USSR (Congress of People's Deputies, Supreme Soviet and Cabinet of Ministers) are obvious, but the government, which took office in September 1990, trimmed the number of economic ministries (which, incidentally, Mikhail Gorbachev signally failed to do until forced by the abortive coup of August 1991), established two liaison committees for the president (a Civil Committee to keep contact with social and political organizations and a Scholarly Committee for links with academics and their institutes). The Great Hural has a standing commission on environmental protection, and the Little Hural a standing committee on women, children and young people. A further demolition of 'mono-archy' was the decontrol of religion. From the persecution of the 1930s until 1990, only a single place of worship was open, the Buddhist monastery of Gandan in the capital Ulaanbaatar (Ulan Bator). Laicized lamas have been encouraged to return to clerical life, desecrated monasteries are being restored and, symbolically, religious service has restarted at Erdene Dzuu, the first monastic settlement on the state's territory, and elsewhere.

2. MONGOLIAN *PERESTROIKA* (*ÖÖRCHLÖN SHINECHLELT*) 1984–89

Sudden and deep-seated as were the political and social changes, the economic transformation justifies the same adjectives, but was preceded by a six-year attempt by the MPRP to liberalize the economy while protecting a centralist polity. Political life between 1939 and 1984 (a pro-China period,

1954–58 apart) had been dominated by two successive leaders, Horloogiyn Choybalsan (until his death in 1952) and Yumjaagiyn Tsedenbal (until his dismissal in August 1984), whose power and attitude to its exercise were Stalinist. The party leader and (from December 1984) premier who followed, Jambyn Batmonh and Dumaagiyn Sodnom respectively, were in the mould of Andropov or Gorbachev on becoming party leader in the USSR, i.e. prepared for economic reform 'from above' without releasing free market forces or political dissonance. In criticism of the state of the economy, the MPRP Central Committee Plenum of December 1984 can be likened to those of the CPSU in June 1983 (Kaser, 1984, pp. 80–3) and of April 1985 (Åslund, 1989, pp. 27–8 and p. 178) and the policies of apolitical reform conformed, though more modestly, to Soviet *perestroika*.

Performance objectives were the first to be changed (on food and agriculture in 1986 and on industrial location in 1987), but were soon paralleled by a Commission for the Improvement of Management and the Economic Mechanism, established in 1986 and reporting to the MPRP Central Committee in June 1987 (Kaser, 1991, p. 100). A British economist, having interviewed senior members of the Mongolian government, listed seven microeconomic measures that had by then been introduced within the 'renovation programme' (Faber, 1990, p. 422). Three were financial – 'the partial introduction of market mechanisms as a guide to a better, more sensitive system of pricing'; cost accounting to value output; and self-finance on the basis of covering such costs. Two were managerial, restructuring incentives and modern training in techniques. The other two policies sought to engender competition with the traditional state enterprise, to allow small family and cooperative businesses and joint ventures with foreign firms. But on the very eve of the *volte face*, the MPRP Central Committee in March 1990 was still claiming as its objective 'a state controlled market economy' (Faber, 1990, p. 427).

The primary enactment of the 'regulated market' period was the Law on the State Enterprise of November 1988, taking effect on 1 January 1989. It allowed the 'labour collective' of each state enterprise greater latitude in negotiating and implementing its planned objectives. Although it supposedly made the collective 'the real master of the land, buildings, machinery, equipment, livestock and other property' on its premises and was termed 'self-management' (for a staff assembly elected the director and a management council, of which at least 60 per cent had to be workers), an annual plan (within a quinquennial and even 10- and 20-year target) remained under the authority of the supervising ministry. The plan indicators which remained for each state enterprise comprised 'realized production taking into account commercially-negotiated contracts', net value-added, profits and specific goals for the quality of goods and services supplied. Autonomous initiative at the microeconomic level was encouraged by devolution within an enterprise to lower sub-divisions ('workshop, department or other primary unit') and by 'self-finance' which implied, in addition to the standard *khozraschet* of the Soviet model, the funding of investment from ploughed-back profit and bank loans. Exactly as under Soviet *perestroika*, the reformed practice was termed 'full' *khozraschet*.

Explicitly to cap any wage-push inflationary pressure, the 1988 Law prescribed that 'the remuneration of staff strictly correspond to the final result and quality of its labour', the supervising ministry establishing the numbers employable and the aggregate wage fund. Within the numbers and payment limits, management could select the wage system (time or piece-rates) and the tariff. Management could only choose among approved tariffs, which were based on a minimum wage (260 tugriks per month, applicable to the food and light industries) and a six-grade scale (each grade paying 15 per cent more than that below) from which 24 tariff-skill manuals were drawn, embracing over 1 700 recognized occupations and qualifications.

Again on the *perestroika* model, enterprises were required to fulfil 'state orders', which the Ministry of External Economic Relations and Supply formulated (under the aegis of the State Planning and Economic Committee) on the basis of the state's requirements for its own 'funds' and for export, and for investment to be executed on centralized finance (including social capital). The new ministry, set up in late 1987 and run by the future president Punsalmaagiyn Ochirbat, ended a series of administrative peregrinations. A central supply system was only founded in Mongolia in 1973. Until 1980 the State Supply Committee was under the Planning Committee; it then became an independent entity directly under the Council of Ministers until, joined by the State Committee on Foreign Economic Relations and the Ministry of Foreign Trade, it became part of the new ministry.

When it began operations the ministry was dealing with some 100,000 product-categories and with over 10,000 state enterprises, farms, building sites and scientific and cultural institutions with a turnover of 5.0 billion tugriks. In its first year it drew up approximately 500 material balances (such as steel products, energy, electrical equipment, building materials and chemicals) and oversaw the distribution of key equipment such as motor vehicles, aircraft and civil engineering plant. But while previous practice was thus maintained, the ministry launched free wholesale trade for a wide range of producers' goods. Until then such decontrolled trade had been a mere 2 per cent of goods supplied, but in late 1987 a central warehouse was established in Ulaanbaatar with an initial list of 700 customer enterprises.

Together, the decentralization to enterprises and the initiation of whole-sale trade required some liberalization of producers' prices. At the time of the reform more than 360,000 wholesale prices were in force, nearly all of which were centrally established. Last revised in 1974, these price lists 'had become somewhat outdated' as the Chairman of the State Committee on Prices and Standards Erdeniyn Byambajav declared, when, in mid-1987, he reviewed the new lists of 1 January 1986. The revision notably envisaged regular review in the light of changes in world prices, which would constitute the base for a uniform wholesale price for exportables and for import substitutes as well as for goods actually transacted in foreign trade. For non-traded goods and services the fixed price was the average branch cost including a charge for capital. With the opening of free wholesale trade and expectations of a profit motive among state enterprises, some decontrol was permitted from 1988, but the 'soft budget constraint' persisted. The budget deficit was almost 19 per cent of GDP in 1986–88 and was cut only to 16.4 per cent in 1989 (IMF, 1991, p. 132). There was much discussion on the break-up of the State Bank, but the 'monobank system' was retained during the *perestroika* period.

The 52 state farms were subject to the same regulations as other state enterprises, but the 255 cooperative-herding associations and their 35 inter-association enterprises were, as in the USSR, bound by procurement quotas instead of by formal plan targets. State prices for procurements were previously being raised (doubling between 1970 and 1985) and from 1986 a 50 per cent premium became payable in any year in which the farm's deliveries exceeded the average of the preceding five years. This was also Soviet *perestroika* practice, as was relaxation of constraints on household production within state and cooperative farms. In the Mongolian case permissible private holdings of livestock were increased from 50 to 75 in standard terrain areas and from 75 to 100 animals in difficult terrain areas.

Finally, among domestic production units, industrial and craft cooperatives were fostered anew by Laws on Labour Cooperatives (1988) and on Cooperation (1989). Tolerated until 1972, when they produced nearly a fifth of gross industrial output, they were then nationalized, the few remaining producing just under 3 per cent of output. The *perestroika* policy revived them and by 1 September 1988 7 000 members were working in 514 cooperatives.

The second major constituent of the *perestroika* measures widened access to the external market and opened Mongolia to Western partners in joint ventures. The Law on the State Enterprise authorised state enterprises to transact directly abroad without compulsory recourse, as before, to the relevant agency of the foreign-trade monopoly: the first firms to be accorded such rights were in wool and leather goods and in electronics. Although many joint enterprises had been established with partners in CMEA countries, legislation on the admission of Western equity was not considered until the *perestroika* period, during which two joint ventures with Western companies were formed prior to the passage of a Law on Foreign Investment in March

1990. Early joint ventures with a UK partner were in wind energy and in telecommunications. Although 100 per cent foreign ownership was not thereby permitted, no upper limit was placed on the external holding, which, furthermore, was guaranteed not to be subsequently nationalized. After payment of domestic taxes (a maximum of 40 per cent on profits but only after a tax holiday of three years, and income tax on employee remuneration) neither tax nor limits were to be imposed on profit or salary repatriation. Some areas of activity could be excluded from the operation of a joint venture and priority was to be given to investment in exportables or import-substitutes, high-technology goods and services and the processing of Mongolian minerals and farm produce, including the conduct of geological survey (for only 4 per cent of Mongolian territory has so far been surveyed on a scale of 200,000 : 1 or 100,000 : 1). The eventual 'internal convertibility' of the tugrik (that is decontrol of the external current account) was posed as an aim and a start was made towards a more realistic rate by separating non-commercial transactions at 20 tugriks to the dollar from 1986, while the commercial rate remained at 3 tugriks. Reform measures had a stimulative effect and the current account deficit fell from its 1986 peak of 36 per cent of GDP to 24 per cent in 1989; trade with convertible-currency partners increased 10-fold between 1985 and 1989 to $52 million (IMF, 1991, p. 132).

3. MEASURES IN MARKETIZATION AND PRIVATIZATION

By the time this chapter reached its final version (May 1991), there had been three turning points in the politics of economic liberalization, namely Mongolia's demonopolized elections in July 1990, the Extraordinary Congress of the MPRP in April 1990 and the Twentieth Congress of the MPRP in February 1991. Public unrest, broadly manifest from December 1989 and undoubtedly influenced by the fall of communist regimes in Eastern Europe, compelled the MPRP to abandon its formal monopoly of political action (the 'leading role' of the party was renounced in March 1990) and to authorize a general election. Although the MPRP gained a clear majority of seats in the Great Hural and its derivative chamber, the Little Hural, one of the first of the latter's acts was to pass a Law for Citizens, protecting basic civil rights.

The Extraordinary Congress elected a new Chairman (Gombojavyn Ochirbat) and adopted a 'Resolution on Basic Policy Directives of the MPRP for Solving the Immediate Tasks Confronting the Nation' which, *inter alia*, called for 'the bold introduction of a state-coordinated market economy, allowing the functioning of various forms of property and providing economic and legal guarantees for industrial and commercial enterprises to develop, within an open economy, direct relations with foreign corporations and organizations'. The Twentieth Congress of the MPRP was the battleground for three factions (conservatives, centrists and reformers), of which the latter were the most numerous but not constituting a majority. The two principal outcomes reflected that pattern. The revised Party Programme omitted Marxism–Leninism as the ideology. Gombojavyn Ochirbat explained in his opening address that 'the names of Marx and Lenin have not been included in the new platform because it has become obvious that the ideology that ruled for decades is not up-to-date in many aspects today ... The MPRP has reached a turning point in its history. The party now allows plurality of views instead of one accepted form of theoretical dogmatism'. He was, however, himself seen as conservative, and was replaced as chairman at the congress by a centrist, Büdragchaagiyn Dash-Yondon. The latter's acceptance speech assured the congress 'that there would be no turning back towards economic and political conservatism' and that it was 'important to transfer towards a market economy'.

That radical path was made manifest in November 1990 by a resolution of the Little Hural on privatization and on a programme of transition to a market economy to begin on 1 January 1991. With the exception of certain key branches, all state enterprises will be converted to joint stock corporations and equity distributed so that each resident Mongolian citizen (adult or child) receives an equal share. The state intends to retain in its own hands existing enterprises in energy, mining, garment-making, meat processing and confectionery, but in February 1991 the Little Hural adopted a law allowing joint ventures to operate in oil exploration. A stock exchange will be set up in each province (*aimag*), but the State Bank would also buy and sell shares. Title to some arable land on state farms would be included in the distribution, but grazing will revert to traditional common lands. Private enterprises were being rapidly set up, some quite large: Mongol Agro, processing sheepskins, has a capital of 1.7 million tugriks, and competitors have emerged to the state tourist agency Juulchin. Privatization of state property began with an auction of shops in Ulanbaatar in May 1991.

In the interim until wider denationalization, the powers of industrial ministries over state enterprises were restricted, only four economic ministries being retained (for National Economic Development, Trade and Industry, Energy, and Finance); overall in September 1990 the number of ministries was cut from 26 down to 12. In August 1990 the State Bank monopoly was terminated and two commercial banks (Mongol Daatgal Bank and Mongol Horshoo Bank) were established the next month.

The second major measure was directed towards reducing the monetary overhang. On 1 January wholesale prices were adjusted closer to world-market relativities and at a higher overall level: coal rose 74 per cent and electricity 94 per cent. On 15 January fixed retail prices were approximately doubled and controls on others were changed to maxima. The effect was of course to halve the value of outstanding cash balances. Deposits in the Savings Banks up to 10,000 tugriks per depositor (equivalent to 18 months average wage) were doubled, and balances in excess of that sum had 10,000 tugriks added to them. In compensation for the price rises, all wages and salaries in the public service and in state enterprises, as well as social security benefits, were simultaneously doubled. Cooperative herdsmen were compensated by a rise in state purchase prices and by the inevitable increase (not necessarily a doubling) of the prices at which they sold their private produce. Members of industrial cooperatives and the few individual proprietors (now to be encouraged) would similarly obtain higher prices on their sales. The retail prices of many necessities remained controlled, but by the end of 1991 80 per cent of retail prices will be liberalized. Further reductions of the inflationary gap are to be expected from cutting the budget deficit and by selling state-owned housing. The latter policy conforms to a broader objective of encouraging private home ownership in towns. In rural areas the traditional felt tent or *ger* has, of course, always been household property.

The third set of measures activated the exchange rate and tariffs as policy instruments. In July 1990 the tugrik commercial rate was devalued from 3 to 5.63 to the dollar and in January 1991 the non-commercial rate was lowered from 20 to 40 to the dollar. Currency auctions (made possible by the allowance of retention quotas to exporters) began in August 1990, the rate then and in subsequent months fluctuating around 40 tugriks to the dollar. Customs duties were applied to all imports (not, as previously, only private purchases) from 1 March 1991 .

4. THE ECONOMIC CRISIS OF 1991

Marketization is, however, taking place in circumstances of economic crisis, such as has not been experienced in Mongolia since the 'leftist excesses' of the 1930s. Its root is the disruption arising from the cessation of many supplies from the USSR and the change in intra-CMEA transactions from the transferable rouble and a special pricing convention to convertible currency settlement at world prices.

Even before the CMEA trade practices were terminated on 31 December 1990, CMEA members were reducing their deliveries to Mongolia. Imports in 1989 were 12 per cent below 1986 by volume and 15 per cent by value, whereas exports were slightly up (2 per cent by volume and 1 per cent by value). During 1990 economic dislocation in the USSR further reduced Soviet exports to Mongolia. The pricing and payments changes of 1 January 1991 substantially reduced exports by other European members. Overall, whereas 90 per cent of Mongolia's foreign trade was with CMEA members in 1990 (92 per cent in 1989), only about 75 per cent would be with those partners in 1991, according to the Minister of Trade and Industry Sed-Ochiryn Bayarbaatar (March 1991).

Deliveries from the USSR began to be sharply cut in the latter months of 1990 and a Soviet trade delegation in Ulaanbaatar in October was unable to conclude a trade protocol for 1991. Mongolia continued in the New Year to deliver under contracts previously concluded and for the first time in many years ran a first quarter surplus with the USSR. Not only did Soviet exports diminish but, given the new requirement for hard-currency settlement and the Soviet delay in payments to Western partners, the USSR Vneshekonombank failed to pay (as the first deputy minister of national development Ravdangiyn Tsagaanhuu stated in March). The cut in imports from the USSR was most serious in energy (oil and electricity) and foodstuffs: power cuts became chronic and rice, macaroni, flour, sugar, tea, dried milk, butter and vegetable oil were rationed in Ulaanbaatar, Darhan, the second industrial city, Sühbaatar and Bulgan. Private leisure motoring was prohibited and, from February 1991, *arhi* (Mongolian vodka) was put on ration (of one litre per household per month except in February, when two litres were allowed for the celebration of the Lunar New Year). An emergency programme of imports ($50 m. of food and industrial consumer goods) was started (Sanders, 1991b).

The failure of CMEA members to deliver spare parts for the plant they once installed led to further interruptions in output, especially electricity generation (the deputy minister of Power, Delgerlyn Misha, noted in March 1991 that only 30 per cent of equipment ordered from the USSR in the first quarter of 1991 had been delivered). Hoarding has exacerbated the visible shortages and the 1990 harvest was not fully brought in: just as in the USSR, 'volunteers' (usually despatched from towns to help in harvesting) refused to go in the new political circumstances.

Mongolia began still more actively to seek trade outside the CMEA. China is the prime partner because of its proximity and good transport links. Political relations have improved, partly because the USSR will have withdrawn all its troops from the Sino-Mongolian border by 1992 and also because of special efforts to renew political relations (the minister of defence, Shagalyn Jadambaa, met a Chinese defence ministry delegation in September 1990 – the first such meeting in 29 years, and president Ochirbat visited Beijing in November). Japan is the second in line; its industrial presence was established in the early 1980s when reparations deliveries (belated, for the Japanese invasion was defeated at Halhyn Gol in 1939) re-equipped a cashmere mill, of which 98 per cent of output is sold for convertible currency, mainly to Japanese importers (Sanders, 1991a). The United States is also targeted: President Ochirbat visited Washington in January 1991, securing MFN treatment and technical assistance, and a joint venture with an American firm is being considered to survey Mongolia's oil deposits; an unsophisticated attempt to exploit oil with Soviet equipment was abandoned in the early 1960s. South Korea and the United Kingdom are other partners already into the Mongolian trade.

Mongolia, unlike the USSR and some Eastern European countries, is not saddled with debt to Western banks: the BIS returns for September 1990 in fact showed a surplus in Western reporting banks for Mongolia of assets over indebtedness. The USSR is Mongolia's largest creditor but has postponed its requirement for repayment (of $16 bn according to President Ochirbat in a speech of 20 January 1991) until the year 2000 (as prime minister Byambasüren announced on 11 September 1990). Membership of the IMF, World Bank and the Asian Development Bank from February 1991 will bring capital inflow, but in nothing like the size in relative terms of programmes established by Western governments for East Europe and the USSR. As a non-European state it does not benefit from EC technical assistance or EBRD capital. Bilateral assistance may be under consideration: the UK could effect a major impact by offering a 'know-how' fund of, say, £1.5 million.

The decline in imports has brought both unemployment and a fall in aggregate production. From 36,000 unemployed in April 1991, the expected unemployment by the end of 1991 is 80,000 (or some 16 per cent of employment). The deputy minister of national development, Ravdangiyn Tsagaanhüü, in March 1991, stated that GNP was projected to be only 7.4 billion tugriks ($1.3 billion) in 1991, against 8.4 billion tugriks ($1.4 billion) in 1990. Both are well below the 8.9 billion tugriks for 1988 stated by Tsendiyn Molom, then deputy minister of external economic relations and supply, on 12 November 1989, when estimates in terms of GNP were first officially announced.

From the Eastern Länder of Germany to Vladivostok the road to a free market system is being rendered more difficult by recession and the disruption of trade and payments (see especially Economic Commission for Europe, 1991, chapters 1 and 4). Mongolia is no exception, but it is the poorest of all the former socialist states in systemic transition. The 1991 GNP estimate just cited, for a 2.23 million population, shows a mere $580 GNP per capita. The danger, in Mongolia as elsewhere, is of social unrest which could upset the parallel trends towards democracy and a liberal economy.

NOTE

Material has been drawn from the following: a note on developments written by Mongolian economists for this chapter; Comecon sources (notably its former journal *Ekonomicheskoe sotrudnichestvo stran-chlenov SEV*); press and radio reports and documentation circulated by the Mongolian Embassy in London and the Anglo-Mongolian Society. Comments by Ian Jeffries and Alan Sanders are gratefully acknowledged. A deviation has been made from standard transliteration in the case of familiar usage – tugrik for tögrög.

REFERENCES

Åslund, A. (1989) *Gorbachev's Struggle for Economic Reform*, London: Pinter.
Brus, W. and Laski, K. (1989) *From Marx to the Market: Socialism in Search of an Economic System*, Oxford: Clarendon Press.
Economic Commission for Europe (1991) *Economic Survey of Europe in 1990–1991*, New York: United Nations.
Faber, M. (1990) 'Mongolia: Moves towards perestroika', *Development Policy Review*, vol. 8, no. 4.
Hicks, Sir John (1969) *A Theory of Economic History*, Oxford: Clarendon Press.
IMF (1991) 'Mongolia restructures its economy', *IMF Survey*, 29 April.
Kaser, M. (1984) 'Human betterment in a planned economy – the case of the Soviet Union', in Boulding K. (Ed.) *The Economics of Human Betterment*, London: Macmillan.
Kaser, M. (1991) 'Economic developments', in Akiner, S. (Ed.) *Mongolia Today*, London: Kegan Paul International.
Sanders, A. (1987) *Mongolia: Politics, Economics and Society*, London: Pinter.
Sanders, A. (1991a) 'Mongolia: Shackled to the past', *Far Eastern Economic Review*, 3 January.
Sanders, A. (1991b) 'Mongolia: Iron rations', *Eastern European Newsletter*, 18 February.

10 North Korea

Ian Jeffries

Like the former GDR, North Korea has suffered from the comparisons continually made to a successful capitalist 'twin' (*The Economist* puts North Korea's per capita GNP in the range $900–$1 500, compared with South Korea's $4 000: 10 February 1990, p. 63). It is no coincidence that the GDR had and North Korea still has an ultra conservative leadership and a command economy. Both Germany and Korea were divided after the Second World War, but, unlike East Germany, North Korea was the more industrialized twin. In 1945 the North accounted for 65 per cent of the total Korean production of heavy industry and 31 per cent of light industry (Halliday, 1987, p. 19).

The Korean Workers' Party has been led by 'the great leader' Kim Il Sung since 1948, a president who practises a strong cult of personality and a policy of *chuche* or 'self-reliance'. This policy helped make North Korea into one of the most isolated of the socialist countries. This isolation is increasing with the 'loss' of Eastern Europe and the successful political manoeuvres of South Korea, which now has diplomatic relations with all the Eastern European countries (including the Soviet Union, but excluding Albania). *Chuche* has been defined by Kim Il Sung himself as 'holding fast to the principle of solving for oneself all the problems of the revolution and construction in conformity with the actual conditions at home and mainly by one's own effort ... man, a social being that is independent and creative, is master of everything and decides everything' (quoted in Rhee, 1987, p. 890). The policy downgrades the importance of material incentives, foreign trade and imitating foreign models (although *chuche* is a malleable concept, e.g. material incentives and foreign trade are currently given greater emphasis).

North Korea has reacted predictably to the events in Eastern Europe since the end of 1989. Kim Il Sung, in a 14 March 1990 speech, determined to 'hoist high the banner of the revolution, without any oscillation, against imperialism and in favour of socialism' (quoted by Kie-Young Lee, 1990, p. 8). On the occasion of his being made president for another four years on 24 May 1990, he declared that socialism 'is the main trend of historical progress and this is the only road for mankind to take'.

177

1. PLANNING

North Korea has a rigid command economy, with economic plans containing very detailed output targets for each industrial enterprise (Pak, 1983, p. 214). Rationing is more prevalent than in the traditional Soviet economic system, with the workshop and residential areas used as means of distributing highly subsidized basic commodities such as rice. As regards manpower, moral incentives are stressed and school-leavers are allocated in groups to particular jobs. In 1958 a sort of Chinese-style Great Leap Forward was begun, involving a mass mobilization of people inspired by moral rather than material incentives. In February 1973 the 'Three Revolution Teams' (ideological, technological and cultural) were initiated. Teams of young people were sent to enterprises to encourage workers to greater effort and to teach them new techniques (Rhee, 1987, pp. 899–900). Campaigns and the accompanying exhortations are still a feature of economic decision making, e.g. a materials-saving campaign began in 1986, while a '200-day battle', 20 February–9 September 1988 concentrated on major construction projects in energy, metals and chemicals. Kim Il Sung's new year address for 1990 called for a new 'speed of the 1990s' in production, involving such aims as the speedy completion of large projects (*EIU Country Report,* 1990, no. 1, p. 35), and for emphasis on light industry (Kong Dan Oh, *Asian Survey,* 1990, vol. XXX, no. 1, p. 75).

2. INDUSTRIAL MANAGEMENT

There have been periodic ministerial reorganizations. The late 1950s saw amalgamations, while in the latter half of the 1980s there was a reverse process. In January 1990 the Mining Industry Commission was divided into the Ministry of Coal Industry and the Ministry of Mining Industry, while the previous July saw a new Ministry for Local Industry established.

Since 1961 the 'Taean (Dae-an) Work System' has been in operation (Kang, 1989, pp. 204–5; *EIU Country Report*, 1988, no. 2, pp. 294–5). This was first applied to an electrical machine enterprise. The industrial enterprise is run by a Factory Party Committee rather than an individual manager. The committee normally comprises 25–35 members, with managers, engineering staff and workers equally represented. Its executive board of 6–9 people carries out day-to-day operations, and is dominated by the party secretary and managers. The party secretary's decision is final.

Some modest enterprise reforms were introduced in late 1984, with a greater emphasis on economic accounting, some increased decision-making autonomy and an increased role for material incentives (Kang, 1989, p. 206).

Increased decision-making autonomy includes greater powers to fix bonus rates and other incentives; to decide the share of profits to reinvest; and to allocate manpower, equipment and materials. Material incentives are boosted by the power to devote up to 50 per cent of excess profits to increasing output and welfare and other benefits (*EIU Country Report*, 1985, no. 3, p. 34, and 1986, no. 2, p. 39). The enterprise success indicators include physical production, exports, profits, costs and inputs, but physical indicators have top priority followed by exports (Kang, 1989, p. 206).

Labour compensation consists of the basic wage, bonuses and prizes (Kang, 1989, pp. 206–7; Kie-Young Lee, 1990, p. 4). The basic wage takes account of factors such as job evaluation, length of service and technical ability. Bonuses, paid to work teams, depend on over-fulfilment of plan targets, while prizes can also be paid to individuals. The *EIU Country Report* (1985, no. 3, p. 34) notes a report that, within some enterprises, teams of four to six workers plan their own work schedules and determine their bonus rates.

Kang (1989, p. 202) reports some spread of the 'associated enterprise system', there having been experiments since 1975. The experiments involved linking geographically adjacent and related enterprises in order to save time and transport costs (Kie-Young Lee, 1990, p. 4). The *EIU Country Report* (1986, no. 2, p. 39) describes the 1985 reforms as akin to the former GDR combines, in the sense that enterprises in related areas of activity (e.g. supplier–user) are encouraged to coordinate their operations in a formal manner. The regionally-based complex reports to the provincial party committee, while the vertically integrated complex has a central party committee to answer to (*EIU Country Report*, 1989, no. 4, p. 35). Each enterprise pays a depreciation allowance and a capital charge (Kang, 1989, p. 206). Some enterprises are allowed to export their own products and import the necessary materials with the foreign exchange so earned (Kie-Young Lee, 1990, p. 6).

Rhee (1987, p. 889) reports the August 1984 mass movement to increase basic consumer goods production by teams of part-time workers from locally available inputs such as waste and by-products. According to Lee (1988, p. 1268), small groups of workers in industrial enterprises, in cooperative farms and at home produce basic necessities for direct sale to consumers in markets. The *EIU Country Profile* for 1988–89 (p. 72) notes that provinces are responsible for consumer goods production, receiving no central investment but having to transfer tax revenue.

3.   THE PRIVATE NON-AGRICULTURAL SECTOR

The dominance of state and collective enterprises in manufacturing can be seen in the figures given by Suh (1983, p. 1990) for 1946 and 1956, respectively: 72.4 per cent and 98.7 per cent. In 1985 individuals were allowed to engage in small private handicraft production such as knitting (*EIU Country Report*, 1985, no. 3, p. 34). There are also a few street food and drink vendors for example.

4. DIRECT FOREIGN INVESTMENT

Soviet aid has been substantial. Van Ree (1989, p. 57) estimates that over the period 1957–76 the Soviet Union may have provided, on average, more than 10 per cent of total industrial investment in the form of grants and credits; aid from the socialist countries in total may have brought this figure up to 25 per cent. Despite a policy of 'self-reliance', North Korea decided to modernize its capital stock by purchasing Western technology, machinery, equipment and even whole plants on a grand scale in the early 1970s. In the period 1970–82 80 per cent of imports and 48 per cent of exports were with capitalist countries (quoted in Rhee, 1987, p. 901). A foreign debt of about $2 billion with the West (about $3 billion in total) was run up by 1982 (*EIU Country Profile*, 1987–88, p. 68); by the end of 1987 $2.8 billion was owed to Western countries and $5.27 billion in total (Kie-Young Lee, 1990, p. 3). North Korea defaulted in 1976 and several debt reschedulings and delayed payments for imports have made North Korea a poor credit risk. In August 1987 Western commercial bank creditors declared a formal default (allowing the seizure of North Korean assets in the West, such as gold and property). This has not helped North Korea attract direct foreign investment.

In September 1984 a joint venture law was promulgated in order to attract Western capital, technology and know-how, but with limited success to date. One hundred per cent foreign ownership is now permitted; the first three years constitute a tax holiday with a possible extension; there is a 25 per cent net profit tax (Kie-Young Lee, 1990, p. 6). Harrison (*FEER*, 3 December 1987, p. 8) estimated that 50 were then under way (44 with Japanese-Koreans). Kie-Young Lee (1990, p. 7) thinks that the partners are mostly pro-North Korea businessmen in Japan and Korean residents in the USA; in the first half of 1985 there were almost 70 and by the end of 1987 100. The North Korean International Joint Venture General Company was founded in August 1986 in partnership with Japanese Koreans. This is a sort of holding company which both establishes and acquires other enterprises (Lee, 1988, p. 1264). Minerals and high technology are the areas favoured, but actual examples include hotel construction (France), clothing, food processing, car components, construction materials, chemical products and department stores (Japan, mostly Japanese Koreans) (Rhee, 1987, p. 888). For example, the Rakwon (Paradise) department store is operated by Japanese-Koreans. Purchases, however, are restricted to hard currency spenders such as foreign diplomats and privileged North Koreans who possess the 'red won' (a special form of currency with a red stamp), which can be converted into hard currency (Harrison, 1987, p. 37). There are also joint ventures with socialist countries, including a shipping enterprise with Poland, joint Soviet–North Korean timber projects in Siberia, and four joint Chinese–North Korean power stations. A joint venture with the Soviet Union for the production of lathes in North Korea came into operation in 1989, while a sea-food joint venture with China was set up on North Korean soil in the same year. In early February 1989 it was announced that the first North–South Korean joint ventures, situated in North Korea, had been agreed upon in principle, involving the development of a tourist area, a ship repair yard, and a railway rolling stock plant. The South Korean government vetoed the last two, however, on security grounds, while North Korea has frozen the other (kindly pointed out by Aidan Foster-Carter). Joint ventures account for only around 1 per cent of exports (Sophie Quinn-Judge, *Far Eastern Economic Review*, 11 January 1990, p. 20). A special economic zone is planned, hopefully in collaboration with neighbouring countries.

REFERENCES

Gomulka, S., Ha, Yong-Chool and Kim, Cae-One (eds) (1989) *Economic Reforms in the Socialist World*, London: Macmillan.
Halliday, J. (1987) 'The economics of North and South Korea', in Sullivan, J. and Foss, R. (eds) *Two Koreas – One Future*, Lanham (MD): University Press of America.
Kang, Myung-Kyu (1989) 'Industrial management and reforms in North Korea', in Gomulka, Ha and Kim (eds).
Lee, Hy-Sang (1988) 'North Korea's closed economy', *Asian Survey*, vol. XXVIII, no. 12.
Lee, Kie-Young (1990) 'Economic reforms and the "open door" policy in North Korea', Hyundai Research Institute (Seoul, South Korea): paper presented to the IV World Congress of Soviet and East European Studies, Harrogate (July).
Pak, Ky-Hyuk (1983) 'Agricultural policy and development in North Korea', in Scalapino and Kim (eds) (1983).
Rhee, Kang Suk (1987) 'North Korea's pragmatism: a turning point?', *Asian Survey*, vol. XXXVII, no. 8.
Scalapino, R. and Kim, Jun Yop (eds) (1983) *North Korea Today: Strategic and Domestic Issues*, CA: Institute of Asian Studies, University of California.
Suh, Sang-Chul (1983) 'North Korean industrial policy and trade', in Scalapino and Kim (eds) (1983).
Van Ree, E. (1989) 'The limits of Juche: North Korea's dependence on Soviet industrial aid, 1953–76', *Journal of Communist Studies*, vol. 5, no. 1.

11 Poland

George Blazyca

1. INTRODUCTION

At the time of writing this chapter, in December 1990, Poland was almost one year into a unique economic experiment designed to do the very nearly impossible: to curb a near hyperinflation while promoting economic growth and recovery. Moreover, this was being done largely in the absence of private enterprise, with highly imperfect domestic market structures and little competitive pressure. During 1990 the first steps were also taken towards the creation of a modern capitalist economy, with the aim of establishing a system similar to that existing in the industrialized West.

When this programme was first discussed in parliament (the Sejm) in December 1989, the finance minister, Leszek Balcerowicz, explained that there was no 'third way' for Poland. If such an alternative did exist it was, he added, a matter for countries richer than Poland to experiment with. It was enough to be, as Balcerowicz told the Sejm on 17 December 1989, 'pioneers' in charting the transition from state socialism to a modern mixed economy.

At the start of 1990 state enterprises found themselves, as a consequence of this fundamental shift in economic policy, in a completely new environment. They were playing a different economic game according to rewritten economic rules. Command planning, which in any case had hardly worked effectively in Poland since the Gomulka period, disappeared almost entirely. The old certainties which used to figure so prominently in the daily life of the state firm (such as ratchet effects, storming, insecurity of supply, hoarding, and the soft-budget constraint) either vanished completely or were displaced by new and highly unusual concerns such as the problem of finding customers, about which more is written below. New certainties started to replace the old, the clearest of which is the iron law that enterprises must pay their way or accept the consequences. As a team of Polish researchers interested in enterprise behaviour put it, 'the stabilization programme of the Mazowiecki government is a major break from the past. For the first time, firms are being forced to think for themselves about costs, markets and survival' (Dąbrowski *et al.*, 1990, p. 60).

Most firms, however, are likely to remain in state hands for some years and so the state will retain a decisive influence on industrial performance.

Precisely how the state will choose to regulate state business is a key issue that was largely unaddressed in Poland in 1990. But it does seem clear that alongside the 'simple' solution of privatization there must be much scope for improving the performance of notoriously inefficient state enterprises.

2. THE ORGANIZATION AND MANAGEMENT OF INDUSTRY

Command planning

Command economies had the virtue of an organizational simplicity that was fairly easy to describe notwithstanding complexities (usually more apparent than real) washed up by periodic waves of 'economic reform'. The typical enterprise was a large, highly integrated (both vertically and horizontally though rarely efficiently so) operation directly responsible to the relevant branch ministry. A 'do-it-yourself bias' (Winiecki, 1988, p. 76) was a key feature of the enterprise's everyday life as they struggled to insulate themselves as far as possible from the difficulties of the notoriously unreliable supply system. Specialization was greatly underdeveloped. The critical task facing the enterprise was to fulfil the plan and 'taut planning' saw to it that this was usually no trivial matter for the firm's management. Occasionally, organizational reforms were enacted that more or less compulsorily brought together enterprises in 'associations' or 'combines', which became a middle tier of management between producers and ministry. The annual plan severely limited the scope for enterprise discretion and ensured that an extreme form of 'short termism' dominated decision making. If the traditional command model was effective in building great heavy industries from scratch, it revealed numerous weaknesses which are well-documented (see for example Nove, 1983, pp. 68–85) and which, worst of all, multiplied rapidly with the passage of time. Of all the problems that became ever more apparent one of the most serious was the inability of the system to adapt and change. The diffusion of innovation was extraordinarily slow and only the clumsiest mechanism existed to support structural change. The system was also characterized by a waste of resources and environmental pillage on a scale that became intolerable.

Reforms

In Poland economic management through command planning was first seriously challenged in 1956, then less seriously in 1970–71, and very seriously again in 1980. As far as industry is concerned, the 1956 episode stimulated a lively interest in the possibility of a 'third way' between Stalinist planning and pure capitalism, namely enterprise management through workers' councils. There had been a strong grass-roots workers' demand for democratization of economic management, which the then party leader (Gomulka) appeared at first to respond to. But by the late 1950s workers' councils had had the stuffing knocked out of them and were totally incorporated in a harmless state-run conference of workers' self-management (KSR – *Konferencja Samorządu Robotniczego*). Enterprises continued to be managed along traditional command lines.

This state of affairs was not challenged again until 1970–71, when the Gierek solution to the problem of effective industrial management was to emphasize the importance of scale and technology. 'Gigantomania' took over. This found expression in mammoth, ill-considered green-field industrial investment funded largely by loans from the West. On the organizational front huge industrial enterprises (*wielkie organizacje gospodarcze*) were also formed, which promised to ease the command-planning overload at the top level of the bureaucracy. In reality, however, these contributed nothing to the development of a genuinely dynamic Polish 'enterprise'. Instead, familiar planning problems were simply relocated *within* the new organizations (see D.M. Nuti in Jeffries, 1981). To make matters worse the centre simply ceased to coordinate or steer the economy at the macro level.

As the crisis of 1980–81 erupted and reform blueprints multiplied, the focus shifted from vast scale to independent, self-managing and self-financing enterprises. Central planning was to be limited to developing a strategic focus and divorce itself from the detailed day-to-day management of firms. Martial law, however, led to the half-hearted introduction of the new system and a crippled central planning was unable to do more than keep the economy ticking over at a low level of activity (see Rosati, 1991a).

The most notable industrial management reform of the 1980s was probably the decision made in October 1987 to abandon the branch principle in favour of the creation of one over-arching industrial ministry to which all firms would be responsible. The then prime minister, Zbigniew Messner, also promised a fundamental shift in the presumption which had governed economic life and which held that 'nothing is permitted unless expressly authorised' and contributed so much to the fossilization of industry structure. Instead, as Messner explained to the Sejm, the new rule guiding economic activity would be that 'anything not prohibited is permitted' (see Economist Intelligence Unit, *Country Report Poland*, 1987, No. 4, p. 7, London).

During the early to mid-1980s, enterprise independence from the centre was partially enlarged, but the idea that firms should be self-financing failed to survive the transition from theory to practice. Workers' self-management suffered a similar fate. The fiscal role of the state grew in importance and became, as in Hungary, a major (if not *the* major) regulatory device in the economy. There was also some evidence in the 1980s, as the data below show, of a badly needed industrial 'de-concentration', a welcome contrast to the 1970s 'gigantomania'. There was little sign, however, of any useful industrial restructuring: the economy was on automatic pilot and the course was drift.

The 1990 upheaval

In 1990 state firms were catapulted into a completely new economic environment. Its main features (discussed more fully below) were a huge squeeze on domestic demand combined with the hardening of the budget constraint and a real liberation in enterprise decision making. The traditional problem of the socialist enterprise, namely finding suppliers, was replaced by a new problem, how to find customers. After a hesitant start to the year, with a certain amount of panic in the air as firms ran down reserves in order to maintain liquidity (especially hard currency bank accounts which could now be converted into zloty at the newly devalued and highly attractive rate), there was evidence of a surprisingly strong attempt to find export outlets as some substitute for reduced domestic demand. But one had to look hard to find signs that a substantial industrial restructuring was under way.

One of the other noticeable features of economic life in 1990 was simply its liberalization. Price setting became essentially a matter for the market place and new independent representative economic organizations emerged for the first time in 40 years. One body, that may turn out to be a Polish equivalent of the Confederation of British Industry, is the *Krajowa Izba Gospodarcza* (KIG), a countrywide chamber of commerce. According to its president, Andrzej Arendarski, this organization seeks to represent business views to the state authorities as well as to promote Poland to foreign business interests. It is open to all sectors whether state owned, cooperative or private and is funded, in the first instance, by members' subscriptions and payments for services rendered. Other organizations, including regionally based 'Economic Associations' (which aim to represent purely private business interests), have also emerged.

3. INDUSTRY: BASIC STRUCTURAL FEATURES

At the end of 1989 some 6 008 independent enterprises operated in state-owned industry. After steadily falling throughout the 1970s, the number has been increasing in recent years. This is largely the result of the administrative dismantling of a variety of 'associations', 'combines' and other multi-plant enterprises. If the 1970s was the decade of Gierek's 'gigantomania', then the 1980s began to witness a reversal of that trend. The number of 'combines' and multi-plant enterprises, for example, fell from 147 in 1985

to 122 in 1989, but the average size of those that remained increased from
6 147 workers in 1985 to 8 680 in 1989. Their share in total employment
changed little. The number of 'associations' fell from 106 in 1985 to 96 in
1988 and the notion of 'obligatory' association, formally at least, virtually
disappeared. In 1988 there were only five such groupings as opposed to 25
in 1985.

In 1989 state industry accounted for 95.2 per cent of total industrial sales
(in constant 1984 prices) and the private sector for 4.8 per cent. For 1985 the
figures were 96.8 per cent and 3.2 per cent respectively. In current prices a
more noticeable shift is apparent, with the state sector share falling from

Table 11.1   Key data – Polish industry

Year	1970	1975	1980	1985	1989
State sector					
Enterprises (no)	5 620	5 142	4 664	5 496	6 008
Employment					
state industry total (000)	4 249	4 946	4 973	4 431	4 177
excluding agents and					
outworkers (000)	4 072	4 730	4 761	4 268	4 053
average					
employees/enterprise	725	920	1 021	771	695
Private sector					
Enterprises (000)	na	na	na	208	291
Employment (000)	204	204	272	446	717
average					
employees/enterprise	na	na	na	2.1	2.5
Total industry					
employment (000)	4 453	5 150	5 245	4 877	4 894
Total labour force (000)	15 175	16 572	17 334	17 144	17 130
Industry share %	29.3	31.1	30.3	28.5	28.6
Agriculture share %	34.3	29.3	28.5	28.9	27.6

Note: Employment figures are averages for each year.

Sources: *Rocznik Statystyczny* (GUS, Warsaw), various years.

96.2 per cent in 1985 to 92.6 per cent of sales in 1989 and the private sector share increasing from 3.8 per cent to 7.4 per cent.

The state industry share in employment fell steadily after the 1980 crisis. In that year state sector employment was 4,973,200, falling to 4.4 million in 1985 and 4.2 million in 1989. Private sector employment increased sharply as the performance of the state economy deteriorated. While private sector industrial employment remained flat during the early 1970s (at just over 200,000), it was 271,700 by 1980, 446,600 in 1985 and 717,400 in 1989.

Production and employment are highly concentrated in a relatively small number of very large state enterprises. In 1988 the largest 113 enterprises had an average employment greater than 5 000. They accounted for 23 per cent of state industry sales and 25.2 per cent of employment. At the other end of the spectrum there were only 625 state enterprises with less than 50 employees and, as would be expected, these accounted for a negligible proportion of sales and employment. The top 428 state enterprises accounted for 47.8 per cent of total industry sales and 52 per cent of employment.

Since the mid-1980s the monthly magazine *Zarządzanie* ('Management') has published annual data on the economic characteristics of the top 500 Polish manufacturing enterprises. In 1989, according to *Zarządzanie*, the top 500 accounted for 65.9 per cent of all manufacturing sales and 49.3 per cent of employment. The leading ten firms are shown in Table 11.2. The spirits firm Polmos is by far the largest firm (by sales) in Poland and also the

Table 11.2   The top ten Polish manufacturers in 1989

Sales		Rankings		
		Net Profitability	Average Employment	Average Earnings
1	Polmos, Warsaw	115	29	131
2	Petrochemia, Plock	139	27	14
3	Huta Katowice	243	5	13
4	Lubin Copper Combine	11	1	6
5	Huta Lenina, Kraków	116	2	88
6	FSO, Warsaw	258	7	96
7	FSM, Bielsko	386	4	172
8	Rafineria, Gdansk	149	317	5
9	POLMAG-EMAG, Katowice	235	3	214
10	Huta Stalowa Wola	45	8	98

Source: Zarządzanie, No 6/7, 1990, pp. 46–7.

exchequer's most important single source of turnover tax. Other leading manufacturers in the top ten include the Plock-based chemicals concern, Petrochemia; three steelworks (Huta Katowice, the Nowa Huta Lenin steelworks at Kraków, now renamed the Tadeusz Sendzimir works, and the Stalowa Wola steelworks); the Lubin copper combine; the heavy engineering combine POLMAG-EMAG at Katowice and the two car producers, FSO in Warsaw and FSM in Bielsko-Biala. Results reported below refer of course to 1989 and the impact of the deep 1990 recession on leading Polish producers remains to be seen. But with light industry and foodstuffs suffering most in 1990 the rankings shown below are likely to be fairly robust.

A recent study of Polish concentration, briefly reported in the government daily paper *Rzeczpospolita* (20 August 1990), noted that in 37 industrial branches (typically, Polish statistics distinguish at branch level around 120 different sectors) the three firm concentration ratio (C_3, that is the share of the top three firms in total industry sales) was greater than 60 per cent and in ten cases it was greater than 90 per cent. These include brown coal, oil refining, copper and other non-ferrous metallurgy, informatics, aircraft, sulphur, coke works and mineral and other soft drinks. The C_3 indicator was below 10 per cent in only 20 branches. The same report also noted that at product level the largest single producer accounted for 60 to 90 per cent of the market for the following: black and white TVs, washing machines, robots, fridges, phones, records, radios and motor cars. For 140 items out of 438 investigated one or two producers only had 60 to 100 per cent of the market.

One of the other new developments worth noting in 1990 was the emergence of an anti-monopoly commission which bared its teeth somewhat ineffectively against the FSO car plant in Warsaw. In early October 1990 FSO was ordered to reduce its prices to the level of the preceding June, but, rather than complying with the commission, FSO immediately launched an appeal. This enabled the enterprise to continue to sell cars at prices of its choice until the issue was adjudicated upon. An appeal hearing in December 1990 ruled that the anti-monopoly commission had exceeded its powers and had no right to take such a detailed view of FSO product pricing.

4.   MACROECONOMIC CONDITIONS AND POLICY IN 1990

When Tadeusz Mazowiecki was called upon to form the first non-Communist government in postwar Poland in September 1989, economic conditions seemed just about as difficult as could be. Production was falling, inflation was spiralling upwards and there was a real danger of deepening economic chaos. The new government had to deal with two major economic issues.

First, inflation had to be brought under control, for without that there could be no possibility of meaningful economic calculation and no prospect of the market mechanism shaping any economy recovery. Second, a start had to be made on system transformation, from exhausted central planning to modern capitalism.

Dealing with inflation was clearly the priority. In January 1990, with IMF backing, Leszek Balcerowicz (the recently appointed finance minister) launched a determined anti-inflation programme. Demand was to be severely tightened through cuts in state subsidies, alongside a sharp devaluation of the zloty–dollar exchange rate and a highly restrictive tax-based incomes policy (in the state sector money wage increases above a centrally fixed norm were subject to a high and sharply progressive tax). Prices were also to be liberalized.

It was expected, of course, that devaluation and the removal of the bulk of prices regulation would give a powerful, but temporary, upward push to inflation. But by de-coupling wages from prices it was also anticipated that this would be transitory, confined in fact only to January 1990.

This expectation proved partly accurate. Although prices increased by 78.6 per cent in January 1990 (over December) money earnings were held virtually constant (up by 2.5 per cent on December) as firms either encountered the tax threshold on wage increases or simply failed to make sales at higher prices and so found themselves, despite all efforts, short of cash. Whatever the cause, the effect was a massive cut of 43 per cent in real earnings in January over December. Demand was certainly squeezed unexpectedly hard and enterprises, particularly those selling consumer goods and foodstuffs, met what the Polish press began to call the 'demand barrier'. The squeeze continued through February 1990 though with less ferocity: real earnings fell by a further 7 per cent, the demand barrier remained in place and production continued to decline. By March the Balcerowicz programme scored its first success as the monthly rate of inflation was brought down to single figures (4.7 per cent).

Inflation appeared to be brought under control by the end of the first quarter of 1990, but at the cost of sharply falling production and accelerating open unemployment. Industrial output in March, as in February, was 31 per cent lower than in the same month of 1989. Unemployment, virtually non-existent before Christmas 1989, accelerated to 267,000 (2.0 per cent of non-agricultural employment) by the end of March 1990. By June 1990 unemployment was running at 568,200 (4.2 per cent of the non-agricultural workforce). By the end of October 1990 unemployment crossed the Rubicon of 1 million (1,014,643, equivalent to 7.5 per cent of the non-agricultural labour force) with vacancies totalling around 56,119. As the vacancies that used far to outstrip unemployment began to be dwarfed by the enormous rise in the jobless, another traditional central planning shibboleth simply vanished. It is worth noting that Government forecasts of late 1989 and early 1990 optimistically pointed to unemployment peaking at around 400,000.

High headline unemployment presented, towards the end of 1990, a less serious political problem than may seem in a society used to 40 years of continuous full employment. This was due to the fact that many of the registered unemployed were either female (not the principal family breadwinner) or actively participated in the large second economy, especially in street trading. The unemployed were to a large extent 'absorbed' in informal activities in 1990. In an area where precise data are inevitably elusive, Polish economists anecdotally suggest that perhaps 30 to 40 per cent of the officially unemployed in late 1990 did not actively seek work. Unemployment benefit (at around 50 per cent of the average monthly wage for up to six months) was available to those registering and this, in the opinion of some Polish economists, created a fairly strong incentive to register. In late 1990 there was some speculation that rules governing eligibility to benefit would be tightened in 1991. Quite clearly during the bulk of 1990 trade unions were inclined to 'cooperate' with the government and chose to avoid making accelerating unemployment a major issue.

First impact of the Balcerowicz programme

In the first half of 1990 industrial production fell by 29.1 per cent over the same period in 1989. This was the result of a 30.1 per cent decline in state sector output combined with a 2 per cent increase in private sector production.

Table 11.3   State industry production sold (% change on same period of 1989)

Jan	Feb	Mar	Apr	May	Jun	Jan–June	Jan–Sep	Jan–Dec
–17.7	–31.0	–31.2	–30.9	–28.6	–28.7	–30.1	–26.2	–25.0

Sources: Polish press and Statistical Office reports.

In early 1990 industries producing consumer goods were hardest hit by the steep fall in domestic demand. The greatest sectoral output slump in the first half of 1990 was in light industry which saw production fall by 42 per cent. Food industry was second hardest hit with a 38.2 per cent fall in sales. Some indication appeared by mid-1990 that light industry was learning that, in a recession of this depth, minimizing price rises might help. The increase in prices in this sector in the first half of 1990 was the least fast among all industrial branches.

Table 11.4 *Production by industry branch (% change in 1990 on same 1989 period)*

	Jan–Jun	Jan–Dec
Fuel and energy	–22.6	–21.2
Metallurgy	–21.3	–19.7
Electrical and mechanical engineering	–26.0	–22.8
Chemicals	–28.2	–24.7
Construction materials	–31.8	–24.3
Wood and paper	–31.7	–24.0
Light industry	–42.0	–37.0
Food industry	–38.2	–25.7
State industry total	–29.7	–25.0

Source: Polish press and Statistical Office reports.

Exports and export structure

One of the most surprising economic developments in 1990 was a surge in hard currency exports. It seems clear that as firms hit the domestic demand barrier then some at least began seriously to look for export outlets. Over January–November 1990 compared with the same 1989 period hard currency exports rose by 32 per cent in volume and this, together with a drop in imports of 20 per cent, contributed to the generation of an end-November trade surplus of $4.1 billion. There is some evidence to suggest a certain 'desperation' on the part of firms looking for export outlets and average export prices in dollar terms fell slightly in 1990.

The commodity structure of Polish exports changed little in 1990. As can be seen from the table below, in the first half of 1990 Poland's top ten exports to the West continued to be dominated by a traditional mix of raw materials and items involving relatively little processing. The usual asymmetry between exports East and West could also be observed with a much greater share of raw materials in exports to the West than to the East. The top ten export items (shown in Table 11.5) accounted for 30 per cent of all exports to the West, but only 10.6 per cent of transferable rouble area exports. Coal was the most important Western export in the first half of 1990 followed by copper, although in both cases export volume fell by around 10 per cent. Coal export value also fell by around 10 per cent, while copper value fell by 22.9 per cent, indicating a major price slippage. With sulphur export volume up by 29.1 per cent and value up by only 6.4 per cent, prices must also have fallen. An interesting asymmetry was evident in plastics trade to West and East. Plastics exports to the West more than doubled for very little price benefit (up 118.3 per cent in volume but only 3.5 per cent in value), while the opposite occurred in trade with the rouble area (down by 41.2 per cent, but up in value by 109.3 per cent).

Two points are worth noting with regard to the export surge that took place in 1990. First, it was most unlikely to be durable and second, in the Polish situation, where exports account for a relatively small share of industry sales (17.1 per cent in 1989), there was little scope for exports to be the locomotive pulling the economy out of the recession (Rosati, 1991b).

Table 11.5   Poland's top ten exports (first half of 1990)

		Value $ m.	Volume % change	Value R m.	Volume % change
1.	Coal	370.6	− 9.1	346.2	2.2
2.	Copper	210.0	−10.4	0.1	−99.6
3.	Steel	192.0	24.4	116.8	− 2.1
4.	Sulphur	112.1	29.1	68.2	−32.4
5.	Textiles	99.8	–	22.1	–
6.	Cattle	96.3	41.3	0.7	–
7.	Oil	80.1	50.4	4.6	8.1
8.	Furniture	75.4	–	20.8	–
9.	Plastics	72.9	118.3	0.3	−41.2
10.	Silver	69.8	5.3	–	–
Sub total		1379.2		579.8	
Total exports		4672.9		5475.4	
Share in total		29.5%		10.6%	

Source: *Rzeczpospolita*, 24 July 1990.

In terms of geographical structure in 1989, and for the first time in the 1980s, Poland conducted most of her trade with the West (49.3 per cent of exports and 52.8 per cent of imports: see *Gospodarka światowa*, 1990), followed by Comecon and then by developing economies. The USSR remained Poland's single most important trading partner (21 per cent of exports and 18.2 per cent of imports). West Germany was not far behind with 14.8 per cent of exports and 15.8 per cent of imports; when this is supplemented by around a 5 per cent share in turnover attributable to East Germany, it seems inevitable that Germany will soon supplant the USSR as Poland's leading trade partner.

During 1990 the trend away from trade within the former Comecon area was reinforced. Over January to November exports to the hard currency payments area increased by 32 per cent in volume while exports to the rouble area fell by 15.9 per cent. Imports from both areas were very depressed though more so in the rouble case where the decline was 38.2 per cent than in the hard currency case with a fall of 20 per cent.

During 1990 Polish firms were bracing themselves for the imminent shock of 1991 and the move to trading within the old Comecon area in hard currency and at current world market prices. In terms of geographical trade pattern firms faced a number of major difficulties in looking ahead to the future. First, manufacturers, hitherto dependent on the vast and undemanding Soviet market, looked with trepidation at a future where their goods would appear increasingly uncompetitive by comparison to Western products. Soviet customers would at least be expected to put a strong downward pressure on Polish sales prices. Second, towards the end of 1990, as economic chaos appeared to deepen in the Soviet Union, Polish firms were by no means certain whether Soviet customers would have the hard currency to pay for goods. Third, Polish firms also expected to lose markets in the former East Germany.

5. JOINT VENTURES

The legislation governing joint ventures was liberalized several times in the late 1980s and was scheduled for a thorough redrafting in the autumn of 1990. Of the 1 231 joint ventures registered at the end of March 1990, most were German (506) followed by Sweden (112), Austria (81) and the US (81). Next came the UK (60) and France (58), only one being Japanese. The scale of investment channelled through joint ventures was exceedingly low, only $162,000 on average, and only in 22 instances did investment exceed $1 m. Of the obstacles discouraging Western investment to Poland, those most frequently mentioned in 1990 included infrastructure (particularly telecommunications and lack of financial institutions) and the limited possibility of profits repatriation (profits made on hard currency trade could be moved without any restraint but only a small proportion of domestically generated profits could be repatriated). There can be little doubt too that the increasingly unsettled political situation, particularly during the autumn 1990 presidential election campaign, made a negative contribution to the inward investment cause. The Polish authorities hinted, in an early June 1990 policy review, that joint venture rules would be relaxed in the nearest future. By the autumn of 1990 new draft joint venture rules had been set out and were about to be discussed in parliament when election fever intervened and slowed the process.

6.   LIFE IN THE 'TYPICAL' ENTERPRISE IN 1990

It was always likely that a determined attack on demand would succeed in reducing inflation and that this medicine would work through quite quickly. At the same time it was understood that it would be very much more difficult to elicit a rapid and positive supply-side response from producers. First, force of habit seemed likely to weigh heavily on production decisions as management cautiously explored the new economic rules of the game in a new intra-enterprise social context. Second, the highly monopolistic structure of Polish industry would probably see to it that much of the demand squeeze ended up in higher prices rather than in greater efficiency or a search for new products and new markets. Third, recent Polish research has shown that a complex internal situation developed within most state enterprises during 1990, which in some cases incapacitated decision making while in others (but relatively few) it stimulated progressive adjustment (Dąbrowski *et al.*, 1990).

It is clear that Polish producers' initial reaction to the fall in demand was to cut production, then to send workers on paid leave and then on unpaid leave. One is struck by the frequency of this response in both the case studies of Polish researchers and press reports. Dąbrowski and his colleagues time and again found firms where, 'as orders fell, the managing director raised prices' (p. 18), or where, even with good profits being made on exports and with domestic prices that were relatively higher still, 'there was no attempt to raise production by lowering the domestic price' (p. 23). Press reports also frequently pointed to many other cases of similar behaviour. In one typical case the Bizon combine harvester plant at Plock, facing falling demand, responded in early March by sending most workers on 'compulsory leave'. In another instance the Autosan bus factory at Sanok in south-east Poland sent its 5 000 employees on two weeks holiday in early April 1990 because of sales problems, by then already the third halt to production in 1990 .

One commentator writing in the weekly *Polityka* (April 1990, p. 3) parodied the thinking of a Polish manager of 1990 in the following terms:

... cannot find sales then reduce production and give the workers a holiday. Still trouble, then substitute unpaid for paid leave. Then it is necessary to lose a few people. If the market still does not want our goods then instead of reducing prices or exporting we again reduce production and let the next group of workers go. In this way the enterprise can die standing up, so long as in the plant there is a single director to turn off the lights.

Of course, in some instances enterprises *did* try to adjust, did try, for example, to shift resources into hard currency exports. But the logic of cutting production and raising prices was also compelling. Managers, unsure about the conditions they found themselves in, tended to react cautiously and take the simplest course of action which was to rein back production. In a few cases a progressive management acted differently, perhaps spurred on by an equally demanding and progressive workers' council or trade union. It is also interesting and somewhat surprising that despite the tightness of the demand squeeze no outright bankruptcies among medium or large state enterprises were reported in the first three-quarters of the year. Instead, what happened, according to the *Polityka* report quoted above, was that Poland developed 'bankruptcy by instalments'.

One of the most interesting of the enterprise level responses to the demand squeeze in 1990 was the development of an inter-enterprise 'payments blockage' (*zapory płatnicze*), that is, the growth of inter-enterprise credits on a large scale. As demand fell and interest rates became clearly positive by March 1990 enterprises increasingly turned away from the banking system and towards each other for credit. In this way they effectively found a way round what was supposed to be a major new monetary instrument and this no doubt helps to explain why the bankruptcies were so few.

The balance of social forces within the enterprise shifted considerably over 1989–90. The authority of the Communist Party suddenly vanished and left many managing directors in a new and difficult situation with no obvious base of support. Workers' councils (*rady pracownicze*) and trade unions (*związki zawodowe*), both Solidarity and 'official', began to wield much greater influence where they were willing and able. Workers' councils in particular began to use to the full legal powers to fire managers: in the first nine months of 1990, over 275 managers were dismissed on the initiative of the councils compared with 44 in 1989 and six in 1988 (*International Herald Tribune*, 29–30 December 1990, p. 7). At the time of writing it was impossible to judge the extent to which this represented the settling of old scores. In some cases in the enterprise a healthily constructive conflict developed, leading, as Dąbrowski and colleagues report, to purposeful adjustment strategies. But in too many other instances the result was stalemate and incapacitated decision making. In the view of most observers this situation will not be clarified until the property rights issue is itself straightened out. As Dąbrowski and colleagues put it, 'state property has decomposed and new rights and entitlements have yet to be defined' leaving no group in effective control (Dąbrowski *et al.*, 1990, p. 62).

It is also impossible to distinguish 'good' from 'bad' enterprises simply by looking at financial results in the first months, indeed in the first year, of the new programme. Dąbrowski and his co-authors favour differentiating enterprises according to their 'capacity for strategic action', but they over-look the fact that this may also be as much a matter of chance as whether firms are profitable. A strong but stupid director or a strong but narrow-minded workers' council or trade union may well be able to act decisively but nonetheless mistakenly. At some stage the 'capacity for strategic action' needs to be combined with a hard analysis of market possibilities. And the authorities may find, as a growing number of critics argued in late 1990, that a tough macroeconomic stance, though crucial, by no means guarantees the emergence of an efficient industrial sector.

With a 30 per cent cut in real earnings from December 1989 to March 1990, it is no surprise to find that the squeeze had a fierce initial impact on light industry, on consumer goods industries and, of course, on food-processing, but it was probably unlikely that a substantial industrial restruc-turing was taking place beneath the sharp decline in production. It may be, as Rosati (1991b) argues, that as the anti-inflation policy began to overshoot some of its targets the Polish authorities should have started sooner to consider more carefully what steps need to be taken on the supply side of the economy. For example, when the anti-inflation policy was devised in the autumn of 1989, it was thought that inflation would be brought down to less than 3 per cent per month by the third quarter of 1990 with a decline in output of no more than 5 per cent and a drop in real incomes of 25 per cent (*Polityka*, 23 June 1990). While third quarter inflation, at 3.6 per cent in July, 1.8 per cent in August and 4.6 per cent in September, was very close to target, it picked up markedly in October (5.7 per cent) and in November (5 per cent). Of course this acceleration was partly due to the Gulf crisis. National income, on the other hand, was heading for a 17 per cent fall and real earnings heading for a decline of 25 to 30 per cent. The finance ministry, however, adopted the cautious view that to relax policy too soon risked throwing away hard won gains. Dąbrowski argues that a supply-side policy should focus on helping firms to generate 'strategic adaptive behaviour'; although this should centre on privatization (with a major role for mutual funds), it should extend beyond to the development of other institutions which will put pressure on firms to restructure. Dąbrowski also believes that local government and trade union organizations should be involved in the development of 'viable adjustment strategies'.

7. PRIVATIZATION

According to some reports, privatization has been such a contentious issue in Poland that the legislation which was eventually placed before parliament on 13 July 1990 had gone through 17 previous drafts. Undoubtedly one of the immediate concerns was to construct a privatization process that would be 'above board'. A limited 'privatization' had been introduced in Poland during 1988 by the communist government headed by Mieczyslaw Rakowski, but this resulted simply in senior managers of state enterprises feathering their own nests by selling to one another portions of the firms they managed. Privatization became cynically regarded by many as yet another nomenklatura privilege.

As the Sejm debated privatization in July 1990 MPs tried to push through around 30 amendments, although most members, including Ryszard Bugaj, a long-standing Solidarity critic of the government scheme, made it clear that even if the amendments fell they would be voting with the government. In the event only one amendment was successful (see below) and only two votes were cast against the government's proposals with 328 in favour. Less than two weeks later, on 26 July 1990, the privatization bill was also accepted by the senate.

This legislation conceived a two-stage privatization process (Jędrzejczak, 1991). In the first, so-called 'commercialization' phase, a state enterprise transforms itself into a joint stock company (*spólka akcyjna*), with all shares held by the Treasury. In stage two, no more than two years later, the Treasury is obliged to sell the shares by public auction or some other highly visible and competitive means. Foreign participation was expected to average 10 per cent of each primary flotation, but special permission (from the head of the Inward Investment Agency) can and probably will be given for a greater initial stake. The employees of privatized enterprises were to be allowed to purchase up to 20 per cent of shares at half price. But the total value of this privilege was to be no greater than average annual earnings (in the state economy over the previous 12 months) times the number of workers in the enterprise. The 20 per cent limit on workers' shareholdings was a major point of contention during the privatization debate. Many Solidarity MPs were keen to create greater space for a more complete form of employee share ownership. However in the only successful amendment pushed in parliament on 13 July, it was agreed that agricultural workers with a long-standing trading association with firms to be privatized should also be entitled to buy shares at preferential rates.

The Mazowiecki government, perhaps stung by Walesa's electioneering criticisms in the autumn of 1990 that it was moving too slowly on privatization, tried to speed up the process and produce some tangible results in the last part of the year. Walesa frequently made it clear during the presidential election campaign that he wanted to see speedier action and 'acceleration' (*przyspieszenie*) became his campaign slogan. But it is hard to see how successful privatization could be made to move more quickly. One major obstacle was the shortage of domestic savings. The authorities may try to overcome this by offering cheap credits to support private share purchases and by issuing, in due course, 'privatization bonds' (exchangeable for shares) to the population at large. Giving shares away is fraught with other dangers: the population may decide to sell immediately on a scale that causes prices to crash, with serious consequences for the development of any 'popular capitalism'; moreover it is hard to see how massive dispersal of shares will contribute anything to the effective management and control of enterprises.

The first state enterprise to enter the 'privatization' stakes, even before the new legislation went through parliament, was the Universal trading organization. Universal specializes in the export–import of white goods. As an apparently profitable enterprise with substantial hard currency activity (exports of $175 m. and imports of $122 m. in 1989) Universal looked likely to be a privatization winner. However, Universal seemed simply to be issuing new shares rather than the state Treasury selling its existing 51 per cent stake in the company.

The first genuine privatizations under the new legislation are likely to be organizations similar to Universal, that is, clearly profitable firms involved in hard currency trade. Over September–October 1990 a number of candidates for privatization were identified. The list was a fluid one but at various times it included: Wedel, the Warsaw chocolates producer; the Norblin metal rolling firm; Exbud, the Kielce based construction company; Prochnik, a Lodz-based garment producer; the Swarzedz furniture enterprise; the Inowroclaw meat processing plant; the Fampa paperworks at Jelenia Gora; and the Silesian cable factory at Czechowice. When the final list of pioneer privatizations was announced Wedel, Norblin and Swarzedz were somewhat mysteriously dropped from the list. Substitutes were found in the Krosno glassworks and the Tonsil radio factory, which together with Exbud, Prochnik and the cable works, became the first five major privatizations in Poland. Share applications were invited from 30 November 1990 until 21 December 1990. This was later extended to 11 January 1991 to allow, according to various reports and depending on which view one wanted to take, either for more time to deal with an upsurge in demand, or else to give more time to boost a demand punctured by the notion that shares might soon be freely distributed by the new president. Alongside those larger sales the less glamorous (but crucially important) privatization of shops and restaurants, mainly by local authorities, made some progress in 1990. This process of 'small' privatization was started in November 1989 and in the first half of 1990 some 12,000 shops (10 per cent of the urban total) were reported to have been sold to private interests (*Rzeczpospolita*, 13 July 1990). By the end of 1990 there was some sign however that some key local authorities were becoming more attracted by the high leaseholds that could be obtained and moving away from outright asset sales.

Parliament also agreed to set up a new ministry to oversee the entire privatization process and to subsume the activities of the already existing 'office for ownership transformation', initially headed by Krzysztof Lis. Poland's first privatization minister, Waldemar Kuczynski, was appointed in September 1990 but, as a close associate of Tadeusz Mazowiecki, he found his term of office lasted only to the end of the year. The new privatization minister was drawn from the devotedly free-market economists close to Walesa, namely Janusz Lewandowski (one of the so-called 'Gdansk Liberal-Democrats').

8. CONCLUSION

Polish enterprises met economic conditions in 1990 the likes of which they had never before seen in the post-war period. A demand barrier or hard budget constraint appeared for the first time as subsidies were all but eliminated and prices liberalized. But their largely monopolistic situation meant that they responded to the demand squeeze mainly by pushing up prices. In a few cases only was there any consistent attempt to adjust production, reduce costs or search for new markets.

Within the enterprise considerable confusion reigned as the collapse in the previous political authority left old nomenklatura directors scrabbling in a void that workers' councils or trades unions sometimes rushed to fill. In a number of cases managers were summarily dismissed by workers' councils exercising newly found muscle.

Privatization is viewed by many as the route to a structure where authority in the enterprises will become dependent on a clear link with ownership. However it is hard to see how an effective 'hands-on' ownership can speedily be created. In late 1990 the situation, following the election of Walesa as President and the resignation of the Mazowiecki government, became considerably confused. Walesa favoured 'acceleration' especially in privatization and in removing the Communist Party nomenklatura from major posts. He also favoured 'correction', where appropriate, of the Balcerowicz programme. But the dangers in this were plain. An accelerated privatization could still leave an authority gap inside the enterprise if shareholders were too dispersed, while a new managerial cadre to replace the old may not be easy to find quickly. Some Polish economists also began to argue more strongly for a set of supply-side measures to complement the clear macroeconomics of the Balcerowicz plan. The lack of any industrial policy, together with discussion on how to improve the efficiency of state business, was perhaps the most serious deficiency of Polish economic policy in 1990.

REFERENCES

Dąbrowski, J., Fedorowicz, M. and Levitas, A. (1990) 'Stabilisation and state enterprise adjustment: The political economy of state firms after five months of fiscal discipline, Poland 1990', A report by the enterprise adjustment and labor market research group, Warsaw, mimeo.
Gospodarka swiatowa i gospodarka Polska w 1989 roku (1990) SGPiS, Warsaw.
Jedrzejczak, G. (1991) 'Privatisation and the private sector', in Blazyca, G. and Rapacki, R. (eds) *Poland to the 1990s: Economy and Society in Transition*, London: Pinter.
Jeffries, I. (Ed.) (1981) *The Industrial Enterprise in Eastern Europe*, New York: Praeger.
Nove, A. (1983) *The Economics of Feasible Socialism*, London: Allen and Unwin.
Rosati, D. (1991a), 'Poland: systemic reforms and economic policy in the 1980s', in Blazyca, G. and Rapacki, R. (eds) *Poland to the 1990s: Economy and Society in Transition*, London: Pinter.
Rosati, D. (1991b) 'The transition from central planning to the market – The Polish experience', *Thames Papers in Political Economy*, New Series, no. 2, London: Thames Polytechnic.
Winiecki, J. (1988) *The Distorted World of Soviet-Type Economies*, London: Routledge.

12 The Romanian enterprise

Alan H. Smith

1. INTRODUCTION

The pace of change in Eastern Europe since the end of 1989 and the proposed transition to a market economy has made a formal analysis of the structure of the traditional Romanian enterprise and changes to the system of enterprise indicators an inadequate guide to the future shape of the industrial enterprise in Romania. Consequently this chapter attempts to analyse the problems that the nature of Romanian society, the pattern of industrialization and the system of industrial administration under Ceausescu will create for the privatization of industry and the creation of a market economy in Romania. The chapter is divided into four broad sections: first, the historic and political differences between Romania and other countries of Eastern Europe; secondly, industrial policy under communism, thirdly, the system of industrial administration under Ceausescu; and finally the debates on and progress of industrial reform since the revolution.

2. WHY ROMANIA IS DIFFERENT: THE LEGACY OF HISTORY

At the time of the overthrow of the Ceausescu regime in December 1989, the Romanian economy was suffering from the classic economic–systemic problems typically associated with an unreformed command economy in an extreme form. In addition, the economic, social, political and historical circumstances confronting the new Romanian government are considerably more severe than those faced by the governments of Central Eastern Europe. The combination of these factors means that the transition from a centrally planned to a market economy will prove to be far more difficult and complicated than in Hungary, Poland or Czechoslovakia.

The most important political factor is that the destruction of 'civil society' was so complete under the Ceausescu regime that the establishment of an alternative form of government and administration that commands popular support at home and trust abroad will be far more difficult. The revolution which deposed the Ceausescu regime in Romania was far more violent and involved considerably more bloodshed than the overthrow of communism in Central Eastern Europe. The overthrow of the Ceausescu regime originated as a popular revolution not only against the Ceausescu family but also against the party nomenklatura and the Securitate (secret police) in particular. However the virtual absence of an organized intellectual opposition contributed to a political vacuum which, in turn, facilitated a *coup d'état* by the National Salvation Front. A major consequence was that many of the political objectives of the popular revolution were not achieved. The leadership of the transitional government, which took power following the December revolution and successfully contested elections held the following May, included a number of figures with a communist background (several of them had held office under Ceausescu in the 1960s and early 1970s) as well as military figures. Similar figures in Central Eastern Europe (or, in many cases, politicians with better credentials as 'reform communists') have largely been swept from power. At lower levels in the economic and political administration, many former members of the nomenklatura and even the Securitate are still reported to be exercising power in central and local government as well as in industry and commerce. The reluctance of the new government to reveal many critical details of the revolution, together with subsequent acts of public violence (including the beating of anti-Front demonstrators in Bucharest by miners, bussed in from the Jiu valley, and ethnic violence in the Transylvanian town of Tirgu Mures), has contributed to distrust of the ruling National Salvation Front. This distrust is felt at home by many Romanian intellectuals and abroad by representatives of many Western governments and international economic and political institutions.

The Ceausescu era was also marked by an extreme degree of centralization of decision making and by the exercise of arbitrary power in both the economic and social spheres; the role of the secret police extended far deeper into everyday life than in Central Eastern Europe, while the isolation of academics and intellectuals from the mainstream of Western ideas and practices was far more extreme in Romania than elsewhere in Eastern Europe, particularly in the 1980s. This will make it far more difficult to establish an independent and, above-all, trusted, professional middle class, while the potential new class of Romanian managers, entrepreneurs, bankers and teachers has a far more limited practical experience of the financial and other skills required to operate successfully in a market economy. Furthermore, those who have travelled and studied in the West are frequently suspected of complicity with the former regime.

3. THE STRATEGY OF INDUSTRIALIZATION UNDER COMMUNIST RULE.

At the beginning of its period of communist government, Romania had the advantage of relatively fertile agricultural land and was better endowed with domestic energy resources (crude oil and natural gas), but was a substantially poorer, more agrarian and less industrialized country than the Central East European economies. According to official statistics, 75 per cent of the working population in 1950 were employed in agriculture, while of the one million industrial employees (12 per cent of the working population) 40 per cent were employed in the food, textiles and extractive industries (*Anuarul Statistic*, 1986, p. 70). The agrarian sector was largely unmechanized, while the industrial sector accounted for 19.8 per cent of the capital stock and 44 per cent of national income (in current prices). By 1989 the industrial labour force had quadrupled and accounted for 43.6 per cent of the working population and 59.1 per cent of national income (*Buletin de Informare Publica*, 1990, no. 3). However, Romania was still the least urbanized and industrialized of the East European CMEA countries with only 51 per cent of the population living in towns in 1987 (*Statisticheskii Yezhegodnik Stran-Chlenov SEV*, 1989, p. 10) and probably the lowest per capita income in Europe (with the exception of Albania and the southern regions of Yugoslavia).

A further result of the low level of pre-war industrialization and the subsequent policy of forced industrialization is that Romania's industrial workforce is predominantly composed of first- or second-generation 'industrial workers of peasant origin' and workers who commute to industrial employment from the countryside. As a result, Romania has developed neither an independent working-class tradition nor a class of independent entrepreneurs who combine commercial and industrial skills . The new generation of industrial workers has become accustomed to an environment of passive obedience to central instructions, backed by guaranteed employment and stable prices for the majority of goods (when available). It may prove exceedingly difficult to win the support of a conservative peasantry and working class for market-orientated reforms, reforms that can be expected to generate considerable uncertainty and insecurity in the short run.

Romania's industrial strategy under Georghiu Dej and Ceausescu was an exaggerated version of the Stalinist growth model, which involved devoting an increasing proportion of national income to investment (at least until the debt repayment programme of the 1980s) and concentrating that investment in building up a heavy engineering sector, while transferring labour from agriculture to industry. The strategy differed from that pursued elsewhere in Eastern Europe in that it included far stronger elements of 'economic nationalism' or 'nationalist autarky'. This involved the construction of a 'many-sided' or broadly-based industrial output structure. The intention was to reduce Romanian dependence on imports of manufactured goods by producing a wide range of manufactured goods domestically and, ultimately, exporting manufactured goods in place of raw materials and agricultural produce. The industrialization policy also involved the concentration of industry into a small number of monopolistic large enterprises, many of which had a wide-ranging production profile (Smith, 1981). In 1985 36.8 per cent of industrial output was produced in enterprises employing more than 5 000 workers; these were also responsible for 32.7 per cent of industrial employment. Only 12.7 per cent of the industrial labour force was employed in enterprises employing less than 1 000 workers (*Anuarul Statistic*, 1986, pp. 86–7).

In practice the policy of 'economic independence' (which involved Romanian non-cooperation in proposals for improved CMEA integration and which was frequently mistaken in the West as designed to achieve independence from the Soviet Union) initially increased Romanian dependence on technology imported from the West (reflected in increased imports of Western machinery and equipment from 1967 onwards and legislation to permit joint ventures with western capital in 1971) and, subsequently, on imported energy and raw materials from non-Soviet sources. Increased industrial consumption resulted in Romania becoming a net oil importer by 1977 with crude oil imports reaching 16 million tonnes in 1980. Similarly, the neglect of agriculture resulted in Romania becoming a net importer of foodstuffs from the OECD by the end of the 1970s.

With the exception of some unsophisticated steel products, Romanian heavy industrial production has remained largely uncompetitive in Western markets, while industrial exports have been concentrated in refined oil products, petrochemicals, textiles, furniture and footwear. The lack of competitiveness of Romanian industrial production meant that the burden of the policy of rapid debt reduction in the 1980s (a policy which was largely determined by the desire to avoid IMF influence over domestic economic policy) was largely achieved by import compression. This enabled Romania to eliminate its hard currency debt entirely by mid-1989 from a peak of $10.2 billion at the end of 1981.

This policy has been vividly described by the Romanian economist Teodorescu (1990), who has analysed Romanian industry in terms of three distinct and separate categories during this period: firstly, an 'enclave' sector of enterprises which 'imported, processed and re-exported raw materials'; secondly, a sector of enterprises which processed and exported domestic raw materials; and, finally, a low-grade domestic sector that was entirely dependent on domestic materials and produced for the home market. Export receipts from the first two sectors of industry were almost entirely used for the repayment of debt, while the industrial capital stock was run down.

According to estimates based on official statistics convertible currency trade surpluses reached a peak of $3.6 billion in 1988, while net exports were equivalent to 9.3 per cent of GNP in domestic prices. The debt repayment programme necessitated not only the imposition of draconian restrictions on household consumption of energy and food, while available resources were directed to the industrial-export sector, but also the virtual cessation of imports of Western machinery and equipment (which accounted for only 4.1 per cent of hard currency imports in 1989: *Buletin de Informare Publica*, 1990, no. 3). This, in turn, has resulted in a failure to modernize industry which has further reduced its long-term competitiveness. Consequently although Romania will not have to bear the costs of servicing a high level of external debt, this apparent advantage over the other East European countries may be more than outweighed by the higher degree of obsolescence of much of the Romanian capital stock. Furthermore, the overrapid repayment of debt meant that Romania destroyed its contacts with the international financial community and, consequently, lowered its creditworthiness, despite virtually non-existent external debt.

4. ENTERPRISE PLANNING AND ADMINISTRATION IN THE CEAUSESCU ERA

The structure of economic administration during the Ceausescu era formally replicated the classic Soviet model of a command economy . Here economic authority was nominally vested in the state apparatus which was, in turn, responsible to the party at both the central and local level. The central organs of state administration in Romania included the State Planning Committee, the State Committee for Material–Technical Supplies, the Ministry for Investment and Construction, the National Bank and such functional ministries as finance, prices, foreign trade and economic relations. The system of industrial administration incorporated a 'Brezhnevian' three-tier system of management. This was headed by sectoral industrial ministries; there was a middle tier of management known as industrial *Centrals* (broadly analogous to industrial associations in the Soviet Union), and whose role was similarly strengthened in 1973; finally, there were the enterprises. During the 1980s approximately 100 Centrals were responsible for the administration and coordination of between 1 750 and 2 000 industrial enterprises, employing 3.5 million workers (*Anuarul Statistic*, various years). The Central was responsible for the formulation of enterprise plan targets, which had to be drawn up in accordance with directives established in the state five-year and annual plans.

Western and Eastern academic studies of the system of planning and industrial administration under Ceausescu have revealed a high degree of both de jure and de facto centralization of economic authority and decision-making and an exceedingly low degree of enterprise autonomy in comparison with other East European CMEA countries. Granick's study (Granick, 1975), based on interviews with industrial managers and economic officials in 1970, indicated that enterprise managers had no authority in making decisions of an economic nature and that their role was virtually confined to questions of technical efficiency. Nearly 20 years later a Soviet study (Shiryaev and Bautina, 1988, p. 151) concluded that Romania still possessed 'a centralized system of economic administration, characterized by a large number of directive indicators and a wide number of plan targets specified in natural units ... over 90 per cent of the value of industrial output is determined by detailed central plan instructions'.

Although Romania published two major reform documents in 1967 and 1978 which had rhetorical similarities with more far-reaching reforms enacted in other CMEA countries, these did not create (and were probably not intended to create) a genuine decentralization of economic authority to the enterprise or to local county authorities. As Ronnas (1990, p. 8) concluded, 'Romania was bypassed by the waves of genuine attempts at reform ... which swept through Eastern Europe in the 1960s and 1970s'. The New Economic–Financial Mechanism (NEFM), which was introduced on 1 January 1979, was intended (in theory at least) to give production units greater economic and financial responsibility for the fulfilment of centrally-determined plan targets and to link workers' incomes directly to plant performance. The basic principles of the NEFM, which introduced the concepts of self-financing (*autogestiune*) and workers' self management (*autoconducerea muncitoreasca*), are broadly similar to the reforms of the systems of economic management introduced in Czechoslovakia in the late 1970s and to the changes in enterprise management introduced in the Soviet Union in the early Gorbachev period from 1985–87. In fact, Ceausescu reaffirmed his support for the policies contained in the NEFM at the Central Committee Plenums of April and June 1986 and Alexandru Babe, who was one of the original designers of the reforms in 1978 (Smith, 1981), was appointed as Minister of Finance in the summer of 1986, while a spate of articles emphasizing the need for the firm application of the principles of self-management, self-finance and payment by results appeared in the daily and technical press in the summer of 1986 (see the survey in the *Economist Intelligence Unit*, 1986, no. 4, pp. 11–16). The concept of self-financing required enterprises to cover operating costs (including wages and bonuses, expenditure on education and training, social services, housing, health and cultural facilities, raw materials, taxes and depreciation) from revenues and to finance a larger proportion of investment from bank credits, rather than state budget grants. The operation of the latter illustrates the real nature of decentralization; the decision to invest remained centralized while enterprises were held to be responsible for the efficient management of the resulting plant and equipment and were required to finance investments from profits and/or bank credits.

Workers' self-management involved the extension of the principle of collective management (initiated by Ceausescu in 1965) by establishing workers' councils, composed of party officials, managerial and technical staff and elected workers' representatives as the nominal highest organ of enterprise management. In practice, the council only meets three times a year (Shiryaev and Bautina, 1988, p. 150) and appears to involve more obligations than rights for workers' committees, which were largely entrusted with the efficient management of the resources according to directives established in the 'Single National Plan'. The basic intention of workers' self-management appears to have been to strengthen the powers of the party and security apparatus in the day-to-day operations of the enterprise at the expense of technocrats in the state apparatus; this was reflected in the decision that the councils be chaired by the local party secretary, not the enterprise director (Smith, 1981). The workers' councils appear to have functioned largely as transmission belts to oversee and implement centrally-determined instructions. The principle of workers' participation in the enterprise was nominally extended in 1982 by legislation which permitted workers to make interest-bearing capital contributions to their enterprise (Jackson, 1986, p. 535). It appears, however, that the purchase of these 'deposits', which could only be transferred or sold under very strict circumstances, were more in the nature of compulsory bond sales to workers, rather than genuine workers' shareholdings.

Even in the late 1980s the industrial enterprise still received an unusually high number of compulsory plan targets and indicators. The most important bonus-forming plan indicators were those for marketed output, net output and the output of important products in physical units. In addition the enterprise received compulsory indicators for the following: the quality of output; targets for the introduction of automation and modernization of plant; labour productivity; the maximum number of workers to be employed and the number of man hours; the wage fund; the number of man hours per unit of output; the level of profits and accumulation; the level of costs and profits per unit of output; cost reductions; the level of payments into the state budget; capital construction and investment; and the source of material inputs and machinery and equipment (Shiryaev and Bautina, 1988, pp. 151–2).

The Romanian authorities also made extensive use of complex systems of money bonuses and fines for the over- or underfulfilment of centrally determined plan targets during the Ceausescu era (Smith, 1981, pp. 77–8). A system of remuneration known as the 'acord global', which is effectively a form of piece rates based on collective contracts, was drastically extended in September 1983 and again in 1986. By the late 1980s it covered over 80 per cent of employees (Jackson, 1986, pp. 536–8; Shiryaev and Bautina, 1988, pp. 162–4).

The basic principles of the 'acord global' (global contract system; broadly similar to the Soviet concept of the labour brigade) were as follows:

1. Workers' incomes were derived from two sources, namely the enterprise wage fund and the fund for workers' participation in profits and production.
2. The normed enterprise wage fund was a function of the level of output in physical units, the level of normed net output and deliveries for export. The fund is determined according to norms linking planned output per worker to planned wage rates.
3. The actual level of the wage fund varied (upwards or downwards) according to the degree of fulfilment of the above indicators plus other additional indicators considered to be important by the authorities (e.g. norms for the consumption of energy and raw materials).
4. Each production brigade or shop-floor was allocated a set of plan tasks specified where possible in natural units. The brigade wage fund was then determined as a function of the degree of fulfilment of planned physical output together with quality specifications and deliveries for export. Individual wages were then determined in proportion to their centrally-tariffed wage rates and their individual fulfilment of plan targets.
5. The fund for profit sharing was formed from above-plan profits arising from exceeding the plan or net output, incurring above-plan savings in raw material consumption and above-plan profits from exports, the majority of which was paid in bonuses to employees.

It is possible that the economists who designed the NEFM in the mid-1970s genuinely intended to create a less centralized economic system giving more authority to the enterprise and more power to workers' committees. But it remains highly improbable that Ceausescu had any such intentions. In practice, however, the Romanian authorities were not allowed to create (and probably did not intend to create) the circumstances which would permit a genuine decentralization of decision-making authority to either the enterprise or even the industrial central. Retail and wholesale prices remained centralized and were unchanged for a number of years, without regard to changing conditions and scarcities on domestic and world markets. Central controls over investment were strengthened rather than liberalized between

1980 and 1983, while central controls over the flow of commodities between enterprises were also strengthened (Jackson, 1986, p. 538).

The system of economic and industrial administration during the Ceausescu era was highly centralized even by the standards of the unreformed command economies, while enterprise instructions frequently reflected the personal whims and directives of Ceausescu himself (Ronnas, 1990, p. 10). The NEFM was not intended to permit a genuine decentralization of economic authority but to exercise strong central control over industrial costs, while a further tightening of the financial controls over enterprises in 1986 and further restrictions on the availability of credit (*Economist Intelligence Unit*, 1986, no. 4, p. 12) gave enterprises little or no room for manoeuvre. The real purpose of the NEFM (at least as it was applied in the 1980s) appears to have been to centralize control over economic decisions and to force enterprises to pass the financial costs of overtaut planning and centrally generated supply shortages onto workers by punishing them for the non-fulfilment of plan instructions. Similarly, strengthening the enterprise's responsibility for financing social welfare payments and facilities simply relieved local authorities from this obligation without providing any realistic alternative form of finance and facilitated a reduction in this form of expenditure, while concentrating resources on centrally-determined projects.

5. INDUSTRIAL REFORMS IN THE 1990S

The various reform programmes of the National Salvation Front

The immediate priority of the National Salvation Front was to win popular support by easing constraints on domestic consumption (particularly food and energy) and by relaxing factory discipline. The government attempted to preserve price stability and full employment in the state sector by retaining price controls and enterprise subsidies, but removed some of the restrictions on the development of a small-scale private sector in the hope that this would bring about a rapid improvement in consumer supplies. The initial economic programmes outlined by leading members of the National Salvation Front gave every indication that the transition to a market economy would be a gradual process and that 'shock therapy' policies would be avoided. It was felt that this was necessary to maintain the support of industrial workers and the urban population, since these would be the sections of the population most severely affected by policies involving the prospect of large-scale industrial unemployment and substantial price increases for basic staple goods.

Silviu Brucan, one of the Front's leading theorists, argued that Romania should avoid the experience of Poland and Hungary in copying Western economic models indiscriminately; the new Romanian economic model should combine the best elements of existing market-based systems in order to stimulate the export-orientated dynamism of the South Korean model with what he described as the social guarantees of the Austrian model. His 'model system' involved a combination of state-directed measures to attract Western multinational investment in 'high-technology' sectors (particularly in micro-electronics and computers) and government policies directed towards ensuring an equitable income distribution, full employment and the creation of a social welfare system (*Economist Intelligence Unit*, 1990, no. 2, pp. 18–19). How these objectives were to be realized was not spelled out in detail.

Brucan's proposals were, at best, only partially reflected in the economic policies outlined in the electoral programme of the National Salvation Front. The programme combined a gradual transition to a mixed market economy (a process which some ministers envisaged would take from six to eight years) with social policies aimed at protecting the less well-off. The electoral programme included the following proposals: to liberalize prices gradually; broaden and diversify the private sector while maintaining state ownership in areas of national interest, including large ventures; encourage foreign investment; abolish the state monopoly on foreign trade; and gradually introduce convertibility of the leu. Social market elements in the programme included the introduction of a 40-hour week; a guaranteed minimum income, with unemployment benefits set at that level; progressive tax policies to prevent the accumulation of great wealth; and measures to ensure better supplies of clothing, food and hot water (see Teodorescu, 1990, p. 17 and the *Economist Intelligence Unit*, 1990, no. 2, p. 18).

Differences in the approach towards the role of the state in the economy and towards the speed of introduction of a market economy between the newly-elected President Iliescu and Prime Minister Petre Roman surfaced following the elections in May 1990. Iliescu's inaugural address confirmed his commitment to the principles of a mixed market economy, which would involve an increased role for the private sector as one of the 'principal components of the economy, but which would coexist with public, cooperative and jointly-owned sectors of industry (*Adevarul*, 21 June 1990). He argued that privatization would begin with the creation of a strong private sector in small and medium-scale industry which would utilize modern technology and would be efficiently managed. Existing large-scale industry would be reorganized by initially converting state enterprises into 'commercial societies with state capital', empowered 'to decide on such matters as organizational structure, wages, investment and wage rates'. Prices would be liberalized under competitive conditions, in parallel with the creation of an ex ante tax system (based on income tax and turnover taxes) and the creation of a social welfare system. Iliescu's programme envisaged a significant 'dirigiste' role for the state in the economy, particularly in stimulating investment in high technology sectors. The state would draw up strategic programmes to promote technical progress and industrial modernization. These would be implemented by measures to finance domestic research and to encourage imports of technology. Thus, although Iliescu recognized that industrial regeneration would require a major input of foreign capital, this would be subject to state controls over the selection and direction of investment.

Prime Minister Roman appointed a young and meritocratic government (many of whose members had been students in the relatively liberal late 1960s), with the major economic portfolios given to genuine advocates of a rapid transition to a market economy. The programmes outlined by the new government have eschewed any reference to South East Asian, Latin American or even Swedish models of economic development in favour of a commitment to the rapid transition to a 'West European type of market economy', with a limited state sector operating according to market rules. It is intended that the economy will eventually become fully integrated into the European economy, involving full membership of the EC. The economic programme, outlined by Roman at the inauguration of the new government on June 28, promised an initial legislative 'shock-therapy' over the following 18–24 months; this would establish the legal basis for a market economy combined with a drastic diminution of the role of the state in the economy (Roman, 1990a, p. 15). All economic activity involving the production and sale of goods and services was to be conducted by a combination of commercial companies (some with state-owned capital in the short run) and autonomous companies involving a form of public ownership limited to mineral resources, energy, transportation, defence production and infrastructure, water and forestry, and some sectors of agriculture (but which would, nevertheless, operate in a market environment).

The government's programme indicated that the responsibility of the state in the economy would be similar to that in a conventional European market economy. In the financial sphere the primary responsibility of the state would be the restoration of a sound currency (which would eventually be convertible) and a sound monetary system. This involves the replacement of the state monobank system by a two-tier banking system incorporating a state-owned National Bank (exercising the functions of a conventional central bank) and a series of independent commercial banks and other financial institutions responsible for providing finance for industrial investment and the newly emerging private sector in industry and services.

The money supply will be controlled by the conventional techniques of open market operations and determination of interest rates. Currency convertibility was to be a medium-term goal. The state's financial role will eventually be limited to raising taxes to finance the newly created social security and state welfare system and defence, but would in the short run be extended to the ownership but not direct management of state industries awaiting privatization. In the short term, at least until a fully-fledged market economy has been established, the state will continue to play a directive or orienteering role in economic strategy involving some elements of macroeconomic forecasting and the use of financial and budgetary instruments to guide producers towards the satisfaction of social needs along French or Japanese lines.

The deterioration of economic performance in 1990

The rapid deterioration in economic performance during the first nine months of 1990 can be seen in a fall in net industrial output (value added) of 27.7 per cent (compared with the corresponding period of 1989). This was used as an argument by Roman that the policy of gradualism should be abandoned in favour of a rapid transition to a market economy (Roman, 1990b). The relaxation of factory discipline following the revolution involved an immediate reduction in the working week and replaced the 'acord global' (which linked wages directly to individual and collective output) with greater security for industrial workers. Wage cuts and fines for the non-fulfilment of plan targets for gross output, export production or for planned reductions in energy consumption were abolished and workers were guaranteed a minimum of 75 per cent of wages if production were halted for reasons outside their control (*Economist Intelligence Unit*, 1990, no. 1, p. 19), while social funds administered by the enterprise were to be maintained regardless of output. One result was that the total industrial wage fund grew by 11.2 per cent in the first nine months of the year, while working time fell by 16.7 per cent (Roman, 1990b).

The decline in industrial output was most acute in the energy sector. Crude oil output continued to fall (by 13.4 per cent in the first ten months), natural gas production fell by 13.9 per cent, but, most noticeably, coal production (where working conditions had been particularly dangerous and inhuman during the Ceausescu era and where worker support was considered essential for the government's survival) fell by over 40 per cent in the first eight months of the year. The fall in coal production was attributed to a cut in the working week of 14 per cent, a fall in the labour force of 18 per cent (largely brought about by early retirement) and a 20 per cent fall in productivity (*Adevarul*, 3 October 1990). This, in turn, contributed to a cut in electricity production of around 15 per cent, while electricity supplies to industry were cut by 35 per cent in order to preserve household consumption. This created critical supply bottlenecks, which had a potential multiplier effect on industrial output as existing stock reserves were used up.

The dismantling of the 'acord global' and improved social security payments contributed to a growth of nominal money incomes of 26.1 per cent in the first nine months of the year (Roman, 1990b). This, combined with fixed retail prices in the state sector, resulted in growing disequilibrium in the domestic consumer market: the visible signs of this disequilibrium were the re-emergence of queues and empty shelves in the state retail sector, the rapid growth of black market activity, the growth of idle money balances and the escalation of prices in the legal and illegal secondary markets. Household money balances (comprising deposits in the State Savings Bank and cash balances) grew from Lei 277 billion at the end of 1989 to Lei 322 billion at the end of August 1990, equivalent to 11 times the stock of goods in state stores (*Adevarul*, 19 September 1990). As these cash balances are entirely uncapitalized they represent deferred demand for basic consumer goods and were equivalent to 104 per cent of the total wage fund in 1989, 108 per cent of total sales in state retail stores, or 64 per cent of total consumption in 1989.

The partial alleviation of domestic bottlenecks by recourse to increased imports and decreased exports could only provide temporary relief as the balance of trade went into deficit and reserves of foreign exchange were rapidly depleted. Hard currency exports fell by 43.4 per cent in the first 11 months of 1990 while hard currency imports grew by 52.2 per cent, resulting in hard currency trade deficit of $1.4 billion in the first 11 months of 1990 (*Adevarul*, 18 December 1990). A trade deficit of 1.5 billion roubles was also incurred in trade with non-socialist countries over this period, much of which will have to be repaid in hard currency following the termination of trade in transferable roubles from January 1991.

The acceleration of economic reform in autumn 1990

It was apparent that the collapse in industrial production and the growing macroeconomic imbalances resulted largely from the relaxation of the regime of harsh factory discipline and the removal of constraints on wage payments, combined with the continuation of enterprise subsidies (which, in turn, necessitated a relatively lax monetary policy in the absence of increased taxes on profitable sectors of the economy). The planning system had ceased to function properly, while authoritarian controls had not been replaced by either the incentives or the discipline of the market place. Consequently it was decided in autumn 1990 to accelerate the pace of reform. A two-year timetable for the transition to a market economy beginning in September 1990 and ending in June 1992, was spelt out in considerable detail in two issues of the new economic journal *Tribuna Economica* (nos 39–40) in September 1990.

On 18 October Roman presented a report on the need to accelerate economic reform to parliament. He argued that this would require an acceleration of the 'legislative shock' and the abolition of arbitrary limits on the private sector (e.g. on the number of employees) which had been established following the revolution. He also advocated a number of positive measures to accelerate the introduction of a private enterprise market economy, including the following: credits to promote the development of a private sector *ab initio* in small- and medium-scale industry and financial measures to attract inward foreign investment; measures to accelerate the introduction of a market-determined exchange rate and currency convertibility and to expose domestic producers to international competition and world market prices; industrial restructuring; the demonopolization of industry; land and agricultural reform; and programmes for macroeconomic stabilization, including price liberalization, accelerated introduction of a social security system and an ex ante tax system in place of the arbitrary system of enterprise taxes (Roman, 1990b). Many of the concrete details of this programme are too unclear at the time of writing, however, to permit a more detailed analysis. The remaining space will, therefore, be devoted to an analysis of the problems of price reform and macroeconomic stabilization, which will critically affect both the prospects for economic reform and the environment in which the enterprise operates and the government proposals for privatization of industry.

Price reform and macroeconomic stabilization

The programme for price reform and macroeconomic stabilization has proved to be the most controversial to date. It threatens to accelerate the split in the National Salvation Front between what may be termed the 'paternalist-populist left' and the 'supply-side social democrats' as well as placing further strains on an already divided community. The advocates of a rapid transition to a market economy argue that rapid price liberalization is essential on both microeconomic (efficiency) and macroeconomic grounds. The microeconomic rationale is that the (eventual) removal of subsidies will allow prices to be determined by supply and demand conditions and will gradually introduce a more rational set of relative prices. At the same time, the introduction of currency convertibility and market-determined exchange rates will enable enterprises to be exposed to international competition and world market prices. The macroeconomic rationale is to equate the value of disposable money incomes (minus voluntary savings) to the value of consumer goods and to remove inflationary overhang by reducing the real and/ or nominal level of savings (by requiring citizens to run down money balances to meet current consumption needs and reducing the purchasing power of money balances through inflation).

The first stage of price reforms, involving the reduction or removal of state subsidies on a large number of basic but 'non-essential' consumer goods (i.e. virtually all goods except basic food products, domestic heating and rents) combined with a substantial devaluation of the leu, was implemented on 1 November 1990. Prices were theoretically liberalized (although government 'guide prices' were published in the press) to allow producers to set prices covering costs. In practice it was argued that guide prices were frequently violated and that retail price increases for affected goods rose by between 100 and 300 per cent. Price reforms proved highly unpopular and led to demonstrations. A second round of retail price increases, which removed (or reduced) subsidies on the majority of food products, was initially postponed from its scheduled date of 1 January 1991 until 1 June but was later brought forward to 1 April. Subsidies for rents and household heating are to stay in place until early 1992.

Central controls over wages and incomes are to be retained during the period of macroeconomic stabilization to prevent the development of a hyperinflationary wage-price spiral. Employees and pensioners have received fixed-sum increases partially to compensate for price increases. A government macroeconomic forecast envisages that roughly 70 per cent of price increases will be recouped by increases in wages and pensions during the course of 1991 and that money balances at the State Savings Bank will be run down by 36 per cent (*Adevarul*, 12 December 1990). Wage and salary increases above government-determined norms will attract punitive taxation. Opposition to price increases has come from both the left and the right. The left argues that compensation for lower-paid workers is inadequate and threatens social stability while speculation and profiteering are rampant. The right argues that price 'reforms' involve simply a move to a new set of higher state-controlled prices, the intention being to erode the value of money balances (in order to restore macroeconomic equilibrium) and to make state enterprises profitable, but not to permit genuine price flexibility as part of the transition to a market economy.

The privatization programme

The government programme envisages two processes for the creation of a private sector. The first stage involves the creation of a small-scale private sector *ab initio* in both services and production. It is hoped this will be achieved by removing existing legal constraints to the development of the private sector and by the creation of financial instruments to channel investment to the private sector. This process will also involve the denationalization of existing small-scale units in the retail and service sectors and their sale to private owners.

The second, more complicated process involves the privatization of existing state enterprises, as outlined in the 'Law on Restructuring State Economic Units as Autonomous Units and Commercial Companies', which was passed by both chambers of the new parliament on 31 July 1990 (*Buletin*, 1990, no. 1). The law, which formally established the National Agency for Privatization (inaugurated in August 1990), envisages that existing state enterprises will fall into two major categories: firstly, autonomous units (encompassing enterprises operating in areas of strategic interest, as outlined above, and remaining in state ownership but operating according to market principles); and, secondly, commercial companies (to be privatized by the issue of shares to the public and to operate as limited liability companies).

The first stage of the creation of commercial companies will involve the creation of joint stock companies, which will, initially, be entirely owned by the Romanian state. The Agency for Privatization will conduct the initial evaluation of state assets, and securities equivalent to 30 per cent of the nominal capital of each joint stock company will be distributed to the Agency for free distribution to the public. Each resident citizen over the age of 18 on 31 December 1990 (except people convicted of certain categories of crime) will receive vouchers entitling him or her to shares worth 5 000 lei, commencing in the first quarter of 1991. This stock of shares can be sold to other citizens, subject to the requirement that both parties must have resided in the country for a year after the period of distribution and that all transfers must be registered with the Agency for Privatization in order to be valid. A proportion (which may differ from enterprise to enterprise) of the remaining shares in each enterprise will be placed on sale to the public. Workers will be consulted about the proportion to be placed on sale, which will differ from enterprise to enterprise. Workers will have preferential rights to buy a proportion (probably 30 per cent) of shares put up for sale in the enterprise in which they work, paying either in cash or by using their voucher allocation. Special credit facilities will also be available to help workers buy shares in their own enterprise. Finally, a block of shares will be reserved for foreign capital. The sale of shares to the public is expected to begin in the last quarter of 1991 (*Tribuna Economica*, 1990, no. 39, pp. 9–10).

6. CONCLUSION

Romania is a relatively immature society by European standards and still suffers from deep-seated ethnic and rural/urban divisions. The total destruction of civil society under the Ceausescu regime, together with popular distrust of politicians and administrators (which is, in part, the historic legacy of subjugation to the Ottoman Empire with its propensity for mendacity and corruption) will make it far harder to establish a system of economic administration and a financial mechanism which commands universal respect. However, the commitment of many members of the Romanian government appointed in June 1990 to the rapid transition to a market economy should not be doubted, although the size of this task (and the opposition to it) should not be underestimated.

The pattern of communist industrialization, which has been described as an extreme case of the Stalinist model of economic development in Eastern Europe (Pecsi, 1989), has led to the creation of economic problems that, while not unique to Romania, appear there to an exaggerated degree. Romania is 'overindustrialized' in relation to its comparative advantage. The service sector is poorly developed, while the agrarian sector has been neglected and run down, particularly in relation to its long-term potential. Industrial policy under Ceausescu resulted in a relatively unspecialized industrial structure with the added complication that a large number of different products are manufactured in relatively small quantities in large enterprises using obsolete technology. As a result it may be very difficult to estimate the long-term viability of industrial enterprises, while enterprise closures will result in high levels of localized unemployment which could exacerbate ethnic tensions. Furthermore, the legacy of Romania's economic and cultural isolation during the 1980s will make it harder to attract Western assistance and foreign investment. As a result, the transition to a market economy will be far more difficult and complicated in Romania than in Central Eastern Europe and is likely to be accompanied by far greater levels of social and political tension.

An update to this chapter is given in the Postscript, page 282.

REFERENCES

Adevarul (Daily newspaper, from 1990), Bucharest.

Anuarul Statistic (Annual Statistical Yearbook), Bucharest: Directia Centrala de Statistica.

Buletin de Informare Publica al Comisie Nationale pentru Statistica (Monthly Bulletin of Statistics, from 1990), Bucharest

Economist Intelligence Unit (London) Quarterly, Country Reports on Romania, Bulgaria and Albania.

Financial Times, London. Reports by Judy Dempsey.

Granick, D. (1975) *Enterprise Guidance in Eastern Europe*, Princeton: Princeton University Press.

Jackson, M. (1986) 'Romania's debt crisis: its causes and its consequences', in Joint Economic Committee of the US Congress, *East European Economies: Slow Growth in the 1980s*, vol. 3, Washington DC: US Government Printing Office.

Jeffries, I. (Ed.) (1981) *The Industrial Enterprise in Eastern Europe*, Eastbourne: Praeger.

Pecsi, K. (1989) 'The extremist path of economic development in Eastern Europe', *Communist Economies*, vol. 1, no. 1.

Roman, P. (1990a) 'Declaration-Programme of the Government', *Bulletin of the Government of Romania*, no. 1.

Roman, P. (1990b) 'Report on the Stage of Implementation of Economic Reform and the Demand to Step Up Its Pace' (distributed copy of his speech of 18 October 1990).
Ronnas, P. (1990) 'The economic legacy of Ceausescu', Stockholm Insititute of Soviet and East European Economics, Working Paper 1990, no. 11 (preliminary paper).
Shiryaev, Yu. and Bautina, N. (eds) (1988) *Predpriyatie v Stranakh SEV*, Moscow: Politizdat.
Smith, A. (1981) 'The Romanian industrial enterprise', in Jeffries (Ed.) *Statisticheskii Yezhegodnik Stran-Chlenov SEV*, Annual Statistical Handbook of CMEA, Moscow.
Teodorescu, A. (1990) 'The future of a failure: the Romanian economy', Stockholm Institute of Soviet and East European Economics. Working Paper 1990, no. 12 (preliminary paper).
Tribuna Economica (weekly economic journal, from 1990), Bucharest.

I have also benefited from invaluable discussions with Romanian officials, economists and politicians while preparing this article. Unfortunately, these cannot be named.

13 The Soviet industrial enterprise in the 1980s

Gertrude E. Schroeder

At the beginning of the 1980s the position of the industrial enterprise in the Soviet Union was little different from that bequeathed by Stalin. This was so despite the many 'reforms' introduced in the preceding 15 years. The enterprise was owned by the state and subordinate to a government agency; it did not have to sell its products or purchase its materials in any real sense, since both output and inputs were allocated through mandatory plans. The enterprise did not have to seek out sources of capital, since investment, too, was allocated by plans. Product prices and basic wage scales were determined administratively, while the enterprise's incentives were orientated toward meeting production targets and satisfying its superior agency; it had little say over the disposition of its profits or the composition of investment. But its position was one of extraordinary security, for it faced neither competition for markets nor threat of bankruptcy. With the dramatic fall in industrial growth and productivity that began in the mid-1970s,[1] the decade of the 1980s, too, has witnessed several new attempts at industrial reform and has ended with an unprecedented programme intended to create in the 1990s a full-blooded market economy with all of its requisite institutions. Nonetheless, at the end of 1990, most of the features of the traditional position of the Soviet industrial enterprise formally remained in place. But specific reforms, along with the erosion of central authority in general, had modified those features enough so as to make the life of enterprise managers enormously more complicated and more uncomfortable than under the old system and had contributed to a marked decline in industrial production in that year.

The industrial reforms actually implemented during the 1980s were of the traditional type, focusing on changes in forms of organization and on expanding the autonomy of the enterprise in a basically unchanged milieu of socialist central planning. That was the nature of the industrial experiments begun by Andropov in 1983, continued by Chernenko, and expanded by Gorbachev soon after he became CPSU General Secretary in March 1985. The same conclusion holds for the assorted measures adopted during 1985–87 and for the major package of economic reforms enacted in mid-1987, which were initiated in 1988 and fully implemented in the industrial sector in 1989 and 1990.[2] To counter the aberrations in enterprise behaviour that were the unintended consequence of the reforms' internal inconsistencies, the government decreed several modifications in various provisions of the

219

package. As industrial performance deteriorated in the final two years of the decade, however, both proposals for reform and the laws actually adopted became more radical, focusing on property ownership and having the potential to alter radically the position of the industrial firm in the next decade.

This paper describes the course of industrial reform during the 1980s and depicts the position of the industrial enterprise at the end of the decade. In section I changes in organizational structures in the industrial hierarchy are considered. Section II deals with innovations in the forms of property ownership. Section III describes the changing situation of the state industrial enterprise in relation to (1) plan, production, supply and pricing; (2) relations with its workforce; (3) investment and finance; and (4) foreign trade. A concluding section assesses the impact of the reforms of the 1980s on industrial performance and the behaviour of the enterprise and evaluates the nature of the reforms now scheduled for the 1990s.

1.   INDUSTRIAL ORGANIZATION

Like their predecessors, the reforms of the 1980s have sought solutions to chronic problems through changes in organizational forms. In 1980 35 ministries (24 all-union and 11 union-republic) managed the industrial sector. Their number increased thereafter, but as part of Gorbachev's 1987 reform package the decision was made to concentrate management of heavy industry in Moscow-based ministries, with consumer sectors to be managed in the republics. At the end of 1990 the number of all-union ministries stood at 15; they were in charge of virtually all enterprises in machinery, defence production, energy, metallurgy and chemicals. Two union-republic ministries managed electric power stations and timber and paper producers. Ministries dealing with enterprises in the light and food processing and construction materials industries answered to various republic ministries. In addition to consolidating ministries and reducing their staffs, Gorbachev's innovations included the setting up in 1986 and 1987 of over-arching Bureaus to oversee the activities of groups of related ministries (for Machinery, for Fuels and Energy and for Chemicals and Timber). In 1989 enterprises directly subordinated to the central government accounted for 61.4 per cent of the total value of industrial production, 64.2 per cent of employment, and 81.1 per cent of the productive capital stock (*Narodnoe Khoziaisvo SSSR v 1989 godu*, 1990, Moscow: Finansy i Statistika, p. 331).

The 1987 package envisioned an altered role for the central ministries. Although they continue to be held responsible for 'satisfying demand for the branch's product', they are forbidden to interfere in the day-to-day operations of enterprises or to infringe in any other way on the broadened decision-making rights accorded to enterprises. In general, the ministries are supposed to monitor the behaviour of enterprises and counter 'abusive' practices, such as monopoly, violation of pricing rules, and restriction of production for goods in demand. Ministries are also responsible for designing and implementing long-range research and development programmes for their sectors.

The drive to amalgamate enterprises into ever-larger entities that had gained momentum in the 1970s continued in the 1980s. At the end of 1989 there were 45,895 industrial combines, associations and independent enterprises, of which 4 689 were classified as associations (p. 313 and pp. 330–1). These associations and their constituent enterprises accounted for 57.9 per cent of industrial production and 60.6 per cent of employment; in 1980, in contrast, 4 083 associations had accounted for 48.2 per cent of output and 50.1 per cent of employment. In 1989 528 associations were so-called 'science-production' types that combined research and development institutes with production facilities. Along with these associations of the traditional type, several new forms of 'voluntary' amalgamations have appeared in the past three years as a result of the greater permissiveness allowed by the 1987 Law on the State Enterprise (Association) and amendments in 1989. In mid-1990 there were 24 'concerns', 17 'inter-branch state production associations', 340 'economic associations', and 40 'consortiums', all numbers being sharply higher than at the start of the year (*Ekonomika i Zhizn*, 1990, no. 14, p. 6 and no. 28, p. 12). Some concerns exist outside the ministerial structure, and many of the inter-branch associations and other entities are comprised of the enterprises formerly subordinated to now defunct ministries or chief administrations (glavki). For example, enterprises of the former Ministries of the Gas Industry and of Mineral Fertilizer are now centrally managed under such rubrics (*Khoziaistvo i Pravo,* 1990, no. 4, p. 24). Thus far, the various new organizational entities have been both lauded as promising large gains in efficiency and condemned as adding to the degree of monopoly and/or merely representing old forms with new and fashionable names.

Soviet industry begins its planned transition to a market economy in the 1990s with extraordinarily large enterprises as compared with Western economies and an extremely high degree of production concentration in individual firms and central ministries. A Soviet study reports that in the mid-1980s the average Soviet industrial enterprise employed 834 workers, compared with 186 in Hungary and 86 in a sample of capitalist countries (*Planovoe Khoziaistvo,* 1990, no. 1, p. 38). In 1987 73.2 per cent of the total number of industrial personnel were employed in plants with 1 000 or more workers; only 1.7 per cent worked in enterprises with 100 or fewer employees (*Promyshlennost SSSR: Staticheskiy Sbornik*, 1988, Moscow: Finansy i Statistika, p. 14). In that year, 1.4 per cent of all enterprises (roughly 550) accounted for 33.6 per cent of the total value of industrial production, 20.9 per cent of employment and 38.9 per cent of the productive capital stock. The shares of small enterprises (those with 100 or fewer workers) had fallen sharply between 1971 and 1987 (*Vestnik Statistiki*, 1990, no. 8, p. 22).

A variety of recently published data depict the extent of monopoly power in Soviet industry. In 1990 the Chairman of the State Committee for Mate-rial–Technical Supply (Gossnab) reported that 1 600 enterprises produced from 80 to 100 per cent of total output in their particular product lines (*Rabochaia Tribuna*, 13 June 1990). According to data released by the State Committee for Statistics (Goskomstat), 83 enterprises have an absolute mo-nopoly on some product (such as sewing machines, tram rails, locomotive cranes and coking equipment); another 85 products are made by only two enterprises, 43 by three and 28 by four (*Voprosy Ekonomiki*, 1990, no. 6, p. 28). Single all-union ministries are sole suppliers for 112 products (*Voprosy Ekonomiki*, 1990, no. 6, p. 30 and *Promyshlennnost SSSR*, 1990, Moscow: Finansy i Statistika, pp. 56–8). Another investigation found that of 239 important products surveyed, 34 per cent were produced by single enterprises, 37 per cent by two, 18 per cent by three and 11 per cent by four (*Materialno-Tekhnicheskoe Snabzhenie,* 1990, no. 3, p. 9). Another source reports that 94.3 per cent of the total number of machinery products offered for whole-sale trade without purchase limits in 1989 is accounted for by firms that are either monopolies, duopolies, or triopolies for their products; the corre-sponding percentage shares are 56.3 for metallurgy, 74.3 for chemical and wood processing, 58.9 for construction materials, and 65.6 for consumer goods (*Ekonomicheskaia Gazeta,* 1989, no. 49, p. 7).

Given the enormous size of industrial firms and the obviously high con-centration ratios, the government has been concerned about finding ways to curtail monopoly power and promote competition as essential ingredients of recipes for moving to a market economy. Pending enactment of federal anti-monopoly legislation, the USSR Council of Ministers on 6 August 1990 issued a decree entitled 'On Measures for the Demonopolization of the Economy' (*Ekonomika i Zhizn*, 1990, no. 38, pp. 2–3). This decree provides for setting up a USSR Anti-Monopoly Committee, which is charged with implementing a wide-ranging programme to demonopolize the economy and economic administration. The decree instructs the central ministries and republic governments to begin in 1990 the selective break-up of entities that have a 'highly monopolized' position; no break-ups are known to have occurred in 1990. The statute also declares illegal a number of practices aimed at restricting competition or abusing a 'dominant' position in the market. Enterprises so classified are defined as those with over 70 per cent of the market: such enterprises would become subject to government price controls and other administrative restrictions. A 'differentiated approach' is to be applied to enterprises having market shares of 35 to 70 per cent, while those remaining are free from controls under the statute. In addition to dealing with industrial enterprises, the statute also aims to demonopolize other sectors of the economy, including wholesale trade, foreign trade and state economic administration. One of the most radical provisions would free the ministries and other central organs from 'direct supervision of the fulfilment of current economic tasks and the operational administrations of enterprises and organizations'. This provision, however, has been suspended while 'urgent measures to stabilize the economy' are being undertaken and pending adoption of new legislation defining the competence of all-union organs.

Other aspects of Gorbachev's reforms have sought to address the monopoly problem through measures to allow new forms of business organization, to promote small enterprises in general, and to expand freedom of entry. The most notable of the first type of action is legislation adopted in 1986 and liberalized in 1988 (*Pravda*, 8 June 1988) that actively encouraged formation of independent producer cooperatives of the type that had existed in the USSR until their abolition by Khrushchev in 1960. While cooperatives have been accorded wide latitude and their number has risen rapidly, they afford only minuscule competition for state firms in the industrial sector. At the beginning of 1990 39,600 cooperatives were classified as producing industrial-type products; they employed a little over a million persons (including part-time workers) and produced goods equivalent to a little over one per cent of total industrial production (*Narodnoe Khoziaistvo SSSR v 1989 godu*, 1990, Moscow, p. 268). Most of these cooperatives were parts of state enterprises, which found it advantageous to set up cooperatives because their output could be counted in the enterprise's total, while the wages it paid could be excluded. Cooperatives as a whole, because their wages were double those in the state sector, did serve to lure labour away from industrial state enterprises and to foster rapid wage growth there.

In another move to encourage formation of small businesses, the USSR Council of Ministers in August 1990 approved a decree entitled 'Measures Pertaining to the Formation and Development of Small Businesses' (*Ekonomika i Zhizn*, 1990, no. 3, Supplement, p. 4), along with draft legislation for submission to the Supreme Soviet. As it applies to the industrial sector, this temporary statute defines a small business as one employing up to 200 workers, but specifies that local authorities may set different limitations. Private employment of non-family members is now allowed. The statute states that small businesses may be formed to engage in any legally permissible economic activity by a variety of entities, namely individuals, families, cooperatives and state enterprises. To encourage their formation, small businesses are accorded a variety of tax and other concessions. The decree proposes the establishment of special funds at local levels, to be financed by 'voluntary' contributions and budgetary revenues, in order to assist small businesses in obtaining start-up capital. The decree establishes a Small Business Committee under the USSR State Commission for Economic Reform to help coordinate and foster a small business sector. Finally, a more general 'Law on Enterprises', adopted by the USSR Supreme Soviet in June 1990 and effective (mainly) 1 January 1991 seemingly allows enterprises of all types of ownership to enter into any kind of economic activity not forbidden by union or republican law (*Ekonomika i Zhizn*, 1990, no. 25, pp. 18–21). If accompanied by the abolition of branch ministries, this law would seem to sanction freedom of entry throughout much of Soviet industry. However, permission to do so and the ability to accomplish it are quite different matters.

2.   EVOLUTION OF NEW FORMS OF PROPERTY RIGHTS

One of the most radical developments in the 1980s centres on the issue of the ownership of industrial enterprises and the property rights given to their managers in practice. At the beginning of the decade these matters were scarcely discussed and orthodoxy prevailed: state property was the 'highest form' of property ownership and ultimately would become universal. The industrial enterprise was owned by the state, which delegated some operational rights. The enterprise's specified rights of possession, use and disposal of its physical and financial assets were severely circumscribed by decrees, rules and regulations issued by the legal owner (the state) and by the de facto owner (the branch ministries). Except for a tiny amount of industrial products produced on collective farms, state-owned entities produced all output and accounted for all employment and capital stock in the industrial sector. So the situation remained until the advent of Gorbachev, who in his first year as General Secretary of the CPSU raised the ideologically sensitive issue of property ownership. At the 27th Party Congress in February 1986, he spoke of the need to create an ownership mentality among workers and managers, and a year later he admitted that in practice socialist property had become 'nobody's property, having no real owner' (*Pravda*, 26 February 1986 and *Kommunist*, 1987, no. 3, p. 7). He also called for 'radical' economic reforms that would enlarge the autonomy of enterprises and accord their employees a voice in management. By the end of 1990 issues of property had come to occupy centre stage, not only in the debates about reform programmes, but also in the laws that were adopted. In the industrial sector new forms of property ownership have been authorized by law and the property rights delegated to the still overwhelmingly dominant state-owned firms have been greatly broadened by new legislation. The laws encouraging private and cooperative enterprises have already been noted. In March 1990 a broadly based Law on Property was approved by the USSR Supreme Soviet; the law recognizes the right to ownership of a wide variety of forms of property (state, communal, collective, joint stock and private) and states that the state guarantees the 'stability' and equal protection under the law for all forms of property (*Izvestia*, 10 March 1990). In July 1990 the USSR Council of Ministers adopted decrees dealing with joint stock and limited liability companies and with the issuance of securities (*Ekonomika i Zhizn*, 1990, no. 27, pp. 12–14). In August Gorbachev issued a Presidential Decree establishing a USSR State Property Fund, with the mandate as one of its 'priority tasks' to 'elaborate and implement a programme to transform state enterprises into joint stock companies and enterprises based on different forms of ownership, while simultaneously carrying out the demonopolization of production' (*Pravda*, 10 August 1989). Earlier legislation had laid out conditions for leasing all or parts of state enterprises by individuals and work collectives (*Ekonomicheskaia Gazeta*, 1989, no. 19, p. 7 and *Izvestia*, 9 April 1989). As of mid-1990, leased industrial enterprises accounted for 4.3 per cent of total industrial employment (USSR Goskomstat, *Preso-vypusk*, 4 September 1990, no. 341). Basically, what has happened is that a spate of new legislation lays the legal basis for a major transformation of property ownership in Soviet industry, but large-scale implementation lies in the future, and its efficacy depends on the extent of progress toward a market economy.

Besides addressing the matter of formal (legal) ownership per se, Gorbachev's reforms have greatly increased the autonomy of the state enterprise, at least on paper. The USSR Law on the State Enterprise (Association) adopted in July 1987 (*O Korennoi Perestroike Upravleniya Ekonomikoi Sbornik Dokumentov*, 1988, Moscow: Gospolitizdati, pp. 3–54) and amended in 1989 (*Izvestia*, 11 August 1989) gives the firm an unprecedented degree of autonomy in the disposition and use of its physical and financial assets, in the distribution of its net income, in the management of its workforce, and in its relations with superior organs. For example, the firm may now take its ministry to court for violation of its rights and may withdraw entirely from its ministry if it is leased or joins a concern. The firm may voluntarily enter into leasing arrangements through contracts, issue bonds and stocks, engage in foreign trade and choose methods of allocating its income or profits. Nonetheless, these laws and other reform documents still seriously constrain the state enterprise in most important areas. These complex matters are discussed below.

3.   THE STATE INDUSTRIAL ENTERPRISE

This section attempts to describe the position of the industrial enterprise and its managers as it is laid out in the 1987 Law on the Enterprise and the 1989 Amendments. Most of the industrial sector operated under the Law's provisions in 1988, and all of it did so by the end of 1989 and during 1990. In general, the original intent was to influence and regulate enterprise behaviour primarily by means of 'economic levers', such as prices, bank credits, incentive funds and profits taxes. Because of the economic consequences of enterprise behaviour under the new law, along with rapidly worsening disequilibrium in the economy, however, the government adopted several decrees using administrative methods to restrict enterprises' freedom of action in a number of areas. Basically, what follows describes these developments and depicts the position of the state industrial enterprise at the end of 1990.

The enterprise plan, production and supply

The 1987 Law on the State Enterprise as amended in 1989 specifies that the enterprise 'independently' formulates its own annual and long-range plan. In so doing, it must take into account 'non-binding' control figures sent down by its ministry pertaining to such matters as levels of production, productivity targets, wages, profits and investment. The enterprise's production plan is developed on the basis of a portfolio of mandatory state orders (*Goszakazy*) implemented through contracts as well as sales contracts negotiated with other customers. The enterprise also receives from its ministry allocations of supplies (limits) required to fulfil state orders, a ceiling on investment, and a set of state-set normatives regulating such matters as the growth of wages and the disposition of profits. Theoretically, there is an obligation to meet the production plan, and managerial bonuses are tied to fulfilment of total contractual obligations, but the ministries may impose additional conditions.

The share of state orders, which may not encompass all of an enterprise's output, is supposed to be gradually reduced. The share was about 90 per cent in 1988 and was intended to fall to about 40 per cent in 1989 (*Ekonomicheskaia Gazeta,* 1988, no. 36, p. 2). Mounting difficulties in the consumer sector, however, prompted the government to issue decrees in 1989 that brought nearly all manufactured consumer goods under state orders in 1989 and 1990 and imposed mandatory quotas on all enterprises to produce consumer goods and services of some kind (*Ekonomicheskaia Gazeta,* 1988, no. 31, pp. 18–20 and *Sobranie Postanovlenii Pravitelstva SSSR,* 1990, no. 6, pp. 143–59). These actions were also intended to curtail 'abuses' by enterprises, many of which had used their greater autonomy to reduce planned output, juggle the product mix in pursuit of profit, refuse to accept state orders and decline to renew contracts except on 'extortionary' terms. As a consequence, state orders issued by both the central and the republic governments apparently encompassed well over half of total industrial production in 1989 and 1990.

With regard to obtaining the raw materials and other supplies required for production, the Law on the State Enterprise gave the firm the 'preferential' right to retain existing arrangements, to expand long-term contractual ties and to select the form of supply. The 1987 reform package called for a gradual transfer from centralized rationing to wholesale trade as the main source of supply; the latter was supposed to comprise some two-thirds of total wholesale turnover in 1992 (*Ekonomicheskaya Gazeta*, 1987, no. 32, p. 6). The State Committee for Statistics reported that the volume of wholesale trade nearly tripled in 1989 compared with 1988 and that about 8 000 different types of products were free of sales restrictions (*Pravda*, 28 January 1990). Nonetheless, a mass of press reporting indicates that obtaining supplies remained the most serious problem for industrial enterprises in 1989 and 1990, and barter deals among enterprises became widespread. To ease their lot, many enterprise managers beseeched their ministries to provide them with supplies. At the same time, the state rationing agency (Gossnab) was finding it ever harder to obtain materials to ration, as regional autarky spread and as many enterprises reduced planned output, failed to meet contracts, increasingly resorted to hoarding and barter deals, and sought to bypass the state trading agencies (see, for example: *Ekonomika i Zhizn*, 1990, no. 1, p. 4; *Rabochaia Tribuna*, 25 September 1990; *Trud*, 8 January 1991; and *Planovoe Khoziaistvo*, 1990, no. 7, pp. 34–43.

The 1987 Law on the State Enterprise also gave enterprises considerably more leeway in setting prices for their products, primarily by sanctioning greater use of contract prices freely negotiated between buyers and sellers. As before, enterprises could determine the prices for new and improved products, but within state-set guidelines. The government, however, continued to fix wholesale prices for the vast bulk of industrial raw materials and manufactures, and enterprises must use these prices as the basis for those that they determine themselves. New and much higher industrial wholesale prices were originally scheduled for introduction on 1 January 1990, but actually introduced by Presidential Decree on 1 January 1991. With the growing disequilibria in the economy during 1988–1990, enterprises 'abused' their newly acquired freedom by increasing the prices of their products substantially and by shifting their product mix toward higher priced goods. In response to such allegedly 'selfish' behaviour, the government in early 1989 and again a year later issued decrees curtailing the freedom of enterprises to fix or negotiate prices by imposing limits on profit rates, confiscating 'excess' profits, and restricting the range of products for which contract prices could be set (*Pravda*, 4 February 1989 and *Sobranie Postanovlenii Pravitelstva SSSR,* 1990, no. 6, pp. 143–59). Subsequently, however, price controls were lifted on a variety of luxury consumer goods, and it was stated that in 1991 there is to be a shift to 'widespread use of contract prices' (*Pravda*, 15 November 1990 and *Izvestia*, 5 October 1990).

Relationships with the workforce
The 1987 Law on the State Enterprise gives the enterprise wide latitude in the area of labour and wages. A part of the total reform package, however, is a decree adopted in September 1986 that mandated a major overhaul of the industrial wage and salary structure, with basic wage rates for blue-collar workers to rise an average of 20–25 per cent and salaries of white-collar workers by 30–35 per cent (Chapman, 1988). The new wage and salary scales were to be introduced in each enterprise when it was able to finance the higher wages from internal funds. Revenues were supposed to be generated by reducing employment, tightening work norms and raising labour productivity. Managers were free to use bonus funds as they saw fit and (with some restrictions) to transfer money from one incentive fund to another. On 1 January 1990 75 per cent of all industrial production personnel worked under the new wage conditions (Goskomstat SSSR, *Preso-vypusk*, 6 June 1990, no. 225).

The 1987 Law on the State Enterprise permitted the work collective to choose between two ways of forming funds for paying workers. Under the first model, the wage fund was formed on the basis of normatives relating it to the growth of net output, and, in addition, workers received bonuses from the enterprise incentive fund formed as a share of profits. Under the second model, total earnings were a residual after deduction from sales of all material costs plus profits taxes and payments into incentive funds (other than the bonus fund) determined as specified shares of profits. Not surprisingly, the second model was unpopular: as of 1989, it was in effect in enterprises that produced only 7.7 per cent of industrial output (*Narodnoe Khoziaistvo SSSR v 1989 godu*, 1990, Moscow, p. 264).

In practice, enterprises raised wages rapidly, but without a concomitant rise in labour productivity. They also needed to raise wages to compete with the rapidly growing cooperatives, where average incomes were more than double those in state enterprises. The government attempted to curtail the increase in wages, first by limiting increases to the growth of labour productivity and later by taxing most wage increases above 3 per cent per year. Both measures were full of exceptions and loopholes and proved ineffective. Whereas average monthly wages in industry had increased by 2.7 per cent annually during 1986–87, they rose at an average annual rate of 9.4 per cent during 1988–89 and continued to rise rapidly in 1990. Total employment in state enterprises, however, fell by 4.7 per cent during 1987–89, and the decline continued in 1990. Part of this decrease reflects the transfer of workers to cooperatives formed within state enterprises.

Another innovation of the 1980s was a drive to install the brigade form of organization of labour throughout industry (Heinemeier, 1987). This campaign was launched in Brezhnev's reform decree of July 1979 with the goal of making brigades the main form of labour organization in industry by 1985. The idea was to promote self-discipline and link effort to reward in these small units. The planners expected sizeable gains in labour productivity and efficiency to be realized. Although 74 per cent of all blue-collar workers worked in brigades in 1985, the hoped-for efficiency gains did not occur. In the Gorbachev era a push was made to put brigades on *khozraschet* (economic accountability). In 1989 a little over half of all brigadiers worked in this type of brigade, compared with 36.7 per cent in 1985 (*Narodnoe Khoziaistvo SSSR v 1989 godu,* 1990, Moscow, p. 369). Workers in such brigades have an incentive to limit the number of members, a fact that may help to explain the decline in industrial employment in 1988–90.

The 1980s have also witnessed a significant move toward industrial democracy through the creation of institutions that give workers more voice in managing their enterprises. A new Law on the Labour Collective adopted in 1983 spelled out in general terms the rights and obligations of labour collectives (*Pravda,* 19 June 1983). In accord with Gorbachev's call for more democracy throughout Soviet society, the 1987 Law on the State Enterprise was much more explicit. It provided for the election of Labour Councils which were to function as permanent bodies in carrying out decisions taken at General Conferences of the enterprise workforce. The Council, required to meet at least once each quarter, was to be elected by open or secret ballot of the workforce for terms of 2 or 3 years. No more than one-quarter of the members could be representatives of management. The Council was given the right to decide on a variety of matters relating to the use of enterprise incentive funds and to the pay, training and disciplining of the workforce. Its decisions were binding on both management and the workforce. The Law also provided for the election of the managers of all key units in the enterprise structure, from the director down to the level of foremen and brigade leaders. Managers of enterprises were to be elected 'as a rule on a competitive basis' at a general meeting of the collective by secret or open ballot for a five-year term. The elected candidate had to be ratified by the ministry to which the enterprise was subordinated. Persons elected to lower-level posts had to be approved by the enterprise manager. Apparently, this experiment in election of officials of enterprises had unintended consequences, most prominently the increased turnover of managers and the election of managers by 'whim' of the workforce (*Izvestia,* 3 October 1989). The section of the

1990 Law on Enterprises that deals with enterprise management (Section IV) took effect in June 1990, even though the Law as a whole became effective on 1 January 1991. Section IV stipulates that managers are to be appointed and dismissed by the owner of the enterprise and that heads of sub-units in the enterprise are to be chosen by the enterprise director. Section IV also provides for creating an enterprise council consisting of an equal number of representatives of the owner and of labour; representatives of labour are supposed to be elected by the workforce unless otherwise stipulated in the enterprise charter. Among other things, the council is given the right to determine the disposition of net profits.

Investment and finance
The 1987 Law on the State Enterprise states that 'as a rule' the enterprise must finance all of its activities from internally-generated funds (amortization deductions, profits and bank credits). If it cannot do so, the state may declare it bankrupt and liquidate its assets. These provisions were intended to impose a hard budget constraint on enterprises. In practice, however, the government continued to subsidize planned loss-making enterprises, which numbered 1 139 in 1989 (*Ekonomika i Zhizn*, 1990, no. 40, p. 15). It appears also that the ministries continued to subsidize unprofitable and low-profit enterprises and to merge financially troubled with successful ones or convert them into cooperatives. In both cases, such subsidization was required because much-needed price revisions did not take place until 1991.

The 1987 reforms allowed enterprises to retain a larger share of their profits and abolished the long-standing practice of making the state budget the residual claimant to profits. Instead, the ministries established normatives (percentages) for deductions from profits into the state budget and into ministerial reserve funds. These normatives included a capital charge and a newly imposed charge for labour. As a result of these changes, the share of retained earnings in total profits of industrial enterprises rose from 36 per cent in 1987 to 43 per cent in 1989 (*Narodnoe Khoziaistvo SSSR v 1989 godu*, 1990, Moscow, p. 620). Nearly all of retained profits are channelled into three major incentive funds, namely the bonus fund, the fund for social–cultural measures, and the fund for development of production and research and development. Allocations of retained profits to these funds were determined by ministry-set normatives, which in practice tended to be enterprise-specific. New federal laws on enterprises and on taxation of enterprises that became effective in 1991 significantly modify these arrangements by fixing uniform federal tax rates and abolishing the system of ministry normatives (*Ekonomika i Zhizn,* 1990, no. 25, pp. 19–21 and *Izvestia*, 30 June 1990).

The industrial enterprise is required to finance as a rule all of its investment from its own funds, now principally from its production development fund, supplemented by bank credits. Besides retaining a larger share of profits, the enterprise now also retains the bulk of its amortization charges, instead of having them centralized in investment banks as before. Thus, a much larger proportion of industrial investment is now financed from decentralized funds and the enterprise ostensibly controls the use of the funds. During 1988–90 the enterprises used their enhanced authority, contrary to the government's wishes, to start numerous new projects and to compete for scarce investment resources with projects financed centrally from the budget. The result was an increase in the volume of unfinished industrial construction from the equivalent of 96 per cent of annual investment in 1987 to 116 per cent in 1989 (*Narodnoe Khoziaistvo SSSR v 1989 godu,* 1990, Moscow, p. 547). This development prompted the government to try to curb enterprises' investment activity in 1990 by various administrative devices, but with little success.

Under the 1987 reforms enterprises were required to conclude annual credit agreements with the banks, which were enjoined to take a much more active role in ensuring that credit extensions would enhance efficiency. The banks themselves were to operate under conditions of full self-finance and were expected to be much more exacting in imposing financial discipline on enterprise borrowers. The latter now received interest on balances in their incentive funds and the banks were allowed to use interest rates on loans more flexibly to penalize enterprises that failed to repay loans on time. Banks also could declare chronically delinquent firms insolvent and demand corrective action from their superior ministries. None of this, however, reflects any radical change in the traditional relationships between industrial firms and the banks. In 1989 and 1990 a number of independent cooperative and commercial banks sprang up. Such banks were often organized to serve particular sectors (e.g. the automobile industry) or regions. They often made loans at much higher rates of interest to enterprises that could not obtain credit from state banks (*Ekonomika i Zhizn*, 1990, no. 10, p. 17; no. 16, pp. 10–11; and no. 20, p. 10). In December 1990 new USSR laws creating a Federal Reserve-type central bank and a network of independent commercial banks were adopted (*Izvestia*, 19 December 1990). A supplemental federal law on investment activities in general was also adopted late in 1990 (*Izvestia*, 17 December 1990).

Foreign trade rights
At the beginning of the 1980s industrial enterprises had almost no possibility of engaging directly in foreign trade, which was a monopoly of the Ministry of Foreign Trade. A major innovation of Gorbachev's reforms was a decree adopted in August 1986 that granted foreign trade rights to 20 ministries and 70 enterprises (*Sobranie Postanovlenii Pravitelstva SSSR*, 1986,

no. 33, pp. 587–91). Exporting enterprises could retain a small part of any hard currency earnings to pay for desired imports. The decree also authorized joint ventures on Soviet soil with firms in capitalist countries. The 1987 Law on the State Enterprise spelled out its rights and responsibilities in the area of foreign trade, but the enterprise had to obtain the permission of its ministry to exercise such rights. A decree adopted in late 1988 greatly liberalized these provisions (*Izvestia*, 10 December 1988). Any enterprise can now engage in foreign trade and joint ventures can be started with 100 per cent foreign ownership (up to 49 per cent before late 1990). Enterprises wishing to engage directly in foreign trade must register with the state. The Council of Ministers is empowered to draw up lists of products and services for which imports and exports are banned or for which licenses are required. In the main enterprises must be able to finance desired imports from their own hard currency earnings or from funds purchased at hard currency auctions that were started in late 1989. In practice many enterprises in 1989 and 1990 were unable to pay for their purchases, helping to bring on a payments crisis that damaged the USSR's creditworthiness in international markets. In response, Gorbachev in late 1990 issued a Presidential Decree centralizing most hard currency earnings, in order, among other things, to bail out delinquent enterprises. Also in 1990 the government banned the export of a list of consumer goods in short supply domestically and imposed high export levies on others.

At the end of 1989 1 274 joint ventures were registered in the USSR (*Pravitelstvennii Vestnik,* 1990, no. 5, p. 10). Most of them had not begun operations and it appears that only a small proportion of these ventures were in the industrial sector. Despite the fact that joint ventures have encountered a myriad of difficulties, most prominently in obtaining supplies and in repatriating profits, their number continued to grow. In its report on economic performance, the State Statistical Committee reported that 'about 3 000' joint enterprises had been created by the end of 1990 (*Ekonomika i Zhizn,* 1991, no. 5, p. 9).

5.   CONCLUSION

At the end of 1990 the position of Soviet industrial enterprises was little changed from what it had been for many decades. Nearly all of them were owned by the state and were subordinated to government agencies that heavily influenced all major aspects of enterprise activities. The bulk of industrial output was produced under mandatory quotas (now labelled state orders), most raw materials and investment resources were acquired through rationing, and most industrial wholesale prices were fixed directly or regulated by the government. Industrial wage and salary scales were established centrally and the allocation of profits was controlled by state-set normatives.

While these pillars of the centrally planned socialist economy remained in place and the bulk of industrial output was produced within that framework, industrial performance had been deteriorating rapidly. Production stagnated in 1989 and declined in 1990. There had been no breakthrough in raising efficiency and quality of industrial products or improving their competitiveness in world markets. At a conference of managers of state industrial enterprises held in Moscow in early December 1990, participants described a rapidly developing barter economy and were prone to describe the situation as chaotic (*Ekonomika i Zhizn*, 1990, no. 51, pp. 4–5). This outcome was largely the result of the government's bad macroeconomic policies of the last half of the 1980s, coupled with the implementation in 1988–90 of inconsistent and contradictory reforms in the industrial sector. In effect, enterprises were given substantially greater production and financial autonomy at a time of fast-growing disequilibrium in the consumer sector, and their actions only made matters worse, especially in the investment sphere. Weakening central control over economic decisions in the republics added to the difficulties. In 1990, especially, local authorities acted to keep scarce supplies from being shipped out of their regions. In such a situation the central government's several efforts to impose restrictions on enterprise autonomy in production, pricing and wages proved ineffective.[3] Enterprises were able to ignore central commands without fear of serious penalties, but also were often forced to find ways to get around central controls in order to survive under the changed financial and market conditions.

Along with all this, however, the final two years of the decade witnessed developments that have the potential to alter fundamentally the position of industrial enterprises in the 1990s. Many laws and decrees were adopted that could lay the legal basis for a market economy. Most important are the federal laws on property, on enterprises, on taxation of enterprises, on investment and on banking, as well as Council of Ministers decrees on joint stock companies, issuance of securities, small businesses and demonopolization. Also notable is a presidential decree establishing a State Property Fund that is charged with 'destatization' of industrial enterprises (i.e. converting them into joint stock companies and other forms of ownership). Even in 1990 some industrial enterprises had begun selling shares to their workers, a number of enterprises had been transformed into joint stock companies, and preparations were made to set up a stock exchange. But the effects of all this legislation will come in 1991 and thereafter. Most of the new legislation deals with the ownership and use of property. Even though much of it is couched in language that is far too general and ambiguous by Western legal standards, this spate of legislation represents remarkable

234 Industrial reform in socialist countries

progress on matters that were ideologically taboo until the advent of Gorbachev in 1985.

Along with adoption of this specific legislation, there was a parade of programmes for comprehensive economic reforms in general, all having the declared goal of moving to a 'destatized' market economy. These programmes included: the 'Abalkin Blueprint' of October 1989 (rejected), the Ryzhkov government programme of December 1989 (approved), a revised Government Programme in May 1990 (rejected), the so-called '500-Day' (Shatalin) Plan in July 1990 (rejected at the federal level), and the so-called Presidential Plan of October 1990 ('Basic Directions for the Stabilization of the Economy and the Changeover to the Market') (adopted). The various programmes differed in many ways, but most importantly on the sequencing of various reform measures, on the speed with which they should occur, and on the division of authority between the federal and republic governments (Hewett, 1991). The acrimonious debates over these assorted recipes for transition to a market economy played out in an atmosphere of increasing tensions between the central government and the governments of the republics. By the end of 1990 all republics had adopted declarations of 'economic sovereignty', and some of them had enacted laws on property and other economic matters that conflicted with federal legislation. President Gorbachev at the end of 1990 sought to resolve the conflicts by drafting a Union Treaty and submitting it to the republics for discussion and ratification (*Pravda*, 24 November 1990). In addition, Gorbachev had sought and received authority to rule by Presidential Decree (from late September 1990 through March 1992). Three such decrees issued during September–December 1990 sought to deal with the rapidly mounting supply difficulties faced by industrial enterprises. These decrees ordered the retention of existing contractual ties among enterprises through 1991, introduced as of 1 January the new wholesale prices on which contracts were to be based, and forbade enterprises and regional bodies from making deals that disrupt existing ties.

As of the end of 1990 the Presidential Plan, approved by the USSR Supreme Soviet on 19 October 1990, constituted the operational document for economic reform in the USSR (*Izvestia*, 27 October 1990). It is being implemented in part by presidential decrees, which are recentralizing in nature and aim to stabilize the economic and financial situation as quickly as possible, while simultaneously proceeding with fundamental reforms as laid out in the Plan. Although the Presidential Plan lacks the specific time-tables and detail of the much-publicized '500-Day programme', the Plan is quite radical, nevertheless, and particularly so when compared with the package of reforms adopted in 1987. The Plan declares that 'The choice of switching to the market has been made, a choice of historic importance to the fate of the country'. Unlike the 1987 package, the Plan calls for gradual 'destatization' and privatization of property. Except to the extent modified by presidential decrees issued during the stabilization phase (18 months to 2 years), the Plan rests on implementation of the many new laws and decrees adopted in 1990.

If all this legislation is fully implemented and with dispatch, the position of the industrial enterprise will need to change radically by the mid-1990s. Central directive plans will have been replaced by a so-called state contracting system of voluntary sales to the state on competitive and mutually advantageous terms. Rationing of producer goods will have been replaced by free contracting between enterprises and a commercial wholesale trade network. Most prices will become market-determined. Substantial progress will have been made toward demonopolization and toward diverse forms of property ownership. The Soviet Union would be well on its way toward a market economy by the mid-1990s, but one that would retain a large state sector in such areas as defence production, transportation, communications and social infrastructure.

There is grave doubt, however, that the Presidential Plan or any other programme of systemic economic reforms can be carried out in practice in the near term. Its success rests on economic relations among regions based on 'recognition of republic state sovereignty and equality and at the same time on the integrity of the Union as a federation, on the understanding that the enterprise is the basis of the economy and the state's task is to create the most favourable conditions for its activity'. But a mutually agreeable accord between the federal and republic governments has yet to be forged. Moreover, both the industrial bureaucracy and managers of state industrial enterprises are profoundly conservative, as the recent conference of managers showed. They can be expected to drag their feet on privatization and resist moves that threaten competition from domestic firms or from imports. The population in general still favours government ownership of large-scale industry, along with a strong role for the state in general, and is deeply opposed to the lifting of price controls, job dislocations and income disparities that would accompany successful market reforms. How these complex and inter-related matters will be resolved remains to be seen.

NOTES

1. Growth of industrial production fell from 6.6 per cent in 1975 to 2.3 per cent in 1982. The causes of this dramatic slowdown are analysed in Schroeder (1985).
2. For details of the reforms adopted during 1985–87 see Schroeder (1986, 1987).
3. We should also note the failure of a government measure intended to obtain a breakthrough in raising the quality of industrial products. Introduced selectively in factories during 1987–89, this measure, known as Gospriemka (state inspection) proved unpopu-

lar, disruptive and ineffective and was allowed to wither away. In 1990 the RSFSR abolished the system on its territory, as did the Ukraine in 1991.

REFERENCES

Chapman, J. (1988) 'Gorbachev's wage reform', *Soviet Economy*, vol. 4, no. 4 (October–December).

Heinemeier, M. (1987) 'The brigade system of labour organization as incentives in Soviet industry', in US Congress Joint Economic Committee *Gorbachev's Economic Plans*, Washington: US Government Printing Office.

Hewett, E. (1991) 'The Soviet plan', *Foreign Affairs*, vol. 69, no. 5 (Winter 1990/91).

Schroeder, G. (1985) 'The slowdown in Soviet industry, 1976–1982', *Soviet Economy*, vol. 1, no. 1 (January–March).

Schroeder, G. (1986) 'Gorbachev: "radically" implementing Brezhnev's reforms', *Soviet Economy*, vol. 2, no. 4 (October–December).

Schroeder, G. (1987) 'Anatomy of Gorbachev's economic reform', *Soviet Economy*, vol. 3, no. 3 (July–September).

14 Industrial reform in Vietnam
Melanie Beresford

Industrial reform in Vietnam is not merely an echo of economic transformations which have taken place elsewhere in the socialist world. Vietnam's economic difficulties of the 1970s and 1980s were generated partly by the 'bureaucratic subsidy system', a feature of administrative planning in general. They were also given a unique configuration by Vietnam's peculiar location as a geo-political battleground, its indigenous revolution and its struggle to unify, under a socialist banner, two diametrically opposed socio-economic systems in the North and South of the country. Vietnamese leaders, well aware that they faced problems which were both similar and highly dissimilar to their counterparts in Eastern Europe and China, have kept one eye carefully on the fortunes and responses of their erstwhile allies, while developing their own strategies for survival and growth. Today, after more than a decade of experimentation, the Vietnamese Communists have achieved a more thorough reform than any of their counterparts – yet retained a degree of political stability which most could not.

In order to understand why this is so, this chapter begins by explaining something of the historical development of Vietnam's industrial sector prior to the introduction of reforms. It then traces the process of reform, commencing in 1979, and discusses its impact on the economy, focusing particularly on the period after the 1986 Party Congress which has seen the most dramatic shifts in policy.

1. BACKGROUND TO THE REFORMS

Output growth was rapid in the Democratic Republic of Vietnam (DRV) after 1954, although Fforde and Paine have shown that signs of the shortage economy were already developing by 1965 (Fforde and Paine, 1987, pp. 56–71). During the next decade, wartime destruction left a rickety infrastructure, requiring major repairs, and wreaked havoc on industrial production. In spite of Soviet and Chinese aid, physical output in 12 out of 26 major industries had failed to recover from US bombing campaigns by 1974 (Beresford, 1989a, p. 169). The South experienced far less industrial development, but was endowed with superior transport facilities by the Americans. After 1975, the US aid embargo, which also affected international lending

237

bodies, and withdrawal of Chinese aid[1] prevented adequate repairs being carried out. This in turn created bottlenecks in supply, especially in the delivery of raw materials to industry. During 1977–78 a series of poor agricultural seasons was another important factor in hampering economic recovery. There were continuing hostilities along Vietnam's borders, at first the highly destabilizing war along the Cambodian frontier and then, in early 1979, a short but destructive war with China to the north. A number of important industrial installations were wrecked, while the high level of Sino-Vietnamese tension in 1978–80 was reflected in domestic ethnic relations and led to an exodus of skilled workers from the Nam Dinh textile mills and the Hon Gai coalfields.

Most of the above difficulties were more or less beyond the government's control, certainly beyond the control of economic policy makers. Yet it is virtually impossible to give any true account of their impact on production because, before 1979, the 'heavy industry priority' strategy and administrative planning model implemented by the Socialist Republic of Vietnam (SRV) government tended to exacerbate the existing difficulties. Because policy changes before 1979 worked in a vicious circle with exogenous factors, it is hard to say which was the more destructive.

However, two major policy steps in the 1970s contributed to the industrial crisis that developed towards the end of the decade. The first of these was the attempt to complete the 'socialization of agriculture' via a New Management System in the North (1974–78) (Fforde, 1989). The second was the 'socialist transformation of the South', begun in 1976.

Both of these policy changes were undertaken in the attempt to overcome contradictions in the operation of the socialist economy, namely the persistence of shortage leading to autarky in most sectors of the economy and inflation in unofficial markets. In the 1970s the view of the majority of party leaders was that these problems were caused by factors such as poor management techniques and deliberate sabotage of the socialist system by reactionary elements, notably within the Southern (predominantly Chinese) business community. The solution was to tighten economic management (by, for example, improving the quality of cadres) and to repress capitalism in the South. These decisions were taken under the acute pressure of developing hostility on Vietnam's south-western and northern borders, as well as American insistence that its allies help isolate Vietnam from the West. The Vietnamese leaders could perhaps be forgiven for thinking that, due to constant pressures of war, the socialist system had never been given a real chance to develop in their country. Moreover, prior to 1978 there was little atmosphere favouring reform in any of Vietnam's socialist neighbours.

2. THE EARLY REFORMS 1979–85

By mid-1979 it was abundantly clear that the measures introduced to 'perfect' the socialist system were having a very different impact from that intended. State rice procurement, the main means by which rural autarky was to be broken, had fallen continuously since 1977, both absolutely and as a share of output (Beresford, 1989a, p. 118). There was evidence that peasants were diverting substantial quantities onto the black market or, given that there were few goods to purchase with income so obtained, feeding rice to the ducks and illegally distilling alcohol (Beresford, 1989a, p. 113). Industry consequently suffered from even greater shortages of raw materials, while workers found it impossible to subsist on the reduced quantities of rice received in their ration.[2]

The Sixth Plenum of the Party Central Committee, meeting in August–September 1979, introduced a programme of economic reforms. The plenum endorsed the principle that investment priorities should be reorientated towards projects offering a quicker economic return, while those projects suffering from excessive delays and cost overruns should be suspended. A degree of enterprise autonomy in areas not covered by the plan was also accepted, as was the idea that the rate of 'socialist transformation' should be slowed, allowing private (meaning family) enterprise in agriculture and artisan industry to play a more important role in stimulating output growth. By the end of the year, small-scale manufacturing cooperatives were able to negotiate directly with suppliers to purchase, at negotiated prices, extra raw materials for production of above-plan goods or secondary products. Similar negotiations were possible between cooperatives producing for export and their (foreign) suppliers, although transactions were still conducted via the Foreign Trade Ministry, which limited any real enterprise autonomy .

Regulations covering state enterprises were not issued until January 1981. These also permitted firms to retain a portion of earnings in order to encourage non-plan investment and/or payment of productivity bonuses to workers. Under the 'three-plan system' the enterprise plan comprised the following: planned output (with inputs provided by the state); above-plan output (with own-procured inputs); and secondary output (not included in the plan) which could be sold on the free market. In the case of planned output profit retention was 50 per cent, for above-plan output it was 60 per cent and for secondary output 90 per cent (Le Trang, 1990, p. 159).

Some efforts were made to improve the system of individual incentives within factories. Prior to the introduction of reforms, it would appear that wage differentials within firms hardly existed at all. In 1978, for example, 88 per cent of workers in the central light industrial sector were on the same wage level (JPRS, 75456, p. 37). Piece rates were first introduced during

1980 and combined with bonuses and penalties for quality of product and efficient consumption of raw materials (JPRS, 80977, p. 36). By 1982, however, only 19 factories had implemented them. One reason for this failure may be that shifting to piece work involved interference with established work practices (see JPRS-SEA-88-009, 24 February 1988, p. 60) and remuneration systems that created conflicts within the workforce. But, in any case, the new wage system could not solve the problem of continuing shortages of food and basic consumer goods. Workers on piece rates may be earning twice the income of time-rated workers in the same plant, but neither group was earning enough to meet the minimum subsistence requirements of workers and their dependents (JPRS, 81347, p. 64; JPRS, 81888, p. 28).

Nevertheless, the initial impetus to production and procurement given by the reforms was encouraging and they were followed in 1981 by the adoption of a major reform in cooperative agriculture in the form of the 'product contract system' (*khoan san pham*). This built on a tendency, already quite widespread in practice, if not receiving official sanction, of cooperatives leasing collectively-owned land to individual households. Under the new system, households contracted for use of a plot of land on which to produce a quota of grain (or other designated crop) at official prices. After meeting contractual obligations, households retained any extra output which they could then sell, either to the state at negotiated prices or on the free market. Cooperatives retained control over a variety of functions including provision of modern inputs (at fixed prices), improved seed and ploughing services.

In general, these agricultural reforms did not affect mechanisms responsible for the supply of industrial goods to farmers. Therefore, in spite of rising farm output and state grain procurement in the next two years, continuing shortages of industrial goods, particularly in North Vietnam, restricted the longer-term impact of the reforms: farmers, unable to obtain manufactured goods, were in no mood to increase their effort. The government's goal of increasing domestic sources of investment by expanding the division of labour between agriculture and industry ran aground on the reef of continuing problems in industry.

Only in the South was there a significant divergence from this pattern. While data are rather fragmentary, anecdotal evidence of the greater volume and quality of goods available in the South since 1980 is plentiful (FEER, 10 April 1986). Ho Chi Minh City is the main industrial centre of the region and produced about a third of national industrial output by the mid-1980s. While industrial employment in the city had grown at an average rate of 2.3 per cent per annum during 1974–80, the rate rose to 14.1 per cent during 1980–84 (Beresford, 1989a, p. 230). The value of industrial output was reported to have risen by over 26 per cent from 1980 to 1981 and by 27 per cent between 1983 and 1984 (admittedly from a low starting point), compared with national industrial growth rates of 1 per cent and 13 per cent respectively (Nguyen Van Linh, 1985, p. 105; Tong Cuc Thong Ke, 1989, p. 143). Consumer goods production dominates in the city, but the crucial light engineering sector also increased its share, from 8.3 per cent in 1976 to 20 per cent in 1984 (Nguyen Van Linh, 1985, p. 106).

Two major reasons for this better performance of the southern region can be identified. The first is that a more rational structure of industry has been developed. The party leadership's strategy for economic unification of the country has been to develop the region's agricultural and light industrial potential in order to complement the heavy industry and mineral resources of the North. Within the South, the local leadership has given priority to intensifying the division of labour between agriculture and industry as the main means of generating growth. The theory of growth implicit in this strategy, though still within a Marxist framework, is different from that implied in the DRV's development model. Instead of focusing on the mobilization of agricultural surpluses to build heavy industry (as in the model derived from such early Soviet thinkers as Preobrazhensky), the South Vietnamese model concentrates on the development of exchange between agriculture and light industry, both to modernize agriculture and to increase the supply of consumer goods and exports (Ho Duc Hung, 1984, pp. 30–1). In this way, the problems generated in the North Vietnamese economy by the overwhelming priority given to heavy industry have been avoided and it has proven possible to achieve quick returns for a relatively small investment.

The second reason is the more highly developed *commodity* economy[3] of the South which has made it more receptive to market-orientated reforms and more open to experimentation. Since the traditional socialist system has never become entrenched in the South, the ability of the vested interests established by such a system to resist reform has been correspondingly restricted. Moreover, ever since 1975 there appears to have been strong practical support within the southern party organization for a much more prolonged 'transition', in which capitalist and family enterprises would play a prominent role than the central leadership was at times prepared to countenance (see Beresford, 1990a, for a full discussion).

Nevertheless, the early success of the reforms convinced many in the party that the process of accelerating socialist ownership in the South could be resumed. A new campaign was announced in 1983 for completing collectivization of southern agriculture within two years and taxation measures were introduced which discriminated against private enterprise, especially in 'non-productive' areas like restaurants and retailing (SWB, FE/7284, 17 March 1983). However, there was no change in the basic direction of increasing use of economic levers, rather than administrative measures, as the mechanism for regulating the economy. The impression among some observers that 1983–85 marked a return to the command economy system is erroneous.

In September 1985 the government moved towards widening the commodity economy by eliminating the subsidized rice rations previously available to all state employees. Because of the enormous gap between the official prices and free market prices, the rice ration had become a valuable resource for state workers who could sell part of it to buy other necessary goods. State wages were certainly not high enough to cover subsistence needs and most workers were compelled to take 'outside' jobs to make ends meet, adversely affecting productivity levels in the state sector itself. Moreover, to encourage farm production, the state offered producers a price far in excess of the ration price and the subsidy thus incurred became a huge item in a widening budget deficit (Spoor, 1988, p. 120). The reform was undertaken to eliminate the subsidy and, simultaneously, to increase wages by a compensatory amount.

Any positive impact this change might have had was completely lost in the aftermath of a currency reform introduced by the conservative State Bank in October. Worried about accumulation of wealth in the private sector, the State Bank introduced a new unit of currency, one new Dong substitutable for ten old ones. A ceiling placed on the amount exchangeable ensured the destruction of much private wealth and also weakened many people's confidence in the continuation of the reforms. At the same time, the Bank's move wiped out illegal cash holdings of state enterprises which were actually necessary for operating in an environment where the black market may be the only place to find the raw materials assigned, but not delivered, by the state. The result was a sharp worsening of shortages of all kinds of goods. The subsidized rice ration had to be reintroduced and inflation then took off as budget deficits increased sharply, covered by cash creation. Conditions in the Vietnamese economy became chaotic, with inflation reaching a reported 700–1 000 per cent within six months and persisting at these rates throughout the next two years (FEER, 10 April 1986, 14 January 1988).

3.   THE REFORM PROCESS SINCE 1986

By late 1986, however, reformers within the Vietnamese Communist Party (VCP) were in a much stronger position. During the previous decade over 10 per cent of the 1.8 million party members had been expelled in a drive to banish 'irresponsible and incompetent cadres', opportunism, formalism, red-tape, parochialism, 'feudal practices' (behaving like mandarins), and 'unqualified members ... degenerate and depraved elements' (Truong Chinh, 1986). A criticism and self-criticism drive was held in the second half of the year, which culminated in substantial changes to membership of local and regional party committees. In December, at the Sixth National Party Congress, the Political Bureau itself underwent a transformation, with the last of Ho Chi Minh's original colleagues being forced into retirement. The Congress took place in a highly self-critical atmosphere, outgoing party Secretary Truong Chinh holding the Political Bureau itself responsible for the economic disasters of the late 1970s and mid-1980s.

Two leaders who were promoted within the party hierarchy at this Congress, Nguyen Van Linh (the new Secretary-General) and Vo Van Kiet (Deputy Premier and Planning Minister) had long political associations with the South. In my view their promotion reflected a shift in the balance of power towards the Southern party organization, which had been eclipsed somewhat in the aftermath of 1975. By 1986, however, the South was clearly the most dynamic part of the country, a fact which is largely attributable to the success of economic reforms there. Northern Vietnam, on the other hand, was again on the verge of a serious economic crisis, with stagnation in food production recorded every year after 1982.[4] Its industry continued to suffer from 'simultaneous abundance and shortage', as well as slow output growth of its intermediate-goods industries (like coal, cement, fertilizer).[5]

The lesson drawn by the new leaders was that there must be a radical restructuring of the economy. They named this process *doi moi* (renovation), which became the catch-cry of the late 1980s. In place of the emphasis by previous congresses on the importance of developing heavy industry sectors, the economic priorities of the Sixth Congress were on agriculture, consumer goods and exports (mainly agricultural and light industrial exports). Transport was another area slated for a larger share of public investment, in order to promote commodity turnover; energy production (coal, hydro-electricity, oil and gas) was also identified in Deputy Premier Vo Van Kiet's Economic Report as a key bottleneck to overcome. Heavy industry was now to be promoted *only* where it could serve the development of these areas (by producing fertilizer, pesticides and veterinary medicines, for example) or national defence.

The yardstick of investment effectiveness laid down by this Congress was a combination of low capital intensity, high employment creation and quick output results. New projects could be started only where increased output was unobtainable by improved productivity of existing establishments. Inessential projects (even those already under construction) were to be stopped and firms unable to produce at a profit were to be closed. The household economy was to be given encouragement in agriculture and handicraft production. Small-scale private capital would be allowed to continue to operate (except in commerce) and investment by overseas Vietnamese was also encouraged. Enterprises and individuals trading in consumer goods were urged to carry out market research and to invite tenders before placing orders, in an effort to reduce costs and improve product quality.

A clear indication was given by this Congress that the system of administrative planning and industrial policy, which so often relied on either exhortation or coercion to achieve implementation of targets, should be replaced by the use of more indirect steering via economic levers such as interest rates, manipulation of retained enterprise profits and incentives to shed bloated enterprise workforces. Legally binding plan quotas were henceforth to be restricted to a few basic commodities and foreign trade commitments. In general, economic incentives should be designed in such a way as to guide investment and production into the desired areas.

Many of these ideas were not new, much of the industrial policy merely reiterating goals of earlier plans and reforms. Yet this was the strongest and most detailed statement so far of the aims of the reformers. It was an indication of how far they had come to dominate political and economic thinking within the party since the late 1970s. Achieving real change, however, was another thing. Powerful forces inside and outside the party continued to oppose the reforms and, in many cases, successfully obstruct them. In the words of Truong Chinh (1986, p. 22):

> The struggle for renovation is not only held back by force of habit, but also runs up against the privileges and prerogatives of some people who stick to the old mechanism. This is the struggle inside the party and the state organs, among comrades and right within ourselves.

Some indication of the continuing strength of this opposition came when the National Assembly, meeting just after the party congress, made no changes to the Council of Ministers. The delay was seen by observers at the time as stemming from the need, felt by the VCP's collective leadership, to ease tension over the recent policy conflicts and changes in personnel. In general, 1987 seems to have been a year of preparation and major reform did not get underway until 1988.

Planning of industrial branches

Regulations issued towards the end of 1987 laid down new guidelines on the planning of industry (*Nhan Dan*, 16 December 1987). The most significant development here was the ending of the administrative planning system in all but a handful of industries. Official targets assigned to state enterprises were reduced to one, namely, a stipulated contribution to the state budget. In only a few 'key' industries are output targets still assigned today. These industries include energy-producing sectors, such as coal and electric power, and rail transport. In all other enterprises, plans are drawn up by the enterprise in accordance with the macroeconomic policies of the state and the market situation facing the firm.

Under these new industrial regulations the output plans are established by a congress of workers, theoretically the highest authority within the enterprise. The enterprise manager is given complete control over implementation of these plans and can decide upon such matters as hiring of workers (on contract, rather than on the basis of lifetime employment), wages policy (provided the minimum is observed), purchase of equipment and implementation of technological changes, market research and establishment of direct contacts with suppliers and customers (in both foreign and domestic trade), disposal of capital of the enterprise, and finding external sources of capital via the banking system and/or by tapping oversea investment resources.

In relation to such external sources of capital, further changes in the rules during early 1989 allowed for the establishment of *joint ventures* in which profits are distributed according to shares in the capital of the enterprise. Adam Fforde has pointed out that such activities had already developed out of the experience firms gained of dealing in parallel markets, which led to the formation of 'own capital' and, as investment began to flow into the most profitable areas in the late 1980s, of profit-sharing arrangements (1989, p. 18). The Bank of Industry and Trade, established in Ho Chi Minh City during 1987, is the first example of such a shareholders' company being given approval. Plans to establish a formal stock exchange in Ho Chi Minh City were announced in late 1990 (ID, 17–26 November 1990).

These new institutional mechanisms were designed to do away with one of the main practical obstacles to enterprise autonomy, namely, interference from above. Under 'traditional' socialist planning, the enterprise management functioned as the lowest level of a hierarchical control mechanism (Fforde, 1990, p. 19). For the enterprise to act in its own interests, establishing direct relations with suppliers and customers, was, in the words of an enterprise manager, impossible 'with "Mr" Southern Metals–Bicycles–Motor Vehicles Corporation ... sitting on top' (JPRS-SEA-88-047, 30 November 1988, p. 28). Breaking this structure of authority has not been an easy process and reports of interference from superior levels have continued throughout the transition to the new system. One of the sources of independent power of local authorities has been their ability to collect their own revenue. The central government has made frequent attempts, for example, to abolish the practice of local authorities setting up road blocks to collect taxes on the transit of goods and people (see JPRS-SEA-88-046, 22 November 1988, p. 24; SWB, FE/0658 B/4, 10 January 1990). This attempt at fiscal autarky not only gives the authorities an independent financial power in the locality, but protects local agriculture and industry from competition (or destroys it as the cadres see fit) and sustains the old patterns of political and economic power.

The abolition of the system of administrative planning of industrial branches does not imply any intention to abandon economic planning. On the contrary, the changes are specifically aimed at increasing central government control over the economy by improving the effectiveness of planning through emphasis on indirect steering via the use of economic levers. One feature of the 'traditional' socialist system in Vietnam had been the creation of relatively autarkic economic structures within sectors and between sectors. There was a rather low rate of commodity exchange and turnover between agriculture and industry. The heavy industrial sector, on which so many investment resources were lavished, also had few linkages to other sectors, while in foreign trade, Vietnam made little progress towards specialization.[6] Attempts to break down the pattern of autarky by administrative means had largely failed in North Vietnam prior to 1979, while the southerners had refused to accept the imposition of the system on their market-based economy after 1975 (see Beresford, 1989a, Chapters 4 and 7, for an extensive discussion). By contrast, the clearly stated goal of the 1980s reformers was to increase the interdependence of the various economic sectors, via increased commodity exchange, and thereby to destroy the self-sufficiency of regions, economic base units and ministries. Only thus could they break the ability of lower levels to resist economic regulation from the centre. The new system of economic planning was to replace administrative controls by economic levers.

Changes to the ownership structure

Two systems of ownership have operated side by side in Vietnam since the end of the war in 1975. In the former DRV, there was a three-tiered system consisting of the state-run, collective and individual (or household) sectors, with the last considered subordinated to the first two. In the former Republic of Vietnam (the South), a five-tiered structure was permitted as a reflection of the 'lower stage' of development of the socialist economy. The five tiers were state, joint state–private, collective, individual and private (or capitalist). Before 1986, although the party leadership in Hanoi often paid lip service to the need for a relatively long transition period in the south of the country, two campaigns were launched (1976–79 and 1983–85) to bring the whole economy more quickly under state and collective control. Neither of these campaigns succeeded and, by 1980, after the termination of the first one, around half of industrial employment in Ho Chi Minh City remained in the private and semi-private sectors (97 per cent of all units) (Ho Duc Hung, 1984, pp. 33–4), while only 50 per cent of agricultural households were in any form of collective organization (Beresford, 1989a, p. 110). By the end of the second campaign, the degree of socialization was higher on paper, although officials admitted that this was not reflected in practice.

The reforms announced in 1988 continued the thrust of the reformers towards greater tolerance of private sector activities. Henceforth six tiers would be recognized across the country and a deliberate policy was enunciated of creating a mixed economy in which a renovated state sector would still play the leading role. The six tiers are state, joint state–private, collective, private, individual and domestic economy. The definition of some of these tiers has also changed: e.g. joint state-private enterprises may now have a majority private shareholding and be treated in the same way as other private enterprises; under the previous rules, they were effectively state-controlled. Private (capitalist) enterprise is now clearly distinguished from individual (family and other small) enterprises, a reflection of the new regulations removing limits on the size of private capital investments and employment of wage labour. The passage of a new Foreign Investment Law at the end of 1987 also clearly encouraged private investment (see below). The new category of 'domestic' economy encompasses those individuals employed in other sectors who take on subsidiary income earning occupations, usually in the informal sector.

In the first 12 months of operation of the new laws allowing expansion of private ownership, Ho Chi Minh City had reportedly acquired 72 such enterprises with a surprisingly large average size of around 140 workers. Hanoi, by contrast, had only 26 units with between 20 and 100 workers each (JPRS-SEA-89-021, 18 May 1989, p. 56). This would represent an increase in employment in the non-state, non-collective sector during 1987–88 of just over 1 per cent (Tong Cuc Thong Ke, 1990, p. 150), hardly a major change in the structure of industry. However, prior to 1988, the data show quite a large increase in the individual sector's share of employment, from 23 per cent in 1985 to 31.5 per cent in 1988. Figures on output are not available for the period after the new regulations, but show a slower upward trend in the share of the individual sector between 1985 and 1988 from 17.6 per cent to 19.6 per cent of industrial output (Tong Cuc Thong Ke, 1990, p. 118). Once again, the differences between the North and South are marked. During 1987, for example, over 40 per cent of Southern industrial workers were employed in the individual sector, compared with 18 per cent in the North. One third of Northern workers were in the state sector, over half of these under central management, whereas in the South only a quarter worked in the state sector and 60 per cent of these were in locally controlled firms (Tong Cuc Thong Ke, 1989, pp. 187–8). In Southern Vietnam, 52 per cent of output was produced in the non-state sector (including collective) compared with 31.5 per cent in the North (Tong Cuc Thong Ke, 1989, pp. 156–7). The South has 42 per cent of all industrial workers, but produces 60 per cent of total industrial output.

Foreign investment
One of the first major reforms of *doi moi* was the new Foreign Investment
Law, passed with great fanfare at the end of 1987. It is widely accepted that
this law is no more 'nationalist' in tone than the foreign investment laws of
its capitalist ASEAN neighbours (Vo Nhan Tri, 1990, p. 218, cites several
sources). The law allows up to 100 per cent ownership by the foreign
investor (compared with 49 per cent under the 1977 law), remittance of
profits and other income accruing and repatriation of capital upon sale or
dissolution (subject to a small tax). The company tax rate is set in a range
from 15 to 25 per cent, the higher rates applying to exploitation of natural
resources like oil (which has, incidentally, received the lion's share of investment so far: AWSJ, 30 July 1990). Tax holidays are allowed for two
years from the first profit-making year, with reduced payments possible for a
further two years (SWB, FE/0820 B/2, 19 July 1990). Losses may be carried
over, for tax purposes, for up to five years. Incentives for firms to reinvest
profits are contained in a provision for tax exemption on the portion reinvested. Conditions set out in the law are that foreign enterprises may not be a
net drain on foreign exchange reserves: all imports must be covered by
export earnings. They must also cover social insurance for their workers and
establish a reserve fund of 5 per cent of profits. Wages must conform to
'collective labour agreements', subject to a minimum set by the Ministry of
Labour,[7] although workers are expected to sign individual contracts. The
exact procedures involved in reaching these agreements were not clear at the
time of writing. Many other conditions are specifically left open to negotiation
with individual investors (SRV, 1987).

As in China, when it first opened up to foreign investment, many firms
have reportedly been able to ignore the Foreign Investment Law altogether,
negotiating their own deal with the government (*Bangkok Post*, 8 October
1988). Other signs of flexibility in the implementation of foreign investment
laws include the 1990 amendment: this allows joint ventures between foreign capital and private Vietnamese companies, replacing the previous
stipulation that only state companies were eligible (AWSJ, 18 July 1990).
The idea here is to encourage overseas Vietnamese to inject capital into joint
ventures with family members or former associates who have remained in
the country.

Industrial development remains uppermost in the aims of the government
in seeking foreign investment. It is not intended that foreigners should invest
mainly in development of primary resources for export. The objective is to
acquire Western technology for the development of light industries, chiefly
consumer goods for the domestic market and export products, using domestically produced raw materials. Foreign investment policy specifically dis-
courages the sort of investment that took place, albeit in a very limited way,

under the US-backed southern regime, in which production for the domestic market was based on remarkably high imported content of raw materials and equipment (Beresford, 1989a, p. 70).[8]

Nevertheless, considerable foreign investment in primary resource development has taken place. Most investment to date has gone into oil exploration and production which remained a priority area for investment during the 1986–90 plan period. It is largely as a result of this investment by (mainly) European oil companies that the South's share of foreign investment during the first 18 months of operation of the new foreign investment law was 80 per cent (SWB, FE/W0086, 19 July 1989, p. A/8). Approval has also reportedly been given for foreign investment in another priority area, rice production in the Mekong delta, which is a truly remarkable development considering the importance of the Communist Party's land reform programme in sustaining revolutionary momentum during the years of war. A Canadian company intends to utilize 50,000 acres with an investment of Canadian $200 million (FBIS-EAS-90-203, 19 October 1990, p. 81).

During 1990 construction was begun on Vietnam's first Export Processing Zone near Ho Chi Minh City. The zone is intended to attract foreign investment and joint ventures in light, pollution-free industries. Interest in the zone has mainly come from East Asian NICs (FBIS-EAS-90-211, 31 October 1990, p. 69).

By late 1990, approved foreign investment projects amounted to some $1.2 billion (ID, September 1990). Much of this may not come to fruition as Vietnam's investment climate is a difficult one. Moreover, once oil investments are subtracted from the total, the sum looks much more paltry. The country remains one of the poorest in the world, with an estimated GNP per capita of $210 in 1989 (AWSJ, 29 November 1990), and its infrastructure, although improving, is in a poor state. It is not a highly attractive location for foreign investors, in spite of its cheap, relatively skilled labour force. Nevertheless, like China a decade ago, it has been able to take advantage of the fact that it is resource rich, a potentially large market and, in a changing international political climate, foreign investors are anxious to have first foot in the door in a market which is beginning to open up.

In some respects then, the passage of the Foreign Investment Law has served less as an attraction to potential investors than as a gesture of goodwill by the Vietnamese government towards the West. When Vietnam passed its first Law (in 1977) in an earlier attempt to open its doors to the West, it was largely ignored. Vietnam was then in a deepening economic crisis, while deteriorating relations with China and the USA were pushing it closer to the Soviet Union. By 1988, on the other hand, its agricultural and industrial production had begun to recover, the impending withdrawal of troops from Cambodia had been announced, and the Cold War was ending.

Price and wage reforms

A major plank of *doi moi* has been the drive to make the concept of 'economic accounting' a reality. During the Vietnam war, the over-riding emphasis in pricing policy had been on stability, which meant that changing costs of production tended to be ignored. Prices were also set to encourage production in priority areas, with the effect that they took little account of realities of supply and demand and often provided signals to enterprises which induced them to behave in a different way from that intended. Artificially low output prices for commodities like coal and electricity, intended to subsidize production elsewhere, caused the energy producers to be unprofitable and encouraged waste of these scarce inputs in user industries. The chronic scarcity of raw materials also forced enterprises to turn to parallel markets to obtain supplies in order to meet production plans. On top of this, the state-subsidized food ration kept wages low, leading to overstaffing and low productivity of labour.

These factors, which are familiar to students of the centrally planned economies, resulted in extensive state subsidies. The subsidies were increased by the production units' tendencies to over-order supplies from the centre as a hedge against uncertainty, to underutilize capacity and to waste resources. These negative influences on industry were largely induced by the state's 'rush' growth strategies, the resultant shortages and the absence of financial discipline. Consumption subsidies have in fact been the largest single item in the state budget, taking 12 per cent of expenditure in 1983 (IMF, 1983, p. 4), and, together with subsidies to state enterprises, make a major contribution to the large budget deficits (Spoor, 1988; Vo Nhan Tri, 1990, p. 201).

The first attempts at price reform, commencing in 1981, failed to make much of an impact because, although prices were revised in line with market movements, the slowness of the adjustment procedure ensured that a multitiered price structure remained in force and continued to encourage diversion of state-traded goods onto the black market. Shortages persisted therefore, while the parallel markets maintained their inflationary spiral. Continuation of the food subsidy system for state workers, which was not permanently removed until 1989, also ensured that the gap between official procurement prices and ration price increased, fuelling the budget deficit and generating further inflationary pressure. During 1988 cash shortages became a major problem, with many firms unable to pay wages and other debts due to non-receipt of planned advances from the state banking system (FEER, 26 October 1989).

The crude attempt by the State Bank in October 1985 to wipe out excess liquidity through its currency reform only exacerbated the shortages. However, a second attempt inaugurated by the financial authorities during March 1989, using different methods, was stunningly successful. Apparently following advice from the IMF, the government pegged interest rates at a few percentage points above the prevailing rate of inflation, thus offering depositors a positive real interest rate in place of the highly negative one available under previous credit regulations (Wood, 1990). At the same time, the authorities undertook large-scale gold sales, causing the price to fall and providing further encouragement to hold savings as bank deposits.

The consequence of the very high interest rates was an immediate dampening of demand for cash. Those firms which were in a strong trading position were able to adjust and survive, but the sellers' market, characteristic of the shortage economy, disappeared, with the result that stockpiles of poor quality products grew and many firms were compelled to send workers on 'holiday'. In spite of a clear intention of government policy that firms unable to operate profitably after a transitional period should be allowed to go bankrupt, this tended not to happen because the State Bank continued, against party policy, to issue credit to state firms at low interest rates. However, about half a million workers were reportedly laid off during 1990, adding to the estimated total of 1.6 million unemployed (AWSJ, 30 November–1 December 1990; ID, 27–30 November 1990).[9]

The interest rate policy carried its own risks. With official rates high and an unregulated financial environment emerging, numerous secondary credit organizations sprang up, offering high interest rates to depositors. In April 1990, several of the private institutions crashed, having been in the habit of lending deposits as soon as they came in, leading to a further crisis of public confidence (AWSJ, 10 May 1990).

Nevertheless, the anti-inflation policy was highly successful in 1989, bringing inflation down to the region of 25–35 per cent. The government promised to sustain positive real interest rates, a promise which it appeared to have broken in the second half of 1990 as inflation began to rise once again in the wake of increasing rice prices.

In line with the changes to the financial mechanism and the industrial planning system, steps were taken to abolish the multi-tiered price structure. The system of official price fixing was ended in all but a few areas and henceforth most prices are to be negotiated between suppliers and customers according to the principle of 'earning a profit'. Since enterprises now have the right to choose between suppliers and to determine quantities ordered, this should have the effect of bringing market forces to bear on output and pricing decisions of firms. Enterprise managers also have power to decide on the form of wage payment (piece or time rates), subject to a minimum wage (this is a subsistence wage designed to ensure 2 000 calories per day to workers). Official policy is for payment in accordance with labour input, but this could work out in a number of different ways, depending on the cost structure and market position of the enterprise.

Coinciding with these changes was an ending of the two-tiered foreign exchange rate system. In the second half of 1988 the official rate for the Dong was allowed to float down to the black market rate. From a rate of 368 Dong to the US dollar in August 1988, the Vietnamese currency fell to about 6 000 in early 1989, before stabilizing at around 3 900 from August 1989 to March 1990. Since then it has fallen again, to around 7 350 (March 1991) (FEER, various issues). Such a major devaluation of the Dong has virtually eliminated the black market, ending speculation in currency and imported goods, and has greatly enhanced the prospects of industrial exporters.

The financial system
In the past the banking system operated primarily as a clearing house for the state sector industrial enterprises. These were required by law to deposit all revenue with the State Bank and to receive cash allocations according to their needs, laid down by the plan. In addition to the State Bank were the Foreign Trade Bank, responsible for all foreign currency transactions, and the Bank for Investment and Construction, through which investment credit was channelled to state enterprises. The private sector, farmers in particular but also small handicraft producers, usually had to resort to unofficial sources of credit.

In 1987, in an effort to give banks more autonomy, they were directed to become self-financing, to lend only on the expectation of an adequate return. However the state-run banks were hampered initially by their inability to attract deposits due to the low official interest rates and high rate of inflation. The first real experiment in the financial sector came with the establishment in Ho Chi Minh City of the Bank of Industry and Trade. This was initially formed as a joint venture between a number of state enterprises as a means of raising capital for their own operations. It was established as the first shareholders' bank, while another major new feature was its offer of competitive interest rates to depositors. Following the passage of new legal provisions allowing greater freedom for private enterprise in early 1989, a plethora of new credit institutions sprang up in the private sector, as many as 200 reportedly in Ho Chi Minh City alone (FEER, 28 October 1989). Some of these engaged in blatantly unsound practices, leading to their collapse in April 1990 and a more general crisis of confidence in the secondary credit system. Nevertheless, by 1990 there was already considerable experience of operating a more market-orientated credit system. It is also worth mentioning here that some of the reforms instituted in Vietnam during 1988–89 had earlier been tried in Cambodia (Vickery, 1990).

Formal agreements were signed with two foreign banks to establish offices in Vietnam as early as the end of 1988, but although several French and one British Bank have opened offices in Ho Chi Minh City, they did not offer banking services (FEER, 26 October 1988; AWSJ, 14 May 1990). It was not until two years later that a joint venture to provide banking services was finally established between the Bank of Industry and Trade and the Indonesian P.T. Bank Summa (AWSJ, 22 November 1990).

Reform of the banking system became a major priority during 1990, especially after the crisis of the secondary credit market in April. But a much more important problem than this, given the weight of state industrial enterprises in the economy, was the need to remove State Bank policies which continued to allocate cheap credit to non-performing firms. A new banking law was passed on 1 October which redefined the role of the State Bank, giving it functions similar to a Western central bank. Under the new law the State Bank is responsible for determining official exchange rates for the Dong and for indirect management of credit (ID, 10–16 November 1990). Changes in the law were followed up by the replacement of most of the senior directors of the State Bank (AWSJ, 8, 9 October 1990), who had failed to implement earlier measures intended to change the Bank's role.

4. CONCLUSIONS

1. A feature of all the reforms is that they have already been experimented with before being implemented economy-wide. Often they have resulted from spontaneous actions taken by individual economic units, and were adapted from developments in the interstices of the administrative planning system. Others have arisen through more deliberate establishment of pilot projects. Much of the impetus to industrial change, namely to search for new forms of efficiency and higher productivity, has come from experimentation with new institutional forms in the southern part of the country.

2. Microeconomic reforms did not work independently of changes in the macroeconomic system, hence the early failure of the 'product contract' system to generate real impulses for growth and the trend towards stagnation after 1983 of Northern agricultural output. Success required wider structural change in the economy. This, in turn, needed reforming the management structure, not only at the level of the firm, but, more importantly, at the macro level.

3. Given the regime's goal of establishing a mixed economy in which the state sector actually holds the commanding heights, an imperative is to make the state sector function efficiently, to enable it to compete with the private and collective sectors. This, in the minds of the party leadership, is what will give 'society' control over the direction of Vietnamese

economic development, rather than leaving it victim of investment decisions by private (non-accountable) individuals. Of course, this societal superintendence depends also on the degree to which economic reforms are accompanied by moves towards a more democratic regime (which does not necessarily mean a multi-party oligarchy). Political reform in Vietnam has concentrated on increasing the degree of openness within the party and mass organizations so that they may become genuine avenues for mass participation in politics. Among communist parties in power, the Vietnamese party has a unique historical record of flexibility and responsiveness to pressure from below which, despite lapses, has enabled it to sustain political legitimacy (Beresford, 1988). Turley (1991, p. 10) observes that

> Perhaps more than any other communist leadership, senior Vietnamese have kept faith that popular participation under party tutelage can combat bureaucratism, maintain an organic relationship between local party organs and the people, and preserve or, in the present, restore mass support for the regime.

If it is to succeed, this type of democratization presupposes the separation of political power (vested in the party) and state function. Danger may lie, however, in the development of previously semi-autarkic fiefdoms into private corporations controlled by cadres and officials in an authoritarian way. Equally it may lie in the obstruction by powerfully placed officials of new industrial strategies which incorporate an increased marketization that erodes their local power. Eliminating this sort of threat is precisely one of the main goals of the Vietnamese reforms.

4.   From the perspective of 1991, it is clear that it is now the southern economy which is more or less the 'engine of growth'. The agricultural cornucopia which had been expected to underpin Vietnam's industrialization in earlier thinking about re-unification now appears to be a real possibility,[10] while Ho Chi Minh City is now the pre-eminent industrial centre, receiving 80 per cent of foreign investment. While all this has been going on, the North has found adaptation to the new system much more difficult. Resistance from the vested interests in the entrenched 'traditional socialist' system has been more powerful, while the quantity of resources tied up in large-scale heavy industry projects has made adjustment of investment priorities slow. It is doubtful whether, without the impetus given by the transformation of the South, the recovery of the Vietnamese industrial economy from the crisis of the late 1970s would have been so rapid or its reform process so deep.

An update to this chapter is given in the Postscript page 283.

NOTES

1. Chinese commodity aid was in fact withdrawn as soon as the war was over, although project aid was not withdrawn until 1978, shortly after Vietnam became a full member of CMEA.
2. The ration fell from 20 kg per month, considered the subsistence minimum, to as little as 13 kg.
3. This term refers to the existence of production for exchange, as opposed to production for own-consumption which prevailed in many of North Vietnam's rural areas. It does not imply the existence of free markets.
4. Per capita food production in the key Red River delta was 354 kg in 1982, but averaged only 249 kg per annum by 1985–87, a figure too low to provide any surplus over peasant consumption requirements. By comparison the figures for the Mekong delta were 467 kg in 1982 and 497 kg per annum on average for the three years 1985–87 (Beresford, 1987, p. 266; Tong Cuc Thong Ke, 1985, p. 87; Tong Cuc Thong Ke, 1989, p. 49).
5. Growth rates of industrial output by region are not available, but some idea of the extent to which the North's heavy industrial structure has held it back can be seen from growth rates of Groups A (producer goods) and B (consumer goods) during the 1980s. The average annual growth rate of real Gross Value of Output 1980–87 was: Group A, 0.7 per cent; Group B, 13.4 per cent (at 1982 prices). The share of Group B expanded from 71 per cent to 85 per cent of industrial output over the same period (Tong Cuc Thong Ke, 1987, p. 153).
6. The pattern of Vietnamese trade is more fully discussed in Beresford (1989b).
7. At the end of August 1990 this was set at $50 per month for a simple labourer in foreign enterprises (SWB, FE/W0145 A/8, 12 September 1990).
8. In 1970 South Vietnam's exports covered less than 2 per cent of the region's import bill (Beresford, 1989a, p. 79).
9. This estimate of unemployment amounts to 5 per cent of the workforce, but other estimates have put the figure as high as seven million, or 22 per cent (AWSJ, 26 June 1990).
10. In 1989 21.4 Mt of staple grain were produced (AWSJ, 15 January 1990, 28 March 1990) and Vietnam emerged as the world's third largest rice exporter, exporting 1.4 Mt (FEER, 10 May 1990).

REFERENCES

Beresford, M. (1987) 'Vietnam: northernizing the South or southernizing the North?', *Contemporary Southeast Asia*, vol. 8, no. 3.

Beresford, M. (1988) *Vietnam: Politics, Economics and Society*, London: Pinter.

Beresford, M. (1989a) *National Unification and Economic Development in Vietnam*, London: Macmillan.

Beresford, M. (1989b) 'Vietnamese trade with the non-communist world', in Limqueco, P. (Ed.) *Partisan Scholarship: Essays in Honour of Renato Constantino*, Manila: JCA Publishers.

Beresford, M. (1990a) 'The impact of economic reform on the South', paper presented to Conference on *Doi Moi in Vietnam*, Australian National University, September.

Fforde, A. and Paine, S. (1987) *The Limits of National Liberation*, London: Croom Helm.

Fforde, A. (1989) *The Agrarian Question in North Vietnam 1974–1978*, New York: M.E. Sharpe.

Ho Duc Hung (1984) *Cong Nghiep phuc vu Nong Nghiep*, Ho Chi Minh City: NXB Thanh Pho Ho Chi Minh.

IMF (1983) 'Vietnam – Staff Report for the 1983 Article IV Consultation', June.

Le Trang (1990) 'Renewal of industrial management policy and organization' in Per Ronnas and Orjan Sjöberg (eds) *Doi Moi: Economic Reforms and Development Policies in Vietnam*, Stockholm: SIDA and SSE/CIEM.

Marr, D. and White, C. (eds) (1988) *Postwar Vietnam: Dilemmas in Socialist Development*, Ithaca: Cornell University Southeast Asia Program.

Nguyen Van Linh (1985) *Thanh Pho Ho Chi Minh 10 Nam*, Hanoi: Su That.

Spoor M. (1988) 'State finance in the Socialist Republic of Vietnam: the difficult transition from "state bureaucratic finance" to "socialist economic accounting" ', in Marr, D. and White, C. (eds).

SRV (Socialist Republic of Vietnam) (1987) Law on Foreign Investment (mimeo).

Tong Cuc Thong Ke (1985) *So Lieu Thong Ke 1930–1984*, Hanoi.

Tong Cuc Thong Ke (1989) *Nien Giam Thong Ke 1987*, Hanoi.

Tong Cuc Thong Ke (1990) *Nien Giam Thong Ke 1988*, Hanoi.

Truong Chinh (1986) 'CPV congress political report' in BBC, *Summary of World Broadcasts*, FE/8447, 20 December.

Vickery, M. (1990) 'Notes on the political economy of the People's Republic of Kampuchea (PRK)', *Journal of Contemporary Asia*, vol. 20, no. 4.

Turley, W. (1991) 'Political renovation in Vietnam: adaptation vs. preservation in a post-communist era', presented at the Southeast Asia/Indochina Seminar Series, under the auspices of the Fairbank Centre and Harvard Institute for International Development, Harvard University, 28 January 1991.

Vo Nhan Tri (1990) *Vietnam's Economic Policy since 1975*, Singapore: ISEAS.

Wood, A. (1990) 'Deceleration of inflation with acceleration of price reform – Vietnam's remarkable recent experience', *Cambridge Journal of Economics*, vol. 13, no. 4.

Periodicals

AWSJ	*Asian Wall Street Journal*, Hong Kong
SWB	BBC, *Summary of World Broadcasts – Far East*, London
FBIS-EAS	United States, *Foreign Broadcast Information Service – East Asia Service*
FEER	*Far Eastern Economic Review*, Hong Kong
ID	*Indochina Digest*, Washington
JPRS	United States, *Joint Publications Research Service – Vietnam Report*

15 Reform in Yugoslavia: The retreat from self-management

Saul Estrin and Lina Takla

1. INTRODUCTION

Just as the institutional structures associated with communist rule have, since the early 1950s, been very different from those pertaining in the rest of Central and Eastern Europe, so the recent process of reform in Yugoslavia has been markedly distinct. The Yugoslavs shifted away from command planning in the early 1950s and by 1965 had introduced many of the elements of a free market system. These included a realistic unified exchange rate and liberalized trade regime, considerable price liberalization and decentralization of most production decisions (including investment) to enterprises and the banking system. The distinguishing characteristic of this Yugoslav 'market socialism' was the unique system of workers' self-management of enterprises, resting on the basis of 'social' rather than state ownership of the means of production. The system regressed significantly after 1974, however, with labour and capital markets 'superseded' by bargaining between decentralized political and economic actors. From the late 1970s economic problems mounted, while governmental decentralization to the republics in the 1974 Constitution neutralized most effective federal policy interventions. With a background of stagnation since the late 1970s, very poor financial discipline of enterprises, banks and local government, and a drift to hyperinflation, a systematic reform process began in the late 1980s similar to that of Poland, with a coherent stabilization-reform package being introduced in 1990.

The principal aim of this paper, therefore, is to explain the reforms enacted thus far, in the light of the prevailing Yugoslav economic conditions and system. It is hoped that this discussion will also help to illustrate why the Yugoslav debate, and transition path to a market economy, are in many ways rather different from that followed in the other economies of Central and Eastern Europe. Because it is our view that some historical information is required for a proper understanding of the current Yugoslav system and how it is to be changed, we provide a brief survey in the following section, as well as a discussion of the country's long-term economic performance under self-management. Reforms commencing in the 1980s, and in particular the package introduced on 1 January 1990, are the subject of the third section, which concerns both the macroeconomic and industrial elements of the programme. A highly speculative discussion of possible future developments is contained in the conclusion.

Our attention is focused on the economic aspects of industrial reform in Yugoslavia. It is futile to attempt to ignore the political problems in a discussion of this sort, however, because these determine both the nature and effectiveness of reforms. In no other reforming country, with the possible exception of the Soviet Union, are inter-ethnic and regional rivalries so strong as to bring into immediate question the appropriate central authority for policy making or, indeed, the survival of Yugoslavia as a unitary state. Yugoslavia is composed of six republics; two relatively developed ones in the north and along the coast (Croatia and Slovenia); one large one in the centre (Serbia); one relatively less developed one with mixed Serb and Croat population (Bosnia Hercegovina); and two relatively poor ones in the south (Montenegro and Macedonia). In addition, Serbia has two ethnically distinct (formerly autonomous) provinces: Vojvodina where there is a large Hungarian minority, and Kosovo, where the population is predominantly Albanian. There have been numerous overlapping conflicts in recent years, in particular between Serbia and Kosovo over the latter's autonomy; between Croats and Serbs over hegemony in the federation and between the developed north and less developed south (including Serbia) over economic development. These rivalries have been exacerbated by both long-term economic stagnation and the election in 1990 of non-communist governments in Slovenia and Croatia, in contrast to a massive vote of confidence in the communist regime in Serbia. It is not clear whether communist and non-communist parties can co-exist in power in a federal system. Recent indications are not encouraging. We return to these questions in the final section.

2.   FIRMS, MARKETS AND ECONOMIC REFORMS, 1952–1988

The Yugoslavs effectively abandoned command planning and a Soviet-type industrial system in 1948. By 1952 the macroeconomic fundamentals of their system (social ownership and self-management) were in place, although the economic environment in which the firms operated altered significantly to the advantage of markets in 1965 (Dirlam and Plummer, 1973; Lydall, 1984; Milenkovitch, 1971). Further reforms in 1974, which established the system operational until the current reform process began, simultaneously reinforced self-management and largely replaced market by bureaucratic coordination processes. Despite the frequent reforms, the economy performed well on the whole until 1979, since when serious problems have emerged.

Company organization

In common with the rest of Central and Eastern Europe, virtually the whole of industrial output in Yugoslavia was restricted to the 'social sector', with the private sector limited by law to an insignificant role. Thus by 1988 some 65 per cent of the labour force was employed in the 'social' sector and 34 per cent in the private sector (primarily small scale agriculture: the share of the private sector in industrial output was negligible). The social sector is so called because, after 1952, all industrial enterprises of any size were 'socially' owned. This Yugoslav concept was devised as the ownership counterpart to the self-management system, whereby workers are entitled to control democratically the enterprises in which they work. It was felt that workers' control could not be effective if ownership were in either private or public hands. Hence social ownership is effectively a form of non-ownership; workers in an enterprise are permitted to appropriate the surplus normally allocated to owners, as well as to make accumulation decisions, but are not permitted to sell the assets or in any way to run them down in order to increase their incomes. These restricted employee ownership rights of '*usus fructus*' could make the privatization process significantly more complex than in countries where an owner (the state) can be easily identified, unless the authorities renationalize as the first stage of privatization.

Workers' self-management means that employees are formally given a central role in the enterprise authority structure. Precise arrangements have varied from period to period, but the primary instrument for employee influence over company decisions has been the Workers' Council. This has the nominal authority to appoint and direct management, typically from a list drawn up by a nominating committee of unionists or local authority representatives, to fix internal pay structures, to determine hiring and firing procedures and policies, and (perhaps most significantly) to determine the allocation of surplus between wages and self-financed investment. There was a considerable debate within Yugoslavia about whether this nominal authority of self-management organs has been effective, or whether enterprise managers, in fact, had decision making as well as operational power (Obradovic and Dunn, 1979).

A corollary to the Yugoslav system of enterprise ownership and control has been an accounting system in which profits are replaced by 'net income'. This is defined as the surplus of gross revenue over material costs, depreciation and taxes, and is available for allocation by the Workers' Council between employee remuneration, collective enterprise consumption (i.e. health facilities or housing) and investment. In principle, therefore, 'wages' are merely an advance by the enterprise against the workers' entitlement to future net income.

Reforms in 1974 extended the principle of self-management from the enterprise to the establishment and the workshop (Tyson, 1980). The communist authorities were persuaded that decision making authority had been usurped by managers rather than the self-management institutions for which it was intended, in part because of the sheer size of Yugoslav enterprises. This conclusion was no doubt coloured by the fact that Yugoslav management, by the late 1960s, were not for the most part members of a communist *nomenklatura* system comparable to that operating in the rest of Eastern Europe. It was decided, therefore, that enterprises should be broken up to units of a size suitable for direct democratic control, either to separate establishments or, in large production units, to technically separable workshops or units. These units, called Basic Organizations of Associated Labour (BOALs), replaced enterprises as legal entities and undertook all their functions. The organizations which had previously been called enterprises formally ceased to exist, and in practice were reconstituted only through the voluntary signature by BOALS of long-term contracts (Sacks, 1983; Prasnikar and Svejnar, 1988).

Markets and market structure
The second important characteristic of the Yugoslav industrial structure is the economic environment in which enterprises have interacted. Three broad phases can be discerned: (1) a semi-planned system between 1952 and 1965; (2) a market based system between 1965 and 1974; and (3) a contractual bargaining system which began formally in 1976 though the retreat from markets can be dated back to 1971 (Estrin, 1983; Lydall, 1984; Tyson, 1980). We shall concentrate on the latter period, only discussing the elements of the former ones in so far as they pertain to current reforms.

1)   Investment decisions and international trade were for the most part planned centrally, and the bulk of enterprise net income was taxed away in order to finance the very high investment share (averaging 34 per cent of Gross Material Product in the 1950s) primarily through the budget. Even so, the share of enterprise self-financing did rise even in this period, from less than 10 per cent in 1953 to 38 per cent by 1964 and self-management organs had some authority over pay structures, employment decisions, welfare issues and, towards the end of the period, wages (Kolaja, 1964; Milenkovitch, 1971).

2)   Reforms in 1965 represented the high-water mark of market-orientated reforms, with a significant freeing of domestic prices and trade, and the

formation of an autonomous though socially owned banking sector to re-place the state's central investment funds. Newly created banks were awarded the balance of state assets and required to fill the gap in the supply of investment funds left by the withdrawal of the state. The share of taxes and deductions in enterprise net income was reduced to less than 40 per cent, and the share of banks as an investment source rose from an average 3 per cent in 1960–63 to more than 50 per cent in 1970. The share financed by enterprises also declined, from 37 per cent to 33 per cent, while the state's share fell from 60 per cent to 16 per cent (Estrin, 1983). At the same time as the functions of the state were being increasingly devolved to firms and banks, the residual activities of the government began to be decentralized from the federal to the republican and even the local government (communal) level.

3) The 1974 reforms were largely motivated by communist fears about the loss of control over the economy implied by 'market socialism'. The disinte-gration of the enterprise into its component BOALs was accompanied by an attempt to improve national economic coordination through consultative committees loosely brought together under an umbrella of indicative plan-ning. Thus, the mediation of economic decisions through markets was, to a considerable extent, replaced by inter-BOAL negotiation and bargaining in the framework of enterprise, industry and regional consultative councils, which were wide open to political intervention. There were intended to emerge as 'social compacts' (which were not legally binding and might, for example, contain a regional incomes policy) and 'self-management agree-ments' between BOALs (which might, for example, specify self-financed investment rates in a sector). While the authorities had no discretionary authority to enforce such agreements, as they would have had in a conven-tional central planning system, self-management agreements were in princi-ple legally binding. In practice, as Ben-Ner and Neuberger (1990) show, the voluntary agreements that were in fact negotiated proved to be incoherent and hard to enforce. They also argue that the collusive rather than competitive nature of the system helped to bring about its downfall by the early 1980s; the system was to all intents and purposes abandoned by 1982, but the attendant framework for widespread collusion and political intervention was retained.

The principles of decentralization of authority and the emergence of policy through the voluntary agreement of all relevant parties was also applied to the political structure. Hence, most policy-making authority was devolved to the republican level, and central economic action had to rely on the unanimous assent of the six republics and two autonomous provinces. This almost entirely eliminated the potential for effective monetary, fiscal or exchange rate policies during the difficult period of adjustment following the second oil shock in 1979. Moreover it meant that local economic agendas came largely to replace national economic questions in the policy-making debate.

The increasing incoherence of economic decision making was accentuated by changes in the status of banks, which were effectively transformed into credit unions controlled by their founders, typically BOALs and their associations (COALs), but also local authorities. The resulting fragmentation of decision-making meant that operational control over resource allocation shifted down to coalitions in small regional units between local authorities, BOALs and banks, acting to a greater or lesser degree in concert and not subject to effective enforcement of either contractual obligations outside the region or the edicts of national economic policies. For example, loss-making BOALs were rarely bankrupted and the industrial sector typically reacted to a credit squeeze by an involuntary expansion of inter-firm credit (Tyson, 1980; Lydall, 1989; Dyker, 1990).

Yugoslav self-management in this period probably also acted to hinder organizational efficiency, not least because the BOAL system took much time and energy from management and employees' representatives on their workers' council, at the expense of attention to production, sales and investment. The breaking up of enterprises to BOALs probably also increased overhead costs (Tyson, 1980) and, by weakening the enterprises' organizational hierarchy, helped to cause problems of 'irresponsibility'. This arose because the system offered no convincing way to penalize workers for poor decisions. Hence, the authorities guaranteed that personal incomes would not fall below a statutory minimum (except in cases of gross mismanagement or fraud) through an inter-enterprise solidarity fund. In law, incomes in enterprises which made losses for a lengthy period would be reduced to these minimum levels, but this has been only rarely applied. Indeed, Sirc (1979) notes that workers in enterprises making losses sometimes had incomes in excess of those paid to their counterparts in profitable organizations. Moreover, there is no penalty through unemployment because layoffs are virtually unknown in Yugoslavia except for cases of criminal misconduct.

The ultimate penalty for poor enterprise decision-making, of course, is bankruptcy. The evidence suggests that during the 1970s and 1980s, a significant proportion of Yugoslav industry was persistently loss-making. The authorities have always been unwilling to permit firms to go bankrupt, however, probably because of the fear of large-scale unemployment. It has been calculated that, even during the relatively successful 1970s, between 10 and 30 per cent of the labour force in the social sector were employed in loss-making firms (Tyson, 1980). Administrative measures were used to stave off bankruptcy, primarily direct budgetary support or unsecured bank overdraft facilities, so that the state acted as lender of last resort to enterprises. Yugoslav self-managed firms have, therefore, operated *de facto* with the same 'soft budget constraints' as their counterparts in centrally-planned economies, though the system in other respects has been rather different.

There is, therefore, no mechanism whereby individual workers, whether in pay or job security, bear any of the costs of poor decisions made by the self-management bodies. This authority without responsibility engendered poor decision making, as well as non-economic or even fraudulent behaviour, and this was underwritten by the public authorities.

Industrial market structure

Reliable data on enterprise size distribution and market structure is unfortunately limited to the pre-1974 period. This is because, as we have seen, the definition of the 'enterprise' was altered by the 1974 reforms: data were collected on BOALs rather than what had previously been enterprises. We therefore concentrate on the 1952–74 period, although there is no reason to believe that competitive pressures or market structures have improved in any way since 1974. Indeed discursive evidence points to the increased fragmentation of the national product market into its republican or even more local constituents, so monopoly power in the relevant market places was probably rising.

Table 15.1 shows the size distribution of enterprises by employment in the Yugoslav social sector. The table reveals the virtual absence of small enterprises; in 1954 only 12 per cent of enterprises employed fewer than 125 workers and by 1973 this had declined to 4 per cent. According to Estrin and

Table 15.1   (a)   *Size distribution of enterprises by employment for the social sector*

Year	15 or less	16–29	30–60	61–125	126–250	251–500	501–1 000	1 001–2 000	2 000
1954	0	1	3	8	12	16	20	41	n/a
1965	0	0	1	7	7	14	18	22	31
1973	0	0	1	3	7	14	18	24	33

(b)   Size distribution of enterprises by employment for the social and private sectors combined

Year	15 or less	16–29	30–60	61–125	126–250	251–500	501–1 000	1 001–2 000	2 000
1959	9	2	4	7	10	13	16	16	23

Source: Estrin and Petrin (1990).

Petrin (1990), this compares with an average for the OECD countries in the mid-1970s of 30 per cent. On the other hand, by 1973, 57 per cent of Yugoslav industrial enterprises employed more than 1 000 workers compared with 35 per cent in the OECD countries at around the same time. This remarkable size distribution, testimony to the survival of the planners' bias for large enterprises well into the self-management era, has prompted Petrin (1989) to refer to the 'black hole' of small enterprises in Yugoslavia relative to Western economies.

The number of enterprises in the Yugoslav industrial sector in the 1952–72 period ranged roughly between 2 200 and 2 800 (Estrin, 1983). One should not be surprised, therefore, at the high levels of market concentration indicated by the four-firm (sales) concentration ratios in Table 15.2. In 1959 more than half Yugoslav industrial sectors displayed concentration ratios in excess of 75 per cent and none displayed concentration ratios of less than 25 per cent. The regional fragmentation of the Yugoslav economy suggests that

Table 15.2   Four-firm (sales) concentration ratios in Yugoslav industrial branches

Industrial Branch	Concentration Ratio in 1959	Concentration Ratio in 1965/1959[a]	Concentration Ratio in 1973/1965[b]	Concentration Ratio in 1973/1959[c]
Coal	58	144.8	100	144.8
Oil	100	96	93.75	90.0
Ferrous metals	86	101.2	96.6	97.7
Non-ferrous	94	96.8	107.7	104.3
Non-metallic	90	98.9	92.1	91.1
Metals	84	63.1	88.7	55.9
Shipbuilding	88	97.7	100	97.7
Electricals	76	110.5	86.9	96.1
Chemicals	78	94.9	97.3	92.3
Blding Materials	56	105.4	89.8	94.7
Wood	27	181.5	53.1	96.3
Paper	53	109.4	89.7	98.1
Textiles	37	108.1	77.5	83.8
Leather	44	154.6	77.9	120.5
Rubber	88	89.8	126.6	113.6
Food	42	111.9	93.6	104.8
Tobacco	51	103.9	113.2	117.6

[a] Four firm concentration ratio in 1965 compared with 1959 (%).
[b] Four firm concentration ratio in 1973 compared with 1965 (%).
[c] Four firm concentration ratio in 1973 compared with 1959 (%).

Source: Estrin (1983).

Table 15.3 Yugoslav economic performance

	1952–60	1960–70	1970–79	1979–85	1981–89
Average Annual **Rate of Growth of:**					
Social Product (%)	6.7	6.0	5.6	–0.9	0.6
Personal Consumption (%)	4.8	6.3	5.6	–0.5	
Personal Consumption per head (%)	3.6	5.7	4.5	–1.3	
Exports (total value $)	12.5	12.8	16.8	2.5	
Imports (total value $)	10.9	13.3	19.3	–4.0	
Social Sector Employment	2.2	2.6	4.3	2.5	
Registered Job Seekers (1 000) (end date)		320	762	1 040	
Net Foreign Debt ($bn) (end date)		4	13.8	18.8	
Share of trade with CMEA (end date) (exports)	32.1	30.8	20.6		

	1985	1986	1987	1988	1989
Growth of Socialized Sector Employment	2.2	3.0	2.0	0.2	–0.2
Exports (total value $)	4.3	4.3	6.0	8.3	6.1
Imports (total value $)	2.4	7.1	–0.8	2.5	12.6
Net foreign debt ($bn) [repayable in foreign currency]	18.4	19.2	20.5	18.9	17.3
Inflation (%)	72.4	89.8	120.8	194.1	1 256.0
Unemployment (%)	13.8	14.1	13.6	14.1	14.0

Source: National Statistics, OECD.

even these figures would understate actual domestic market monopoly power at the republican or local level. Levels of concentration did drift downwards during the period of market socialism in a majority of sectors, although it still rose in one-third of them and was only reduced by more than 10 per cent in two sectors.

Economic Performance 1952–79
Yugoslav economic performance was impressive between 1952 and 1979, despite some obvious problems. As can be seen in Table 15.3, the economy grew very quickly until the 1970s, and this was reflected in per capita consumption levels. Yugoslavia also achieved rapid export growth with hard currency countries: in the 1950s and 1960s exports to CMEA were at 30 per cent of total exports, with a slightly lower proportion for imports.

There have, however, also been long-term problems. Unemployment has been rising since the late 1960s and is regionally concentrated (OECD, 1990). The balance of payment has been in persistent deficit. Even between 1953 and 1960 the deficit was 3 per cent of Gross Material Product on average. Exports were only equal to 66 per cent of imports, and for the convertible area only 60 per cent, in the mid-1960s. Between 1952 and 1979 imports grew persistently faster than exports, especially in the rapid expansion of the final three years. Initially, the deficit was increased by US grants and income from workers abroad, but the country became increasingly dependent on foreign loans, the foreign debt reaching some $19 billion in 1979.

The economic record in the 1980s
Real gross social product per head declined by an average annual rate of 0.2 per cent from 1981–89; living standards thus fell and unemployment rose. The economy also gradually drifted towards hyperinflation. Inflation was more or less stable until 1983, and then accelerated continuously to attain around 72 per cent in 1985, 90 per cent in 1986 and to peak at 1 256 per cent in 1989. Output growth was 0.6 per cent on average in the period 1981–89, against 6.4 per cent in the period 1974–80. Job creation schemes forced firms to increase employment even in the face of declining demand so employment increased at an average rate of 3 per cent per annum throughout the 1980s and labour hoarding has been estimated to have reached 20 per cent of the labour force in 1988 (Bartlett and Estrin, 1990). Enterprise losses increased from 3 per cent to 15 per cent of GNP in the second half of the 1980s. The only bright element in the Yugoslavia of the 1980s was the improvement of the current account associated with the low level of domestic demand. The current account surplus of 1989 was $2.4 billion.

Yugoslavia thus entered the period of reform ranking first amongst socialist countries in the extent of her development of a market system and of trade relations with the West. In 1980 Yugoslavia exported $5 665 million worth of goods to the West and $3 322 million to Eastern bloc countries (Bartlett and Estrin, 1990). It was also unusual among Central and Eastern European countries in having always permitted some degree of open unemployment. Yugoslavia also had no monetary overhang and the *nomenklatura* in the enterprise was not open as in the rest of Central and Eastern Europe. By the 1980s, however, the Yugoslav system resembled other Eastern European countries in the existence of soft-budget constraints, political intervention at enterprise/industry level to retain full employment, significant restrictions on free trade (OECD, 1989–90), and a poor domestic supply structure.

3. MAJOR REFORMS SINCE 1988

In this section, we concentrate on the reform process at the federal level. However, it is important to stress that many aspects of the federal reform programme have either ended in failure or have ended as frameworks for the development of separate reform programmes at the level of each individual republic. The gradual breakdown of the federal structure in the past few years is associated with the political upheavals of 1989, which opened the way for free elections in each of the republics. These produced nationalist–democratic governments in Slovenia and Croatia, but reaffirmed the highly nationalistic socialist (communist) regime in Serbia. Federal reforms make the obvious first starting point to study the transition process in Yugoslavia, but the outcome to date suggests that researchers in the future may have to abandon this unified framework in favour of a separate treatment of reform in each of the main republics. Such an approach is beyond the scope of this paper, particularly because the appropriate political structures and policy frameworks have not yet fully emerged. Major economic reforms have been introduced in Yugoslavia since 1988 which, if implemented and developed, could amount to the introduction of a new economic system. They have tackled fundamental issues, including self-management and privatization, and introduced an IMF-inspired stabilization plan similar to those of Poland and Latin American countries to deal with inflation and foreign exchange convertibility. Since November 1988, 39 amendments to the Federal Constitution have been made and 20 new laws adopted by the Federal Parliament.

The reform programme
The sequencing of the stabilization plan of January 1991 was as follows. First, exchange rate and price corrections were undertaken before the plan was put into effect. Since 1988 the government has implemented a policy of

Table 15.4   Summarized description of the Yugoslav reform programme

---

Incomes/prices policy
6-month freeze on: nominal wages, excluding some vulnerable households, with pay remaining stable in DM; energy and other public sector prices (20 per cent of the consumer price index) after corrections in December; freeze on rents; partial price freeze covering 25 per cent of industrial goods including metal products, pharmaceuticals and utilities; all indirect price controls abolished in December 1989.

Fiscal policy
Expected fiscal adjustment of 5 per cent of GNP.

Monetary policy
Controls on net-domestic assets of the Central Bank with growth target slightly negative in the first two quarters of 1990; M1 growth set at 24 per cent for 1990. Note: the Yugoslav programme was preceded by a substantial monetary expansion in December.

Exchange rate and trade policy
Creation of a new unit of currency: 1 New Dinar = 10,000 Old. This new currency was made externally convertible and pegged to the DM (1 : 7); unified foreign exchange market to replace multiplicity of shadow rates.
    Creation of a single exchange rate for both private and public sectors in all regions; reduction of quotas and relaxation of licenses – some quota restrictions maintained amounting to 13 per cent of imports; phased liberalization of imports (10 per cent of all imports in 1988 rising to 87 per cent in 1989); export processing zones to be established: enterprises to benefit from tax privileges on the condition that 70 per cent of their output is exported (exports must however exceed $30 million per annum).

Enterprise and bank reforms
Enforcement of bankruptcies through a 60-day tolerance limit for arrears; a new labour law introduced in 1989 to remove the commitment of enterprises to maintain full employment; redundancy rules made simpler; bank restructuring programme evolving programmes for enterprise restructuring and privatization.

Enterprise Law (December 1988)   replaced the 1976 Law on Associated Labour; freedom to establish any type of enterprise (socialist, private, cooperative or mixed); also possible for a private company to acquire a stake in a socialist enterprise, although the process is not yet clear.

Law on Social Capital (December 1989) 'Social capital' defined as belonging to republican state organs (Development Funds); facilitates the transformation of socially owned enterprises into other forms of ownership: workers' councils or local authorities allowed to sell part of their enterprise capital either to socially-owned firms or to private firms or individuals. Superseded by Law on Social Property 1990.

Foreign Investment Law (January 1989) Foreign companies and individuals can establish wholly-owned companies or engage in joint ventures with Yugoslav public or private enterprises.

Financial Operations Act (February 1989) Simplifies the system for restructuring illiquid enterprises: if enterprise fails to agree rescheduling of its debts with its creditors, it may be declared bankrupt (thus the abandonment of selective crediting and the subsidization of priority sectors); commercial banks transformed into shareholding companies challenging the control of founders (enterprises and local government) *but* the power of shareholders still constrained and inter-bank competition limited; June 1989 autonomy and authority of National Bank of Yugoslavia (NBY) increased: majority voting decision-making instead of unanimity, influence over granting commercial credits and linking them to credit-worthiness.

Law on Rehabilitation of Banks (December 1989) Allowed NBY to impose solvency ratios (a ratio of equity to assets of 15) and ceilings on foreign credit and to initiate restructuring procedures for the banks and to license new commercial banks.

Law on Social Property (August 1990) 'Internal' shares (i.e. issued to pension funds and workers, not general public) defined as main instrument of privatization.

Law on Personal Incomes (August 1990) Enterprises to give internal shares as well as basic wages to workers as part of their regular incomes.

price liberalization: in 1987 only around 40 per cent of prices were freely determined; in 1989 the figure rose to 75 per cent and in December 1989 all indirect regimes of price control (i.e. prices requiring approval by the Federal Price Office) were abolished. An associated reform was the liberalization of imports, which by the end of September 1989 resulted in 87 per cent of all imports being free and only 13 per cent subject to licences (compared with 48 per cent in 1987), though tariffs remain in place. Secondly there was a monetary programme, preceded by a large increase in base money stock in December 1990 (25 per cent) resulting from increased domestic credit and foreign credit inflows, mainly by Serbia's banks in Vojvodina. Finally, microeconomic reforms have been continuous, but since summer 1990 efforts have concentrated on privatization.

The programme comprises measures to stabilize inflation at low levels and to change the structure of the economy. Table 15.4 illustrates the main components. The first step was the December 1988 Enterprise Law, which replaced BOALs by enterprises once again as the legally defined organization responsible for production and increased the decision-making authority of managers *vis-à-vis* self-management organs, which in principle become advisory. It also allowed private enterprises and mixed ownership forms to co-exist on roughly equal terms with the social sector. Explicit or implicit subsidization of inefficient enterprises was tackled through new bankruptcy procedures, with a 60-day tolerance limit rule as a trigger mechanism. This means that a debtor who has not paid his or her debts in 60 days is declared insolvent and subject to bankruptcy procedures carried out by regular courts. In practice, firms getting close to the limit have typically borrowed for one day, and thereby delayed the process for another 60 days. The Banking Law was intended to transform banks into profit-maximizing, joint stock institutions and allowed some foreign ownership joint ventures. The bank restructuring programme also aims to help here by creating a centralized system of payments. A bank rehabilitation agency, supported by budgetary resources, was created in mid-1990. Progress in the area of enterprise restructuring has been slower, pending the setting-up of regional specialized institutions. The privatization programme is now centred around the Law on Social Property (1990) via the gradual sale of internal shares.

Results of the first phase of the programme (January–June 1990)

The results of the stabilization plan are illustrated by the economic indicators in Table 15.5. The plan was effective in reducing the rate of inflation. Consumer prices were increasing at a monthly rate of 38 per cent in January, 13 per cent in February, 3.8 per cent in March and actually began to decline in May and continued to decline at a rate of –0.3 per cent in June (Bartlett and Estrin, 1990): accumulated inflation from end December to end June

Table 15.5   First results of the Yugoslav programme 1990

	First stage	Second stage
Inflation Rate:	Q1 = 9%, Q2 = 0.1%	Retail price index rose by 2.1% in July and 1.9% in August, 7.1% in September, 8.1% in October and 3.0% in November. Inflation likely to exceed 100% in 1990.
Wages:	32% of average in 1989*	8.5% in July, 9% in August, 6% in September.
Output Growth:	first 6 months = −10% industrial output = −15.4%	
Current Account:	surplus: first quarter 1989 non-seasonally adjusted: $97 million first quarter 1990 non-seasonally adjusted: $70 million	Gross social product likely to fall 6% in 1990.
Black Market Premium:	reduced to zero in December increased to 15% in the first half of the year	
Share of foreign Exchange deposits in M3:	December 1989: 65% June 1990: 52% Q1 = −7%, Q2 = −15%	
Employment:	in industry: fell by 30,000 in 12 months to May 1990	
Unemployment:	very slight increase in rate unemployment at 11.7% in May public sector: 69,000 jobs lost net of new jobs over 12 months to May 1990	Unemployment rose by 43,000 Jan-Aug, with employment falling by 173,000.
Trade Balance	deficit: half year results 1989: $0.5 billion half year results 1990: $1.6 billion	

Source: World Bank, Economist Intelligence Unit.

was of around 30 per cent only. The wage freeze held for the most part, but it is difficult to assess the impact of the various measures on wages. Real personal incomes fell by 27 per cent in the first half of the year. Nevertheless, it is likely that there were differences across households and enterprises; some enterprises were still able to afford wage increases, but without necessarily operating efficiently. Retail sales fell by 26 per cent over the first six months compared with the same period in 1989, national output by 10 per cent, and industrial production by 15.4 per cent in the year up to June 1990. Unemployment also rose, but the exchange rate against the DM was held until early January 1991, when the dinar was devalued from DM = YD7 to DM = YD9. The share of foreign exchange deposits decreased from 65 per cent in December 1989 to 52 per cent in June 1990. Households do not appear in general to have converted their stocks of foreign currency into domestic currency deposits despite the frozen exchange rate and the higher rate on domestic deposits (deposit rates stable at 12–15 per cent per annum).

The question is whether there was much structural and behavioural change as a result of the first phase of the programme. We will first survey the impact of the Enterprise Law. The bankruptcy legislation does not seem to have been used extensively in practice. In 1989 7 per cent of all enterprises were declared insolvent, but only five had bankruptcy proceedings taken against them. During the first part of 1990, however, the effect of stabilization became apparent with a rise in enterprise illiquidity. The removal of credit subsidies had a strong impact on the enterprise sector during the first period. Seven thousand enterprises were reported to have had difficulties in meeting payments, 3 000 had accumulated arrears for 30 days and 350 were declared bankrupt. The power to implement bankruptcy procedures lies in the hands of republican authorities. Serbia, for one, refused to implement a full reform programme (*NRC-Handelsblad*, 18 September 1990) and this leads one to ask whether other republics are likely to follow suit. Turning to examine the effect of the reforms on firm entry, we find that some 20,000 small enterprises were established in 1989 and a further 40,000 in the first seven months of 1990 (interview with Markovic, *NRC-Handelsblad,* 10 October 1990). A smaller figure was mentioned in Bartlett and Estrin (citing Privedni Pregled, September 1990); 24,000 new enterprises were allegedly established in the first six months of 1990.

Weaknesses in the first stage of the programme included the freezing of the exchange rate (the real exchange rate in Yugoslavia became seriously overvalued in the first phase and this was not corrected in the second phase), the introduction of new wage policy (as the wage freeze was removed) and the need for a reduction in external debt servicing as funds were channelled towards fiscal support for the restructuring programme. In addition, the government did not act decisively with regard to either the restructuring and privatization of enterprises or the development of labour and financial markets. Although many reforms were concerned with the structure and operation of banks and enterprises, there remained ambiguities about ownership, property rights, management powers and labour relations. The dissociation of banks from enterprises was not for the most part achieved and by all accounts banks have continued to remain dependent on their clients. They were supposed to be 'refounded' under the new Banking Law at the beginning of 1990, but the process is taking longer than expected: 80 banks have been registered and it is doubtful whether they should all qualify (EIU). A major problem remains the losses of the banking sector, estimated to be cumulated at $12 billion (Uvalic, 1991).

Description of the second stage of the programme July–December 1990
The second-stage plan was introduced at the end of June 1990, with further laws on banking, enterprises and labour relations. Special emphasis was placed on privatization. At the macroeconomic level the objective was to encourage exports and investment-led growth, while maintaining a low inflation and a stable exchange rate.

Under the Law on Social Property, the main agents of privatization are to be the workforce. The government appears to wish to replace social ownership with worker ownership. This contrasts with the approach of the 1988 Enterprise Law which allows for free competition between various forms of ownership. An unstated proportion of shares will be sold to both former and actual employees at the discretion of the enterprise management board at the book value of the enterprise and at a progressive discount rate of up to 70 per cent (depending on years of service). Republican Development Funds will oversee the process and receive the proceeds from the sales, except for shares to raise new capital. It is expected that when the workers are given authorization to sell, their shares will end up in the hands of financial institutions, especially pension funds, although some will still be held by employees. Most of the republics now have their own separate privatization schemes, with the Slovenes and the Croats likely to rely less on sales to workers and more on the public, institutions and foreign direct investment than the federal proposals.

The government has tried to replace the wage and price freeze by an incomes policy linking the sale of shares to wage increases (Law on Personal Incomes). Enterprises that pay more than the average wage increase in their republic must do so in the form of shares. This has proved unpopular with employees and wages increased fast after July. Real wages rose by 13 per cent in June 1990, 6.5 per cent in July and 7.0 per cent in August. However, in September they fell by 1 per cent and real personal incomes declined by 4.6 per cent. A partial wage freeze was agreed by the federal government with the republics with wages to be held to the September–November 1990 average for the whole of 1991, with greater budgetary control to be exerted by the republics. It remains to be seen whether this will hold.

The wage increases have been aided by a relaxation of monetary (credit) policy. Both the economic and political prospects of Yugoslavia have worsened over the past few months. In the second half of 1990 the powers of the central government have weakened as Serbia, Croatia and Slovenia have gone their own way. This has meant the inability of the federal government to control the expenditure of the republics including the subsidies they provided to enterprises. The Central Bank, although given more authority, has had the degree of its independence undermined by its inability to control monetary developments in the republics. The federal government budget had been projected to be in surplus in 1990 (0.8 per cent of GSP). However, ceilings on spending have constantly been exceeded and the republics are reluctant to cede control over any of their spending to the federal level. On the trade front, export subsidies are being abolished and replaced by the reimbursement of domestic taxes as in other OECD countries.

Data on the second stage of the programme are preliminary. Inflation is re-emerging. Money in circulation rose by 138 per cent in the ten months to the end of October, compared with an increase of retail prices of 110 per cent, revealing that monetary policy was not an effective restraint. Inflation began to rise in the summer: a monthly rate of 2 per cent in July and August, reaching 7 per cent in September and 8 per cent in October before falling to 3 per cent in November. In the nine months between January and October 1990 prices rose by 48 per cent (an annualized rate of 68 per cent) compared with only 28 per cent (an annualized rate of 53 per cent) in the seven months to August. The annual inflation rate is still likely to have exceeded 100 per cent in 1990.

The current account of the balance of payments has deteriorated over the same period. As of August, exports fell sharply. As a result, after five years of current account surplus, a deficit is likely for 1990 (when figures for the whole year are available) and one is certainly in prospect for 1991. Although the devaluation of the Dinar in early January 1990 (from DM = YD7 to DM = YD9) led to slightly improved export prospects, this improvement in competitiveness will be lost if inflation is not brought under control.

Industrial production in the 9 months to September 1990 fell by 10.6 per cent compared with the same period the previous year. This had caused a gradual contraction in public sector employment with a fall of 74,000 between May and August compared with a fall of 40,000 between February and May. Official figures show unemployment rising by 43,000 between January and August, with employment falling by 173,000. The same sources exhibit a rise of 17,000 in those employed in the private sector since the beginning of 1990. Given the employment and unemployment figures quoted above, private employment seems to be officially underestimated. Unregistered private employment is estimated at 2.8 million (EIU). GSP in 1990 as a whole is expected to drop by 6 per cent with a 1 per cent drop forecast for 1991 (EIU).

At the microeconomic level, the process of privatization has been very slow, but is beginning to take shape. Bankruptcy procedures have now started against 71 companies and in November 1990 proceedings began against a commercial bank. According to Uvalic (1991), 5.4 per cent of the Yugoslav wage bill was paid out in internal shares, and it is estimated that some 600 companies have sold shares to their workers, including some of the largest in the country. There has also been some diversification of property types under the Enterprise Law. An official announcement on 8 November 1990 claimed that over 300 enterprises had already been converted into joint stock companies. It is reported that sales are being held up by republican governments who are keen to retain control over large enterprises in particular. By 30 September 1990 some 74 per cent of the more than 50,000 enterprises in Yugoslavia were privately owned, 21 per cent were socially owned, 2.5 per cent were cooperatives and 2.0 per cent were in mixed property. These figures are misleading however because the majority of new private firms are very small: the contribution of the social sector to GNP was still more than 85 per cent. It also seems likely that the bulk of new enterprises are concentrated in the service sector. There was also considerable expansion in the number of new joint ventures; 578 in 1989 and 2 588 between January and November 1990, with a value of more than £700 million.

4. CONCLUSION

Yugoslavia began its latest phase of reforms in the late 1980s in a different situation from that of the Central and East European neighbours. The long experience of market exchange and trading relations with the West had been dissipated by the bureaucratization of the post-1974 economic system. The economy was in decline during the 1980s, and the inability of the federal authorities to exert monetary control or to enforce financial discipline on firms had allowed price changes to reach hyperinflationary levels. The underlying economic system, based on self-management and social ownership, required different reforms from those being developed elsewhere in Eastern Europe. Perhaps most importantly, there is no general agreement on the desired path of reform or the appropriate outcome, not only within the federal government but also between the various republics.

Despite this discouraging background, the stabilization element of the 1990 reform programme was surprisingly successful in its first phase, and probably only began to fail because monetary policy was allowed to become too lax in the second. However it is arguable that the array of microeconomic and structural reforms outlined in Table 4 lacked a systematic basis for forging a viable new economic system out of the existing structure. In particular, reforms to the enterprise and banking sector were not adequate enough to ensure systemic change. There are several reasons why, despite numerous well-thought out initiatives, the Yugoslav reform process has been so confused and incoherent by the standards of, for example, Poland. In the first place, as we have seen, there are conflicts about means and ends between the federal authorities and several of the republics, in particular Slovenia and Croatia, as well as between the republics, most notably Serbia and Croatia.

A major stumbling block is that an effective reform programme requires a strong central government able to enforce a strict monetary and fiscal policy and financial discipline on enterprises and local government. The republican governments were never willing to hand back the power given them by the 1974 reform to Mr Markovic's federal government, although the ability of the central bank to control the money stock has in principle been somewhat strengthened in 1990. Even this advance has been brought into question by the Serbian government's unauthorized use in late December 1990/early January 1991 of approximately half the entire 1991 national monetary emission to pay civil service wages and pensions.

The republics have been unwilling to recentralize authority to the federal level because they do not agree about the appropriate make-up of the Yugoslav state. The northern republics favour a transition on Polish or Czechoslovak lines, while the central and southern ones have been more circumspect about their objectives, particularly with regard to privatization. It is not clear whether two economic systems can sensibly coexist under one central government. Slovenia and Croatia therefore want Yugoslavia to decentralize further into a loose confederation, a less closely knit unit than even that currently pertaining, since they believe that their market based economies could survive without any political link to the less developed south. In contrast, the Serbs see economic as well as political benefit from maintaining the existing federation.

The situation has steadily deteriorated in recent months. In October 1990 Serbia imposed trade tariffs on Slovenian and Croatian goods, although this was found to be contrary to GATT rules and Serbia was ordered to lift the duties by the Yugoslav constitutional government in January 1991. A Slovene referendum in December 1990 and a Croatian one in February 1991 approved secession if a confederal structure does not emerge. While these acts do not necessarily indicate the automatic disintegration of the country, that has clearly become a significant possibility. Federal economic reform, if not reform in particular republics, must be a second order issue until these constitutional questions about the nature and survival of the state are resolved.

An update to this chapter is given in the Postscript, page 284.

ACKNOWLEDGEMENTS

The authors would like to thank Paul Hare, Michelle Ledic, Zoran Popov, Emille Primoric, Jan Svejnar and the editor for valuable discussion and comments. The analysis and interpretation of events, however, remain our own. Financial support from the ESRC is gratefully acknowledged,

REFERENCES

Bartlett, W. and Estrin, S. (1990) 'Inflation, external debt and national tensions: the Yugoslav experience', Paper presented to the IUM World Congress on Soviet and East European Studies, Harrogate, July.
Ben-Ner, A. and Neuberger, E. (1990) 'The feasibility of planned market systems: the Yugoslav visible hand and negotiated planning', *Journal of Comparative Economics,* vol. 14, no. 4.
Dyker, D. (1990) *Yugoslavia: Socialism. Development. Debt,* London: Routledge.
Dirlam, J. and Plummer, J. (1973) *An Introduction to the Yugoslav Economy,* Columbus, Ohio: Merrill.
Estrin, S. (1983) *Self-Management: Economic Theory and Yugoslav Practice,* Cambridge: Cambridge University Press.
Estrin, S. and Petrin, T. (1990) 'Patterns of entry, exit and merger in Yugoslavia', in Geroski, P. and Schwalbach, J. (eds), *Entry and Market Contestability,* London: Blackwell.
Kolaja, J. (1964) *Workers Councils: The Yugoslav Experience,* New York: Praeger.
Lydall, H. (1984) *Yugoslav Socialism: Theory and Practice,* Oxford: Oxford University Press.
Lydall, H. (1989) *Yugoslavia in Crisis,* Oxford: Clarendon Press.
Milenkovitch, D. (1971) *Plan and Market in Yugoslav Economic Thought,* New Haven: Yale University Press.
Obradovic, J. and Dunn, W. (eds) (1979) *Workers' Self-Management and Organisational Power in Yugoslavia,* University of Pittsburgh, Centre for International Studies.
OECD (1989–90) *Country Report on Yugoslavia.*
Petrin, T. (1989) 'Restructuring the Yugoslav economy through the entry of new firms', University of Ljubljana (mimeo).
Prasnikar, J. and Svejnar, J. (1988) 'Economic behaviour of Yugoslav enterprises', *Advances in the Economics of Labor-Managers and Participatory Firms,* vol. 3, London: JAI Press.
Sacks, S. (1983), *Self-Management and Efficiency: Large corporations in Yugoslavia,* London: Allen and Unwin.
Sirc, L. (1979) *The Yugoslav Economy under Self-Management,* London: Macmillan.
Tyson, L. (1980) *The Yugoslav Economy and its Performance in the 1970s,* Berkeley, California: Institute for International Studies.
Uvalic, M. (1991) 'How Different is Yugoslavia', Paper for European Commission (DGII) within Phase II Programme.

Postscript

CHAPTER 1

Ian Jeffries

Things change at a bewildering pace these days in the Soviet Union and Eastern Europe. Fortunately the August 1991 Soviet coup attempt failed and gave the reform process a shove. Indeed, throughout Eastern Europe the road to 'political democracy' and the 'market' is now seen as the only one, although difficult decisions remain about the speed of the transition and the exact type of system to be striven for.

The Soviet Union and Yugoslavia are disintegrating and one important question is whether at least some of the emerging 'bits' are able to agree on some sort of loose, sustainable economic and political union. Albania is in a desperate economic state. The other East European countries have their varying problems, but there are signs of hope. Paul Hare reports that in Hungary trade is continuing to do well, inflation is about as expected and total output, again as expected, is still falling. Restructuring and privatization are proceeding apace and the country has been relatively successful in attracting foreign investment. Nicholas Denton (*The Financial Times*, 29 October 1991, p. 26), however, reports the postponement of the *Danubius* hotel chain privatization and general difficulties with the 20-company programme.

In Poland the Bielecki privatization programme was unveiled on 27 June 1991, in which some 400 large industrial enterprises (accounting for about 25 per cent of industrial sales) were listed. Between 5 and 20 National Wealth Management Funds were to be set up, which would be endowed with 60 per cent of the shares; 10 per cent were to be given free to the workers in their own enterprises and 30 per cent were to be retained by the state. Each adult Polish citizen was to receive vouchers worth one share in each of the Funds. The Bielecki government began to take a sectoral (industrial) approach to privatization and, indeed, to slow down the whole programme because of the social consequences (especially unemployment). A more interventionist approach to state industry could be detected in government policy, aspects of this emerging 'industrial policy' including advice on restructuring. The Polish general election was held on 27 October 1991. The turnout was dismal (a provisional 43.2 per cent) and no clear-cut winner emerged from the mass of competing parties. The Democratic Union, led by Mazowiecki, appeared to

278

be only marginally ahead of the ex-communists' Alliance of the Democratic Left. It seems to be an ominous comment on Poland's 'shock' experiment.

In Bulgaria the second free general election was held on 13 October 1991. The Union of Democratic Forces (UDF) won 110 seats in the 240-seat Grand National Assembly, with 106 going to the Bulgarian Socialist Party and 24 to the Movement for Rights and Freedom (MRF) (representing the Turkish minority). The UDF intends to form a minority government with parliamentary support from the MRF. The political and economic reform programme is set to continue.

There has been increasing recognition during 1991, spurred on by the abortive Soviet coup, of the need for larger-scale Western aid and a more welcoming stance by the EC towards Eastern Europe.

China and Vietnam are still broadly proceeding with their economic reform programmes, while maintaining tight control by the communist party. North Korea and Cuba still reject market-orientated economic reforms. At the Fourth Congress of the Cuban communist party, held 10–14 October 1991, only marginal political and economic changes were conceded, e.g. concessions to individual private activity (plumbers, carpenters and mechanics etc.). Cuba has already started to prepare for a belt-tightening 'special period in a time of peace' and is now engaged in a 'zero option', a reaction to a world of increasing shortages and the prospects of a life without Soviet aid and subsidized trade

CHAPTER 2: ALBANIA

Adi Schnytzer

According to all reports, the Albanian economy virtually collapsed in 1991. Industrial output in the third quarter of the year was down by over 60 per cent compared with the same period of 1990 and the absence of well-defined property rights has led to widespread theft of public property (see Åslund, A. and Sjöberg, Ö.: Privatization and Transition to Market Economy, in: Stockholm Institute of Soviet and East European Economics Working Paper No. 27, 1991 for a detailed discussion of the current state of affairs). Under these circumstances, transition costs are probably no longer a relevant consideration in the contemplation of economic reform: there are few costs left to be borne.

The present government has stated its intention to initiate economic reform based on the following points:

1. Privatization of agricultural land.

2. Development of a legal framework appropriate for a market economy.
3. Commercialization and privatization of state enterprises.
4. Macroeconomic austerity.
5. Price and foreign trade liberalization.
6. Limited convertibility of the Albanian lek.
7. Creation of a social safety net suitable to a market economy (G. Pashko, 'International Assistance for Democracy in Albania', Mimeo, 1991).

It is too soon to predict the outcome of such reforms or even the speed with which they will be implemented. Success is assured only to the extent that things can hardly get worse.

The postscripts for Cuba and Bulgaria are to be found at the end of this section.

CHAPTER 6: CZECHOSLOVAKIA

Ludek Rychetnik

After the January shock of price liberalization and a sharp devaluation, accompanied by the disintegration of the former Comecon markets, external and internal demand barriers depressed production in all industries. Personal consumption decreased by 37 per cent in the first half of 1991 compared to the same period of 1990, and unemployment reached nearly 4 per cent. Consumer prices in June 1991 were nearly 50 per cent above December 1990, although half of the inflation (and the most of it in food prices) occurred in January. On a more positive note, the trade balance with developed market economies resulted in a surplus of 6.3 billion Koruna. Gross foreign debt reached $8.8 billion but this was significantly better than expected (Zpráva..., 1991).

Many state enterprise managers found themselves in an entirely new situation of having to serve a Western or a changed domestic (now essentially buyer's) market. With outdated products, technologies and management style, they were unable to cope; enterprises had to cut production, working time and labour, and an already widespread liquidity crisis deepened. A new 'Consolidation' Bank, set up in March, took over a part of the older bad debts. Another attempt to relieve the critical situation of potentially viable enterprises was launched in October; commercial banks would be recapitalized by convertible bonds issued by the National Asset Funds against their future receipts. The banks can swap the bonds for the equity of (corporatized) enterprises in compensation for a bad debt write-off. Also the bonds hedge the banks against losses from bankruptcies.

But the main reform effort was directed towards major privatization. Enterprises were preparing privatization projects and competitive variants were encouraged. The choice was between different structurings of the business and various combinations of the privatization methods proposed. The first wave of the investment coupon (tokens) auctions was planned to start in January 1992 (Závazná osnova, 1991).

References

Závazná osnova a metodický návod K zpracování privatizačních projektů (1991), in *Hospodářské noviny,* nos 29, 32, 33, 18 July, 8 and 15 August.
Zpráva Federálního statistického úřadu o ekonomickém a sociálním vývoji ČSFR v prvním pololetí 1991 (1991) in *Hospodářské noviny* no. 165, 27 August.

CHAPTER 7: EAST GERMANY

Ian Jeffries

It seems as though output was beginning to bottom out in the latter half of 1991, with construction and services (especially retail trade) in the forefront. Even so, national income fell again in 1991, while industrial output declined by 43 per cent over the year to July 1991 (Quentin Peel, *The Financial Times,* 16 October 1991, p. 3). A rise in national income is generally expected in 1992. The five German economic research institutes' autumn report was published in October 1991 (*The Financial Times, International Herald Tribune* and *The Guardian,* 22 October; Deutsche Bank, *Unification Issue,* 1991, no. 61). Their estimates give a 20 per cent fall in EG national income in 1991 and a rise of 10–15 per cent in 1992. Unemployment will average 1.4 million in 1992 and reach a peak of 1.5 million in the summer of that year. The inflation rate in EG is estimated at 12 per cent for both 1991 and 1992. They point out the danger represented by rapid wage increases and a burgeoning budget deficit (estimated all-German budget deficit in 1991 of DM 130 billion or 4.6 per cent of GNP). They see no signs of a *sustained* recovery in EG: 'Above all, the forces for self-sustaining economic growth are lacking', i.e. the recovery is largely being driven by government inflows from WG. The Deutsche Bank's forecasts indicate a 20 per cent fall in GNP in 1991 and a rise of only 5–10 per cent in 1992; inflation is estimated at 18 per cent in 1991 and 15 per cent in 1992.

The figures for unemployment are as follows:

	Unemployment		'Short-time' working
	Numbers	Rate (%)	
July 1991	1,068,600	12.1	1,620,000
August 1991	1,063,200	12.1	1,451,000
September 1991	1,030,000	11.7	1,300,000

The fall in unemployment in August and September is expected to be followed by a further rise at some point. Christopher Parkes (*The Financial Times*, 10 October 1991, p. 2) provides some very interesting further information on the labour front for the end of September 1991: 450,000 East Germans were employed in West Germany, i.e. commute daily; more than 300,000 were involved in job creation schemes; 225,000 were in early retirement at reduced pensions; and 300,000 were taking part in vocational training programmes.

By August 1991 nearly 3,400 large enterprises had been privatized (reducing the number still under the control of the THA to about 7,000), DM 12.5 billion had been raised from these sales, and foreigners had bought 156 of these enterprises (Deutsche Bank, *Unification Issue,* 1991, no. 58, p. 2). The THA would like to involve a larger number of foreigners. By the end of September the number of enterprises privatized had gone up to 3,788.

CHAPTER 12: ROMANIA

Alan H. Smith

The prospects for the transition to a market economy in Romania remained in the balance at the end of October 1991. Violent demonstrations in Bucharest 25–28 September by 6,000 miners complaining about the impact of the doubling of prices, the slower growth of wages and the threat of unemployment were followed by the fall of Petre Roman's government. Theodor Stolojan, a technocrat who had resigned from the post of Minister of Finance in the Roman government in April 1991, after complaining that the pace of reform was too slow, was nominated as the new prime minister on 1 October. A coalition government that contained representatives of the opposition parties and nine independents was approved by parliament on 18 October. Stolojan himself is not a member of a political party and stated that he would not stand at the elections, which it was hoped would be held in the spring of 1992.

Stolojan argued that his government would continue with the policies of macroeconomic stabilization and would accelerate the transition to a market economy, including measures to accelerate reforms to the banking system, the creation of small private businesses, land distribution and the accelerated sale of houses. These measures are both aimed at increasing economic efficiency and creating a middle and entrepreneurial class who would support the continuation of reforms. It was also hoped that a government decree to unify the exchange rate and to introduce residents' convertibility (originally scheduled for 1 October but abandoned following the miners' intervention and the fall of the Roman government) would be implemented in November. Stolojan also appointed Adrian Severin, a major moving force behind rapid reforms (who had also resigned from the Roman government in protest at the slow pace of reforms) as his replacement as head of the National Agency for Privatization. Stolojan announced the continuation of a price freeze on fuel and energy, staple foodstuffs, rents on state properties and state services announced by the outgoing government which has been criticized by the opposition as anti-market.

There are therefore indications that the fall of the Roman government could actually result in an acceleration of economic reforms, although the manner in which the government had fallen has damaged Romania's international standing. The official line was that Roman had failed to head warnings about popular dissatisfaction with the reforms and would have been forced to resign without the miners' intervention. This view was supported by reformers who argued that Roman's failure to explain the reforms properly to the people had contributed to their unpopularity.

Reformers argue that although the economic problems facing the country are serious and great hardships are to be expected in the winter of 1991–92, the costs of reform are exaggerated while the benefits (or the costs of doing nothing) have not been properly explained. A critical political problem is that the supporters of reform are dispersed between the political parties and tend to engage in bitter disagreements about the detail of reform rather than concentrating on the factors that unite them

On the negative side, a strong feeling persists that opponents of reform still excercise considerable power in local and national government and the media and will attempt to use the economic crisis to exploit popular unrest as a pretext for a return to more authoritarian government.

CHAPTER 14: VIETNAM

Melanie Beresford

The last twelve months have seen a process of consolidation and adjustment of the reforms in Vietnam rather than any major new departures. There has been a large volume of regulation and legislation designed to iron out anomalies and cope with difficulties arising. Provisions have been made, for example, covering bankruptcy in the private sector and worker redundancy in unprofitable state enterprises. Legislation governing bankruptcy of state enterprises has not yet been passed, however, and this is already causing problems in sorting out the debt servicing obligations of defunct state firms (FEER, 26 September 1991, p. 57).

Approved foreign investment had doubled by late 1991 compared with a year earlier. While primary resource development and tourism continued to attract the majority, manufacturing investment now accounts for about a fifth of the total (AWSJ, 19–20 July 1991). Whether these approvals will come to fruition, however, is another question. A major blow to the Vietnamese economy in 1991 was the collapse of Soviet economic support. Vietnam's principal source of external investment finance has all but dried up, deliveries of imported Soviet fuel and fertilizer are frequently not made, while exports were dramatically down in the first half of 1991 compared with 1990. Industrial and agricultural output have both suffered and inflation has risen again. Hardest hit have been the local state and collective industrial enterprises, which have lost their export markets in Eastern Europe, and the private sector which has found the investment climate unstable and uncertain. The collapse of a major external prop thus has the potential to undermine significantly the gains made in previous years.

Offsetting this, trade with the West has steadily increased since 1985, while aid flows have also begun to circumvent the continuing American embargo. Possibly the Vietnamese economy has acquired enough resilience through the reforms already in place to ride out this latest storm without imposing yet more severe burdens on its long-suffering population.

CHAPTER 15: YUGOSLAVIA

Saul Estrin and Lina Takla

The political situation in Yugoslavia has deteriorated dramatically during 1991, with serious fighting between Serbs and Croats having already claimed more than 2,000 lives, and the country teetering on the brink of full scale civil war. Economic issues of all sorts, let alone the complexities of transition, have faded into the background, and seem unlikely to head the political agenda until the fighting stops.

These recent appalling developments have a number of implications for the reform process. In the first place, it seems impossible in the light of recent events that Yugoslavia can be re-established as a single political entity. At the very minimum, Slovenia and Croatia will have a significant degree of independence from Belgrade, and the same could apply to Macedonia. This prospect brings into question whether, or in what form, a single currency can be maintained. Slovenia has already officially abandoned the Dinar for internal transactions. There are also remains the issue of how the remaining large foreign debt will be allocated between the successor states.

Secondly, it seems likely that recent tragic events will have fundamentally weakened Yugoslavia's (or its successor states') economy as it enters the difficult process of transition. The problem is deeper than war damage to people and property, and output losses as the economy moves to a war footing. In the past, balance of payments problems have been financed by remittances from abroad and by tourism and both now seem likely to dry up. Moreover, in an area competing hard for foreign capital, political instability will be a significant negative factor in the minds of potential foreign investors.

The most worrying feature about recent events, however, is that the shape of the future South Balkans has not begun to emerge. Slovenia, Croatia and Macedonia seek total independence, though it is not clear whether any of them are viable as independent economic units. No one is proposing institutions to ensure the maintenance of future trades relations in the region, though, despite recent fragmentation, there have been gains from inter-republican trade. The rhetoric of war has driven out the painstaking effort required for a successful evolution from single to multi-states in the region. Until such attitudes begin to soften, it is hard to see how successful economic reforms can begin.

CHAPTER 5: CUBA

Andrew Zimbalist

As of mid-October 1991, the economic and political crisis in Cuba has deepened profoundly. The continued political disintegration in the former Soviet Union, the 30 per cent diminution in Russian output and the late summer, aborted coup have all reverberated devastatingly on the Cuban economy. Cuba's revolution was able to survive only because it was rescued from the US embargo by the Soviet Union and the CMEA. Until 1991, most of the decrease in Soviet trade with and aid to Cuba came gradually, albeit that the disruptions were severe for certain products. With the turmoil of 1991, the disruptions became more acute, more frequent and more pervasive. Further, much of the development and price-subsidy aid, which was already on the wane, was cut off. With 1992, all aid is scheduled to end and Cuba will do well to preserve a good share of its trade with depressed enterprises in the various Republics. The United States has only tightened the embargo, substantially reducing the amount of permitted transfers from members of the Cuban exile community to the island.

Living conditions in Cuba are severe. Almost all goods are on tight rations, and often the promised rations are not available. Soviet shipments of meat, dairy products, grain and cereals have fallen drastically as have shipments of raw materials essential for the production of consumer goods. Cuban industry has virtually halted production of many goods essential for household health and cleanliness, such as soap, detergents, brooms, textiles and underwear. Cuba's special food plan has yet to yield important benefits. Growing shortages have also further undermined the motivation to work and further instigated the motivation to pilfer state materials. The economic mechanism teeters on the edge of breakdown. The population sees little reason for hope in the revolution's present course and the Party leadership has proven itself, most recently at the Fourth Party Congress, unwilling or unable to take the necessary bold measures of economic and political reform.

CHAPTER 3: BULGARIA*

Robert J. McIntyre

Soviet–Bulgarian–American relations: rivalry and reform
Seemingly irrational Bulgarian economic policy makes sense if it wins American approval and thus IMF support. US government involvement in Bulgarian internal affairs expanded rapidly during 1989–91 and included participation in formulation of UDF political tactics, as well as use of the American Democratic Party, Republican Party and AFL–CIO as surrogates to finance the UDF and the oxymoronic 'Thatcherite trade union' Podkrepa (*Financial Times*, 3 May 1991, p. 6). Bulgaria was especially hard hit by the collapse of CMEA trade, which resulted largely from the withdrawal of Soviet subsidies, but Western reporting of a Bulgaria wistfully regretting its abandonment by the USSR ignores the pursuit of the US as new patron. It should be recalled that the American play for hegemony in Bulgaria after 1989 is a reprise of ultimately catastrophic 1943–47 events, and that the Soviet–Bulgarian chill pre-dates *perestroika*, beginning in the Andropov period in 1983 (reflecting Soviet impatience with poor quality Bulgarian exports, waste of energy and raw materials, accidents, corruption charges and perhaps of Todor Zhivkov explaining Bulgarian success as the result of having the USSR as an economic colony).

Workplace reorganization and trade union in the new politics
After measures in 1979–83 increasing DSO financial accountability and

*The editor wishes to disassociate himself from the contents of this postscript.

self-financing, reforms in 1986–87 emphasized workplace democracy and election of managers. A complete and well thought out legal structure of self-management was created within Soviet-type forms (Wallimann and Stojanov, 1988, 1989). In January 1989 enterprises were converted into 'firms' and provision was made to distribute shares to employees. The possibility of 100 per cent foreign ownership was also established.

Labour organizations were at the centre of the political transformation of 1989–90 and will be a major force in determining the concrete forms of economic organization that eventually emerge. The 400,000 member independent trade union Podkrepa has monarchist–monetarist leadership and strong foreign connections. The official Bulgarian Trade Union declared its independence of the BSP, changed its name to CITUB, and quickly emerged as an active relegitimized force, calling for rapid marketization and privatization. The CITUB defines these terms quite differently from Podkrepa, using privatization to mean some form of worker or local collective ownership, rather than anything approaching classic capitalist conceptions. CITUB success in reestablishing its reputation and retaining 70 per cent (3,000,000) of the work force as members is partly the result of avoiding the taint of foreign control (Engelbrekt, 1991).

A new political–economic constellation of forces
The coalition government formed in January 1991 introduced drastic price 'liberalization' directly negotiated with the IMF, leading to falls in output and employment so sharp the President congratulated the population for accepting an even greater collapse in living standards than have the Polish population. The BSP, which earlier called for a 'mixed and socially-oriented economy, functioning on market principles', generally supported the austerity programme which resembles its stalemated 1990 efforts. The coalition government passed several significant legislative acts, including a new land code allowing (but not carrying out) privatization of agriculture land. The remarkable October 1991 election results pointed towards further chaos: the BSP remained the largest party, but its vote fell to 34 per cent – only slightly less that the vote of the 20 party UDF coalition. The UDF can only govern with the support of the Turkish minority party (MRF), which was the only other (of 55 new parties) represented in parliament. The large unrepresented vote, the ability of the BSP to block any legislation requiring a two-thirds vote and the unpopularity of the MRF suggest unlimited potential for future instability.

Reference
Engelbrekt, K. (1991) 'Bulgaria: partnership or opposition?', *RL/RFE Report on Eastern Europe*, vol. 2, no. 13, pp. 19–22.

Index

'Two Hundred (200 day) battle' 178
Tyminski, S. 27
Tyson, L. 260, 262

Unemployment 13, 20, 48, 55, 101, 136–
8. 161, 175, 189–90, 210, 251,
262, 266–7, 271–2, 274–5, 280–2
U-Uchevarria, O. et al. 108
U-Uchevarria, O. and Trueba, G. 109
Union Treaty 38–9, 123, 127, 234
Uvalic, M. 273, 275

Vacha, V. 111–12
Van Ree, E. 180
'Velvet revolution' 16, 112, 120
VHJ (Czechoslovak industrial associa-
tion) 15–16, 111–12, 114, 116
Volkskammer (People's Chamber) 133–
4
Von Czege, A. 22
Vo Nhan Tri 248, 250
Vo Van Kiet 243
VVB (association of nationally owned
enterprises) 19

Wages *see* Labour and wages
Waigel, T. 136

Walesa, L. 26–7, 197–9
Wholesale trade 24, 33, 52, 169, 222,
227, 235
Wienert, H. and Slater, J. 151
'Wild' ('spontaneous') privatization 23,
160
Winiecki, J. 69, 183
WOG (Polish large industrial enterprise)
26, 184
Wong, C. 13
Wood, A. 251
Workers' committees 16, 29, 207–8
Workers' councils 15, 26, 41, 183–4,
195–6, 199, 207, 259

Xi, W. and Du, H. 78

Yavlinsky, G. 35
Yeltsin, B. 35, 38

'Zero Option' 279
Zhao Ziyang 81
Zhivkov, T. 6, 11, 63
Zieleniec, J. 120
Zimbalist, A. 14–15, 97
Zimbalist, A. and Brundenius, C. 98
Zimbalist, A. and Smith, W. 106